ROBERTSON DAVIES

A Portrait in Mosaic

ROBERTSON DAVIES
A Portrait in Mosaic

VAL ROSS

[A DOUGLAS GIBSON BOOK]

McCLELLAND & STEWART

Library and Archives Canada Cataloguing in Publication

Ross, Val
    Robertson Davies : a portrait in mosaic / Val Ross.

"A Douglas Gibson book".
ISBN 978-0-7710-7775-3

    1. Davies, Robertson, 1913-1995. 2. Authors, Canadian (English) –
20th century – Biography. 3. Oral biography. I. Title.

PS8507.A67Z84 2008   C813'.54   C2007-905918-X

We acknowledge the financial support of the Government of Canada through the
Book Publishing Industry Development Program and that of the Government of
Ontario through the Ontario Media Development Corporation's Ontario Book
Initiative. We further acknowledge the support of the Canada Council for the
Arts and the Ontario Arts Council for our publishing program.

A Douglas Gibson Book

Printed and bound in Canada

This book is printed on acid-free paper that is 100% ancient-forest friendly
(100% post-consumer recycled).

ANCIENT FOREST
FRIENDLY

McClelland & Stewart Ltd.
75 Sherbourne Street
Toronto, Ontario
M5A 2P9
www.mcclelland.com

1 2 3 4 5   12 11 10 09 08

For Morton, of course

"Successful relationships are genuinely mysterious."
Chapter 38

CONTENTS

ROBERTSON DAVIES

A Portrait in Mosaic

MEETING THE SWAN

On a morning in September 1991, I walked into the book-lined downtown Toronto offices of Robertson Davies's Canadian publisher, McClelland & Stewart. There he was: a dapper, magisterial man of 78, in full Edwardian rig of blazer and flannels. He spoke with an English inflection to his vowels – remarkable for someone born in Thamesville, Ontario, who had spent seven of his eight decades on this side of the Atlantic. I was then a reporter covering books and authors for *The Globe and Mail*, and we were supposed to be discussing Davies's latest book, *Murther and Walking Spirits*. We did that – but he also treated me to what I thought was a wonderful spell of gossip.

A tale that delighted him concerned a current campaign to have the nineteenth-century English theologian John Henry Newman canonized. "The problem is, a man must have three well-attested miracles attributed to him before he can be named a saint," RD told me with visible glee. "They're having trouble finding miracles for Newman, but the English Jesuits have come up with a marvellous explanation: they say Newman was too much an English gentleman to resort to anything as *showy* as miracles." Davies roared with laughter. "As if Christ were just some sort of *low tough!*"

Why was he telling stories about Cardinal Newman, of all people, to a strange journalist? Because, I suppose, he was beguiling me – like a magician, misdirecting my attention. All his life, Davies was shy, and by the time I met him he was wary of the press, having been a journalist himself for three decades. The one message that he conveyed directly that day was his wish to warn people – me, my readers, anyone who was listening – not to underestimate him, or to assume they had his number.

Asked what mythic animal he identified with, he toured his mental library of myth only briefly before pulling out his answer: "If I had to choose a character standing for myself, it would be the Ugly Duckling. You see, no one thought much of him when he was a duck. But when they found out he was a swan, opinion changed. I may not be the world's fore-most swan, but I am not a duck."

In metaphor, swans are both magnificent and vain, staring at their own shifting reflections. Still, "swan" seems an odd choice, until you recall that Davies's most famous novel, *Fifth Business*, is written in the form of a letter by an indignant schoolmaster on the eve of retirement, whose vanity is stung when a humble college newspaper produces a reflection of his life in ways he feels are inadequate. Another Davies novel, *What's Bred in the Bone*, is narrated by two angels as they watch an earthly biographer floundering and failing to understand his subject's life. Davies wrote *What's Bred in the Bone* while Judith Skelton Grant was at work on her authoritative biography of him, *Robertson Davies: Man of Myth*, and Davies seemed to be embedding his own feelings as a biographee in its pages: Don't presume you can ever fully understand the reasons behind another person's achievements and eccentricities.

It was, and still is, hard to assess this man. Davies has always been wil-fully eccentric, or "ex-centric," as Bruce Powe noted in his perceptive essay "Odd Man Out." His voice was "a voice of someone off-centre from the volatile neighbours, like *Fifth Business* and Canada itself, a character who is 'odd man out,' on the periphery of the true action."

What has made Davies an even more complex subject is that at times he resorted to tricks to protect his privacy. One of his biographers, Elspeth Cameron Buitenhuis, told me, "He was not at all a truthful man." Those who knew him for years were sometimes stunned to learn late in their relationship of aspects of his emotional life they had never suspected. His wide-ranging, sometimes scatological, interests could nonplus those who categorized him as a somewhat proper Edwardian gent. His daugh-ters, sorting through his voluminous diaries, say they are still astonished by some of their father's private thoughts.

Yet despite his passion for privacy, Davies lived large. He made impressions, sometimes very deep ones, on many people. In this oral history – a collection of spoken memories and impressions of the man – it is my hope to cast an image of this shape-shifter of an artist.

– V. R.

Chapter 1

WALKING SPIRITS

Robertson Davies's father's family made their living for centuries in and around a border town in northeast Wales, a place where shaggy mountains shadow blackened brick houses strung along the hillsides. To the North American eye, Welshpool, Montgomeryshire, looks like a good place to have come from. Yet the Davies family emigrated from this place reluctantly. Once, they were community leaders. The patriarch, Samuel Davies, a tailor who made servants' uniforms, had risen through Welshpool's hierarchy to be elected on the Liberal platform as mayor. Then a late-nineteenth-century economic downturn undercut the family's good fortune. In his memoir, *Far-Off Fields*, Rupert Davies dodged the question of whether Samuel did, in fact, go bankrupt, but his son RD was very clear about the effects of this period on the family's reputation. In his semi-autobiographical novel *Murther and Walking Spirits*, he wrote, "Bankruptcy! The hobgoblin, the obliterating shadow of the commercial world of Samuel's day! For in those days a man could be bankrupt but once; there were no second chances, no histories of repeated bankruptcies. It all happens within a few months. Samuel retires to a cramped life in the premises over the tailor's shop and the black day approaches when he must, in the local phrase, 'go up the Town Hall steps' and be formally declared a bankrupt."

RUPERT DAVIES (from *Far-Off Fields*)
[My father Walter] was definitely of a studious bent. He taught school when a young man and as far as he was able to go in seeking higher education he was succeeding very well. . . . He received his certificate from Oxford University giving him the degree of A.A., Associate of the Arts; I understand that meant he was acceptable as an undergraduate. . . . [But] the kind of business our family was in was going downhill. . . . Family

financial problems, which need not here be related, descended upon my father, and he was hard hit all around.

In 1876, Walter married a schoolteacher, Janet Jessie Robertson. Her brother, John Robertson, married Walter's sister Mary Ann Davies, so the two families were doubly linked: the entrepreneurial Davieses and the scholarly Robertsons. Their younger son, Rupert, born on September 12, 1879, grew up acutely conscious of his family's fall from prestige, particularly when, as the economic depression persisted, he was required to press some of the Davieses' tailoring customers to pay their bills.

RUPERT DAVIES
Many times I had to eat a hurried dinner and make calls on some of our "slow poke" debtors to try to collect enough to meet a cheque at the bank that day from a wholesale house. My recollection is that somehow or other we used to meet the cheques, and thus appease the wrath of the bank manager, of whom I was sore afraid. However, it was not easy.

Rupert's granddaughter Kathryn Davies Bray, Robertson Davies's niece, says this period shaped Rupert.

KATE [DAVIES] BRAY
Rupert always felt that the Davieses had come down in life, in nineteenth-century terms – from a grandfather who had been mayor of Welshpool to living above the tailor shop. I don't know if Rupert ever got over the need to get the family back up.

In 1891, Rupert's uncle John Robertson and his wife, Mary Ann Davies Robertson, left for Canada. Three years later, Rupert, then aged 15, and his older brother Percy, 17, were sent out to join their aunt and uncle in Brantford, Ontario. The boys sailed on September 13, 1894.

RUPERT DAVIES
The first two days, I was very homesick, and I recollect that I tried to persuade Percy to get off with me at the northern Irish port at which we called. . . . We arrived in Quebec very early on Saturday 22nd . . . [and] in Brantford late on Sunday afternoon and we were given a hearty welcome by all the Robertson family. . . . On Monday morning I was

taken to the office of the Brantford *Expositor* to be interviewed. I started [as a printer's devil] on Tuesday morning, sweeping out, running back and forth to the post office for mail (three times each morning) and generally making myself useful.

By the time the rest of the Davies family emigrated to Canada in 1895, Rupert was apprenticed at the *Expositor*. He brimmed with ambition. But his father, Walter, the would-be scholar, found the New World more difficult.

RUPERT DAVIES
When we were going through our hardest times, my mother would gather us around the table and read the Bible and pray. Our mother was a very religious woman and she had great courage. When my father failed to find employment for several months, he had fits of depression and doubts as to whether he had made the right move when he brought his family to Canada. But my mother never had any doubts. . . . My father had a long siege of unemployment, but we got along. Percy and I earned three or four dollars a week between us. Mother was a careful manager.

In a 1995 letter to his friend Horace Davenport, Robertson Davies wrote about Walter's money anxieties.

RD
My grandfather, an admirable man whom I remember with affection, used to cry, in agony, when the family expenses seemed about to overwhelm him, "You'll have me in the workus – the workhouse – among you!"

By his late teens, Rupert was clearly a young man on his way. He studied at night school; on special occasions, he dressed up in dapper vests and bow ties – a sort of salute to the family's tailoring background. At the age of 20 he went to work in printing in New York City. But then he fell ill. Melancholy and alone, he headed back to Brantford. RD's wife Brenda met Rupert for the first time when he was in late middle age, and was able to see how he responded to stress.

BRENDA DAVIES
Rupert was the same as Rob – prone to depression. He was very up and down. He would sometimes go to bed for the whole day, to escape. That was his idea of a holiday. Very Welsh and very temperamental.

These were not the qualities of his dour new fellow townspeople, as he discovered when he joined a church choir in Brantford, where he met Florence McKay. She was clever, well read, and loved theatre and music – pleasures not shared by her Loyalist pioneer forebears.

RD
The pioneers were not a cheerful, high-hearted lot. They were coura-geous and enduring, but they were pretty hard to live with. I can speak with some certainty about that because on my mother's side all my family were pioneers, and there was a long series of family stories about that going back several generations. Oh, they were a grim lot! They sus-pected joy, they suspected an unforeseen good fortune, they suspected strangers – they were suspicious of just about everything. Mind you, if you spent your whole winter eating salt pork and pumpkin sass, *you'd* get suspicious.

The McKays traced their lineage back to May Jones Gage, widow of a captain in a British regiment who had been killed in action in the Revolutionary War. In 1790, she fled the new republic in a canoe, and, with her two children, paddled the rivers north to Lake Ontario. This tough woman's granddaughter Sarah married a Loyalist of Dutch descent, John Langs. They had eleven children, the youngest of whom, Lavinia Catherine Langs, begat Florence McKay, mother of Robertson Davies. In a letter, written in 1991 to Robert Finch, RD wrote:

RD
The Dutch strain ran strong until the death of my grandmother, Lavinia Langs, who died in 1924. She had been nowhere near Holland, nor had her forebears for nearly three hundred years, but in the certificate of death she had to be described as Dutch because at that time there was no such thing as Canadian nationality. She was Dutch clear through. Every week, every keyhole in the house had to be cleaned out with an oiled feather; everything gleamed – spic and span wasn't the word for it. But it is amusing now to recall that the old lady thought a bath once a

week was foppish. After all, if you kept a clean house, how could you get dirty? She never lost a few Dutch words. The verandah (fashionable Portuguese word) was always the *stoep* to her.

RD's eldest daughter, Miranda, heard tales about her formidable great-grandmother.

MIRANDA DAVIES
My ideas about the McKays are derived from *Murther and Walking Spirits*. . . . The mother is sitting by the fire hating everyone. . . . I was told that as a young woman Florence had had tonsillitis, and after removing her tonsils the doctor sent her home on foot. She fainted outside the house of the local prostitute, who took her in and comforted her. The McKays' response to this was to reprimand Florence for having anything to do with "that woman."

RD described his grandmother in a letter he wrote in 1970 to the author Margaret Laurence.

RD
[She] was poison-pious. "I'll get to the market tomorra – *if I'm spared!*" she would say, casting a gooseberry eye at me to see if I was appropriately impressed by the vanity of human wishes and the Conqueror Worm. She was spared to a great old age, and as generals have horses shot under them in battle, she outwore two old-maid daughters. My mother was the only one who had the "sand" (a much admired quality) to marry, having to run away from home and have a row with her parents to do so.

In another letter, written in 1991 to Robert Finch, RD mentioned one reason for that row:

My mother gave grave offence by marrying an "Englishman." He was a Welshman, but they couldn't make that distinction.

Another reason why Florence's family opposed her marriage to Rupert was that her father, William McKay, didn't live with the family, nor did he support them. Florence worked as a secretary to help provide for her mother and sisters. Rupert's second son, Arthur Davies, described the McKay family's situation in his memoir, *Green Pastures*.

ARTHUR DAVIES

William McKay had been a skilful carpenter and in time became a successful small contractor, building houses in Brantford for resale. He suffered from asthma, and his brother-in-law, a medical doctor practising in Niagara Falls, New York, taught him to give himself injections of a narcotic to relieve the pain. The result was, of course, that he became addicted to the drug, and sometimes, under its influence, he abused and frightened his wife and daughters. After several years of such alarms and excursions, Grandmother McKay and her unmarried daughters left him and set up their own household. The addict . . . was placed in the home for indigents.

Florence fled this unhappy household to wed Rupert on October 16, 1901. Rupert had just turned 22. Florence told him that she was about the same age (though the marriage certificate listed her as 27). On June 10, 1902, their first son, Frederic Rupert McKay Davies, was born – less than eight months after their wedding. Had Florence trapped Rupert into marrying her? A second son, Arthur Llewellyn Davies, arrived on August 18, 1903. Fred's daughter Kathryn heard family stories about her father and uncle's early years.

KATE BRAY

Florence's second son, Arthur, was born with spina bifida. He was smaller and less robust than my father, though bright, very bright. Florence undertook to teach Arthur a lot. I'm not sure if she did home schooling with Arthur, but my father always talked about the time she spent with him.

Rupert supported his growing family by working as a typesetter for two different Brantford newspapers, the *Courier* and the *Expositor*. Keeping on top of their two different printing technologies, he wrote in his memoirs, "nearly finished me." A doctor warned him to find new work "unless I wanted a nervous breakdown." In 1907, Rupert writes in his memoir, he decided he would be better off running his own newspaper.

RUPERT DAVIES

I decided to try for the *Thamesville Herald* . . . [and] with a cash total of about $400 sallied forth to Thamesville to seek my fortune. . . . It was an uphill fight. . . . The first three years or so, I went back to the office and worked three and four nights every week. I worked very hard. My wife, Florence, also worked hard; whenever there was any folding or work of that sort to do, she was always on the job. When they got old enough, Fred and Arthur also worked in the office after school.

KATE BRAY
My father was a big, strong boy and very mechanical. He could lift anything, fix anything. Rupert was not above using people, and my father was very useful to him. That's how you get ahead in life, I suppose: you find someone to do the heavy lifting and the grunt work. Arthur naturally spent more time with his mother, learning her business acumen. . . . Heavy lifting wasn't work that Arthur could do.

ARTHUR DAVIES (from *Green Pastures*)
The whole family spent considerable time in the *Herald* office, for my mother was determined to do everything she could to help my father succeed in this new venture. She learned to set type by hand, to fold newspapers, to fold and assemble job printing, and she insisted upon housecleaning the premises.

At this stage in their marriage, Rupert was impressed by Florence. Her superior education contributed not only to the raising of their sons, but also to raising the family's social standing.

RUPERT DAVIES
[In Thamesville] there were regular lodges and several other organizations. An important one was the Thamesville Art and Music Club, which had been formed by a group of ladies who tried to develop culture in the village. For a time, my wife Florence was secretary of this society, and on one occasion I recall, she delivered a paper on some chap named Theseus, of whom, up to that time, I had never heard.

Amid their hard work, Rupert and Florence took trips to Toronto to see plays and concerts, and they joined the Thamesville Dramatic Society. Then Florence lost a third child, and got pregnant a fourth time.

ARTHUR DAVIES (from *Green Pastures*)
The year 1913 was an important year in Davies history. While Fred and I were enjoying a summer holiday in Brantford, we were informed on

August 28 that we had a baby brother back in Thamesville. We didn't consider this good news. We had the companionship of one another, and a brother ten or eleven years our junior didn't sound like much fun.

A few days later we were returned to Thamesville, and I remember our introduction to the new member of the family. Dad escorted us upstairs to the "big bedroom" in our very small house. There was our dear mother in bed, and cuddled with her was the smallest, reddest, most wrinkled baby I had ever seen. This is understandable when I confess I had never seen a six-day-old baby before. Fred and I were embarrassed and far from enthusiastic. We kissed our mother and then retreated downstairs and outdoors in a dismal frame of mind to discuss this ominous occurrence.

I am sure our mother and father were disappointed at our lack of enthusiasm, but Robertson, the cause of our dismay, paid us no heed. He probably made up his mind at that first encounter that he didn't want or need the approval of older brothers.

If the birth of William Robertson Davies upset his brothers, it triggered a seismic shift in Florence's relations with Rupert.

MIRANDA DAVIES
Rupert discovered her true age after she gave birth to Robertson. When he asked the doctor how she was doing, the doctor said, "She's done well for her age."

By 1913, Florence was almost 43, nine years Rupert's senior.

MIRANDA DAVIES
Up to that point, Rupert had regarded her as his wife and helpmate. My father depicted the sense of betrayal in *Murther and Walking Spirits* as he had had it from his father, that she had lied to him. An ideal had been smashed.

Everything I knew about the early years was filtered through RD. He was of such a different temperament from his brothers. Fred was very attached to his mother, and RD was very attached to his father.

My take on that, from the point of view of a child psychotherapist, is that there was a failure of early attachment because, at the age of 43, she had difficulty breastfeeding and caring for the baby. I think she may have been a bit invalidish at the time. She may have been depressed, too.

I suggest this as a way of understanding why he did not thrive very well as a baby and was susceptible to the severe smallpox he had when an infant, which left him partially deaf in one ear. He often told us that he had been "despaired of." As he makes clear, he never felt close to his mother. The hypothesis that she had a post-puerperal depression could be helpful in beginning to understand his defences, his vulnerability and his wonderfully constructed personality.

KATE BRAY

By the time Robertson came along, I think there was a very different dynamic at work in the marriage. . . . I do not think Florence was well treated in the marriage. I don't think Rupert abused her, except in a psychological way. I often wonder how much the pressures she lived with – Rupert's sense of betrayal – had to do with her health.

Rupert was seriously upset by the revelation about her age. A serious bone of contention. As for her being older than Rupert, that's so stupid! Men are like that.

Chapter 2

THAMESVILLE TO

DEPTFORD

Western Ontario is a land of flat, seemingly dull farmland. Odd that the Scots, Welsh and Irish immigrants who settled there should have produced so many notable writers.

ALICE MUNRO

I didn't know Robertson Davies very well, but in 1986 I was in New York City at the big PEN International event. . . . On the last evening, he asked me to come and have a drink with him. So I did. And it was like being with a member of my family. It was very comfortable. I felt so relaxed! And he was making me relaxed, of course, by letting me have the sense of our being alike, from small-town, southwest Ontario.

Yet we are not really alike. We come from different classes. I was the kind of girl who would have come to do his mother's ironing. And he was usually a man who valued class – no, not class, *breeding* – because it made life pleasant. He was a conventional man in many ways.

In his later, public re-creation of himself, RD seemed to have sprung from somewhere between a private boy's school and an English theatre troupe. His mid-Atlantic drawl gave little hint of his birth in a small, white frame house with no indoor plumbing in Thamesville, a town of around eight hundred homespun Canadians. In a 1975 radio interview, Judy LaMarsh, a politician turned broadcaster, challenged RD on the way his rural Ontario origins had been expunged from his personal legend.

JUDY LaMARSH: I find the same stories repeated over and over again. I suspect you're a phony.
RD: Quite right, quite right.

JL: You seem to have come to life when you were an actor at the Old Vic. But you *did* live up to age 23 or more in Canada. You were born in Thamesville! I know where Thamesville is.

RD: Not very many people do. They keep confusing it with Thamesford, which is not very far away. . . . When I was a small boy, Thamesville had a very keen sense of its identity.

The writer Kildare Dobbs, raised in Ireland and widely travelled, was nonplussed by the place when he first arrived in Canada.

KILDARE DOBBS
Thamesville people were mistrustful of outsiders. They'd tell me, "Well, sir, you'll soon get used to our ways." That was because I dug worms at home and then went to the river to fish, whereas they dug their worms *at* the river. . . . Thamesville was a weird place. The people there pronounced it Th-aymes-ville, and they said it was on the River Th-aymes. I spent one night and then I took a taxi – I took *the* taxi – from Th-aymes-ville to my new home, Florence, Ontario. The taxi driver heard my accent and said, "You're from England. You got lords over there?"

I said, "Yes."

He said, "There is only one Lord, and that is Jesus Christ."

That was Th-aymes-ville!

Television producer Ann MacMillan returned with RD to Thamesville when she produced a documentary on him in 1983.

ANN MacMILLAN
Thamesville was a town with five or six churches. . . . The whole town was dominated by these buildings. His mother was depressive, and I did get the feeling that the church and his mother were burdens for Robertson Davies.

By the time William Robertson Davies was born, the Davies family had secured a place in the small-town Ontario middle class. But the new baby arrived at a time of tensions at home and abroad. Just after Robertson's first birthday, Britain, and its colonies and dominions, entered the First World War.

RD
I heard a great deal of gloomy talk almost as soon as I learned to talk myself. And it seemed to be that the war was hardly over before there was further gloomy talk about the war that was to come. . . . I became acquainted with the accents of despair almost as soon as I began to pay attention to conversation.

The older Davies boys, Fred and Arthur, who were close to their mother, must have sensed that the newcomer's arrival coincided with difficulties for the family. Martin Hunter, a theatre director and author who knew the family well from the 1960s on, was struck by Arthur's reticence in recalling that period.

MARTIN HUNTER (Theatre director and friend)
I met Arthur. He was a smart, capable, amusing character, an interesting man, with a kind of Yankee gumption. He said, "I will talk to you about my family, but not about my brother [Robertson]."

But he did say that he and Fred had been very close in age, and when Rob came along they didn't think much of him. At one point, he and Fred put Rob in a baby carriage and rolled the carriage down a hill, hoping . . .

With a war on and a family to support, much responsibility rested on Rupert, who must have feared that the family would face ruin if he fell ill. Then he did fall ill.

ARTHUR DAVIES
Dad contracted smallpox in November 1917. It was a dismal period for all of us, but we survived. . . . My most vivid recollection of this event is of some dollar bills hanging on a clothesline to dry after being washed in a fumigating liquid following Dad's recovery, but before the quarantine was lifted from our house. It seemed normal to me that we should all be washed and fumigated and that the house should be fumigated, but somehow it seemed strange that those desirable dollar bills should have to be cleansed.

In November 1918, Canadians celebrated the war's end twice – once unofficially, and once with pomp and circumstance.

ARTHUR DAVIES

November 1918 brought the False Armistice and the Real Armistice to our village. To my mind, the False Armistice was by far the most exciting because the celebration was spontaneous. On the occasion of the Real Armistice, the celebration was organized and to my mind dull, although Dad and Robertson marched in a parade of the village's leading citizens.

I was jealous of Robertson's preferment on that occasion, but Dad had selected him because he couldn't include all his sons.

Rupert, who had become an ardent member of the Liberal Party of Canada, also chose young Robertson to accompany him on political forays.

RUPERT DAVIES

I attended the nomination meeting in Alvinston and declined [to stand] in a speech from the platform, with Robertson standing beside me (aged four), hanging on to one leg.

The child was old enough to notice what was going on, as he writes in *One Half of Robertson Davies*.

RD

When I was a boy, I used often to go with my parents to political rallies, where candidates for Parliament appealed for votes. These men were no fools. They included in their entourage an entertainer, who put the audience in a good mood. After the entertainer had delighted us with his comic songs and imitation of a Red Indian reciting *The Charge of the Light Brigade*, we were softened up for the political address. As a boy, I had no vote; if I had been enfranchised, I should unhesitatingly have voted for the entertainer. I learned a lesson at those meetings, and it was this: if you haven't got a professional entertainer on your side, you should do your best to be entertaining in your own person.

Entertainment in Thamesville tended towards melodrama and spectacle. Thamesville had its own small theatre, and Rupert and Florence propelled their youngest boy to the stage. RD recalled this in a memoir he wrote under the name of his fictional creation, Samuel Marchbanks.

SAMUEL MARCHBANKS
[Robertson Davies] first appeared in public at the age of three in the
Ferguson Opera House, Thamesville, as an Israelite child in an opera
called *Queen Esther*; he was one of a chorus of children in bathrobes and
turbans who hailed the victorious Mordecai in a spirited number in
which the words "We triumph, we triumph" were repeated with typical
operatic persistence.

RD (in a 1983 CBC radio interview with Marilyn Powell)
I became interested in nineteenth-century drama because I was brought
up to it. Both my parents were keen playgoers. On the wall of my father's
study hung a picture of Henry Irving in *The Bells*. And my mother had
a picture of William Fanshawe in *Julius Caesar*. . . . What nineteenth-
century melodrama was was the kind of theatre people thought reflected
deep within themselves what they were or wished to be. . . . It was also
founded on a principle that was, that *is*, very dear to humanity: poetic
justice – people getting what's coming to them.

**The Davies family's musical tastes ranged from opera, hymns, Welsh
ballads to popular ditties.**

RD
In our household, music was not a hobby or a pastime; it was one of life's
preoccupations. My father sang and played the flute and directed a choir;
my mother sang and played the piano; one of my brothers sang and
wrought manfully with the cornet. I sang myself – a piece which began:

> *A little pink rose in my garden grew*
> *The prettiest rose of them all;*
> *'Twas kissed by the sun*
> *And caressed by the Jew . . .*

"The dew," the voice of authority would say. But the next time the Jew
would be sure to get into it, and I saw no harm in him. After all, was
not Mendelssohn, an effigy of whom sat on the piano top, a Jew?

**In 1919, Rupert took his sons to Toronto to the Canadian National
Exhibition. Fred went off on his own. Arthur looked at art exhibitions.**

Little Robertson was taken around by his proud father. What he saw would intrigue him all his life.

RD

In the recollections of my contemporaries, the midway plays a prominent part, but it was not so with me. . . . I liked to gape at giants, dwarfs and malformed persons, but this was considered, quite rightly, to be a displeasing characteristic in a child and was not encouraged. But my curiosity was in no way cruel; deviations from the commonplace attracted me strongly, as they still do, and to me the hermaphrodite and the living skeleton were interesting . . . because such people did not often come my way and I hoped that they might impart some great revelation to me, some insight that would help me to a clearer understanding of the world about me.

Chapter 3

THE LAND THAT
GOD GAVE CAIN

In May 1919, on hearing that a newspaper in a Northern Ontario town near the Quebec border was for sale, Rupert took a train to the Ottawa Valley to investigate buying the *Renfrew Mercury*.

RUPERT DAVIES
The price, including the building, was quite high for me, but in those days I was young and venturesome . . . The *Renfrew Mercury* was a test of my business ability. . . . I built the business up during the six years I was in Renfrew to more than double what it was when I bought it. It took a lot of work.

JUDY LaMARSH: You've said you had a happy childhood . . . so where does the pain come from in your books?
RD: My parents were very kind and very supportive. But my parents were also extremely demanding and could be very severe. They made heavy demands on all their children in the sense that they wanted them to measure up to particular standards. The two strains that were dominant in my family, Welsh and Dutch, are not in the least aristocratic nations. They're peasant nations and they work like Billy-O all the time.

A logging town surrounded by bush, Renfrew was rougher and more isolated than Thamesville. As the family discovered, its people were sharply divided, French and English, Catholic and Protestant. Years later, RD told documentary filmmaker John McGreevy that he learned about his new home through the stories Rupert brought home from work at the *Mercury*.

JOHN McGREEVY
He told me of how his father would come home and regale the family
with high gossip, who was doing what to whom . . . because of his
father's position as newspaper publisher, he knew secrets that most
others would not. That intrigued him. That sense of ordinary people,
extraordinary lives. Rob grew up expecting the unexpected.

**In a 1967 letter written to his friend and fellow journalist Scott Young
(father of the singer Neil Young), RD recalled prime Renfrew gossip. It
turned up again in RD's novel *What's Bred in the Bone*.**

RD
The old Senator [O'Brien]'s son-in-law, Joe Murray, always held his head
very high, and on one occasion, when my father was publisher of the
Renfrew Mercury, he called in at the paper to say that in future, in any
reference to him, he was to be spoken of as "Sir Joseph Murray," as the
Pope had just appointed him a Knight of the Order of St. Gregory
the Great.

My father treated this announcement with coarse Protestant hilar-
ity, and Joe was deeply annoyed. It was not very long, however, before
some busybody made it known that Joe was more than ordinarily interested in his secretary, a girl named Blondie Dolan, who wore rolled
stockings and smoked. As a result, the Holy Father retracted the
Knighthood and Joe was right back among the common people. This
caused a lot of ill-natured giggling in Protestant circles among people
who have never had any real appreciation of tragedy.

**Rupert had his own social ambitions. He joined Renfrew's board of trade
and the Rotarians, became president of the South Renfrew Temperance
Association, and campaigned for the Liberals. He expected his family to
keep up with him.**

RD (from *Writing Away*)
I did not like travelling on trains. My father, on the contrary, liked
nothing better. He was a newspaperman, and knew people everywhere,
as it seemed to me, and no sooner had we boarded a train than he set
out to walk its length, to see what acquaintances might be offering on
the green plush seats. . . . I was told to sit and look out of the window,
and that after a while he would return.

I did as I was told, but in terror. Figures of authority – the brake-man, or, most awesome of all, the conductor – appeared at my side and looked at me with what I now suppose was benevolence, but which seemed to me to be the questioning glances of mighty officials who could put me off the train if I had no ticket.

And I had no ticket. My father always had all the tickets and all the money and was not in the least awed by men in caps with stiff peaks and ponderous silver watch chains. My father's most disquieting habit was to leap from the train whenever it entered a station in order to buy a newspaper. . . . Would he be left behind? I agonized. Certainly not, but it was his debonair habit to swing up on the steps of the last car on the train as it moved out of the station, while I sat on the green plush seat (the plush penetrating my shorts and teasing my skin), dying a thousand deaths. No ticket, no money. What would become of me?

Like his brothers, RD contributed to his father's newspaper. Perhaps it was a good way to get Rupert's attention, as RD's wife suggests.

BRENDA DAVIES
Early on, Rob was working in journalism. That was his family's life. He had covered a meeting in Renfrew at age nine. . . . He was paid twenty-five cents and said, "This is the life for me!"

> (*Renfrew Mercury*, **February 16, 1923**)
> **MR. RADLEY LECTURES ON SHAKESPEARE**
> **To Interested Audience in the Methodist Church**
> **– Numerous Illustrations Shown**
> A very enjoyable lecture was given by Rev. Mr. Radley in the Methodist Church on Friday evening last on "William Shakespeare and His Country." . . . The evening was a very enjoyable and instructive one, and many of those present expressed their appreciation of Mr Radley's address. During the evening Mrs M. H. Winter sang "Husheen" very accept-ably . . .

Rupert expected his older sons, Fred and Arthur, to perform nuts-and-bolts machinery and reporter jobs. His expectations for his youngest son were loftier, and possibly even more onerous.

KATE BRAY
We always felt that Robertson was the son who could do no wrong in Rupert's eyes. The others were beyond the pale. Rupert approved of us, his grandchildren, but I don't think he approved of my father. . . .

By the time Robertson came along, the family was in a much better financial position, and Robertson stood to benefit. Whereas Fred, my father, did all that was asked of him – driving the cars, fixing things, all that was asked. He was expected to provide the muscle, and never had those opportunities.

Rupert's sons were conscious that their father chose to stand apart from Renfrew's rail workers and lumbermen. Rupert was so clothes-proud, RD recalled, his sons nicknamed him "Queen Elizabeth" – after the Tudor monarch who, according to legend, never wore the same outfit twice. Perhaps embarrassed, Fred and Arthur blended in with Renfrew's conservative fashion sense. Their little brother opted for Rupert's strategy.

MIRANDA DAVIES
I remember Rupert's smell: he had a splendid cologne and was very fastidious. Nice, square hands, clean nails, gold cufflinks with "W R D" on them, which my father wore after he died. . . . He wore grey suits and yellow dial socks. My father called him a snappy dresser. My father was the same.

Unlike his older brothers, RD identified with his father, and with a grander world, a choice remarked upon by the journalist Robert Fulford.

ROBERT FULFORD (in *Queen's Quarterly*, spring 2007)
Davies's alter ego [Samuel Marchbanks] announced at one point his agreement with Theophile Gauthier, the nineteenth-century Romantic poet, who divided "men into two groups, The Flamboyant and The Drab." Marchbanks/Davies placed himself firmly among The Flamboyant.

His far from flamboyant mother, Florence, made few friends in Renfrew. She was becoming more reclusive, which was not lost on other Renfrewites such as Kay Derry, who was a child at the time, and who remembered, tactfully, that Mrs. Davies "seemed to enjoy being at home."

ROSAMOND [DAVIES] BAILEY

In the early years of my grandparents' marriage, she helped out at the newspapers and helped to move his ambitions forward. Later, when he'd made a lot of money and a wife was supposed to be involved in social life, she was bored with these little teas. My father always said if she had lived in a different time, she would have had a career, and she would have been much happier.

BRENDA DAVIES

Florence was lonely and shy in Renfrew. Her group of Presbyterians broke off and joined the United Church, and that was a blow to her. . . . Rupert had a public life and she did not. They were growing very cool with each other.

The more estranged Rupert and Florence grew, the more both parents insisted that their sons, particularly the youngest, show Florence respect, as RD recalled years later to his publisher, Doug Gibson.

DOUG GIBSON

Rob did once mention to me that his mother was put on such a pedestal in the family that he at least once had to apologize to her on his knees. Every family of boys is taught that mothers are to be respected – but this went much further. Rob shook his head over the memory as he told me of having to get down on his knees.

He also told documentary filmmaker Harry Rasky about Davies family discipline.

HARRY RASKY

He told me that with his father, you never knew when he'd be easy-going, you never knew when he'd be strict. You never knew where you were. Caprice and whim ruled the family.

Davies didn't mind corporal punishment. He told me Rupert disciplined him with a cane and he felt "cleansed and restored." But he said his mother used a pony whip, and you got it on the bottom.

MIRANDA DAVIES

Rupert was a hugely forceful personality. His family could well have felt pressure under his heel. My mother remembers Rupert and Florence having horrible arguments at the table, which is why RD suffered such horrible digestive problems.

JENNIFER [DAVIES] SURRIDGE
When Dad was young, his family would always fight at meals. As a result, he had a terrible nervous stomach. . . . When he got nervous, he'd get indigestion. . . . He was very conscious of his guts all the time. His mother used to give him colonic lavages. Awful! His mother had a rage for high colonics *and* she also made him wear special shoes. Which didn't do him any good.

RD (letter to Horace Davenport, April 23–25, 1987)
As you are well aware, I have all my life been much troubled by my tripes, as was my father before me. . . . Sometimes I used to wonder if I had not eaten more barium meals than Christmas dinners.

Colonic lavages and special shoes were bad, but the North Ward public school was worse.

BRENDA DAVIES
Rob despised and hated Renfrew. When he took me to Renfrew in 1954, I recall he spoke of the oppressive kids there. Rob had hated every minute of it. They all had. It was a very rough town, very cut off.

He told me how the boys tortured frogs and blew up their cloaca with straws, and wore their underclothes all winter, which was why they smelled.

The story of RD's 1954 visit to his former public school is still told by some people of Renfrew – and their children.

SARAH GIBSON BRAY
The Renfrew Historical Society tells of how he came for a visit and they took him to see his old schoolhouse, and his comment was, "The school still smells of piss and shit."

BRENDA DAVIES
He had to walk to school two miles, part of the way across a cold and very windy cable bridge with wooden slats over the [Bonnechere] River. It swung. Wind blew over the bridge. And he got beaten up by Polish boys.

JENNIFER SURRIDGE
He always had a revulsion to [physically] dirty books in public libraries. It must have come from his school days in Renfrew, when he had to look things up in the public library. At home, Rupert had a lot of books, and RD had a feeling for good books and how they should be treated.

KAY DERRY (Renfrew resident)
Robertson always said he didn't like Renfrew. He didn't like the school. Kids pick on all strangers. It's children being children, I don't know why. But it wasn't a tough school. Most of us survived it!

Years later, in a letter written on January 21, 1980, to Lisa Balfour Bowen, one of his former students from his days spent teaching at the University of Toronto, RD hinted that if he was picked on in Renfrew, at times he gave as good as he got. Perhaps he was not always as victimized as he later recalled.

Many thanks for your note about the boy who was killed by a snowball. . . . I am not surprised; snowballs are much more serious affairs than people generally imagine and I am amazed that we do not hear of more people losing an eye or suffering some severe injury from them.

When I was a boy and snowball fights were in prospect, we used to make the snowballs and soak them with water so that they became, in fact, balls of ice, and I suppose it was only because we were not strong enough that we did not kill a few people with them.

The outside world was savage. But like his mother, RD found a sanctuary and a wonderful world in books. Florence read aloud to him, and discussed how language worked.

ROSAMOND BAILEY
Dad never stopped complaining about Florence and what a difficult person she was. But he also said he thought his imagination and literary sense came from her. She was educated. She was the eldest of a family of girls and the only one to marry, the only one to escape possessive and tyrannical parents. She was the one who told my father, "A comma counts for one beat, a semicolon for two," as in music.

Meanwhile, Rupert was not only seizing opportunities, he was creating them. He ran for the presidency of the Canadian Weekly Newspapers Association, and in 1923, from that position, organized a tour of Europe for Canadian newspaper owners, editors and their wives, "to meet the Empire's great statesmen and discuss Imperial questions." This trip was such a success, he organized a second tour the next year, taking Florence and young Robertson, aged nine, with him to show them the battlefields of Belgium and France – and his own native Wales.

RUPERT DAVIES
We left Montreal about the 10th or 11th of June, 1924, one hundred and seventy-five strong. . . . It was a good trip. We were received by the King of the Belgians in his palace in Brussels, by the President of France at the Elysée Palace and at a Buckingham Palace garden party by King George V and Queen Mary.

BRENDA DAVIES
Rob always spoke of how wonderful that trip was and how it opened his eyes.

That same year, Rupert bought Renfrew's other newspaper, the *Renfrew Journal*, thereby cornering the local printing business. During the town's annual fall fair and Old Home Week, he produced a special-edition newspaper and printed all the official programs, posters and small bills needed by the fall fair organizers.

RUPERT DAVIES
That was some week. Everybody worked hard and everyone was well paid for his or her work. From the time I got up from my bed on the Monday morning of Old Home Week, I did not crawl into it again until about three o'clock the next Saturday morning. . . . [Fred] ran the newspaper press all night. Every night at 12 o'clock, Mrs. Davies and Robertson arrived with thermoses and jugs of coffee and lots of sandwiches. As a result of that strenuous week, . . . I was able to wipe out the loan which I had floated at the bank when I bought out the *Journal*.

Fall fairs weren't Renfrew's only source of entertainment. The town had its own theatre, the O'Brien Opera House. Here, Robertson was taken to see plays, magic shows and movies.

RD
The 1925 movie *Phantom of the Opera*, starring Lon Chaney, was absolutely transfixing! There was one scene where the foolish girl pulls the Phantom's mask off. A horrible face is revealed. He takes her hand and pulls it down his face. It is dragged down. Strips of stuff like Plasticine come off. . . . That movie taught me something . . . about taking off people's masks.

The great magician Harry Blackstone performed at the O'Brien Opera House in February 1925. RD went to see the show.

BRENDA DAVIES
He sometimes talked about Harry Blackstone and said he had tried to do magic himself. But he was so ham-handed! All his life he was interested, though.

And all his life RD pondered how magicians construct their illusions. His view was a dark one, that magicians were effective manipulators of human perception.

RD (from *Wizards of Awe*, CBC-TV, 1992)
You cannot love a magician, or he's not a magician. You must admire him. You can be fascinated by him. But you don't want to become too familiar with him, because you don't know what he might do next.

In the twenty-first century, magicians are seen as entertainers. In the 1920s, notes one of RD's former students, Vincent del Buono, people had more interest in the occult.

VINCENT del BUONO
You have to unpack RD's interest in magic. Later on in life, he was a very good student of Jung; he understood the role of the Trickster – who, when you think you're going in one direction, takes you in another. He understood that the Trickster exists within you. He understood the feint, the illusionist. . . . In Canada in his youth, the Spiritualist movement was very strong. We all know now that Prime Minister Mackenzie King talked to spirits and clairvoyants. I suspect that in small-town Ontario this was prevalent. This would have been part of his cultural context early in life.

Small-town Ontario was where the Davies built their wealth. But, aside from Rupert, no family member recalled the Renfrew period with happiness.

RD (letter to Margaret Laurence, February 18, 1970)
Renfrew, in the Upper Ottawa Valley, when I was a child there, was certainly the Land that God Gave Cain. Rural Ontario or rural Manitoba, the spiritual deprivation is the same, and for the sort of perceptive child who later becomes a writer, the sense of being strange and alone is all-pervasive. I know now that what I suffered from most painfully was unrequited vivacity: I wanted to be merry and lively, and the leaden spirit of those sour-spirited Scotch kids, whose vivacity expressed itself in torturing animals and jeering at the crippled (the town boasted a notable dwarf who hanged himself eventually, so jolly had life been made for him). . . I was terribly oppressed. Was life really like this, I wondered. . . . Oooooh, how Canada marks us, and mars us and maims us.

Chapter 4

KINGSTON / SALTERTON:
"TWICE A CITY"

Early in 1925, J.E. Atkinson, proprietor of *The Toronto Star*, urged his young, ambitious newspaper colleague to look into acquiring and turning around yet another newspaper. Unlike the rest of the family, Rupert was pleased with life in Renfrew, where his paper was increasingly profitable. The challenge of taking on one in a larger city filled him with such doubts, he wrote in his autobiography, "I got out of Atkinson's office as fast as I could," and he added that for the next two weeks he was "under doctor's care." But Davies's ambition trumped his anxiety, and soon Rupert was in Kingston, looking over one of its two newspapers, *The British Whig*.

RUPERT DAVIES
The year before I took over *The British Whig* it had lost between $5,000 and $10,000 . . . [t]he business was being run for an estate, and those on the paper did not worry very much. . . . When we took the paper over, Fred took on the job room management . . . Arthur joined the news staff.

Kingston could not support two daily papers, Rupert realized, so he approached a London, Ontario, editor, Harry B. Muir, whom he knew through his Canadian Press connections. Muir bought the Kingston *Standard*. The two men amalgamated the newspapers on December 1, 1926.

ISABEL HOPE MUIR
My husband's father [Harry B. Muir] and Rupert made the *Whig-Standard*. . . . Rupert looked after the editorial half and Wally's dad, Harry, looked after the business side. They did well, you're not kidding! After Wally's dad died, Rupert bought out the family.

As in Renfrew, the Davies family did not socialize widely.

ISABEL HOPE MUIR
My husband worked at the *Whig* with Arthur before World War II. He was news editor before he left for overseas. I don't know that the Davieses were active in the golf club. I don't think that was their thing at all. Rupert was in politics. No one ever saw Mrs. Davies.

Beatrice Grant Corbett, daughter of a professor at the Royal Military Institute, was a child in Kingston in the 1920s.

BEA CORBETT
My father did not like Rupert Davies. My father loathed the Liberal Prime Minister, Mackenzie King, and Rupert Davies didn't. In Kingston, Rupert wasn't popular so much as respected. He was known to be a strong Liberal – a bagman, someone said, though I don't know how true that is. Certainly he was someone for whom public recognition was important.

Also, my father liked talking to everyone, and the Davieses were reclusive. None of my parents' friends ever said they had gone for tea there. I remember at a wedding in 1942 in the Cathedral, when General Armstrong's daughter was getting married, my father turned around in the middle of the ceremony and said, "Good heavens! There are the Rupert Davieses!" It was a surprise to see them. The few people who knew her said Mrs. Davies was very intelligent. But she just didn't mix.

Kingston was a far more sophisticated place than Renfrew. But even among Kingstonians, Rupert drew attention with his elegant clothes. So did his youngest son, now entering his teen years and enrolled in the local high school.

BEA CORBETT
There were certainly many eccentrics in Kingston. But Robertson Davies was in a class by himself! . . . My sister, Constance Grant Dickson, was a contemporary of RD at Kingston Collegiate Institute, where he went for a year. Kingston Collegiate in the 1930s was a very superior high school, with a lively drama scene. At Kingston C.I., he

was Shylock in a production of scenes from *The Merchant of Venice* . . . around 1927. . . . There's a picture of him, in full makeup.

After Renfrew, Kingston, the former capital of Upper Canada, with its old mansions, institutional buildings and impressive waterfront, struck young Robertson as physically beautiful and sociologically intriguing. So he recalled in a 1973 CBC radio interview.

RD

Kingston has something that is very rare in Canada, and that is actual, real civic beauty. . . . I had, until we moved to Kingston, lived a lot of my life in small towns and in virtually rural Ontario.

Kingston isn't a small town. Kingston is twice a city. It contains two cathedrals, and is the seat of two bishops, and when you lived there you certainly knew it. . . . Believe me, between them, those two men swung a terrific amount of power, and the Roman Catholic bishop had a very substantial amount of political power.

BEA CORBETT

In the Kingston in which I grew up, there were only two or three Catholic families which seemed to mingle. And they were very well-to-do. The Catholics kept to themselves. And they did not trust the Protestants, whom they all lumped together. The Presbyterians were a strong force here because of the Scottish presence. Religion was a strong force.

RD

Another thing which made Kingston a fascinating city to me; a city of gothic romance: there were many strange people. . . . One was spectacularly strange, and that was the very old Roman Catholic archbishop who had, in the Irish phrase, "survived his wits" and who lived as a highly respected, much honoured invalid in the Bishop's Palace, while a young, very strong, dark-faced coadjutor bishop ran the diocese.

On great occasions such as a visit from the papal nuncio, you saw the old archbishop carried through the streets. Two young priests held him under the arms. He had his mitre on. He obviously didn't know where he was or what he was doing, but there he was. It was, to me, wonderful. . . .

The Davieses had no Catholics in their social circle. They attended St. Andrew's Presbyterian Church.

JEAN RICHARDSON (Kingston contemporary)

I saw Robertson Davies sitting reading a book during the sermon. He always had a purple handkerchief in his pocket, sticking out. But if he blew his nose, he'd dig for an ordinary white one. That's what we'd sit and watch for. We sat across from him; we engineered it so we could see. And it was worth watching!

The Davieses' first house in Kingston was a modest place on Albert Street. But by 1928, *The Kingston Whig-Standard* was sufficiently profitable that they could afford to move into a grander house. One that was available for a good price was Calderwood, built around 1850 in the Tuscan villa style. It had been damaged by fire. Florence and Rupert repaired and refurbished it.

KATE BRAY

Calderwood's gardens were full of the most gorgeous bluebells in the spring. I will never forget the peonies and cana lilies. I also visited Florence at Calderwood, where I remember her in the library, doing her jigsaw puzzles, which were huge.

RD believed that Calderwood was haunted – or so he told Flora Betts, descendant of another Calderwood family, in a letter sent March 11, 1987.

RD

I can assure you that the tale that Dr. H.A. Betts either drowned or permitted his daughter Augusta to drown in the bath at Calderwood, was very widely circulated in Kingston at the time that I lived there and my family were frequently rallied on the subject of living in the house where it had happened. . . . We were given to understand also that it was precisely because Dr. Betts was a man of impressive personality that no investigation was made into this curious happening. There were dark hints as to Dr. Betts's reason for wishing to get rid of Augusta, but, of course, such things belong to the realm of rumour.

Another feature of RD's new life in Kingston was that the city, which lies between Montreal, Ottawa, and Toronto, was a stop for troupes of professional theatre companies.

TIMOTHY FINDLEY (from *Journeyman*)
I once did an interview with Robertson Davies on the subject of nineteenth and early-twentieth-century theatre in Canada – and one of the most telling images he evoked was of the great English actor-manager John Martin-Harvey.

Martin-Harvey's career bridged the turn of the century, and he often took his company on tour across the U.S. and Canada. Consequently, as a small boy, Robertson Davies saw Martin-Harvey perform. But more importantly, he saw him walk down the street.

It was winter. There was snow. A figure of majestic proportions strode towards the young boy, who was on his way somewhere in the company of his father.

Everything stopped.

There were scarves flying back in the wind. There was a Trilby hat pulled down above the eyes. Even full-face, there was the power of a gorgeous profile. A cape was appended to the shoulders of a great-coat. And there was a walking stick . . .

"Who . . . who . . . who was that?" said the boy.

"*That*," said Rupert Davies, "was Sir John Martin-Harvey – the actor."

Rupert was generous when treating his family to theatre and music, but as a self-made man, he took a controlling attitude to the family's money.

KATE BRAY
Rupert could be a pretty tight chappy. I know he had the reputation for having the first dollar he ever earned. If Robertson was on an allowance, I am not sure Arthur and Fred got allowances at all. . . . Rupert's sister Elsie never married, Mary married but was widowed, and Florence's sister Aunt Matt had nobody. So all were sort of dependent on Rupert. But I don't think he kept them lavishly. . . . Rupert often brought Aunt Matt to come to Calderwood to look after Florence. She wouldn't have cost him anything but food.

Florence did not need servants to "do" for her. . . . Florence did not see the need for a grand house. She was not happy with Rupert's aspirations to grandeur. It did not make her comfortable.

Despite their deepening estrangement, one thing Rupert and Florence agreed on was that their youngest boy was floundering in mathematics and Latin at Kingston Collegiate. After his first unimpressive year, they decided to send him to the most prestigious boys' boarding school in Ontario, Upper Canada College in Toronto.

Chapter 5

AN ELEGANT SEAT
OF LEARNING

Rupert's eldest son, Fred, went to Renfrew Collegiate and then went off to work at the Canadian Linotype company, probably before he was allowed to complete his studies (his daughter Kate is unsure). Arthur Llewellyn attended Renfrew Collegiate, though his parents did allow him to study art for one year at Northern Vocational School in Toronto. Their young brother arrived at Upper Canada College as a boarder in September 1928, aged 15. The schooling he got compared to that given his brothers was a factor in family dynamics.

MARTIN HUNTER
The older boys certainly never got to university. They worked for Rupert. I think they resented the fact that Rob didn't have to go through this.

Writing in *Maclean's* magazine in March 1951, June Callwood also noted that RD was the first in his family to attend a prestigious private school.

JUNE CALLWOOD
Fred and Arthur were . . . older than Robertson, and during their school years missed the ensuing prosperity. Robertson, however, was enrolled in Upper Canada College. He arrived at that elegant seat of learning attired in a wing collar with a four-in-hand tie and similar accessories down to somewhat Elizabethan shoes with buckles. A young boy in such affected dress has two choices: He can submit to ridicule and beatings or he can attempt to carry it off. Robertson chose the latter course. "How he did it, I have no idea," recalls a classmate. "His arrogance rather paralyzed everyone. He stared us all down."

RD's main biographer suggests that the reasons for RD's sartorial flamboyance had less to do with arrogance than with a simple error.

JUDITH SKELTON GRANT (RD's biographer)
At UCC, Davies had old-fashioned collars, but he told me that was because his parents had an outmoded clothes list from the school. As soon as they realized the collars were out of date, he got rid of them.

But other UCC alumni suspect that RD's dress and behaviour were part of an elaborate system of self-defence, as John Fraser, writing in *The Globe and Mail*, noted in 1975.

JOHN FRASER
The son of a self-made giant of a father, he was sent to Upper Canada College, where he had to learn very early on how to survive. Unless you've been immersed in that sort of masculine, waspish, jockish world – unfit for athletics and doomed with an imagination – it's a bit hard to realize the profound effect it can have. If you don't want to sink, you develop an act to keep the bullies at bay and the philistines beneath contempt.

HARRY RASKY
He told me that he'd felt that the other boys at UCC had very little curiosity and very few opinions which weren't inherited opinions. He said this was because they had been brought up in such a "terribly Tory" way.

How was he to hold his own in such a school?

RD
Quite soon I acquired a reputation for eccentricity. This was not surprising, for if you tell a boy he is odd, he is likely to become odd, even if only to be obliging.

MARTIN HUNTER
Freddy Mallett, Jane's husband, was a master at Upper Canada College and once, when Davies was mentioned, Freddy said, "Davies? Ah, yes. Odd chap. Wore a monocle." Though he didn't say whether Rob was wearing one just in preparation for a role he'd taken in some Gilbert and Sullivan play.

JOHN FRASER
There are some people who swear that when he was at UCC he wore both a monocle and a cape. Davies denies it with a chuckle, although he readily admits that life there necessitated some sort of performance. When I told him the name of the master who claimed he wore an eyepiece, he whooped with laughter.

JUDITH SKELTON GRANT
He said he wore a monocle because they were regularly worn by actors who couldn't otherwise see on stage. A monocle gives you half-vision without acknowledging that you are having terrible seeing problems. Rob especially had these problems on stage in the semi-dark. But the monocle didn't survive long.

JENNIFER SURRIDGE
One of the reasons he developed his personality, one of the reasons he developed a character at Upper Canada College, was he didn't like people to learn things about his personal life.

RD
Fortunately, there were others who understood that I had simply not acquired the knack of doing the expected, which was at that time – and still is to some extent – the secret of passing tests.

> *RD's marks in first term, November 1928*
> Form VB-1 [not the A form, but the form for the lesser scholars]
> W.R. DAVIES: Latin, 43; French, 43; English Literature, 80; Algebra, 0; Geometry, 19; Chemistry, 27.

The archivist at UCC, Marian Spence, points out that RD attended the school in an era before grade inflation. A mark of 57 was considered not bad, a 70 very good.

RD (from "A Chapter of Autobiography," *UCC Old Times*, 1979, Jubilee edition)
My earliest days at the school were clouded by several rebuffs. Not more than three days had passed before I was summoned to the headmaster's office, and I still recall exactly what he said to me: "Davies, I think you

ought to know that you won that scholarship for which you competed, but I have decided to award it to Blank instead of you; his mother, as you perhaps know, is a clergyman's widow, and your father can well afford to send you here."

My contribution to the conversation was "Yes sir," but I wished afterward (and I wish still) that I had the courage to say, "Why not give Blank the money and me the scholarship?" I should greatly have liked to be a scholarship boy, and I think it would have made a difference to my school years, because UCC respected brains, and I thought I had enough to take my place with others who bore the scholarship mark. . . .

I was put to share a room with Blank, the son of the needy widow. . . . He was an uneasy companion. He walked in his sleep, and twice took my clothes while in a trance and put them in a room on a lower floor, so that I had to trace them in the morning. Somnambulism – which he attributed to disturbed nerves – upset his digestion, and while sleeping he vomited in the washstand basin. Every night. This sounds like a grossly farcical invention, but I swear by all that I hold sacred that it is strict truth. . . . It gives me keen pleasure to add that Blank was expelled before the end of his first year. I think it was because of gambling, on which the school cast a cold eye. He was last seen by me driving down the avenue in a taxi, smoking a large cigar. This was educational: I have never trusted the son of a deserving widow since, nor has the principle ever failed me.

Did Davies embroider the story of "Blank" and his comeuppance? School records show that his roommate for a major part of 1928–29 was Edward Wade Devlin, with whom RD exchanged Christmas presents in 1930. Devlin and RD remained in contact into the late 1980s. Even if RD's account of the scholar he named Blank is true, there are other instances of RD's embroidering his UCC years.

RD
I recall my housemaster, William Mowbray, assuring us that we harmed our characters irreparably if we wore our slippers to breakfast, because Sir George Parkin [first secretary of the Rhodes Trust for Rhodes scholarships, and father-in-law of UCC's headmaster, W.L. Grant] had said that a man who did so revealed a lack of moral stamina.

RD wrote that in his *College Times* memoir in 1979. Yet, twenty years earlier, he sent this admission in a letter to Raleigh Parkin:

Yes, I can give you the source of the quotation which was attributed to your father, the late Sir George Parkin; it came entirely out of my own imagination. However, when I was a school boy at Upper Canada College, I heard your father quoted so often, particularly by my housemaster, William Mowbray, that he has always figured in my mind as a source of wise sayings. Unfortunately, Mowbray's favourite gem from your father's collection was "A gentleman never appears at breakfast in his slippers," and this was always followed by a detention.

> *Final marks, June 1929*
> W.R. Davies: Latin, 48; French, 85; English Literature, 88; Algebra (blank); German (blank); Chemistry, 57; Ancient History, 70.

With the above marks, RD ranked third in his form. However, in terms of the school's athletic culture, he was a failure.

KATE BRAY
When Robertson came along, he was not as good at sports as the older boys. . . . He didn't learn how to do boy things.

His inadequacies were reinforced in summer when he was sent, like many of his fellow UCC students, to a rigorous summer camp for boys, Ahmek, in the middle of Algonquin Park.

MIRANDA DAVIES
He was physically self-conscious and inhibited, and his mother's attitude was overprotective. She didn't allow him to swim or learn to ride a bicycle. You can imagine the effect this would have on a boy at camp, with everyone canoeing, swimming and trekking in the woods. He was rather clumsy and much preferred to read a book or play the piano. He mockingly called one lake with an Indian name "Lake Ohwhatawetness."

So it was something of a relief to return to school in the autumn. The schoolmasters, particularly the headmaster, Dr. W.L. "Choppy" Grant, opened young RD's eyes to a loftier and more beautiful world.

RD
A gentleman, as defined by Dr. W.L. Grant, was one who claimed his place in the world by devotion to high standards of honesty and courtesy, and maintained his claim by unrelenting hard work for some aspect of the public weal. . . . I recall a Sunday evening service of prayers where Dr. Grant startled some of us by shouting the great cry of Luther: "Live in the large; avoid sin if you can, but if you must sin, *sin nobly!*"

Alas, his math teacher was not so life-enhancing.

RD
For two years, his daily litany of contemptuous abuse, directed at my stupid head, was worse than anything I have had to endure since – and writers become acquainted with bitter criticism. At last the headmaster excused me from maths on the grounds of "invincible ignorance."

MIRANDA DAVIES
My understanding is that he did unusually well in virtually every subject, and senior matriculation [the university entrance examination] didn't present any difficulties for him. His problem arose because they required twelve papers for students to complete high school. And mathematics had to be one.

Mathematics continued to give him nightmares well into our lives. When we were older, he told us that he would wake up sweating from a horrid dream about a mathematics exam.

VICTORIA WOOD
My husband Jade [James Douglas Wood] had been at Upper Canada with Rob. Rob didn't have a very happy time there, but my husband loved it. Both were in a Gilbert and Sullivan operetta together, and in the three years they overlapped at Upper Canada, that was a bond. But at school Rob was absolutely no good at maths. Rob's humiliation in front of the class left a terrible scar.

JUNE CALLWOOD

Young Robertson Davies's mathematics were so bad he was unable to graduate from Upper Canada College, but he left his mark in the school's literary paper *In Between Times*. The brilliant satirical couplets he wrote have never been forgotten by his contemporaries, who also remember him for his buffoonery in the school's Gilbert and Sullivan operettas.

RD (from the UCC student journal *In Between Times*, 1931–32)

> On spinach and with Sun-Wheat biscuits fed
> What boy would say life's staff was puny bread?
> His health is moulded like a desert land
> Spinach and cakes supply the rock and sand.
> (And Camels are partaken of by some
> In secret when the evening meal is done).
> Dessert now hastens to adorn the board
> Anticipation fills the hungry horde.
> Will it be tapioca's fishy eye?
> The dread ingredients of a nameless pie?
> A pudding fashioned by the cook's deft hand
> 'Til it resembles nought on sea or land?
> Boys who reject such luxuries as these
> Are spoiled at home and are too hard to please.

ROSAMOND BAILEY

At Upper Canada College, they told my father on his report card, "Davies is incorrigibly frivolous." That's the *last* thing you would think about Dad!

Happily, RD could excel in the school's drama society. A 1931 *College Times* article on a school production of *Arms and the Man* reported:

> W.R. Davies as Captain Bluntschli showed, as he has shown before on the College stage, that he gives all the attention and care to his part that most people neglect to give their books, and that care, combined with a very good sense of dramatic value, went far towards making the production successful.

In a 1934 letter to a friend [Eleanor Sweezey], RD confessed that the school's theatre program was the setting for many adolescent male crushes.

RD
Ryerson (a friend from Upper Canada College) had quite a homosexual spell, and adventures in that mode with several people I know, but is now mad for girls. Every boy I have known has had something of the sort, some lasting a short time and some longer (my own was a week during which I was blinded by a lad who played Maria in *Twelfth Night* at UCC, in which I was Malvolio, but I said nothing to him about it, but hugged my passion as a secret).

Mavor Moore, then a student at a rival boys' school, was struck at drama competitions by RD's theatrical flair.

MAVOR MOORE
Upper Canada College had a lively tradition of all-male Shakespearean revivals. . . . I saw Rob as Malvolio in *Twelfth Night* at Upper Canada College. What struck me was that he brought out the clash in that role – the clash that occupied Davies a great deal in his later writing. . . . Not the clash between rich and poor, but what Dickens had also gone after: the clash between the pretentious and the pompous and the true and the natural. . . . That's what the role of Malvolio needs. He is a much put-upon character. Davies found the heart in that. He himself was misunderstood.

> *Marks, March 1932*
> W.R. Davies: Latin, 69; English Literature, 68; English Composition, 70; Modern History (NR – not recorded); Algebra (NR); Geometry (NR).
> Winner, the Wallace Rankin Nesbitt Cup in Extemporary Speaking and the John Martland Exhibition Medal in English.

In 1932, Rupert took his youngest son for another summer visit to England and Wales. Here the two of them looked at country property, and Rupert bought a house called Fronfraith just outside of Rupert's native Welshpool.

RUPERT DAVIES
I cabled Robertson's mother, on his suggestion, and she came over. Together we went to London and bought some furniture. My wife came back with me in 1933, and we did some more furnishing. She next

came back in 1936. That was a bad summer, and with her predilection to bronchial asthma she found the wet weather very trying. She did not come again.

The Davies family spent the summer of 1932 going to plays in Stratford-upon-Avon, to the Malvern Theatre Festival and to London. They must also have puzzled over the problem of what would become of Robertson, who had won prizes in public speaking and English literature at Upper Canada College but failed to graduate.

Chapter 6

QUEEN'S AND THE
"SPECIAL STUDENT"

Several influential people pitched in to help resolve the conundrum of RD's further education. Dr. Duncan MacArthur, chairman of Queen's admissions, developed a "special student" category to cover cases such as RD's. Later, when he became Ontario's minister of education, MacArthur did away with mathematics as a prerequisite for university admission. But that was too late to help RD, who, despite attending the lectures and working hard, never qualified for a Queen's B.A. – which surely embarrassed him.

GEORGINA ROSS MATTHEWS
He's not in the Queen's alumni directory. But I recall him at Queen's. And I heard him in the 1970s, at Guelph Spring Festival, talking about how introspective Queen's was in the 1930s and how unaware of the coming war . . . of how professors tried to speak to the students about gas attacks and so on, and about how Kingston was hit hard by the Depression, with many male students living in boarding houses where their rent was the only source of income for the families, because the husbands had been laid off. At the time, nobody realized . . .

The early 1930s were a quiet time in Kingston, so an eccentric such as the young Robertson Davies made a strong impression on people such as Bea Corbett, Jean Richardson, Georgina Ross and her future husband Joe Matthews.

GEORGINA ROSS MATTHEWS
He was noted on campus, oh yes, as a bit of a character. . . . He had an English accent, and he dressed differently from the other young men. He had a very fine tweed jacket with leather patches on the elbows, the

only one on campus. He wore a broad-brimmed brown felt hat, somewhat in the style that Pierre Trudeau wore. Everyone on campus knew who he was.

JOE MATTHEWS
I thought he was a professor. He certainly wasn't one of the gang. I didn't see him at hockey, I only saw him in the library, with his round black glasses and his furled umbrella. Always in the library.

BEA CORBETT
Sunday teas were great in those days. Mother was going to give a tea, and my father, a professor at Royal Military College, looked at the invitation list and said, "The girls are fine, but the men are a dull bunch. Why don't you invite Davies?" So we invited RD and the party went so well, everyone stayed for dinner. Robertson Davies was a Kingston character even then.

JEAN RICHARDSON
My sister wrote Robertson Davies a letter once, and told him all these things she could remember about him in Kingston. He wrote back a very nice letter and said it was good of her to remember him. But he said she had got one thing wrong: he never wore a cape. But he did!

BEA CORBETT
He certainly did!

JEAN RICHARDSON
I am so glad you remember. Perhaps it was a caped coat. And in summer, Robertson wore a broad-brimmed hat.

At Queen's, RD enrolled in Honours English. He also took courses in history, philosophy and psychology. Among his professors, James Roy stood out. A friend of J.M. Barrie, who wrote *Peter Pan*, Roy's specialties were the romantic poets – Keats, Shelley, Coleridge, Byron. As a character, Roy turns up in RD's *Murther and Walking Spirits* as James Alexander King, and in the play, *Fortune My Foe*, he is Idris Rowlands.

BEA CORBETT

Professor Roy was considered a great catch for dinner parties. We all thought he went on a bender every spring, when he would disappear for two weeks. But he was a very, very good professor, very good at getting information across to students and at keeping them interested. Robertson had a soft spot for him.

After Professor Roy had been at dinner one night and was a little the worse for wear, he took a wrong turn by the courthouse on Court Street and he hit the city fountain with his car. He went to jail for a week.

Robertson Davies and Bill Wilgar were the envy of their classmates when they took tea to Professor Roy in the jail and had a special seminar in his cell. My sister wanted to go to the jail, but my parents would not hear of it. In any case, time in jail did not affect Professor Roy's social standing. He was still invited to dinner parties.

RD found time to work on dramatic productions at Kingston's churches.

BEA CORBETT

When I was 10, I was one of three angels in the St. George's Anglican Cathedral Nativity Play at Christmas 1932. I had been plucked from Sunday school when the third angel became ill. I quickly learned my four lines, with cues, facing the prompter. But as I stood there, I began thinking about how, a week before, our Sunday school teacher, Miss Austin, had taken us around the cathedral and told us, "This is the chancel . . . it leads to the altar, the holiest place in the church."

As I stood there thinking of this, suddenly I felt a sharp jab to the ribs. My lines! I was forgetting them! The prompter was hissing at me. He was furious. Someone covered for me, and then we angels all trooped out, and the prompter gave me a baleful glance as he ran his hand through his thick mane of hair. That furious prompter was Robertson Davies.

The Kingston Drama Guild mounted a pantomime, *Alice in Wonderland*, in the fall of 1933. Arthur Davies, who had cut short his art studies to work for the family newspaper, volunteered to paint masks and sets; Robertson played two roles, the King of Hearts and the Gryphon, as well as taking it upon himself to advise the director.

BEA CORBETT

The rehearsals took place in a home not far from where we lived. We children would hide behind the sofa and watch. Then we would go into fits of laughter. I was nine or ten, and from my vantage point, he, Robertson Davies, took himself quite seriously. He never spoke to us.

He would interrupt the director, Mrs. [Daisy] Miller, and she had had dramatic training in England. What's interesting is that she never minded when he would interrupt her. He would be very self-confident, and she would certainly listen to him politely. I can still see him, sitting on the throne of the King of Hearts, saying how he thought things should be done!

RD turned 21 in August 1934. Yet he impressed people as a much older and more experienced man.

GEORGINA MATTHEWS

I was in Sophocles' *Oedipus, King of Thebes*, for the Queen's Dramatic Guild, the students' dramatic society. He was directing, and I saw a lot of him. Now, that was in the fall of 1934. I'd gone to Queen's as a freshette at 16 years of age, and I thought he was really old – about 30!

Under his direction, *Oedipus* was a very dramatic production, especially where the messenger comes in at the end, in a bright red tunic. He threw up his arms . . . [she demonstrates by throwing her arms up above her head] . . . with the announcement that *Oedipus* was dashing out his eyes. I was in the chorus. We were in yellow tunics – Grecian things with crisscrosses on the breast. We had a brief little speech to make. Under his direction, we'd step forward to the centre of the stage, three at each side.

As a director, he didn't intimidate people. He had a lovely, velvet voice, really. You had the feeling that for him, the voice was very important.

This was a very different play for Queen's students. The Classics department would have known the play, but for the rest of us, Robertson Davies took us into new territory, a new way of presenting a drama.

Working as a tutor for Queen's English students, RD was already feeling some of the formidable impatience with ignorance that would later daunt his university students. So he confessed in a 1934 letter to Eleanor Sweezey.

RD

The pay for the tutoring racket is beggarly, but one is accorded certain privileges in the University that make it worthwhile. The part of the job I really hate is giving "interviews"; that means sitting in a horrible room with sixteen corners and a slanting roof under the eaves of the Arts Bldg. and receiving students hour after hour, and explaining to them that there is no such word as "termendulously" or that a sentence without a verb is frowned on in literary circles.

Each night, when RD went home to Calderwood, he re-entered Florence's domain. Rupert was working hard at his small newspaper empire, and Fred and Arthur were adults. Florence lived more and more through her sons.

ROSAMOND BAILEY

Fred used to come in after dates and sit on his mother's bed and tell her all about them. My father told us this story as if it were a negative thing. . . . And he told me she would only be happy if all her three sons were at home at the same time and in bed. He regarded that as a negative, too. He regarded mothers as Not a Boy's Best Friend.

In April 1932, Fred Davies married Muriel Porter (the marriage lasted only five years). In May 1934, Arthur married Muriel's sister Dorothy. In a letter, RD explained how this would affect him.

RD

A most remarkable change has taken place in my home life. Despite the fact that I outraged convention by returning home at 5 a.m. on two successive nights, no word of reproach has been directed against me, and indeed my parents have been vying with one another to be nice to me. . . . I can only conclude that, as I am the only son now at home, my stock must have risen with my parents.

RD's late nights occasionally involved student escapades with pals. But more often, he was simply roaming Kingston's dark streets.

RD

I used to go for walks every night when I lived in Kingston . . . after I'd finished my studying . . . generally between 11 and 12 at night. I walked through that city in every possible season, and it would be hard to say when it was most beautiful. But I think it was perhaps most beautiful in winter, and as I walked through it you had a sense of nineteenth-century and early-nineteenth-century Europe.

At that time, I was interested in Russian novelists and German writers, particularly Heinrich Heine, and you know, sometimes as I walked through those streets, lyrics would force themselves upon my attention because so very often you felt that you were in a place all kinds of people before you were doing what you were doing then.

Now, what was I doing then?

I was a romantic young man and I was always in love with some girl or other, and quite often when I went out for my refreshing walk at night I walked past her house. It was a very beautiful house, not a house of wealth but a house that had the beauty of having been built well and been loved by a lot of people. I thought of that lyric from *Der Doppelganger*:

> *Still is the night, it quiets the streets down*
> *In that window my love would appear. . .*

I thought, here am I, looking at that girl's window, and I'll bet there have been at least a half a dozen people who've done exactly the same thing for a different girl at that window.

Chapter 7

FIRST LOVES

The romantic young man who was "always in love with some girl or other" could not impress his Juliets on the football field, but at campus theatre productions he excelled.

BEA CORBETT

In 1933, when *Alice in Wonderland* was produced, he seemed to be very enamoured of the girl who played Alice, Elizabeth Stewart. We could tell he was enamoured of her – the way he spoke to her and sought her out.

ELIZABETH STEWART KAMOFF-NICOLSKY

My father was Colonel, later Brigadier-General, James Crossley Stewart. The university people did not mix with the army. . . .

When it went around town that the Kingston Drama Group were going to have a wonderful production of *Alice in Wonderland*, Valerie Hora and I went along. I was in high school then. I was 17. We thought it would be fun to volunteer to be either the Dormouse or someone else at the Mad Hatter's tea party. But because I was the only one to come out who had long hair, I was picked to be *Alice*. I haven't the faintest idea who did the picking. But, of course, I remember Robertson Davies, because every day he and Mrs. Dorothea Goodfellow gave me private coaching in how to play Alice.

We went to Dorothea's house. She and Robertson Davies started from the beginning. I went almost every day, and I missed Latin class at school because of these drama classes. I failed my last Latin exam! But they taught me everything. Whatever Robertson Davies did, he was very good at. They taught me how to say my lines, how to move, gestures, timing. As Alice, I was on stage the whole time, and I never stopped talking.

Did they tell you how he looked in those days? He was very tall; he used to wear a large, black hat and a flowing tie, tied loosely at the neck. And his feet went like this – flap! flap! – the feet turned out, like Charlie Chaplin. And he carried a cane. He was very elegant with the cane. He looked like an artist from 1900.

I cannot believe he was only 20. Robertson Davies was very old for 20. He was an imposing figure. You couldn't miss him. When I think of him looking like that, walking through all those dreadful students at Queen's! I thought he was much much older. He had an English accent even then. It was an unusual voice. I can hear his voice as clear as a bell.

After the private acting lessons were underway, Robertson Davies informed me that I needed much more education. He was always saying that I should be better educated than I was. So he said he would take me to a concert. He arrived at my house in his father's car, a large car driven by his father's chauffeur. It was very grand. When he escorted me to the car I was very impressed with the chauffeur. I was ushered into the back seat.

I haven't the faintest idea what the concert was. It was classical. After we sat down, he kept trying to make me laugh, all through the concert. He was saying things *sotto voce*. He was not explaining the music to me! He was very amusing. I don't think he was making cracks about the musicians or the performance; he was not that kind of person. He was a very nice man. But it was funny.

Afterwards, he took me back to his parents' house, Calderwood, out on Union Street, to meet his mother and father. I remember his father, Rupert Davies, a very good-looking man with a mustache. His mother was a nice woman. One of his brothers was there with a girlfriend. I was there in the evening, and it seemed to me a very pleasant, warm room.

And then, a few days later, he came to tea at my house. I don't know why. I do not think he met my father, though he met my mother. She did not tell me what she thought of him. My mother did not make personal remarks. Robertson Davies wrote me a letter after that tea which was very amusing. I only went out with Robertson Davies that one time. . . . No, after that there was one excursion to the theatre as well.

BEA CORBETT

I can still see them, Elizabeth and RD, on the stage together. He was the Gryphon and the King of Hearts and she was Alice. Elizabeth was not tall and had lovely long hair and she would look up at him. As an actor, Robertson Davies has been called a ham. He certainly would not take a back seat at any production he was in. . . . I can still see Elizabeth at the end of that play, screaming, "You're nothing but a pack of cards!"

Alas, Elizabeth Stewart was more interested in military men than theatrical ones.

ELIZABETH STEWART KAMOFF-NICOLSKY
All my family was Presbyterian and went to St. Thomas, but I went with Jean Richardson to St. George's because the cadets were up there in the gallery. At the time of *Alice* I was very keen on a certain cadet. He was a most attractive man. Some of them were rogues! I never thought of Robertson Davies as a date. I liked him and thought him a most interesting man, but my family was in the military and the army is not given to great intellectuals. He was the one person I am sorry I never met again. He was the only intellectual I ever knew.

The young theatre director's passion next fell on a Queen's student and campus actress named Eleanor Sweezey. As he wrote half a century later in his novel *The Lyre of Orpheus,* "We all have an early love whom we keep in our minds all our lives."

BEA CORBETT
Then Robertson Davies's interest in Elizabeth seemed to pass. . . . Now, Judith Grant's biography of Robertson Davies was wonderful, but you could tell she was not from Kingston. In *Robertson Davies: Man of Myth* she refers to "a Mrs. Sweezey." But to someone from Kingston, this was *the* Mrs. Sweezey: Harriet Watson Sweezey.

    Harriet was in my mother's book club. She was a strong character and very pleasant. Her father had been a philosophy professor, Dr. Watson, and Watson Hall at Queen's is named after him. I can just remember Mother telling me that Dr. Watson was to present a paper in Vienna and fell ill, and Harriet took his place to deliver the paper.

RD wrote notes about the remarkable Sweezey family for his biographer, Judith Skelton Grant. He also edited, bowdlerized and extracted material from letters he wrote to Eleanor Sweezey between 1933 and 1937. The italics and brackets are RD's.

RD

THE LETTERS FROM WHICH these extracts are taken were written to a girl with whom I was in love; she returned them to me several years ago, which was considerate of her, for I would not have liked to have them fall into strange hands. There was nothing in them I was ashamed of, but they were, like most love letters, wretched stuff to anyone not a partner in the affair – overwritten, extravagant and foolish in all the ways that men in love are foolish. . . . But I am not reproachful – not now – for I see that I must have been a considerable nuisance. She was a scholarship student in philosophy at Queen's, with a strong leaning toward mathematics, and neither of those studies is a great friend to passion.

From Notes Made After I Had Known the Family Three Months
I first met Mrs. S. on December 9, 1933; I had been acting in a Christmas play which she had seen, and she asked me to meet her, through my friend Bell. I knew nothing of her except that her husband had been involved in the Beauharnois Scandal, which filled the papers for a time. I had only the vaguest recollection of this affair, and was surprised when she introduced the subject and seemed offended when I said I knew little about it and was not interested; she pressed newspaper cuttings on me and insisted that I inform myself as quickly as possible (why was that?).

In 1932, it had been discovered that the Beauharnois Light, Heat and Power Company, of which R.O. Sweezey was director, had given money to the Liberal Party in return for permission to divert the St. Lawrence River thirty kilometres west of Montreal to generate hydroelectricity. R.O. Sweezey testified that the company had contributed more than $600,000 to federal and provincial Liberal Party campaign funds. He served a brief prison sentence. RD put his own interpretation on all this in notes to his biographer, Judith Skelton Grant.

RD

Mrs. S. is frequent in her eulogies of her husband's character and genius; he is reputedly a brilliant engineer, though the circumstances of the scandal showed that he understood little of people, and particularly that devious sub-section, politicians. She plays the role of the faithful, much-tried wife, but says she has contemplated divorce. Meanwhile, she is a rival of her daughters, and warns me against becoming involved with E. [Eleanor], who is, she says, cruel and inconstant. (There was some truth in this, as I subsequently discovered, but not to anything like the degree her mother suggested.) A peculiar, unhappy household, but with the attraction of what is strange. So unlike the home life of the Davies family, where angry passions and discontents are sternly repressed and boil beneath the surface.

Mrs. Sweezey asked RD to produce a play for her New Year's party, *The Importance of Being Earnest*. Here he met her husband and his brother, who may have suffered shell shock in World War I. Two Sweezey daughters appeared later. At first they teased him, but soon were laughing at his jokes. And as he suggested in his letter recollecting snowball fights in Renfrew, RD was no victim, but was capable of physically defending himself.

RD

The uncle, when Mr. S. returned to Montreal, asserted that he was the guardian of the morals of his nieces . . . and once knocked me down in the course of a row; I am glad to remember that I made him regret that, for though no great fighter, I was bigger than he was, and neither drunk nor sick of the pox. . . .

The daughters were divided in their loyalty, the younger one favouring the mother. They were not really rich; their fortune was in ruins, and the household, though it was conducted on a lavish scale, had an atmosphere of fallen grandeur. . . .

At New Year, I was a guest at the house party for a week, and became increasingly convinced that these people were very odd indeed, but they were amusing as other people were not. And I fell in love.

Which did not escape the notice of other young people in Kingston.

JEAN RICHARDSON

I remember RD in church, in St. George's, on a Sunday night with Eleanor Sweezey. It was a winter night. She was just a dream girl, she was so lovely. It was evensong. They would just go on Sunday night to be together. They would sit in the middle of the church. . . . They definitely did not go for the sermons!

ANDREA SWEEZEY CAMERON

I never knew about [my aunt] Eleanor's relationship with Robertson Davies until Judith Grant's biography came out. My grandmother Harriet studied at Queen's when she was in her thirties. Her husband, R.O. Sweezey, was in Montreal much of the time on business, while the family lived a fair bit of time in Kingston at Pine Ledge, their summer house. It was built in 1929 on the St. Lawrence River. It was stone and shingle. Oh, it was beautiful. The walls were this thick. Amazing . . . an English country house.

In RD's final year at Queen's, 1935, the Drama Group presented an outdoor production of *A Midsummer Night's Dream*. Daisy Miller was the producer-director; RD co-directed. Rupert and Florence agreed to let the Drama Group stage its production of *Dream* in the grounds of Calderwood. Rupert even joined in, as another young participant recalls.

MARGARET GIBSON

He played the Duke of Athens. He was a rather dramatic man!

BEA CORBETT

When *Midsummer Night's Dream* was held at Calderwood, I think I was about 11, in Grade 7. I had to lead the other fairies in from one side. This play was staged for three nights. Robertson was Lysander and whenever I see the play now, I hear Lysander as Robertson. He played opposite Eleanor Sweezey, who was Hermia.

I remember him being quite bossy. Mrs. Miller directed and Peggy Miller was Titania, the best I ever saw. But RD kept interjecting with his views. He was certainly flamboyant. Other people in the cast were used to him, people like Pyramus, Jim Conacher, who later became a classics prof at University of Toronto. People knew what to expect from Robertson.

MARGARET GIBSON

I remember Robertson only as a little girl, when I was just a little fairy in that play and I was wearing my bathing suit with a little cheesecloth wreath on it and wreaths in my hair. But I remember that it was marvellous to be able to stay up late and dance under the moonlight.

BEA CORBETT

When Robertson played Lysander and Eleanor was Hermia, there were offstage romances. The couples would come back into the woods. We children, when we weren't on stage as fairies, ran around flashing our torches on recumbent couples and then darting away. Darn it, I never saw Robertson with Eleanor. But you could tell that he was sweet on her. She was doubtful about him.

When Judith Skelton Grant was preparing her definitive biography of RD, she questioned him about this relationship, which he hadn't discussed with even his closest friends, and began to sense how it still haunted him.

JUDITH SKELTON GRANT

In his relationship with Eleanor there was always an element of resentment. He felt himself the supplicant, not in control of the situation. Later, he found it deeply satisfying in reading Jung to see he was not the only one to fall prey to an uncontrolled element in his psyche.

JENNIFER SURRIDGE

I have worked on RD's diaries, and there are times when I want to throttle Eleanor. From 1933 to 1934 he never shut up about her. A 20-year-old can get tedious. His infatuation was understandable, though. He so craved someone to give him affection. . . .

I didn't like typing this diary. He went on and on and on about her. The 1933 diary is about 150 typed pages and as I typed, I would go, "Please! Get over yourself!" After he went to England, he had a kind of mental breakdown.

RD left Canada to study at Oxford in 1935, but continued to court Eleanor by letter and during holiday visits home. Her reluctance to commit herself only deepened his emotions.

BRENDA DAVIES

He had had an unfortunate experience falling in love with Eleanor Sweezey. He was frightfully romantic. . . . He told me about Eleanor. It was obviously painful. He quoted poetry and he expected the world to be very much more than it was, colourful, exciting and rich.

ANDREA SWEEZEY CAMERON
He wrote to my aunt Ellie from Oxford in 1936 that he was in the hands of a Dr. Gillespie, undergoing psychoanalysis, and that he had had a nervous breakdown, which he referred to as his third. But he added that he was much, much happier now. He signed that letter "Love, Bob."

The story through my mother was that Robertson Davies had expressed love for Ellie, but her father wouldn't allow it. Maybe that was just Ellie's excuse. The truth was, her sister Maggie was very dominating. As a child, I was always in fear of her . . . and Maggie was not going to let Ellie go.

Eventually, Eleanor and Margaret Sweezey moved to Montreal. Eleanor worked as a medical illustrator, a meticulous job at which she excelled. She never married. In his notes to his biographer, RD offered a dramatic explanation.

RD
Marriage may not have been to her taste. . . . But I suspected then, and suspect now, another reason, which is that there was madness in her family: her grandfather, a noted authority on Kant and a double-dyed Calvinist, died mad, as did his daughter, her mother. She may have feared to continue that strain. . . . She was not a girl of strongly reciprocating passion, but she was a person of strong principle.

RD's gothic explanation of Eleanor's reluctance to marry has little in common with the Sweezey family's understanding.

ANDREA SWEEZEY CAMERON
Ellie would work all day, then come home and look after her sister, who never had a job. . . . As life went on, Maggie's health worsened, related to excessive smoking and drinking. . . . Ellie also looked after her father, as he grew older. I think she sort of gave up her own life.

Chapter 8

A LOST OXFORD YEAR

The challenges which Rupert presented to his bright, eccentric, youngest son were daunting. Technically, RD had never passed Grade 13 nor graduated from Queen's, yet Rupert wanted him to right an old family wrong: the sacrifice his father, Walter, had made when he cut short his studies at Oxford.

ROSAMOND BAILEY
My dad saw himself, in terms of his parents, as that he did't have much to offer. He couldn't get his Grade 13, he failed math, he didn't get into Oxford until Rupert came in with extra pull or something. . . . Rupert made sure that Oxford got some very strong letters of recommendation from a Queen's professor.

JUDITH SKELTON GRANT
His father had been instrumental in getting him into Oxford. RD had applied, and had had no response, so Rupert Davies dropped into Oxford to find out what had happened to RD's application and discovered that there had been a change in registrars and the application had gotten lost. RD's Queen's profs had done a laudable job in presenting an unconventional student who would do a good job at Oxford. They'd sent a sample essay and letters of recommendation. Rupert had a lot of chutzpah.

Finally admitted to Oxford, RD sailed to England on the *Empress of Britain* in the fall of 1935. In a letter to Eleanor Sweezey, he reported that also on board were Oxford-bound friends from UCC, including Douglas LePan.

RD
Sometimes LePan and I walk around the first-class decks, hoping not to be detected, but they are much more suited to longish walks. . . . I sit at a table with two girls, 13 and 14, who are very nice and believe that I am the cardinal's Protestant secretary, which is what I told them; it is vile to play upon such innocence, but the temptation is overwhelming.

RD moved into his rooms in Oxford's Balliol College on Wednesday, October 9, 1935.

My rooms are right at the end of the Garden Quad, off a small court-yard which is reached through an arched passage. I have a sitting-room, fireplace with a big mirror over it, and built-in bookcase which nicely accomodates [sic] the two huge chests of books I have brought; the stone floor is covered with a thick carpet of garish design; all very Victorian and pleases me greatly. I have hired a piano, a "little mini," as the man called it, and slaves have dragged it up the two flights of stairs; good tone. Some personal things have made the whole place mine. . . . I have bought a few pictures: Dürer's *Madonna with Many Beasts*, and my great favourite, Bronzino's *Allegory of Time*; most undergraduates run to Van Gogh's *Sunflowers*, a dull, safe choice.

I have bought a Balliol scarf, which is in stripes of navy blue, white and a sort of cerise; bold in effect and six feet long; no need to wear an overcoat. . . . Yesterday I was lying on my sofa reading *The Golden Ass* when who should burst in but Curtis, the Presbyterian parson; ticked me off for reading Apuleius, which he described as tawdry, degenerate stuff. I countered by demanding that he bring back my Spenser, which he had borrowed. What gall.

Among the many UCC grads at Oxford whom RD already knew, one was from a family with which he would have a lifelong connection.

Lionel Massey is also here, the youth who sought my advice about what one should do if one had a wet dream while a guest at Rideau Hall. Obviously, he thought it would be the talk of the breakfast table. He means well but is petrified with fear of doing something that is not "good form"; his life is a hell of anxiety. Several times a day he bursts into my room with some revelation about whether one is supposed to walk on the grass, or spit at the Dean, or whatever. He doesn't think my eyeglasses are good form because he has not seen anybody else wearing them. He even asked me if I thought one was supposed to empty one's jerry into the slop-pail or leave it for one's scout [college servant] to do. A moot point; why not pee out of the window? . . .

Lionel asked me to a party, which was decent of him, for all his blue-blooded friends were there. . . . Not the brightest spirits in the coll., but they took me to their noble bosoms and laughed heartily at all my jokes, so there must be some good in the nobility after all.

RD also made another life-long friend in an American medical student, Horace Davenport. His son was named after RD.

ROBERTSON DAVIES DAVENPORT

My father had been at the California Institute of Technology and got a Rhodes scholarship to study physiology at Oxford. He spoke a lot about Robertson Davies and their time together at Balliol. Partly what brought them together was that they were both foreigners in Oxford – my father the American, Rob the Canadian. They had a group, with William Sachse and John Espey, which they called the Long Christmas Dinner Society, and they would get together to make up riddles and poems. . . . My father, Horace, appreciated the depth and sophistication of the humour. They'd exchange puns. I don't know how this started, but Rob wrote a satirical poem about a empty box and my father wrote a sonnet on the theme of the empty box, which was bawdy, the box being a vagina. This was the sort of humour they shared.

My father had a different background from Rob. He had very little money at Oxford. Rob probably had a lot more, even if his father kept him on an allowance.

After RD's death in 1995, Horace Davenport wrote down the ideas he would have liked to share with his friend in a document he called "A posthumous conversation with Robertson Davies."

HORACE DAVENPORT

When Robertson Davies and I met in Balliol College in 1935–36, we began long conversations to find out what each other was like. . . . We talked most frequently in my rooms on Staircase XV, but sometimes later, after Hall, Rob would invite me to his rooms, where we would sit in front of his fire, drinking stout or Gin and It. . . . At Balliol, I told

Rob Davies something about my problems with my mother. He had a Tartar himself to contend with, and he knew what I was saying. . . . When we were old men, I reviewed with Rob all the miseries that had made my mother what she was. I ended by saying rather sententiously, "To understand is to forgive." Rob said, "Horseshit!"

RD (from his précis of letters to Eleanor Sweezey)
Another Scot, one Macgregor, besieges me for sex counsel. . . . Is it all right to "feel" girls if you wash your hands first? He is a medical student, and when I had given satisfactory answers to all his questions, he diagnosed me as a case of insufficient thyroid. . . . What it is about me that inspires this sort of confidence? . . . Somebody referred to me the other day as "The Havelock Ellis of Balliol." I wish I were. But the fact is that I am extremely curious, and will listen, and this nosiness consumes a lot of time.

On rare occasions, RD had got into physical scraps back in Canada, and was once "knocked down in the course of a row" in the Sweezey household. This unexpected side of him surfaced again at Oxford.

RD
Got into trouble on Guy Fawkes Night; the university had been warned not to create any "demonstrations". . . . But returning from the innocent and childlike pleasure, found suddenly that I was in the middle of a fight between univ. people and townees, who were very tough; but I found myself enjoying it, holding my specs with one hand and punching likely subjects with the other. There were a lot of cops about, and one of them tore the seat out of Eliot Emmanuel's pants – not an easy thing to do, but perhaps they have a technique for it. The University Proctors were surging to and fro, with their bullers (Univ. servants, fleet of foot and hard of fist), but we seemed to be all right till we met a drunk we knew who had a great idea: we should seize the back wheels of the next car that passed, bringing it to a stop and astonishing the passengers; so he dived at the car, and Emmanuel followed him, and I was about to follow when I was nabbed by a buller, who said in a gentle voice, "The Proctor wants to see you, sir."

I attended upon the Proctor at 9:30 Thursday; he was merry and bright and still licking bits of breakfast out of his teeth; discharged me and Emmanuel with a severe warning about brawling (me? a brawler?) but no fine.

At this point, RD's précis of his Oxford letters to Eleanor (which he made for his biographer Judith Skelton Grant) skips from the autumn of 1935 to the autumn of 1936 and deals at length with his growing involvement with theatre and the Oxford University Dramatic Society.

RD

I have been asked by the OUDS to be their stage manager for their forthcoming big production, *Richard II*. . . . As stage manager, I have to be continually attentive, but it is not in the least wearisome. [John] Gielgud is quiet and authoritative. . . . Every now and then something really marvellous is done by JG. Everybody says, "How does he do it?" I know how he does it; what I don't know is how he thinks of it.

A stage manager has a lot of jobs to do, great and small, but at rehearsals he must "sit on the book" – i.e., make notes of every move and effect the director wants in the large prompt-copy, which eventually becomes the Bible of the prod. And of course, if something goes wrong, it is always his fault, and sometimes even is so. . . . New officers elected today and to my surprise I am elected to the committee; I wasn't there and only heard of my election by chance. This is considered meteoric!

And later in 1936:

I am now Treasurer of the OUDS, and my whole life seems to be spent in accounts, and sending duns to people, and issuing writs against debtors. . . . Previous secretaries have been so lax that the OUDS is now owed over £1,700 in unpaid debts, and I am determined to get as much as I can, for we are not a large affair, and can't afford that kind of thing (I did get about ¾ of it). Can you imagine *me* as a man of business; I am a positive Scrooge, and recently had a man nabbed just as he was embarking for the U.S.A., and £50 was ripped off him on the dock, to his dismay.

Reading RD's synopsis of his letters from Oxford, a reader can only infer that these years were great fun. This wasn't a complete picture. One hint was this:

RD (from the letters to Eleanor)
My status has now been changed, and I am an advanced student, working for a B. Litt. [a research degree]. So I shall never be a B.A. or an M.A., but perhaps people won't notice.

When she read RD's précis five decades later, Judith Skelton Grant did notice. She also noticed that RD had skipped over much of early 1936. She told him that she needed to go over that period more closely, which led to what Grant terms her first "major crisis" in writing RD's biography.

JUDITH SKELTON GRANT
At the end of that first chat on Oxford I said, "The next time we meet I want to ask you about someone named Dr. Gillespie." In putting his name on the list, I thought Dr. Gillespie was someone Davies had worked for. . . . I'd transcribed every interview Davies had done at the CBC and I had a body of material which he had thought was irretrievable. That's where I got Dr. Gillespie's name. I did not know that he had been Davies's psychiatrist. And after the first interview on that Oxford period, I spent the weekend with some British friends who'd been to Oxford. I said, "There's something wrong here with the structure and the chronology." My friend said, "It should have taken him two years to do this, and here it took him three." So when I went back for week two of the Oxford interviews, intending to ask him about Dr. Gillespie, he said before I began, "I think we'd better start over."

He had not told me about Eleanor Sweezey. Nor about the major psychological breakdown. He had not told me about Dr. Gillespie. He had not told me that he had flunked his exams at the end of the first year in an absolute tizzy.

RD's breakdown at the end of his first-year studies at Oxford was in part due to ill health, and to the stress of trying to meet his parents' expectations.

BRENDA DAVIES
Walter Davies [RD's grandfather], had had to leave Oxford, so it had been very important to the family and to Rupert. I wouldn't be surprised if there was too much pressure on Rob at Oxford.

JUDITH SKELTON GRANT
There may well have been a string pulled [to get RD into Oxford]. Rupert knew people in the social hierarchy. So when RD flunked that year, he would have lost face with his father.

And there was also the beating his ego had taken when Eleanor rejected him. He made light of his talks with Dr. Gillespie when writing to her, as can be seen from the précis he gave to Judith Skelton Grant.

RD's version of his letter to Eleanor
I have also been going every Saturday to London for talks with Dr. R.D. Gillespie – not analysis, but an outside view of my affairs, and it is going splendidly; I make him laugh, and I don't suppose many patients do; a brilliant man, and the picture of a London physician of the fashionable sort – top hat and morning dress when he goes to his hospital, St. Bartholomew's, in his Rolls limousine.

BRENDA DAVIES
Rob only went to Dr. Gillespie for a short psychoanalysis. Dr. Gillespie thought that he had been very badly brought up, which was liberating for Rob, and let him take a fresh look at his family. . . . Rob was a very nervous man. He had a lot of bad dreams. He was very affected by personalities and by everything that happened to him. I always thought he had one skin too few. . . . When he told me that he had had a nervous breakdown at Oxford and had gone to see a Dr. Gillespie, I didn't pry, I didn't push it. In those days, psychology was not widely trusted. And he didn't want people to think that he was strange and different.

After RD told Grant about Dr. Gillespie, he sent her this addendum to his memoir of that period:

RD
Gillespie talked me into some sort of reasonable estimate of this love affair [with Eleanor], which he saw as disastrously one-sided – an anima projection of a not uncommon sort, except that every instance is individual and the rules are never quite the same.

With the exception of Brenda, RD never discussed this period of his life with anyone.

HORACE DAVENPORT (posthumous letter to RD)
I visited Rob three times at ffrontfraith [sic], his father's summer home in Montgomeryshire. . . . In front of a coal fire we talked for hours. We learned a lot about each other, but by no means all there was to tell. When Judith Grant wrote Rob's biography, she ferreted out a great body of information about Rob's family, childhood, schooldays and early romantic involvements that I had known nothing whatever about.

I think that I was a bit more candid than Rob at Balliol and in our subsequent conversations.

Nor was RD fully candid about his experience with psychoanalysis with his later, younger friends, including a former student who became a professor of drama at Guelph University, Peter Brigg.

PETER BRIGG
RD once said to me in some context that he had never had analysis, which I took to mean a proper full-scale Jungian analysis. But as we now know, he had had a Freudian psychoanalyst when he was at Oxford.

Think about what that means, and think about a man whose background includes having had nervous breakdowns at Oxford, the man to whom life has come with shocks. Compare that to the man rowing with a steady stroke through life, as depicted in some of the biographies.

Did Rupert know about Dr. Gillespie? It's very likely that he knew that RD was seeing a London doctor because Rupert retained considerable control over his son's finances during this period.

RD (letter to Eleanor Sweezey)
Have been spending all day paying bills and getting ready to close this place [Fronfraith] up when I go back to Oxford. I have to keep strict accounts to be gone over by my Father.

JUDITH SKELTON GRANT
Rupert gave Robertson hellish problems over money. RD was never openly critical of his father, but his father would say, "Go and buy X and Y," and then the bill would come and his son would have to justify every

cent. The big difference between RD and his brothers was that RD was the son of a rich man. But he still had to justify every cent he spent.

Returning to Oxford for the 1936–37 year, RD took great pleasure both in theatre and in practical jokes. Both gave him a sense that he could convince people of a different reality.

RD

Prospects for the next term are bright; a Balliol group wants to do Milton's *Samson Agonistes* and Max Patrick, who is something of a giant, will make a good Samson; I am to direct; also, my tutor wants me to play Touchstone in the OUDS summer prod of ASYLI [*As You Like It*] . . . several people questioned me about what the OUDS were going to do about lighting in Magdalen Grove?

So I told them of something that Davenport and I have devised; he is doing the lighting, at which he has experience gained at the Pasadena Playhouse. We say we are going to use a new German device, called the Boehmann Frame; causes light to bend, and thus go *around* objects instead of falling directly on them, thus avoiding ugly stage shadows.

They all swallowed it, and it is a goodish hoax. Davenport can be extremely technical in support of it, and I think Einstein comes into it, somewhere. Actually we are just putting spots and floods in the trees – but cunningly, so they do not show, giving an effect of sunlight or moonlight. Davenport is always teasing the OUDS, who are very solemn about Americans.

Thanks in part to sessions with Dr. Gillespie, RD graduated in the spring of 1938 with a genuine sense of accomplishment – and an impressive thesis on Shakespeare's boy actors. He described his thesis defence in a letter to Douglas LePan.

I was glad to hear that you had got a good job at Harvard. . . . For my part, I got my B. Litt., and with some distinction, if I may blow a bit. My examiners were Sir Edmund Chambers and Dr. Percy Simpson, a couple of tough Elizabethan babies, but they gave me a ten-minute viva, complimented me on what they called "a valuable and original piece of work," advised me to publish, & bade me Good-Day. I had anticipated an awful struggle & vomited twice before going into the viva, so you may judge my relief and ecstasy. The thesis, in fact, attracted some attention and even won me the congratulations of the Master of Balliol, sour-puss though he is. To me, the despised and rejected, this was nectar, and I took the degree with a feeling of relief that the struggle was over and that I was now a certified Wise Man. I was amazed that I had no difficulty in getting a publisher.

Something else happened during his final year at Oxford, though RD did not realize its importance until later.

RD (letter to Eleanor Sweezey)
I am working hard on the stage management of *As You Like It*. . . . Stage managing is a dog's life. . . . One actor was stabbed in the leg with a dirty sword from a costumer's and has a nasty infected wound (Willoughby Gray).

BRENDA DAVIES
I had met Rob in June 1938 when Willoughby Gray invited me to go down to Oxford to see the Oxford University Drama Society production of *The Taming of the Shrew*. . . . Rob was playing Christopher Sly, who acts as an audience and is on stage all through the show. Afterward, at supper, Willoughby introduced me to Rob, who offered me his bacon and eggs. . . . I hadn't had any supper, yet I refused. I thought his need was greater than mine because he'd been working all day.

And I was exceedingly independent and did not wish to accept favours from strange men, not knowing what they would want in return.

Chapter 9

IN LOVE AND WAR

Brenda Ethel Mathews Newbold was born in Australia on January 17, 1917. Like RD, she came from a family with money, colonial attitudes and cultural ambition. Like RD, she was insecure about her academic short-comings (she never went to university because of undiagnosed dyslexia).

Brenda's childhood was unsettled. Her mother, Muriel Larking, was just 22 years old when she married Paul Mathews, the son of a private-school headmaster. Paul had graduated from Cambridge with a first-class degree in mathematics. It was 1914, and the beginning of the First World War; Paul, a conscientious objector, took his wife to Tasmania to grow apples. The young idealists had no sense of what they were getting themselves into, and survived only thanks to Muriel's dress allowance from her mother. Their first daughter, Maisie, was born on September 1, 1915. Shortly after Brenda's birth, Muriel left Paul and returned with the babies to her mother and the upper-middle-class comforts of Melbourne. Brenda had no early memory of her father, but if she or her sister got into trouble, Muriel would threaten to "send them to Paul." Muriel's second marriage, to an alcoholic named Newbold, ended when Brenda was 16. At 19, Brenda left to study drama at the Old Vic in London. Muriel and Maisie arrived soon after.

BRENDA DAVIES

At the Old Vic I was a good deal more mature for my age than the English students who had come right out of boarding school, and had no experience compared to the freedom we had in Australia. I had driven a car since I was sixteen – in the country, as you couldn't get a licence until you were eighteen. I had helped run a house, been hostess at dances in our house, and I had travelled a lot.

And she had gumption.

BRENDA DAVIES

When we were on Baker Street, my mother, sister and I decided to go for a holiday to the south of France. At the train station, I remembered that I had not got my passport. I took a taxi back to the house, which was locked. I decided to burgle it by climbing up a ladder. The window wasn't locked, so I climbed in and got my passport – and got back to the station just in time to see the train pull away. I had to go on to Paris on my own, and I spoke no French. Fortunately, I had the hotel address.

BASIL COLEMAN (friend)

Brenda and I were students at the Old Vic. She and I got on awfully well. I was from Rhodesia. We probably bonded as colonials. And we both thought that the Old Vic's director, Tyrone Guthrie, was so exciting – daring, in an interesting way. When he did *Henry V* and Laurence Olivier did that speech, "Once more unto the breach, dear friends" – he had Olivier climb a wall and we students came on stage and shone lamps on him – it had never been done like that before. I suppose Tyrone Guthrie was a father figure to all of us. He was larger than life in every way, and remained so in life for me.

BRENDA DAVIES

It is a great disadvantage to be brought up without a father's influence to balance the family of women. It is no wonder I took on Tyrone Guthrie as a father figure when I went to the Old Vic.

Rob Davies, the young man she had met at Oxford, joined the Old Vic in December 1938 at Guthrie's invitation. His jobs included bit-part actor, dramaturge and lecturer. The theatre building was squalid, but RD felt at home.

BRENDA DAVIES

The Old Vic had no showers and no facilities except a stinking men's room in the basement. This was a period when actors' social standing was not very high, and they weren't expected to have comfort. The dressing room was a mirror along one wall, a couple of hard chairs, and a shelf for makeup.

BASIL COLEMAN
He struck me as very mature. I am always in awe of people with an intellect. He'd been to two universities. But it was a very warm encounter. This was a highly professional company, and though Rob had had no training as an actor, it never occurred to anyone that he was anything but a professional actor. He was always a *big* man, and in those days clean-shaven. Pleasant and happy. . . . Rob never mentioned his mother to me, but he mentioned his father as having gone from rags to riches. He admired that.

BRENDA DAVIES
When Rob first came to the Vic as lecturer to the students on the history of the theatre, and to play small parts, he was listed as "William Robertson Davies." I was getting all the lists of names, which was one of the stage manager's jobs, and I went to his dressing room to ask him if his name was hyphenated. He was known as Rob – he'd dropped the William. He said it wasn't hyphenated.

But after I'd gone, he heard one of the other actors say, "Oh, that's Brenda Newbold. It's tuppence to speak to Brenda!" I was only 21 and I was trying very hard to be official because of my extreme youth. A Cockney backstage said, "Stage managers! I've seen them grow!" I suppose I *was* formal in those days. I was driven to it!

I remember we were doing a production of *Romeo and Juliet* with Robert Donat, and Rob was playing old Capulet. He was 25! And Basil was the suitor, Paris, who comes to Juliet's tomb. Rob could hardly see in the dark and he could not wear his glasses with his costume – and was extremely short-sighted without them. He and Basil had to climb up a very dark and steep stair to enter the tomb scene. Basil was thin and Rob was square and six feet. They'd climb in from a ladder backstage and go down into the tomb from above. I think they scrambled and faltered. He was grateful for Basil's help.

BASIL COLEMAN
Now that my sight is so bad I realize what a handicap it must have been for Rob. . . . Rob, we felt, was an intellectual, an academic, not an actor. I remember him on stage. He was not great, but he was competent. I would say that Rob just didn't have enough experience as an actor. It takes time.

BRENDA DAVIES
Tony [Guthrie] was very hard on an older member of the company, Ben Webster, who was then in his late seventies. RD was fascinated by this Webster because he had worked on the first production of *Lady Windermere's Fan* and remembered Oscar Wilde. And he had worked with Sir Henry Irving on one of his tours of America. Rob was thrilled, and Webster was pleased to find a young man listening to him. RD was a great listener and helped him with his lines. . . . When he forgot, Webster felt badly, and Tony made cutting remarks in front of the whole company. . . .

Rob and I both romanticized Tyrone Guthrie. He was always a very life-enhancing person. Things brightened up when he was there. We had huge regard for Tony, but the head of a theatre is someone you don't get to know very closely. It wasn't until later on that we began to understand his character.

Early in 1939, when Guthrie went on tour, he promoted Brenda to stage manager. She was the first woman in that job in the theatre's history, and was then 23.

BRENDA DAVIES
There is a picture of me on the wall of the Old Vic, hanging on the stairs to the lower lobby. It was taken during a rehearsal of *A Midsummer Night's Dream*. I am standing on a basket, talking to Tyrone Guthrie and Laurence Olivier and Anthony Quayle, and I am identified as "Member of Staff." Jennifer pointed it out to me on a visit to London in 2005.

At Christmas 1938, the Old Vic mounted a production of *A Midsummer Night's Dream*, accompanied by Felix Mendelssohn's music.

BRENDA DAVIES
The overture was to play a certain number of bars and then the curtain would go up, and I was to signal that. I don't read music. And so, when I saw that RD had been talking in the stalls to Tyrone Guthrie about Mendelssohn and how to fit the music with the production, I went to him and asked him if he'd come and give me the nod. He was playing one of the Rude Mechanicals. He was shy . . . though a great man for covering it up. But he was shy. He certainly came most faithfully. Just

stood by me in the prompt corner, which in those days was just beside the stage. He was always perfect.

RD (in a 1938 letter to Douglas LePan)
Now, what about you? Are you married yet? Everybody else is. John is and Sachse and everyone else I know except Horace, who is wedded to science. . . . But marriage is definitely in the air; I had to go away to be best man to a friend this summer, and, as is usual at weddings, everyone predicted that I would be next. God forbid! Much as I like the nubile and beautiful, I cannot even contemplate the prospect of a lifetime with one. So much of my time is given to the struggle after eternal things, and a wife would probably deride that and make me wash napkins (baby's, not sanitary). Not, mind you, that I have suffered from any feminine persecution yet; the customary indifference prevails.

JENNIFER SURRIDGE
There was another woman in England, Birgitta Rydbeck, a very interesting woman who later taught voice for the Swedish state. At the time, she was a 19-year-old drama student at the Old Vic. RD invited her out early in 1939. He projected feelings on her and she said, "Absolutely no way!"

In March 1939, the Old Vic and Sadler's Wells held their annual costume ball. Brenda suggested RD take a Miss X. Davies did so, but it gave him the idea that Brenda might be more in need of a worldly defender than she let on, for she was unaware that Miss X had a reputation as a loose woman.

BRENDA DAVIES
I think I acted out of fright, out of fear that he might ask me! I suggested he take this girl to the party, not knowing that she was very questionable indeed. He faithfully took her. The Vic-Wells Ball was a huge thing, fancy dress. I went with someone else, I can't remember who. The one thing I do remember is getting him to ask the wrong person. I suppose I did sense that he was becoming interested, and I did sense that things were dangerous. I'd seen in my own family bad marriages and I was very uneasy taking up with anyone in a strong way.

Despite Brenda's defensive manoeuvres, RD convinced her to go on long walks around London. Their friendship deepened.

BRENDA DAVIES
It was very chummy. We'd go to dinner. There was a Chinese place on Shaftesbury Avenue, across the river. When we started to go out together I continued to insist on paying for my own meals, which amazed him. I was always very independent. I did not want to be beholden to him. I was alone in London, and I had to be careful.

Then Rob used to walk me home to Baker Street, and then to Chelsea when we moved to Tite Street. That's when you'd have long conversations. We occasionally got to Sadler's Wells for opera and ballet. And Rob was always on time. My family was always late. But he was faithfully there.

Rob and I understood each other very well. . . . Our backgrounds were in many ways the same. My great-grandfather went to Australia from the Shetland Islands – he had nothing and he went to the colonies and made a lot of money. Rob's father, of course, did the same. We had the same sort of pushing, the "getting on" in our backgrounds.

And then Brenda introduced her Canadian friend to her mother and sister.

BRENDA DAVIES
My mother and RD got along very well. They used to tell each other stories. She was very ladylike, but she'd try to shock him, and Rob didn't expect this from women, but my mother was a generation younger than his parents. They'd talk about current affairs, absolutely anything. I think she approved of him. He was very different from the young Australian men she'd known, more highly informed and educated. He'd been to Queen's and graduated brilliantly from Oxford. He'd had his thesis published. And he was a wonderful talker, a great raconteur. . . I think he used to rehearse his stories. That was very Welsh of him.

In the late 1930s, Brenda's sister Maisie became engaged to a young Australian painter.

BRENDA DAVIES
The four of us would go out: Maisie and her fiance, Peter Purves-Smith. Mother would pack a picnic in the hamper, egg-and-bacon pie, with fruit and coffee. Rob always said my mother made the best coffee in London. . . . We used to go on picnics in Pete's car, of which he was very

proud, to places like Brighton. Rob and Pete worked up a merry war at this time: Pete drew caricatures of Rob and Rob wrote satirical poems about Pete.

RD

> *You, Pete, with mere artisan rascality*
> *Paint what you see, and call the result, Reality,*
> *Shunning the Artist's nobler task of Seeing,*
> *Stripped of his outer guise, the Essential Being. . .*
> *This Baroque exterior conceals*
> *More than mere trumpery talent ever reveals;*
> *Pencil can never capture and control*
> *The Perpendicular of my Gothic Soul.*

BRENDA DAVIES
This gave us a lot of merriment, which we needed, as the [war] situation was so threatening and parting was so near.

In late August 1939, the Old Vic troupe travelled to the Buxton Theatre Festival in Derbyshire. On September 3, Prime Minister Neville Chamberlain announced that Britain had entered the war against Germany. Actor Basil Coleman recalls that day.

BASIL COLEMAN
Tony Guthrie had a wonderful idea: to tell us that we were at war, he ordered everyone to the theatre at 11 a.m. He said we were not to be miserable, and so that night we would have a party. Everyone was to be back at 5, back at the theatre for the party. He was determined to keep the morale of the company together. Someone in Buxton told us the war would probably last for five years.

BRENDA DAVIES
Then they closed the theatre and all our salaries were cut off. So we had to find cheaper places to stay. We stayed in Buxton a week, wondering what was going to happen and what we were going to do. I thought I'd have to go back to Australia. . . . The theatre reopened after a week. This was the period of the "phony war." So we went on with our tour – Manchester, Streatham, Cardiff – into the blackout. It was very peculiar indeed.

You'd arrive in a town, find somewhere to live and then go to the theatre that night. Then you'd have to find your way back in the blackout. People were very kind and they would tell you where you were. Rob couldn't see in the dark. His eyesight was very poor. So we took digs in the same place so I could help him get home at night. And yes, to some degree you would have to hold hands – to get down the steps. But Rob was very independent.

BASIL COLEMAN
The blackouts! Brenda had to find lodgings, theatre digs. I remember the terrible lodgings with the terrible wet sheets. We caught terrible colds.

BRENDA DAVIES
I never volunteered for the war. I'm against it in principle! RD did, but he was not accepted, because of his flat feet and poor eyesight. Rob and I did discuss the war and whether we would stay in England. We did discuss going to Canada. Where did he propose? Up in Buxton. It was one afternoon in early September in one of the dressing rooms. He got around to asking would I marry him. He didn't go on one knee; if he had, I would have laughed. It came out of the blue. He didn't even give me an engagement ring. That came later on.

My experience with Mum's marriages made me feel that I did not want to marry – the risk was too great. But when I met Rob, all that went out of my mind. You know, he talks in his work about friendships. He means a profound understanding that you're not only carried away by passion and sex; so much of that kind of love is our projection on the other. I think he was getting past that.

RD and Brenda decided that despite the blackout, they would tell Rupert in person of their engagement. This meant a trip to Wales.

BRENDA DAVIES (from her privately printed memoir *Beads on a String*)
We decided we would start after the performance on Saturday night and returning in time for the Monday night show. The blackout was in force. We couldn't have the car headlights on. Fortunately, it was a moonlit night. Now and then we would stop to look at road signs, so it was a slow trip. After we got there, Rupert was rather formal and distant with me – he wanted Rob to marry a Welsh county lady.

RD (letter to Eleanor Sweezey, January 11, 1940)
Thank you for your letter of congratulation; its generosity was characteristic of you. When war broke out the Old Vic Co. was at Buxton Spa. . . . [T]he head of our drama school was needed for more immediately important work, and so had to depute quite a lot of her duties to me. The twenty-five students behaved, on the whole, very well but some had special problems, as they were in danger of becoming enemy aliens. In this hour of need Brenda gave me invaluable help, and showed immense gumption, as a lot of extra work fell on her, as stage manager of the touring co., whose head [Guthrie] had to be in London a great deal. We shall do very well together.

BRENDA DAVIES
Tyrone told me I should not marry Rob, because he was a Welshman! There were a lot of bad stories about Welshmen. But I think now that it was that Tony didn't want me to be influenced by anyone else. It's hard to say what Tony really thought, because he'd change his position. I guess he felt proprietary, possessive.

At the wedding I had a blue coat and skirt – it was a grey blue with a velvet collar, and the hat had a snood at the back. We had chosen the ring together, from a jeweller on Regent Street, Garrard [the Crown Jeweller since 1843]. Rob was used to dealing with the best shops; when I met him I didn't know anything about his background, because in theatre we never discussed outside life.

We were at my mother's the morning of the wedding, and my sister Maisie said, "You look like the cat that swallowed the cream."

Tony joked that the wedding got more publicity than the theatre, because of Rupert Davies's presidency of the Canadian Press. CP had a reporter and photographer at the church and sent the news to several papers with pictures.

The wedding took place on Friday, February 2 at Chelsea Old Church in London. RD had no family members present. The only guest on his side was Elsbeth Herbert-Jones, the daughter of Dora Herbert-Jones, whom RD knew from a stately home near Rupert's in Wales, where lived two aristocratic sisters. Dora was their secretary, oversaw their private printing press and art collection, and collected Welsh folklore, according to Bruce Ubukata, a musician who years later became a friend of RD's in Toronto.

BRUCE UBUKATA
Elsbeth had known RD since she was 15. Her mother was a connoisseur of Welsh folk songs and sang them beautifully. Gustav Holst wrote settings for the songs that Dora Herbert-Jones had collected.

BRENDA DAVIES
After we were married, we had a lunch and took the train for Wales. . . . Then we went back to London and then took the train from London to Liverpool. My mother came, with daffodils, to see us off. We boarded the ship for Canada in Liverpool on March 1, St. David's Day. There was already torpedoing in the Atlantic, and our ship carried depth charges in the back for protection. The boat was all blacked out at night. But we were too much taken up with each other to be alarmed.

BRUCE UBUKATA
Not long after Rob and Brenda's wedding, Elsbeth Herbert-Jones sailed for Australia with a ship of refugee children. Her ship was torpedoed and she was lost at sea. All of this happened in the earliest days of their marriage.

Chapter 10

CHEATED BY CANADA

The ship carrying RD and Brenda to Canada entered the St. Lawrence and docked at Quebec City. When they went ashore to tour the Old Town, a taxi driver cheated the newlyweds.

BRENDA DAVIES
Rob was very annoyed. He felt his own country had cheated him!

From Montreal we took the train to Kingston and arrived at 2 a.m. Rob's brother Fred met us at the station and drove the car back to the house, where all the family were up and waiting with coffee. I think they greeted each other quite formally. They were not a passionate family. Perhaps they shook hands. Certainly the brothers never kissed – my God! The most welcoming member of the family? I wouldn't say any of them were! Of course, they must have felt, here was their son with a Wild Australian. And I knew that Rupert had been terribly keen that Rob marry a county girl in Wales.

The in-laws did not grow much warmer over time.

BRENDA DAVIES
It was a bit of an ordeal, but I was prepared to put up with anything because Rob did not have to go to war. Florence had a big tea to introduce the Wild Australian to the family friends – Rupert's friends, as Florence did not socialize so much and Rupert was very, very sociable. At that tea I kept my head down.

As a hostess, I think Florence was quite good. She had servants, of course. I had been working at the Old Vic for very little money and this was an entirely different world. There was always lots of food at the Davieses'. It was very lush. And Rupert was always very generous with the booze.

Florence in those early weeks in Canada took very little notice of me, as little notice as possible. She talked to Rob all the time. She was very possessive about her sons.

The one thing I had brought her from England was our wedding cake. I had carried a big piece of it from England, and I gave it to her and it never appeared again. I must say I was hurt by that.

Florence never did anything; she just sat in a chair all day. Oh, once she gave me a set of sock stretchers . . .

The newly married couple camped at Calderwood for six difficult months.

BRENDA DAVIES
I now realize it must have been difficult for the Davieses to have us stay for so long. It was also difficult for Rob, standing between his parents and his new wife. I had been stage manager at the Old Vic, an important and responsible job, and suddenly I was the low man on the totem pole, and knew only the Davies family.

Kingston society's preoccupations struck her as odd.

BRENDA DAVIES
They talked a lot about religion – what religion everyone belonged to – which was categorizing in a way I found very strange. In Canada, what religion you were was frightfully important at that time. And Rob had changed his religion at Oxford. After he had decided that the Presbyterianism he had been brought up with was hard and cruel, he had been baptized by a bishop. . . .

The Davieses were terribly old-fashioned. I thought they were my grandparents' generation, not my parents'. We'd all have dinner together. His mother would come down for dinner, wearing dark colours, always keeping everything at bay. She wasn't interested in a lot of things – only in her sons. But they were all great talkers, so I didn't have to talk. I just kept quiet.

Being Welsh, they all talked about relatives and friends all the time. The Welsh always know their relatives very closely. When we lived at Calderwood I didn't know any of the people they were talking about. It was all over my head. . . . I did not know that Fred had been married before, to the sister of Arthur's wife Dorothy. He and Muriel had divorced in 1937. I didn't know about that for years.

Families like the Davieses drop subjects and they never come up again. They were great talkers, but there were things they Did Not Discuss. This was a family on the up-and-up, and you pass people on your way, you move into different groups, and you have to drop your past.

Often, the talk would be about politics. Rupert, by now a major publisher, continued to work actively for the Liberal Party, as RD later recalled in a 1974 CBC interview.

RD

I remember in May of 1940 sitting at a dinner table where a former premier of Ontario, Mitchell Hepburn, was assuring my father that by the middle of June, Hitler would be sitting in Buckingham Palace dictating peace terms. And I was aware that Mr. Hepburn was giving himself extraordinary pleasure and he was doing it by trying to scare the wits out of the rest of us.

In Canada, the war played out in minor dramas. RD was called up for military service but was rejected on the grounds of poor eyesight. Meanwhile, as an influential newspaper publisher, Rupert kept in close contact with the prime minister, Mackenzie King. In 1942 King appointed Rupert to the Senate of Canada.

RUPERT DAVIES

I do not know what impelled Mr. King to appoint me to the Senate. I most certainly did not seek the honour . . . but I had done several things for Mr. King which were fairly important. . . . He called me up one Saturday during the war and told me that France was going to fold up over the weekend. He asked me to call by telephone every editor of every daily paper in Canada and ask them to play it down as much as possible. It took me from Saturday noon until Sunday night to reach all of the one hundred and six editors, but I found them most co-operative. Perhaps the matters I have mentioned influenced the Senate appointment; or it might have been the result of long friendship.

MICHAEL DAVIES (Arthur's son, Rupert's grandson)

Rupert was an acquisitor; Rupert was a driver. As the proprietor of a small Canadian newspaper, he became the head of the Canadian Press.

He was a political animal for sure. He was extremely pleased with how life had turned out for him.

At Calderwood, family tensions worsened, especially whenever Robertson or his new wife tried to assert their independence. One issue was the car.

KATE BRAY
I think the older brothers were downright mean to him. I've heard something about Robertson trying to learn to drive and hitting a gate, and the brothers would have teased him for that.

BRENDA DAVIES
On Saturdays at Calderwood we'd borrow the car and head off to park by the river and listen to the Metropolitan Opera on the car radio. Fred didn't like this. Fred was a real man about town. He was a great driver. He did not like me driving the family car when we stayed in Kingston. He was very nasty to me about it and said I only got a licence in order to drive his father's cars. When I drove the car, he felt I was trying to take the car away.

In March 1940, Brenda told her husband that she was pregnant. With a baby coming, RD needed to find steady work and move his family into their own home. In July 1940, for $40 a week, he began to write a regular column for the *Kingston Whig-Standard*. At first, it was called Cap and Bells, a name he explained in his column of August 1.

RD
Why Cap and Bells? . . . The object of this column is to amuse and entertain. That has always been the job of the man who wears the cap and bells. But to amuse and entertain is not always to be funny; no one is more dreary than the man who is always funny.

RD's sense of humour provoked more family disagreements. Arthur, by now general manager of the *Whig-Standard*, believed that a funny column during wartime was a bad idea. Rupert must have sided with Robertson, for RD continued to contribute the column, under the byline "Samuel Marchbanks," for both the *Whig* and *The Peterborough Examiner*, which Rupert had acquired.

MICHAEL DAVIES
My father was mild, easy-going. Robertson was aggressive. He wasn't really interested in acquiring newspapers and doing what his father did. He was interested in becoming an author and a playwright, and to do that you have to expose yourself and wait to see what the reaction is. Robertson was intellectually aggressive. He had a goal – a quest for immortality, perhaps.

This quest, and the need to establish independence beyond two forceful parents, prompted RD and Brenda to move to Toronto.

BRENDA DAVIES
In Toronto he applied for a radio job at the Canadian Broadcasting Corporation, but there was no job there. Finally, at *Saturday Night* magazine he got a job as the literary editor. I was in Toronto with him when he got the *Saturday Night* job and we went to Eaton's College Street Round Room, now the Carlu, to celebrate.

At *Saturday Night* Rob worked with Hector Charlesworth and B.K. Sandwell. He admired them a great deal. B.K. Sandwell taught Rob a lot. B.K. taught him about style, about how to approach an article.

Finally, we were able to move out of Calderwood and into a place of our own, on Aylmer Avenue in central Toronto, one of a row of houses built for the servants who worked in Rosedale. We had a sitting room, a dining room, a big kitchen and, upstairs, two bedrooms and a bathroom, for $45 a month.

Rob was earning $100 a week. I'd make him a picnic lunch and he'd take it to work – peanut butter sandwiches; he had a passion for them, with jam. He'd walk downtown to work – we didn't have a car – and he'd be away all day.

While RD wrote, and assigned others to write, book reviews for *Saturday Night*, and also produced music and theatre reviews and unsigned editorials, Brenda also found work.

MAVOR MOORE
Brenda did several radio programs for CBC. I thought she was very charming indeed and had a great sense of humour. I do remember her telling me how much she missed London, and that she hadn't known what she was coming to when she came to Canada to be with Rob.

Their first baby, Miranda Nichola Rhiannon, was born at noon on December 24, 1940, in Toronto. Meanwhile, more interesting jobs began to come RD's way. One was through Duncan MacArthur, the professor who had helped RD enter Queen's as a special student. Now minister of education in the provincial government, he suggested that RD talk to W.H. Clarke, publisher at Clarke Irwin, a major educational publishing firm.

BRENDA DAVIES
Rob was asked to write a book for schools, with extracts from Shakespeare. He wondered if it was any use doing it in the face of the war, but was finally persuaded. It was called *Shakespeare for Young Players* and was published in 1942.

DAVID GARDNER (actor and theatre scholar)
When he wrote *Shakespeare for Young Players*, I remember the opening sentence: "Are you an interesting person?" That's a very provocative opening for a young reader. I think Rob spent his life trying to explore who he was. For Rob, being an interesting person was terribly important, and that would hit a 13-year-old boy reader right away.

BRENDA DAVIES
That book contained short pieces suggested as suitable for acting in schools and was illustrated with line drawings by Grant Macdonald, an artist Rob had known from Kingston. The book brought us a little much-needed money.

It also brought them new friends.

AMY STEWART
We met the Davieses first through Grant Macdonald. I think I was in Grant's room in the Windsor Arms Hotel, and they came to his door. I was there because Grant was going to do my portrait. Brenda was very elegant – she is still. And Rob, oh gosh, he was so impressive. He didn't have a beard at that point. . . . Then they came to our house on Poplar Plains Crescent. We saw them in their house, a little house overlooking a park, a house totally full of books. All their houses have been totally full of books.

CLAIR STEWART
They were our natural friends from the first.

AMY STEWART
He was funny and entertained us always. My reading was entirely transformed when I met Rob. I remember him talking about Mervyn Peake.

CLAIR STEWART
We used to argue about Sigmund Freud. I didn't like any of those fellows! I thought they were all . . . shysters.

AMY STEWART
He gave up on you, Clair!

CLAIR STEWART
Oh, yes he did! I used to enjoy goading him about putting any faith whatsoever in psychoanalysis. In these discussions, Brenda was right in there.

AMY STEWART
She has her own opinions . . .

CLAIR STEWART
. . . which were pretty much aligned with Rob's. We'd have these discussions over dinner. She was a splendid cook. Rob, he was a big meat eater. And always at these dinners we'd have red wine. No way we'd have a dinner without wine!

The Davieses were building themselves a social circle and a working life in Toronto. Then, while they were visiting Calderwood for the 1941 Christmas holidays, Rupert announced that the editor of *The Peterborough Examiner* had suddenly died and that RD should take over. RD understood that this was less an offer than an order. But he was 28, with a family to support. RD and a pregnant Brenda reluctantly moved to Peterborough with fifteen-month-old Miranda in March 1942.

Chapter 11

JUST A PINCH BETTER
THAN PETERBOROUGH

For a young and creatively ambitious couple who had known Oxford and London, Peterborough (which then had a population of about 30,000) was little more than dismaying. And the Davieses' alienation wasn't hard to spot, according to people such as the filmmaker Norman Jewison, who years later became a friend and neighbour.

NORMAN JEWISON

I got him to tell me a lot of stories about his time in Peterborough. He told me how stifling it was, what a small town, hardly anyone to go to dinner with. I always felt Rob had very strong opinions about everything. A natural teacher, impatient with fools. It got so that I felt he was kind of putting Peterborough down. Finally, I said, "Well, wait a minute, Rob, all of my people came from there, they were a bunch of farmer immigrants from Yorkshire. What do you expect? This was a farming community!"

Sassy Waddell, a neighbour who befriended the Davies children, had a similar reaction.

SASSY WADDELL

I lived on Hunter Street, two blocks from the Davieses. In those days Peterborough was *Leave It to Beaver*. It was school and church every Sunday. There were no divorces and goings-on – and if there were, they were whispered about through pursed lips. It was an industrial town, with Quaker Oats, an Evinrude motor factory and a big General Electric plant. Like the mill towns in England, the GE plant had a whistle, and the workers would knock off work at noon and go home for lunch. You could hear the whistle all over town. The fact that Rupert ordered Rob to Peterborough – this has got to have coloured their feelings about Peterborough. This was *not their choice*.

Brenda found a brick house at 572 Weller Street and asked her husband to check it out as a prospective home. In a letter of March 2, 1942, he wrote:

> My dearest Pink:
>
> Congratulations on your Extreme Cleverness in getting us such a truly excellent house. . . . I thought the back garden a tremendous Feature, and see many a lazy afternoon there in the summer. Sunbaths for Pink, sunbaths and romps in the hose for Nemo [the unborn baby]. . . . In front of the verandah, Ma [the owner and vendor] tells me that there are hydrangeas. Now isn't it odd that about two months ago or so I had one of my foreseeings, or Visitations, in which I was talking to an old Deefie on a verandah about hydrangeas? If only one could harness these things. . . . I give you full marks and a bonus as a house-picker. *Clever, discerning, tasteful* Pinkie! . . . Dearest Pinkie, I am so anxious that this shall be the right move for us, and that we shall be happy here. The opportunity for me is a big one, and I must make the very most of it, but that is only half. It must be a good thing for you. It is a curious fate which brings you from Australia in order to be the wife of an editor in a Canadian small city, and I don't suppose that it is one which you ever contemplated. . . . [But] somehow this place *smells* adventurous, though a bit crude.

Rupert's company bought the house on Weller Street for his son's family. They paid rent. Rupert also loaned RD and Brenda money to furnish the house, which had four bedrooms, a study, and a maid's room overlooking the back garden. Gwen Brown still lives in a house a few doors away.

GWEN BROWN

When they moved here, to Weller Street, Rob was clean-shaven. Brenda was pregnant. They were very interesting to the people of Peterborough: the new editor of the *Examiner*.

My first impression? I was probably, in 1942 – heaven's sakes alive, I was 19. I wouldn't say they were standoffish, but Peterborough was a little in awe of them. I was young and talked to them, of course.

Brenda had this accent. A delightful person. She wasn't effusive . . . but never mind! When Rob started to grow his beard and sported rather fun clothes like a coat with a cape, a flowing tie and a hat at a jaunty angle, he was an imposing character. How did Peterborough react? Anything people don't understand, they take a negative attitude towards. He couldn't have cared less!

For most men of RD's generation, the Second World War was a defining experience.

AMY STEWART
I'm sure he was upset that he couldn't join the war. But his eyes were no good. He couldn't even drive.

CLAIR STEWART
I can remember we made a visit to Peterborough, and we were all lying on the lawn or sitting, having a drink. I liked the fact that Rob could demolish a drink. He always liked to flatter me by drinking a dry martini, because that's all I drank – all I still drink. We were lying out on the lawn. I was keen to become a pilot, and this Avro Ensign came over flying quite low. Rob said, "That thing shouldn't be flying, that's nothing better than a threshing machine." . . . And there I was, an admirer of those boys, those fliers – and Rob was knocking them down!

The news from England was grim. In 1941, Chelsea Old Church, where RD and Brenda had married, was destroyed by bombing. More bad news was to come.

RD (letter to Gill Purcell of the Canadian Press news service, 1944)
Many thanks for sending me the Canadian Press Reuters dispatch about the Old Vic. I knew that it had been bombed, and that the whole side of the large rehearsal room had been blown out. . . .

I am most grateful to you for bringing this to our attention, as it apparently did not come to us on our wire, or else nobody paid attention to it. I am intensely interested in everything that happens to the Old Vic and keep in touch with the director of the theatre by regular correspondence.

But as a newspaper editor, RD had to learn to take Peterborough's dramas seriously, too.

GWEN BROWN
We had a big St. Bernard dog, King, who was the pride of the neigh-bourhood. Rob did not like dogs. He liked cats. But this one day, my father's nurse was walking King, and this little dog started jumping and yapping, and King grabbed the little dog and shook him. Then a strange man walked up and kicked King, and just killed him!

The war was still on, and my brother Jim was overseas. When I went to my dad's bedside, he saw my long face. Dad said, "Is it Jim?"

I said "No, Dad, it's King."

My father said, "You tell that Davies chap to do a story, to do something about the perpetrator."

I was embarrassed to do this, but my father had told me to. So in fear and trepidation, I went down to the *Examiner* and knocked on the door.

RD said, "Oh, nice to see you."

I said, "I've come because my father asked me," and I told him what the nurse had seen.

RD said, "I know the dog. A magnificent specimen."

I said, "This is a terrible imposition, but my father thinks if you wrote something . . ."

And he did, on the editorial page. He said it was a nice dog and a tragedy.

My father read it and thought this was wonderful. And a few days later there was a knock on the door. A man came to confess, "I am the one who kicked your dog. I feel terrible. I only meant to separate the two dogs fighting."

While the war wound down, RD worked long hours at *The Peterborough Examiner* and at his desk at Weller Street, producing twelve thousand words each week under his own name or in the form of editorials. By the mid-1940s he had transformed the *Examiner* from a mediocre regional daily to one of English Canada's most quoted newspapers.

WILLIAM FRENCH (journalist and former literary editor of *The Globe and Mail*)
One of my earliest encounters with the name Robertson Davies was in the spring of 1947, when I was about to finish my third and semi-final year at the University of Western Ontario. My class would become the first to graduate from a journalism course in Canada, so naturally there

was considerable interest among editors about these strange new creatures. The managing editor of *The Globe and Mail* asked the head of the course (Professor George McCracken) if he would recommend a student to work at *The Globe* for the summer. I was chosen, but only later did I learn that Professor McCracken had chosen another student who had already agreed to go to *The Peterborough Examiner* – and preferred that job over *The Globe* because of Robertson Davies. That was the kind of reputation the *Examiner* had in those days.

ROBERT FULFORD (from *Queen's Quarterly*, Spring 2007)
In the 1940s, Hugh Kenner was an adolescent in Peterborough who had never heard of James Joyce. One day, glancing through the *Examiner*, he came upon a piece about him by Davies. That article arrived at the right time in the right hands. Kenner became an interpreter of modern literature and produced three books about Joyce. While Davies did not make Kenner the wonderfully articulate scholar he became, he helped open him to the possibility of a larger world – roughly the goal of all the journalism Davies produced.

MICHAEL DAVIES
For a small newspaper, the *Examiner* got a lot more than its share of national press – and it was successful in economic terms. . . . It's difficult to please everybody. But as for local fights with the police chief or the clergy, that's standard fare with newspapers. Robertson was definitely running an upscale production. . . . He was a provocateur, but he could write. And he was bright enough to realize that 90 percent of subscribers didn't have his tastes. If you produce only what pleases you, then you won't be successful commercially.

RD's most talked-about contribution was his Samuel Marchbanks column, which he wrote for his father's newspapers from 1941 to 1953 – two thousand words a week. Some Peterborovians were baffled by his humour. Others, such as a high school English teacher named Fern Rahmel, were enchanted.

FERN RAHMEL
When he began doing the Diary of Samuel Marchbanks, people couldn't wait for Saturdays to come around to see what he'd say. . . . But

many people didn't like him because they didn't understand him. And there were thinly veiled portraits of local people in Samuel Marchbanks.

MICHAEL DAVIES

We all looked forward to reading Samuel Marchbanks. I know there were code names in Marchbanks's columns that my father would relate to and tell us about. My father was the character known as "Fairchild." That was his code.

ROBERT FULFORD

Davies used to tell a story about Stephen Leacock. . . that someone from Leacock's home town of Orillia said, "We never liked Leacock because he didn't like us." RD said, "Why the hell should he like you?" – the very idea that a humorist should be liking the people he wrote about didn't make sense to Davies.

MARTIN HUNTER

He'd also perform as Samuel Marchbanks. I think I saw him once at the Art Gallery of Toronto, as it was then. I was a teenager. Of course I laughed. It was at a time when saying something like "balls" was considered highly naughty. He was sort of impersonating Marchbanks. He liked to assume the persona, just as he later did when reading his ghost stories at Massey College. In both cases he was an arch performer, rather precious, but he had good comic technique. Miranda told me he used to get dressed up as Marchbanks.

Like so many stories about RD, this one has been embellished.

MIRANDA DAVIES

I know of one occasion: RD took a photo in the mirror over the fireplace at Weller Street of himself as Marchbanks. He was wearing a pair of those spectacles with a big false nose from the joke shop and perhaps had tousled his hair and maybe added a scarf at the neck. My memory is of the false nose.

The war ended, and paper shortages and censorship were over. RD contacted his publisher, Clarke Irwin, and proposed a book of the collected columns of Samuel Marchbanks. *The Diary of Samuel Marchbanks* appeared in 1947, with graphics by Clair Stewart. *The Table Talk of Samuel Marchbanks* was published in 1949. Both books found readers in high places.

PRIME MINISTER MACKENZIE KING
I cannot thank you too warmly for your kind thought in sending me, with your good wishes for my birthday anniversary and for the Christmas season and the New Year, a copy of your book, "The Diary of Samuel Marchbanks." As you know I have long enjoyed a friendship with your father, Senator Davies, and any book written by a son of his would naturally commend itself to my attention. "The Diary of Samuel Marchbanks," however, has its own especial interest for me, not the least because it speaks, however frankly, of so many aspects of Canadian life. . .

Marchbanks books also turned up in the homes of poets such as E.J. Pratt – and of people who would grow up to be poets.

E.J. PRATT (letter to RD, February 17, 1948)
It is a bit belated, but here is my personal tribute to Samuel Marchbanks. My wife gave the diary to me as a New Year's present and I have read every word of it and enjoyed it immensely. There is nothing else like it in this country. . . . I had an enjoyable trip from Kingston a month ago and I had the good fortune to be sitting beside your "grand" (not lineal as a term) father. . . . He informed me that you had sold several thousands of your book. Well, that's a reflection of the good literary taste of this country.

Give my regards to your lovely Scotch lady.

MARGARET ATWOOD
I met Robertson Davies through the diaries of Samuel Marchbanks. My family bought all the volumes of Samuel Marchbanks. I read them in the 1950s and thought Marchbanks was a curmudgeonly old man. But when he wrote Marchbanks, Davies wasn't old. And he wasn't really curmudgeonly at all.

Or perhaps he was . . .

MIRANDA DAVIES
Marchbankian attitudes: I think of them as *de haut en bas* – so that although Marchbanks is disguised behind the mask of the curmudgeon, he is excoriatingly critical of the society he is observing. Father was like that at home when talking about all and sundry, extremely critical.

SASSY WADDELL
The Davieses may have felt isolated, but in a small town you have to go with the flow, and I do *not* think the Davies were willing to bend. You know the survivor skills you learn, when you kinda bend here and there?

I think he was incredibly shy. . . . But also there was a certain amount of arrogance. The feeling that "I've got the big picture and these local people are the ants running around." It was a comic sense, but underlying it was a sense of "we're just a pinch better."

This seems clear in a letter dated January 8, 1946, which RD sent to the American essayist and philologist H.L. Mencken after Mencken sent a letter to the *Whig-Standard* asking about Canadian usage.

RD
It may interest you to know that this town . . . is officially Peterborough, but the railway stations have shortened it to Peterboro for their signs, and clownish folk have taken up this spelling. . . . May I say how much I have been delighted by . . . [your book] *The American Language*, as well as by the fugitive pieces which I see here and there. In return for that pleasure, may I offer (if I may do so without seeming pushful) to provide you with Canadian raw material when and as you want it? I am a bit of a crank about language, have a good ear, and Canadian and Oxford degrees in English, and was an actor for a time, so I think I can hear what is really said, and reproduce it accurately.

Mencken seems not to have responded to RD's offer to mine his neighbours' speech patterns for raw comic material. Which is just as well, for he was beginning to matter a good deal to some of them, says John Whyte, a childhood friend of the Davies children.

JOHN WHYTE
When I spent my youth in Peterborough, my impression then was that Davies's thing was owning his dark side. Samuel Marchbanks is over and

over again bringing a boundary to unconventionality. "I had an experience in town today . . . ," and he goes on to say, in effect, "My reaction is not the same as others, but here it is and here is my boundary."

We were neighbours. When my brother Terence went to Europe, Marchbanks wrote a column on how important it is for people to leave and go away and travel. It was a very admiring column about the idea of "going" – about becoming who you are through travel.

The enemy in Marchbanks was convention, and the Marchbanks series was a continuing letter to Peterborough: This is how people think about this town – but there can be richer, funnier ways of seeing.

Chapter 12

THE CHILDREN OF THE
MAN WITH THE BEARD

Two more daughters were born to RD and Brenda: Jennifer Minerva Angharad in 1942 and Rosamond Bronwen in 1947. It was with his eldest daughter that RD had the strongest childhood bond.

MIRANDA DAVIES
My earliest memories are of the living room at 572 Weller, sitting beside him and listening to the Metropolitan Opera broadcast. I would have been old enough to listen to music. I thought he was so wonderful that what he would do, I would do. It was just the two of us, alone. The others wouldn't have been interested enough for this heavy stuff.

At Weller Street, when you go in the front door, on the right is an open archway to the sitting room with the radio, the gramophone, the baby grand and Daddy's desk. This room was magical to me: it had music in it.

I remember one Christmas, sitting on the stairs outside that room in the evening and listening to *The Cherry Tree Carol* playing on the gramophone. I had been given a baby doll that I christened Polly Baby. I was listening to the song and singing along, "When Joseph was an old man, and an old man was he, he married Polly Baby, the Queen of Galilee." There you have the Electra complex!

I emulated him. I shared jokes with him. I was interested in literature and good at school. I was *all right* as far as he was concerned. I was quick of tongue, glib, saucy, and we would make up silly jokey things together. To the tune of *Jingle Bells*, we'd sing his version: "Ginger ale, ginger ale/ Ginger all the way!/ Bubbles goes/ Right up my nose/ Makes me feel so gay – hey . . ."

When we played duets together, we'd share music like the Diller-Quaile easy version of the *Ruy Blas Overture* of Mendelssohn. He'd do it with "expression" and "worm" the keys, sort of wobbling, as if to bring out the tone. We'd end these duets with a theatrical flourish and he'd shake my hand as if I were first violin. It was such fun. That home seemed full of love. Babies were loved, fathers were loved. If you had a secure and happy childhood, you loved the house.

JENNIFER SURRIDGE
Miranda and I are only twenty-two months apart. Miranda was the kind of child who led with her chin forward, who was defiant, always in trouble. I would simply cry. . . . He was so mercurial, you never really knew what he thought. Even in his diary, one day he says somebody is the total pits and then he'd find out something redeeming about them and take the other side. . . . For a child, this was pretty confusing. You never really knew where you were.

ROSAMOND BAILEY
I was afraid of him as a child, afraid to make him angry. He was very explosive and unpredictable. You never knew what would upset or irritate him. He was very impatient. And he found the physical world difficult. He was not dextrous with his hands, he couldn't see well. It was challenging for him. If you are very intuitive, and are not capable in the physical world, you become frustrated.

Having such a mercurial, gifted and exotic father set the Davies children apart.

JENNIFER SURRIDGE
When we lived in Peterborough, we were all thought to be different. Our father was unusual – and in the 1940s and '50s in Peterborough, "unusual" was not really liked very much. And RD had a beard. We were the children of the man who had the beard.

MIRANDA DAVIES
Rude boys would yell at me, "Hey, Davies, why don't yer old man get a razor?" He would walk to and from *The Peterborough Examiner* twice a day, and he would go between the Bishop's Palace and the Catholic primary school. The kids would yell rude things at him because he had a beard and a homburg hat. The kids would yell "Santa Claus" or "Why you got a beard?" This ordeal stirred up all his early Renfrew experience – that mean, corrosive hatred of the Other – whereas he

wanted to embrace all that was enlarging of the spirit. He was put through the fire. Don't forget, at the time he was vulnerable. He was then a young man carrying a heavy responsibility for his father at *The Peterborough Examiner.*

Aware of what was riding on her husband's shoulders, and of her own mother's failed marriages, Brenda took pains to create a peaceful, orderly household.

BRENDA DAVIES
I just wanted to protect him. I had great confidence in those days! Look how many people marry to reform someone . . . it never works! But I got Rob to a steadier plane where he could use his imagination constructively.

He liked quieting foods. I used to make a lemon soufflé that he liked, and a rice pudding with raisins. He was very keen about food and I was quite a good cook.

Though neighbours thought RD grand and aloof, he did some practical chores. And the elegant Brenda was the family's all-round fixer.

MIRANDA DAVIES
The image of the parents needs modification . . . in fact, she was flushing out the diapers and he was chucking wood into the cellar. It would have been unusual, but I recall khaki shorts and English sandals (he actually had very good legs, but he was extremely modest and self-conscious). . . .

Mother's got that Oz, get-on-with-it, making-do, gung-ho know-how. This meant we got to be adventurous as children. Father had complete confidence in her. She'd execute a good three-point turn in the car and Daddy would say, "Huzzah! Huzzah for the daring and intrepid Mummy!"

Brenda tried to keep the children from bothering RD in the evenings so that he would be free to work, recalls John Whyte's sister Wynne Whyte.

WYNNE WHYTE
"He's writing a book," Miranda would say, and we had to be very quiet. We'd go gently upstairs. Mr. Davies was a pretty private man.

Usually he was in his study working, and there was no horsing around allowed.

JENNIFER SURRIDGE

When we were really little, we had a table in an alcove where we ate because Mum didn't expect us to have meals with the adults, and so they could have some quiet times. So we had a housekeeper, Sylvia Pedak. She came to us when Rosamond was very young.

SYLVIA PEDAK MacFADYEN JONES

I was born in Estonia in 1923. During the German occupation I was in a German labour camp. . . . We were liberated by the British and then the United Nations. We were called "DPs" – displaced persons, a very derogatory term. Once I was released from the labour camp I worked in Berlin with Save the Children. The Davieses were looking for someone with a background with children. I came as a nanny to take care of the girls, and the Davies family was very protective of me.

Robertson Davies was then the editor of *The Peterborough Examiner* and very busy, and Brenda was very interested in the theatre. That left the children in my hands. I can't say the family were my employers. They became my family. I would travel with them. They protected me from the status of being a DP.

I had a background in piano, and Brenda immediately made an arrangement for me to continue with piano studies in Peterborough. Robertson Davies became my mentor. He made me read Shakespeare, which I had read in Estonian. It was interesting for him to discuss with me how different the translations were.

My political background was strongly socialist, and Robertson Davies was monarchist. At Weller Street, we had terrible arguments. But then he started to call himself a "socialist monarchist. . . ."

Brenda had a little nursery school in the house on Weller Street, run according to the method of Dr. William Blatz. They got me into his school, the University of Toronto's Institute of Child Studies, to study early childhood education. Once I graduated I became part of the Toronto Nursery School Association, and then made early childhood education my career in British Columbia. The Davieses always treated me as a person; they took seriously my interest in children, and got me into child studies.

Sylvia Pedak sponsored her mother, Anna, who took over as the Davieses' housekeeper/nanny just as Rosamond was learning to walk and talk.

SYLVIA PEDAK

Other people called my mother "Anna." Brenda called my mother "Mrs. Pedak."

MIRANDA DAVIES

I think Mum wanted to move Mrs. Pedak out of being downgraded and downcast. In Estonia, she had been an officer's wife.

While helping the Pedaks to integrate into Canadian life, the Davieses simultaneously asserted their own aloofness from it.

JENNIFER SURRIDGE

We were an island unto ourselves. We spoke a different way and acted a different way. . . . RD didn't want us to casually reveal things to play-mates. So I grew up with the sense that I'd have to be very careful of what I said. He would say ridiculous things about people, but I would not repeat them because I never wanted to offend people.

MIRANDA DAVIES

Father would *not* take us to church. He wouldn't let us go to Sunday school, for which I was miserably teased by children on the street. When I asked Daddy about it, Jenny and I were at his knee, and he said, "Well, we will have Sunday school at home and I will tell you about the seven deadly sins and the three cardinal virtues." He did so. That cured us of wanting Sunday school.

The other children had Mission Band and Brownies and Girl Guides. We were not Brownies or Girl Guides – same reason. I think it arose from the kind of religious and social snobbery that you can see in his novels. . . .

We were separated from our neighbours by Father inveighing against the society in which we lived. His idea was that he and we must drag ourselves out of the mud. But some of the ways in which he did this were mischievous. At Weller Street, he had put above the archway in the hall a mask of a satyr, and he had put sequins in the eyes and given the face more contour by shading in the hollows. He knew my girlfriend Wynne Whyte came from a devoted United Church house, so when Wynne came to play, he told her the mask was the Devil.

WYNNE WHYTE
I don't remember the mask, but I remember that for their birthday parties he would write a special play and put on a puppet show, and some of the characters were scary. The puppets would be based on people in the community.

MIRANDA DAVIES
Oliver M. Steer was the principal of Queen Mary Public School, and Daddy wrote a puppet play for us when we were home from boarding school for the holidays, to perform at a family party. We had been given hand puppets – a devil, a Mr. Punch. Our heroine was a blonde bride doll. His version of the story of Rumpelstiltskin was based on our experiences at Queen Mary – that knack he had of referring to real people in the guise of another character! I think Oliver Steer might have been the king who locks up his daughter until she can weave straw into gold.

As well as staging private entertainments at home, RD took his children to selected amusements – not sporting events, but fireworks displays and films at a local cinema owned by Harry Yudin, one of the few Jews in Peterborough. He established a cinema club to bring in special-interest movies.

SANDY YUDIN
My dad, Harry, brought in *Die Fledermaus*. RD was sitting right behind me with Miranda. I don't remember what it was that tickled his funny bone, but at one point in the film, he near blasted my head off with his right-from-the-toes laughter. He had what you would nicely call a booming laugh.

JOHN WHYTE
Rob and Brenda loved a celebration. I do remember them coming to the 24th of May fireworks celebration in the Knoxes' backyard on Weller Street. RD liked things which were irrational, wasteful and exuberant. He was a good man.

WYNNE WHYTE
One time we were holding fireworks, individual sparklers, and I handed Rosamond one, and it burned her hand. Mr. Davies got very mad at me. He thought I had done it intentionally. That was scary. But as soon as he realized it wasn't intentional, he said, "Oh, I am sure she'll be all right." This gave me an idea how much he loved and protected the girls.

With their father as protector, the Davies girls developed a reputation for daring.

MIRANDA DAVIES
He was very mischievous and naughty to us about our teachers. In person, he would be exemplary with them, but he really was rather subversive.

When I was in Grade 7, my teacher was a young man named Duncan Watson. Mr. Watson was overimpressed by me because I did so brilliantly in those multiple-choice reading comprehension tests – I would get 98 or so. And I was very naughty, and made myself one of the boys.

One day, when Ronald Sinclair in front of me was snapping his wrist for Mr. Duncan Watson's attention, some ink from his pen flew back and spilled on my blouse. I spoke out and was reprimanded by Mr. Watson. I did not like this. Later, when Mr. Watson was bent over Ronnie's desk, his bottom was turned towards me. A boy nearby made a gesture of stabbing Mr. Watson on the bottom with a pen. So I did!

In a voice like a roar, Mr. Watson said, "Who did that?"
I smirkingly replied, "I did."

A day or two later, I did something else. And then Mr. Watson gave me the strap. I then had to go to the principal's office and Mr. Steer said to me: "With your background! You should grow up and when you have your own children you will understand. And you should confess to your parents what you have done . . ."

I scampered home and confessed to my parents right away. And they just roared with laughter! They were subversive. It was a whole attitude of superiority that was imbued with their attitude towards my teachers and to Peterborough.

RD's treatment of his daughters impressed their playmates.

WYNNE WHYTE

He adored his children and respected them as people. He spoke to them in an adult way, with no rudeness, no loudness. It was real, pure conversation.

The girls themselves had a different perspective.

MIRANDA DAVIES

One summer afternoon at 572 Weller, my parents' friend Graham MacInnes and Daddy were talking. We sat on the verandah and looked down the lawn to the street. They were talking about politics. When an opportunity came – I would never have cut in – I asked, "What's a Liberal?" I recall that Daddy came and sat beside me in an equal way on the steps. It was not *de haut en bas*, but Graham was very much above us listening to the conversation.

Daddy said something like, "The Liberal Party is the open-minded, forward-looking party and wants to move with the times, while the Conservatives want to keep things as they are." Graham was grinning away, because of the ironical tone, which meant that Liberals are good and Conservatives are bad.

It was very kindly meant, but it was pitched to his real audience, which was Graham. I became very familiar with this: sometimes Daddy would talk to the children with an ear to the adult nearby.

Through their parents, the Davies children learned about adult matters.

KATE BRAY

Obviously, Robertson and Brenda talked about lots of things in front of their children that our parents didn't. Initially, my father, Fred, and my uncle Arthur married sisters, and then there was my father's divorce. Muriel Porter went on her merry way and married someone else, but Dorothy Porter remained with Arthur. Divorce was not a thing that was chatted about in those days. My sister and I did not find out about Muriel Porter until we went to Kingston for Christmas and Robertson's girls told us that our father had had another wife. That was an odd thing to hear from cousins who were younger than you were.

MIRANDA DAVIES
He'd had a very difficult relationship with his family, a lot of animosity with his brothers, a great deal. There was that buildup of frustration, tension, energy. You have to imagine him as young – teasing, annoying, boyish, uxorious, childish. He was a bit fascinated by anal stuff. He really liked to disgust us. He really tried to get a rise out of us, testing Mum to turn on him and give him a clout and say, "Oh, *Rob!*"

BRENDA DAVIES
He'd try to stir me up. He wanted everyone stirred up. He thought ordinary life was dull. But I didn't stir easily. I was the steady person in the house. I thought he was childish but merry. I thought it was great.

Then, suddenly, in the summer of 1947, RD developed difficulties breathing. In November, medical specialists in Toronto diagnosed him with Hodgkin's disease and warned that it might be fatal. He was prescribed radiation.

FERN RAHMEL
RD was down in Toronto quite a bit, but I got no sense from anything he said that he was ill. But Mary Hale, the wife of Lloyd Hale, who was head of English at Peterborough Collegiate Institute – Mary was a talky woman, and I remember her telling me, "Rob is really quite sick." She had made a point of taking over casseroles.

One friend who did know about RD's illness was Arnold Edinborough, an academic at Queen's, recently arrived from England. He and his wife became close friends of the Davies through theatre work in Kingston.

KILDARE DOBBS
I first met him when I was with Arnold Edinborough. We went to see him in hospital in Toronto. He and Edinborough were "talking bawdy," swapping crude remarks. . . . When I saw Robertson Davies first, in hospital, my sense was he was theatrical, even in being a sick person. He did that quite well.

AMY STEWART
The doctors thought he had cancer. He came and stayed with us in Toronto for several weeks. That was a scary time. If he had had this, it

was the kind of cancer that you can't do anything about. He would never let on that he was frightened. But *I* was frightened!

CLAIR STEWART
He was by himself at our house on Poplar Plains Crescent, with our cook and the nursemaid. We went to Mexico. We went away and left him. . . . He didn't talk to us [about his fears], not really, as he was a very private person.

MIRANDA DAVIES
November to May is a long time in a child's life. . . . My father feared he had slowly progressive cancer. But the parents spilled nothing to us. They kept it to themselves to spare the children. By 1947, I was six. Do I remember it? No, but it has left its mark on my psyche: a general sense that All Is Not Secure. That there was an emotional experience . . . that things can change . . . another war could break out . . . we could lose everything . . .

RD (letter to Rupert Davies, April 3, 1948)
As I understand the matter, this thing can either be acute or chronic and when it is chronic the problem is to keep it under control. . . . In its acute form it is very unpleasant. They seem to be sure, however, that as they have caught it very early in my case, they can keep it well under control. . . . I don't think there would be any point in mentioning this to Mother.

With good wishes, I am
Yours sincerely
Robertson Davies, editor

By the summer of 1948, RD had recovered from whatever had ailed him – probably a misdiagnosed bout of mononucleosis – just in time to confront the seriously deteriorating health of his mother.

BRENDA DAVIES
Florence was a terrible hypochondriac, and Rupert would ring in the middle of the night and say, "Get down here, she's dying." . . . When we got a call from Calderwood, we'd leave the children. I remember driving through the night – I did all the driving – from Peterborough

and arriving in Kingston at 3 a.m. I'd stay on the sofa, while Rob went to the hospital. It was pretty hard on Rob. By the next morning she would have recovered, and Rob would be relieved and going back home.

ROSAMOND BAILEY

I believe Florence and my father had a real bond, but it was filtered through anxiety. He thought she was a possessive, devouring and fearful person. He told me her highest aspiration for him was that he become a pharmacist. He resented that terribly. My mother once let go and said, "Your father is *hipped* on his mother." Can you imagine? She so rarely talked like that!

RD told me that he went to Kingston when Florence was dying. He told me that he was sitting in the next room from her bed, all night, because he was afraid to fall asleep. He thought if he did, he would die, too. That's a participation mystique if there ever was one!

BRENDA DAVIES

When she died, in December 1948, I had to stay in Peterborough because we were doing the Nativity play, so one of the men from the *Examiner* drove Rob down to Kingston. He was there alone when she died. That night he went to bed and had such bad dreams that she was coming to get him, to take him with her, that he stayed up all night. I know that he dreamed she was going to kill him after she died.

It was arranged that the family would have a railway car and we would take the train from Kingston to Brantford, where she would be buried in the McKay family plot. So we all went to Brantford by train – fighting. Fred and Rob fought on the train, about me, apparently. Fred probably said something about me and Rob took offence. . . .

It was a difficult relationship with his mother, but profound. Rob was a very complex person. He used to get depressed a great deal . . . so many colds and flus. But then he'd get back to work, and that would get him through.

Chapter 13

"TONIGHT WE ARE ACTORS"

Even while building his newspaper, RD tried to maintain a connection to his old life in theatre. During the war, he wrote mini-plays to raise money for Victory Loans. These met with mixed reviews; some agreed with RD's brother Arthur that the humour in his scripts was inappropriate in wartime. In the last days of the war, RD turned his frustrations into a play, *Hope Deferred*. It tells of a seventeenth-century Quebec drama troupe whose creativity is crushed by the colonial authorities.

ARNOLD EDINBOROUGH
My wife and I acted in *Hope Deferred*, Rob's French-Canadian play; she was Chimene, the Indian girl. RD was interesting to me. I was a new Canadian, and here was a man imbued with the Canadian spirit. . . . He realized what a raw society, culturally, Canada was. If you were having a career at the Old Vic, would you think of coming back? Rob had gone to England saying, "There's nothing for me in Canada." Then he came back and realized that he was on the eve of a renaissance in Canada.

In the summer of 1945, RD resumed work on a script he'd started while visiting Wales as a student at Oxford. The plot dealt with politicians trying to manipulate superstitious Welsh voters by using a gypsy fortune teller to prophesy an election. Late that summer, RD finished *A Jig for the Gypsy*.

JAMIE CUNNINGHAM (child actor friend of the Davies family)
Robertson Davies was part of the establishment in Peterborough and later at Massey – and yet he identified with the gypsies of the theatre. In fact, he wrote that play about gypsies. Gypsies are always camping on the outskirts of town. . . . perhaps his conflict was between establishment and gypsy.

The mid-1940s was a productive period. A third play, *Overlaid*, was completed in December 1945. In it, a romantic old man and his hard-headed daughter argue about whether to spend a windfall on one grand trip to New York to hear music, or on a respectable gravestone. Like *Hope Deferred*, this play dealt with a society's crushing of creativity. But when RD sent his new plays to W.H. Clarke for possible publication, he too was crushed. When he mailed his scripts to the Canadian Broadcasting Corporation, he got a similar rebuff. Yet he persisted.

BRENDA DAVIES
In many ways, Peterborough was a huge opportunity for him. We didn't have much of a social life, so he had evenings free to work.

MIRANDA DAVIES
He wrote in the living room at a little desk. I'm sure you've heard: "Quiet children, Daddy's writing."

Under a pseudonym, he submitted *Overlaid* to the Ottawa Drama League's competition for best one-act play. At last, some good news: it beat out forty-six competitors, winning $100 and a production by the Ottawa Drama League in October 1946. That fall, RD wrote the one-act play *Eros at Breakfast*. By June 1948, he completed *The Voice of the People*, another one-acter about the havoc wreaked by letters to the editor of a small-town paper (this foreshadowed the plot device of his later novel *Leaven of Malice*). By summer, RD had completed his first full-length play, *Fortune My Foe*.

BILL NEEDLES (actor and friend)
It was in 1948 that I met him. I was called in by the Arthur Sutherland Players in Kingston, Ontario. Arthur called and asked if I'd do a part in *Fortune My Foe*. I said, "Who's *that* by?" So Arthur Sutherland gave me the script. I was to be Szabo. There would be good people in it. . . . We went into rehearsal, and then – Rob appeared. My first impression? He was awe-inspiring. I stood in fear. And he was encouraging to *me*. We did the play with a fair degree of success. As I remember, Rob may have given me some notes about the part. But Rob never interfered with people given authority to direct. He may have felt like doing so, but he never did so. . . . He had an acerbic tongue, though.

In 1948, the Ottawa Drama League took RD's *Eros at Breakfast* to the Edinburgh Festival in Scotland. RD, Brenda and the cast were to be the guests of the Scottish Drama League. In her memoir, *Life Before Stratford*, actress Amelia Hall wrote:

> The little reconnoitring force of Canadians arrived in Edinburgh in August 1949, not to take the British stage by storm but to test the temper of the natives towards Canadian theatre. . . . On September 13 and 14 we were in Glasgow, playing at the Atheneum Theatre, under the auspices of the Glasgow Torch Theatre Club. . . . *Eros at Breakfast* got a better reception there than anywhere else.

Then came Edinburgh. An English theatre critic, Philip Hope Wallace, covered the Canadian visit for *The Globe and Mail*.

> Let us face it. The Third International Festival of the Arts, which has just finished in Edinburgh, was a success. Canadian participation was not. . . . It was in every way a pity that this excellent cast and excellently played production of *Eros at Breakfast* cut so little ice. . . . It did not draw the crowds or the notices it deserved.

However, at last people in Peterborough were growing aware of the theatrical talent in their midst, particularly since 1946, when the rector of St. George's Anglican Church, E.C. Moore, asked RD and Brenda to help stage a Nativity play for Christmas. The Davies did more than stage it; they made it memorable.

BRENDA DAVIES
I remember making bishops' mitres out of old sofa material . . . we used old paper from the *Examiner*. We used our children's marbles set in sealing wax, which looked like medieval jewels, glowing rather than glittering. I made someone an orb out of a root vegetable. We painted it gold and put on more marbles. This was our line of country!

With its ambitious professional production qualities, the Nativity play was an eye-opener.

FERN RAHMEL

I went as a spectator to their first production. It was the Coventry Nativity Play at St. George's Anglican Church. It was simply done, it was well done. It was a moving performance. Nothing like this had been done in Peterborough. It made me feel rather proud.

And St. George's Anglican Church was "beyond the railway tracks" – does that phrase mean anything to you? It was working-class people. Very much so. I was born in Peterborough and brought up in that area. I had lived on the wrong side of the tracks. . . . I had never seen this kind of play, and I was thrilled. . . . It was a miracle – and a kind of miracle play.

The Nativity play's success started people thinking about other projects.

GWEN BROWN (neighbour)

I've always thought that one of the reasons Rob was willing to take on theatre projects was so that Brenda could have an outlet. At St. John Players, we didn't have any money and we were just another church group – but we asked her to direct us in a three-act play. She said yes, she would, but on a professional basis. She would have to be paid. So we gave her $50 and she promptly gave it back to the players. . . . Rob did the makeup and everything else. The programs he did were marvellous, done in the period style. For instance, in *Trelawney of the "Wells,"* he uses *f*s for *s*s:

> *Thursday, the company of the players of St. John's Parifh in the City of Peterborough, in Upper Canada, will revive the late Mr. Arthur Pinero's original comedietta in Four Acts, concerning Rofe Trelawney, a Young Actrefs. . . . Wigmaker and Drefser, Mr. Davies . . . At Common Prices. Vivat Regina.*

FERN RAHMEL

Then came the Peterborough Little Theatre. It got its impetus from a public school principal, a Colonel R.J. Bolton. He had been in the First World War and walked with a limp, which he turned into a swagger. There had been a lot of criticism of teachers and the teaching profession around this time, with letters to the editor about teachers getting too much pay and two months' holidays.

Bob Bolton was rather provoked by it. So there was a meeting in a classroom at Central School, of which he was principal at that time. Bolton thought, to raise the prestige of teachers, we should do something completely different from our routine. He talked very persuasively about starting to do drama.

I can remember at the meeting, after he had finished his speech, there was a long silence. Then we started to say we'd never done it before. And who would we get to act?

I remember someone saying the Davieses would *never* consider helping us. But Bob Bolton said, if they'd do the Coventry Play at St. George's, then they could work with a group of teachers. Nobody thought that Davies would be interested in the slightest.

But the Davieses came to the next meeting, with suggestions.

FERN RAHMEL

First, they thought, we should start out in a small way, with three one-act plays. They suggested Shaw's *The Dark Lady of Sonnets*, and Anatole France's *The Man Who Married a Dumb Wife*, and then they asked the meeting if anyone had any suggestion for the third one-act play. Someone spoke up – I have a feeling it was me. I said, "Would you let us do one of your plays?"

I had never talked to Robertson Davies before. But I knew he wrote plays and I think he had submitted one to competition that had won the Ottawa Little Theatre Prize: *Overlaid*. I don't think I'd read it. In any case, he replied, "Oh yes, if others were agreeable."

Soon the whole thing was thrown open. Bob Bolton got copies of the plays, and they were passed around. We met again, sitting in a circle in the kindergarten room with Rob and Brenda. They cast all the parts and said they needed at least three people backstage for every person onstage – set designers, props makers, stage managers.

Rob asked me to be stage manager for *The Man Who Married a Dumb Wife*, and he taught me how to set up a stage manager's book. He saw us making notes and said, "Fern, what are you doing?"

I said, "Stage manager's notes."

He said, "Don't you know how to set up a stage manager's book?"

When Rob was stage manager at Oxford, John Gielgud had said to Rob what Rob said to me: "Don't you know how to set up a stage manager's book?"

Here's what you do: You get a big, empty loose-leaf book. You take the pages out of your text. Then you either staple or paste one page at a time with a blank page opposite. You need nice, wide margins so you can write things down in pencil – because directors change their minds. . . .

There was an attic in the school where we whacked together planks to make a stage. We rehearsed there. Rob and Brenda gave it endless time. Three nights a week, at least.

Just before opening night, RD surprised Fern Rahmel with a script for her to introduce the evening.

I said, "What gives you the idea that I can do this?"

Rob said, "Oh, go on, you can do it." That was typical. You found that you *could*. At dress rehearsal, Brenda had said to me, "You've got to have long white gloves to carry this off." I said, "Why would I have long white gloves?"

Rob said, "Brenda, do you have long white gloves?" So I wore Brenda's gloves.

On opening night, January 20, 1948, Fern Rahmel came on stage, swathed in a black scholarly robe.

I said something like, "Although teachers are thought to be academic and dry, tonight we are not teachers, we are actors!"

Then I took off the academic gown to reveal a tight bodice, off the shoulders, and a full skirt. . . . After that first triumph, we were all very happy.

MIRANDA DAVIES

One time he brought a number of actors home to Weller Street to teach them about makeup, Number 9 and Number 5, and how to apply a beard, and how to brighten the eye with a little white. This was the father I knew: someone who *knew his stuff*. That was the way he liked to be. He wasn't someone for muddling through. He'd prepare his productions with meticulous care.

FERN RAHMEL
After the three one-act plays, we didn't want to stop. . . . The next year, Rob suggested that we do *The Taming of the Shrew* with John Londerville as Petrucchio. It was a marvellous group. Colonel Bolton had been correct: there was a lot of talent among the teaching staff.

But public school teachers are very easily shocked. You can't do Shakespeare and mince words, and Rob never minced words. There was all sorts of racy stuff in *Shrew*, and we did it as a tremendously active play – a play within a play, with Christopher Sly on a mattress dreaming the play.

Shrew was very well received. But I remember one of the teachers, a very proper woman, saying, "I enjoyed the *Shrew*, but I am little put off by some of the language." I think Rob just ignored such comments.

Early in 1949, the Peterborough Little Theatre took *Shrew* to the Dominion Drama Festival, where it went up against Ontario's leading theatre troupe. Elsa Franklin was then a member of that company, the Ottawa Little Theatre.

ELSA FRANKLIN (Television producer and publicist)
There's no question the Ottawa Little Theatre was the best theatre troupe in the country. We were the usual stars at the Dominion Drama Festival. And then these actors from Peterborough turned up. We did not like Robertson or Mrs. Davies. They seemed like big shots, big cheeses. He was so dramatic in his look that he put a lot of people off. I saw Robertson Davies onstage and offstage and I had the feeling of his being superior. I thought he sounded like a pompous ass. At the time, I was too young to appreciate him. But you know, the people who worked with him loved him.

DAVID GARDNER
The Royal Alex in Toronto is where I saw RD act. This was a rare occurrence. It was in 1949, when he directed a production of *The Taming of the Shrew*. Brenda was Katerina. RD had a bit part in this production, as the tailor. It was an Alfred Hitchcock thing to do, to direct and then to appear.

He appeared suddenly on stage, on he came, like a ballet dancer! He was so light on his feet! And he was a big man. But he was light and airy, and he danced across the stage with a piece of cloth streaming from his arm. The audience laughed and cheered in recognition. It was only a short moment – the tailor just has a few words. He appeared and then was gone. But so graceful!

Somehow, being on stage transformed the nearsighted and clumsy RD into a man of unexpected grace.

GWEN BROWN

When he was directing here at the summer theatre, I asked him if I could come and watch rehearsals. He said, "Yes, you may," but he wasn't crazy about the idea. So I sat quiet as a mouse at the back of the house.

I remember there was one scene, there was a gal who was talking and taking off her glove, and it wasn't synchronized with the dialogue. So he jumped up on stage – it was so graceful! I can still see him, talking away as he was taking off the glove. He was a big man, but he just jumped up on stage. I bet he was a good dancer!

Imaginative in his staging of classics, when it came to his own scripts, RD was protective.

FERN RAHMEL

Once he snapped at me. I was directing *The Voice of the People*. There's a scene where one character is writing a letter to the paper. . . . I told the actor who was doing it to change a couple of words to give the play a local flavour. Rob ticked me off about it, justifiably so. Directors do it all the time and they don't think to ask the writer. But Rob was upset, and I certainly coveted his good opinion.

He gave his theatre-related opinions generously.

BILL NEEDLES

A young Irish director called Michael Sadlier came to Toronto, an entrepreneur if there ever was one. He asked me if I knew if there was anywhere in Ontario that we might be received if we were to start a summer stock theatre company. I said I knew Robertson Davies through theatre, and that he was the editor of *The Peterborough Examiner*. So we went to see him, at the newspaper. I remember it was a small office, very orderly and neat. He was in a sort of swivel chair. He had a commanding presence.

I put the proposal for a summer stock company to Rob. I said, Would he support us? Rob put it succinctly in a deep voice, with a mid-Atlantic accent: "If you are prepared to allow me to direct one or two plays occasionally, and you are prepared to allow my wife to play a part, then I think I might, yes."

We had good people with us: Kate Reid, Anna Cameron and young Tony Perkins. Yes, *the* Tony Perkins, later the star in *Psycho*. He was about 17, and his mother had asked us to take him along because she couldn't do a thing with him. He was maybe third props assistant.

JENNIFER SURRIDGE

One day, Rosamond was outside at Weller Street, sunbathing nude in the garden. She must have been around two years old. She took off from the front garden and started tearing down Weller Street. Father took off after her. He wasn't very athletic. Just at that moment, the summer theatre truck came by. That was the summer Anthony Perkins was in the summer theatre company, and he was one of the ones who went by in the truck. The actors were all cheering RD on.

Like Tony Perkins, William Davis, who later played "Cancer Man" in the 1990s TV show *The X-Files*, was a young actor when he first met RD.

WILLIAM DAVIS

My first acquaintance with Rob was when I saw *Fortune My Foe*, at age 12. I was greatly moved by the story of a Canadian trying to succeed. Rob certainly had an impact as a writer and as a director on me and on my love for the theatre. . . . By the time I was 14 my cousins Donald Davis and Murray Davis were running Straw Hat Players in Gravenhurst and Bracebridge. We did *Ten Nights in a Barroom* . . . and he, Robertson Davies, directed. My character was the son of a bartender, and I served drinks a lot. Donald Davis had had success with *The Drunkard* in the late 1940s, and so they had reprised that music and those songs. That year I was 14 and my voice was breaking, and I was required to sing. RD took me aside and said, "Are you happy in that tenor part?" His main encouragement to me was about my voice. He was a very pleasant presence. He was very sweet, always in control and very relaxed and gentle.

Alas, RD's growing theatrical reputation didn't mean the end of clashes with Peterborough sensibilities.

FERN RAHMEL

We had cast parties back at their house on Weller Street. They were very hospitable. I do remember one party when the women were taken to the Davieses' bedroom to leave their coats, and there over the bed was [a print of Botticelli's] *Venus on the Half Shell* [The Birth of Venus]. One of the teachers was shocked. Imagine having *Venus*! It was so suggestive!

In the third year of The Little Theatre we did a Synge play, *The Tinker's Wedding*. This really riled the local Catholics. Rob directed it. *The Tinker's Wedding* presents the Catholic Church in an unflattering light. The local bishop wrote to the paper. That sort of thing bothered Rob. He put a good face on it, but it hurt him.

But RD's contribution was valued at Ottawa's Canadian Repertory Theatre in 1951.

AMELIA HALL (actor)

On January 9 we presented Robertson Davies's new play, *At My Heart's Core*. . . . About the play, Robertson Davies has written, "The point which I am trying to bring out is that the physical hardships which the pioneers suffered were very great, but that many of them suffered at least equal pain from the intellectual frustration which they endured." . . . The play ran fifth in box-office appeal of all fifty plays the CRT had presented so far. . . . One letter to *The Ottawa Citizen* thanked the paper for introducing its readers to Davies through his column; otherwise he might not have gone to the CRT to see *At My Heart's Core* and thus would have missed a grand play, well done.

FERN RAHMEL

When we did *Riders to the Sea*, one of the actresses came down with measles and Rob said I had to take over in her role. He coached me. I am sure he thought, "Fern, how can you be so stupid?" But he was patient. He talked about emotion: Be this person. It was a different aspect of acting than I had ever thought of. Anything I knew about acting and directing I learned from him.

I think RD was very conscious of the Canadian tendency to push people down. What I admired about him was he pulled people *up*. I would never have thought I could be a successful director of plays. But I eventually became one. RD saw the possibility in me and he encouraged me to try. I think he did that with many people.

Chapter 14

TEMPEST IN WALES

Smarting from the cool reception *Eros At Breakfast* received in Edinburgh in 1949, and from the brush-offs his plays received when he sent them to English producers (one informed him, "You must realise that no one, but no one, has any interest in Canada"), RD began to ask himself if he should focus on writing books.

RD (letter to Horace Davenport, November 23, 1949)
I was very surprised to hear that your friend named Kittredge in Arizona likes my books. . . .

If he really likes the books, I would be very happy to receive his address from you, and I will send him a copy of the *Marchbanks' Table Talk*. I am still in that stage of authorship where I am so cringingly grateful to anybody who likes my books that I am prepared to give away free copies in the most reckless manner.

He wondered if an idea he'd had for a play might make a better book.

BRENDA DAVIES
He felt the trouble with plays was that they were taken out of his hands and messed about with. With a novel, it was just Rob and the readers.

JENNIFER SURRIDGE
Turning to the writing of novels was strategic, because he was a person who loved to do things on his own, and he was terrible at letting anyone help him.

MARTIN HUNTER

He told me that he read Aldous Huxley's *Antic Hay* – after reading Dickens and Trollope – and said to himself, "Oho, so you can do that – you can be light and still literary!"

His first novel was light, but it also explored the anxieties RD was beginning to feel as the father of three daughters. He created a character, a Mr. Webster, father of two pretty daughters, who muses, "Girls were such unpredictable creatures. He came of a generation to which any girl, until she is married, is a kind of unexploded bomb."

BRENDA DAVIES

Daughters as "unexploded bombs"? Rob never wasted any material. Rob would use that line "unexploded bombs" around the house. When he thought up a good line, he'd use it! . . . Rob used his writing as an outlet. . . . He'd always foresee trouble long before it came.

RD delivered the manuscript of *Tempest-Tost* in May 1951 to his publisher, Clarke Irwin. Annoyingly, the editor asked that he tone down his slightly scatological humour. So RD revised the manuscript on a family trip to Wales, to see Rupert and his second wife, Margaret McAdoo, Rupert's former secretary. Senator Davies had formally retired (though he never stopped critiquing the family newspapers). In 1951, he was appointed High Sheriff of Montgomeryshire. That year, he and his new wife moved into a grand house with turrets and a gated driveway, Leighton Hall, which still stands on the outskirts of Welshpool.

BRENDA DAVIES

When Rupert got married and bought Leighton Hall, the plan was, the older brothers would leave when we arrived. The brothers criticized Margaret terribly, particularly Fred, who was loyal to his mother. It was a great stress for Margaret, who hadn't been married before. She tried so hard, washing and sending out Rupert's clothes to be cleaned after one use. Fred was terribly against this marriage because he had been Florence's favourite and was honouring Florence's memory. He was a very difficult man and he was critical of all the children. . . . He had such a weight behind these things, of anger and cruelty.

KATE BRAY

Mother and Dad and Jane and I were there for July and August. Arthur and Dorothy and their sons Michael and Chris came for the first half of the summer. We roamed everywhere! We walked to Welshpool if we felt like it. Then Robertson and Brenda came over with their three girls, and there was a week or so overlap. We had had the most wonderful summer until then. When they arrived, it went to hell in a handcart.

MICHAEL DAVIES

There was discontent in the air. . . . Apparently there was more going on that month that I wasn't privy to. They'd given us grandchildren all a pony, and I was far more interested in the riding teacher's rear end as she sat on the horse ahead of me than I was in the family's internecine wars.

KATE BRAY

We kids had a tremendous amount of freedom. We had to muck out the stables and take care of our own ponies, but we had the afternoons to ourselves. We all played with the Smiths, who had six kids and lived on the property. We were a gang all summer. In fact, we still correspond. I owe Moira Smith a letter. . . .

But when Robertson and Brenda arrived, they were horrified by the amount of freedom we had been permitted and what they considered the lower-class friends we were hanging out with. They definitely had some very interesting ideas as to who it was good to associate with. They had a British attitude towards class. . . . Rosamond came up to the stables one day and said to the Smiths, "We are not allowed to play with you because you are common." Awful!

MIRANDA DAVIES

We were sitting outside the stables, Rosamond on the swing, and she said, "Anyway, Daddy says we are not to play with you because you are common." So Jenny and I had to hurry Rosamond away before Leo Smith got out his slingshot.

KATE BRAY

There was a great row. The Smiths were terribly hurt and extrapolated from this that Jane and I felt that way as well. It seemed like forever when we could not get through to them at all. There was a huge, hurt rift. And Mrs. Smith was a wonderful person. Somehow it got patched up. Miranda and Jennifer were not to play with them – but we could. But it was never the same, and we were expected to play with Miranda and Jenny.

BRENDA DAVIES
Kate is right in a way. There were deep divisions in the family in attitudes towards child-rearing. The attitudes were so different!

When we arrived in Wales, Rupert complained about Fred's daughters Kathryn and Jane rushing around. He wanted them to come in for tea and to behave properly. It was Rupert who didn't want them to play with the Smiths. *We* were not trying to bring up other peoples' kids! As for the Smiths, that was Rupert. Wales is so class-ridden!

JENNIFER SURRIDGE
I remember Rupert saying we couldn't play with the Smiths because they were the help. That's just the way he was. His family had to conform to his standards. Self-made men can be funny. . . . RD wanted to please Rupert, and we were ruled by what Rupert wanted.

MIRANDA DAVIES
What Rupert wanted done had to be done. This was reinforced by my mother when we stayed at Leighton Hall. If Rupert invited another family with children over for tea, we were expected to be there with our dresses on. . . . Whereas Kate and Jane might not turn up.

Meanwhile RD indulged in his own sense of play, although he must have been aware that on June 22nd, that very year, the British Parliament passed "The Fraudulent Mediums Act" "for the punishment of persons who fraudulently purport to act as spiritualistic mediums. . ." If he did know of this new law, provocatively he flouted it.

MIRANDA DAVIES
Near Leighton Hall, there was a country fete. RD got himself dressed up as the Veiled Prophetess of Ecbatana [the name of a priestess in *The Golden Ass* and also the mock-identity of a character in Aldous Huxley's *Chrome Yellow*]. Daddy sat in a little tent and told fortunes and read palms.

KATE BRAY

Robertson dressed up as a fortune teller, Madame Swami or whatever he called himself. I remember a turban and a shawl. He did like acting!

But the summer visit among the Davies brothers remained difficult. Mealtimes were particularly stressful.

MICHAEL DAVIES

I do remember one gigantic argument at Leighton Hall. Three families were there with their children, and Rupert and Margaret, all in the big dining room. At one point I remember Fred saying, "I wish you'd tell Rose [the cook] to keep her goddamned hair out of the soup." Margaret was horror-stricken. Someone, I don't know who, got up and left the table.

KATE BRAY

Poor Margaret, in this giant decaying pile of stone – poor, poor Margaret, planning all these meals with very limited staff. It was unbelievable. My mother and father would have left if they could have. . . . I know they tried desperately to get on a ship, but couldn't find one. They wanted to get out of there. . . . Arthur and Dorothy and Mother and Dad were just weeping.

Finally, RD and Brenda decamped for London, accompanied by a Welshpool girl hired to look after their daughters.

JEAN POWELL NOY

When we got to London, the parents went out quite a bit. I remember the children's parents: she was very smart and he was big and jolly with a big beard. . . . We'd have our evening meal together and then they'd go out. The girls I remember as very happy girls.

MIRANDA DAVIES

While we were in London, the parents went to a play every night. They saw the Oliviers in *Caesar and Cleopatra* and *Antony and Cleopatra* – the Shaw and the Shakespeare. They went off to see Peggy Ashcroft in *A Winter's Tale*. Jean Powell had to babysit us at night when the parents went to the theatre. She probably had to deal with my disappointment.

BRENDA DAVIES
We were able to leave them with Jean when we went to theatre in the
evenings. In those days we could put the girls with her into a taxi and
send them back to the hotel. The girls behaved very well. They knew
how to behave. . . . London was the Great Good Place. Rob was keen
about nice restaurants and second-hand bookshops. He was extremely
interested in alchemy and Jung, and he was frightfully interested in
circus oddities, so he would go to a bookstore in Holborne. . . . He
carried notebooks. He was always making notes. He carried a Smithson's
in his pocket and he'd write huge numbers of things. He had huge
numbers of diaries – a travel diary, and a theatre diary of where we went
and who we met and what we saw.

**At summer's end, the family returned to Peterborough to await publica-
tion of *Tempest-Tost*, which was published by Clarke Irwin in October
1951. Canadian reviews were good, and readers, especially in Kingston,
were very intrigued.**

BEA CORBETT
He wrote those Salterton books in the 1950s, but they were about
Kingston in the 1930s. When I read *Tempest-Tost*, I remembered that
production of *Midsummer Night's Dream* all those years later. . . . I used
to be able to identify most of the characters. Robertson did like gossip,
and Kingston left its mark on him. Puss Pottinger in *Tempest-Tost* is
Mabel Guildersleeve.

**But when the American and British editions followed the next spring, the
response was more muted.**

18th November 1952
Chatto and Windus
London WC2

Dear Mr Davies,

I have been meaning for some time to write to you about
Tempest-Tost, and I am now reminded to do so by having
passed to me the account of its sales. . . . The account shows
a total to date of 1,700 sold, which I cannot pretend is a

very exciting record. On the other hand, many a first novel nowadays sells far fewer copies. Several of the reviews were complimentary. . . . Out of curiosity I took a ruler and actually measured the total space, even including mere two- or three-line mentions. It came to forty-seven inches – little more than a total of two columns in *The Times*. . . .

Anyway, even if *Tempest-Tost* cannot be described as a success, it has been noticed by quite a few folk who are eagerly on the look-out for a new source of merriment in this melancholy world. Alan Melville is one of them, and I only wish his broadcast had not been on the Light Programme on a Sunday afternoon.

I wonder what you are at work on now? . . . Whatever form a new work of yours may take it can be assured of eager readers at Chatto's.

Yours very sincerely
Harold Raymond
[Director, Chatto and Windus]

Response to his first novel gave RD little reason to believe that fiction was his future.

AMY STEWART
Rob never said anything to us, but I think from talking to Brenda he was always disappointed in the reviews.

Chapter 15

FAMILY GAMES ON
PARK STREET

In 1951, the summer of their trip to Wales, RD and Brenda moved their family to a new house in Peterborough. Built in 1848, 361 Park Street North is surrounded by lawns and an aura of history. It is now the home of Tom Symons, the first president of Trent University, and his wife.

TOM SYMONS
In this house we have found traces of RD's life here, but also of people long before him. One of the Gilmours (the founders of McMaster University) had carved an initial with a date, 1871, and that's still here, cut into the glass. . . . We had one or two chats with RD about the ghosts of the house. . . . He enjoyed confirming some community thoughts that he had an understanding of the mysteries of the ghost world.

When RD and his family first moved in, they decided something had to be done about the previous occupants' taste in wallpaper.

MIRANDA DAVIES
We were allowed to crayon on the walls all over the feathers of the grey-blue wallpaper in the living room. The thrill of being allowed to do it! And then the room was re-papered in something calm and light.

We moved our much-loved furniture there – a long, dark brown, heavy table you could crawl around underneath. There was an oriental rug in dusty rose by the piano.

The house had a central hall, with RD's study off to the right. . . . On his table was the typewriter: he told us he typed with his two index fingers, but he'd worn them out, so now he typed with his two middle fingers. . . . His work table faced the window, while as you came in, facing you was the fireplace – never used. On the back wall was the door to the small toilet he called the Men's, in which he hung a large poster of the Versailles Hall of Mirrors. It wasn't a room that we frequented much. We were not supposed to use the Men's. So if we did, we'd whip out pretty quick.

TOM SYMONS
Go into the Throne Room [the bathroom] and you'll see a card written by Robertson Davies above the "throne." When we moved here he gave me this useful motto: it is on *Peterborough Examiner* editor letterhead:

Ne Illegitimus Carborundum. . . . RD.

[Daviesian Latin for "Don't let the bastards grind you down."]

As at Weller Street, the Davieses didn't socialize with their nearest neighbours. But the door was always open to people involved with the theatre.

GWEN BROWN
Brenda asked me if I'd come down to her Park Street house and talk to her about this section of a play we were doing that she wasn't happy with. As we were talking, Rob came in the front door and the kids came out to greet him. He was wearing a big fur coat. He got down on the floor and was going ROWRR, ROWRR – on all fours, being a big bear! He loved dress-ups.

JAMIE CUNNINGHAM
I'd been a boy actor since the age of seven. At 13, I went to Peterborough to play in summer stock, and Robertson Davies was directing *Ten Nights in a Barroom*. As a director I thought he was great – very focused. For him, work and play connected.

It was the first time I'd been away from home. He recognized that I was lonely and he introduced me to his family. I was the same age as Miranda and we became friends.

They had this wonderful house, big and spacious, and made me feel welcome. Meals were very festive. It was all lots of fun, a big romp. They had a wonderful housekeeper, Mrs. Pedak.

Robertson Davies reminded me a lot of my own father, a very dominating presence, surrounded by females, the daughters, the wife and the housekeeper. He once wrote that everything remarkable that has been achieved for good or ill was by men and women who never lost touch with their three-year-old self, the self who wants all the power, all the money, all the attention. That was Robertson Davies.

MARTIN HUNTER
When he was young, my brother-in-law Jamie would go to dinner in Peterborough at the Davieses' and RD would go into this tremendous performance, telling stories, making jokes – bowel diseases and afflictions also permeate Davies's books. He always liked shocking people in that slightly schoolboyish way. Jamie said, "Looking back, I wonder, why was he going to all this trouble for a 14-year-old boy and his own daughters?"

JAMIE CUNNINGHAM
At dinners I was made aware that Mr. Davies was a performer, and a full-blown performance was going on. Like all people who have food issues, he was obsessed by elimination. . . . Conversation was civilized and then suddenly down and dirty . . . but the atmosphere was extremely genial, lots of laughter and good humour.

SASSY WADDELL
At dinner there was a lot of talk and kidding each other. And the "What did you do today, dear?" talk was on a much more erudite level than I was used to: my mother was a stay-at-home mum and my father was with Canadian Tire. But the Davieses were talking ideas and concepts and that kind of stuff, not about the price of meat. I loved it. I thought it was terrific. I thought they all seemed so smart and articulate. There were a lot of family jokes. As they say, too clever by half. Which dazzled me.

But there was a strong code of behaviour.

BRENDA DAVIES
As parents, were we strict? Yes, in a way. I remember one of the children, Miranda, complaining that we had to have three meals a day in our house and the other children at school were allowed to forage for themselves. We did not want our children to become Little Peterborovians. Rob and I were very keen on words, and we disliked phrases such as "in back of" and actual misuse of grammar. Miranda said to us, "Mummy, you and Daddy can say what you like at home. But I have to get along with these people." The girls had to speak two languages, one at home and the other at school.

SASSY WADDELL
Always they had dinner in the dining room. A relatively formal dinner. I remember cloth napkins. I remember I thought it very strange that they all had cloth napkins and napkin holders. I thought, Why the hell would you do that if you just have to wash the napkin?

JENNIFER SURRIDGE
When we were punished, it was because of something we had done or because we had been rude to Mum. RD got more angry with us on Mum's behalf than on his own. He had a stick called Tickler. We were always being threatened with Tickler. I can remember being spanked with Tickler, but I can't remember why. We may have answered back to Mum. . . . He'd get very upset if you were neglectful of someone else. We were given a very moral upbringing, ways of behaving that even then were stricter than a lot of our friends.

RAMSAY DERRY (friend of Miranda and later a fiction editor)
The Davieses were very hospitable people in a formal way. They entertained their children's friends with dinners or even overnight. We had a very good time, but you were aware with the Davieses that they had a sense of how things should be done. . . . This could have a puzzling effect on some people who saw them as pretentious or phony. I didn't. I saw it as a theatrical sense, wanting to perform a role and wanting to do the right thing, socially – and morally. It struck me that Miranda was immensely proud to be her parents' daughter, and liked to be part of their lives. I know very well there was a downside that came to be manifested more openly later on.

Despite his dependence on his wife, RD understood that their marriage would be stronger if each partner respected the other's independence. In 1952, leaving Anna Pedak to look after the younger girls, Brenda went to visit her mother and sister in Australia. In a March 18 letter, RD wrote:

RD
Really of course I ought to be there, so that you could see me in the surroundings which will probably always be the backdrop of your most intimate thoughts. Then you could decide whether you are really going to keep me or not. . . .

I don't see why, when Boodie [Rosamond] is a few years older, we shouldn't travel a great deal. I weary of Pboro and Canada. . . .

You know that I have a strong feeling for the continuity of life; one is a bead on a string, and it is good to know what the other beads are like. Perhaps that is how we seem to God – all generations milling about, without regard for accidents of Time. . . . Let me say how very happy – deeply happy – I am that you have made this journey, for I feel it will be a turning point in our life together. . . . Coming to live in Canada was a wrench and a nervous adventure, and I never forget or undervalue the great courage and trust in me which you brought to it.

JENNIFER SURRIDGE
RD was half a person when Mum was away. I guess his emotional dependence on her was very strong, as was hers on him. When she wasn't there, there was nobody for him to tell his deepest thoughts and feelings. He thought of marriage as one long conversation, and that conversation in marriage is more important than sex. Which is true.

So he'd retire into himself. He wasn't good with young children. Never was. He did his best for us when she was away, but he didn't quite come out of his work.

As he had promised in his letter, RD and Brenda began to do more travelling in the late 1950s. In Britain they'd visit Rupert and go to theatre in London. In 1958, they also went to Manchester to reconnect with Paul Mathews, Brenda's biological father, of whom she had no memory.

BRENDA DAVIES
Rob encouraged me to contact my father, and it was a good idea. It's not good not to know anything about your past. Rob wrote me a wonderful letter when I went to Australia about the importance of reassessing your roots. My father and Rob got on very well.

And they travelled to New York for special classes in the Alexander Technique of physical exercises to reduce emotional stress, and to see Broadway plays.

ROSAMOND BAILEY
They were always going away. And Jenny was always saying, "It's my birthday and they're away again."

JENNIFER SURRIDGE
It seemed that way! And what's implied: they'd never miss my sisters' birthdays! My birthday is in October, Rosamond's at Easter and Miranda's at Christmas. . . . The parents were always travelling in the fall. It may have been irrational for me to say that, but it seemed they were always travelling. And life was not as much fun when they were away! The conversation was not as good.

When they were old enough, RD showed his children where their father worked, and what his professional values were.

MIRANDA DAVIES
Daddy took us to *The Peterborough Examiner* print room where we could see the pages laid out in type. We had our names given to us back to front in lead pieces. His office was big, with big windows and a large desk and a typewriter. I think he pointed to the typewriter and said, "There, children, is the machine that I use to win bread."

We were taken to the press room, and watched newspapers when they came out at the end. Every tenth one was at an angle so they would be counted. The paperboys would take them away in big sacks. Daddy would get into a rage if the paperboys delivering the paper missed our verandah. He'd want to get a BB gun. . . . What impressed me was his sense of service to the community. One day a woman phoned to say she had not got her newspaper. And Daddy piled us all into the car and Mum drove us to her house and he delivered it himself. I thought that was honourable and fine.

The Davieses wanted their daughters to be challenged beyond the horizons of the local public education system. So as each finished elementary school, they were sent to board at Bishop Strachan School in Toronto, the sister school of his alma mater, Upper Canada College.

MIRANDA DAVIES
In my last year, when I was in Grade 7 at Queen Mary Public School in Peterborough, I was telling people that I would be leaving to board at Bishop Strachan in Toronto the next year. I told Daddy, "The kids are teasing me – they're saying things like 'Whatsa matter, Miranda, why you leavin' Queen Mary – not good enough fer ya?'"

Daddy was no use at all! He said, "Tell them you are being sent away to be made a lady of." I may have said this to them. I was very much my father's daughter.

JENNIFER SURRIDGE

Whenever one of us went away to school, or whenever Mum was away, he seemed very cold to me then. Recently, I found a piece in his diary that whenever anyone went away or back to school, he wrote that he felt extremely emotional, as if he might break down, and he had to fight to keep a leash on his feelings and not show them. I wish I had known that!

We children got the feeling that when Mum went away, or when we went away, he never gave it another thought. He was an emotional man, but he was brought up so that it did not show.

ROSAMOND BAILEY

All my life I've had the sense that domesticity and creativity are linked. At our house, my dad wrote plays, he wrote puppet plays for us, he wrote letters and used sealing wax. My mother sewed, they made props, we'd all play charades. It was magical. Dad even made Christmas decorations. He *loved* Christmas. He loved any excuse for a pageant, a celebration. . . . When they went away, I felt left out, because there was always so much going on. . . . None of us wanted to leave the house and go to boarding school.

JENNIFER SURRIDGE

At BSS we had chapel every day and had Grace Church on the Hill on Sundays. When I was being prepared for confirmation, the chaplain, who was also the minister at Grace Church on the Hill, was a terrible, unctuous man, Canon Craig. My friends and I would have bets on how soon his sermon would turn to money and what his parishioners should give.

Because I wanted to raise hell in class, I asked him about the Virgin Birth. I said I didn't understand why Catholics believed in it and we Anglicans did not. Canon Craig thought I was trying to get him into sex talk. I was humiliated! In the basement corridor after the class I yelled, "I *hate* Dr. Craig." I was called in to the principal of BSS. And I was told that I must write to my father and say, This is what I did, this is why I am being punished.

When I did, RD sent me a telegram, "I support you in your stand. I will back you" – in effect saying that Dr. Craig should have talked to us about my question. Then RD came to the school and spoke to the principal. The upshot was that another man was assigned to take our confirmation class, and I was confirmed.

Each Christmas, the girls returned from boarding school and the family celebrated lavishly.

JOHN WHYTE
For years and years they had the best of Christmas parties. Miranda's birthday is December 24, so these parties were associated with Miranda's birthday. But they had the quality of "revels" – that's a word RD would have used. I remember going to one when I was at Trinity [College at the University of Toronto]. I remember driving back from Toronto furiously to get to the Davies party. I associate these parties with mince tarts. I remember the parties as being not a meal, but with lots of food, sweets.

There were games, and there would be a point at these parties where he would step through a door and do seer-and-soothsayer stuff, tapping the mysterious and the spooky. He'd wear a cloak and a bright red waistcoat. This was in the 1950s and men did not wear beards, so his beard was a kind of costume, too. And maybe a kimono or smoking jacket or cloak. And we would also play charades, but it was beyond ordinary charades. As with the rest of the Davieses, it was larger than life. You were more engaged, more amused than in ordinary life. We knew we were a little bigger than we would normally appear to be.

The other big thing at these parties was "Murder." There's someone who is the murderer, and no one knows who it is. The house was plunged into complete darkness and you could go anywhere you liked. But you could get killed. Then you had to lie still. The idea is to do it when the victim is isolated. RD was enthusiastic about this game, beyond measure.

MIRANDA DAVIES
Once, the family was at home playing Consequences, the game in which each player writes part of a story, folds the paper and passes it on.

You start with a description, then a man's name, then a description, then a woman's name; you invent something that happens to them, and then "he said to her," and "she said to him."

We were reading Daisy Ashford's *The Young Visiters* at the time, and Rosamond wrote down on the He Said to Her sequence: "Without you my life will be sour grapes and ashes." Of course, Rosamond got the biggest laugh and the biggest reaction to this. It outshone Daddy's line, which was also funny. But to my astonishment, he *minded!*

Of the three sisters, Rosamond had such a lively, attractive personality, she got away with murder. She was enormously competitive with our father and he Did Not Like It. Rosamond liked to see how far she could go. She was more impulsive and free than Jenny and me. She would also stand up to him or even be saucy.

ROSAMOND BAILEY

I seem to have taken it upon myself to feel that he allowed me to compete with him. I could see that the others weren't willing to do that. But I got pleasure out of it and he tolerated it. And if he said something, I felt I could question it.

Family dynamics escaped the notice of most guests, who were simply enchanted by the Davieses' revelry.

JOHN WHYTE

I remember walking home with a group of people, up Park Street, after one of these parties, enjoying the night, still full of merriment.

There were also tobogganing parties on Television Hill. RD and Brenda owned the property, from which Rupert's TV station, CHEX-TV, was broadcast.

ARNOLD EDINBOROUGH

On one occasion, Scott Young and his wife Rassie [parents of the future singer Neil Young] joined us and we sent all the kids off tobogganing. Then we said, "Why don't we all go?" Scott and Rassie and Brenda and Rob and myself were all on one of these sleighs, going down the hill. Rob had a wonderful time. He went down several times and tumbled off, too. Then one of the kids went down the hill and broke a leg and had to be taken off to hospital.

Despite such shared crises and celebrations, RD never felt at home in Peterborough.

ARNOLD EDINBOROUGH

You can't imagine. They were very much outsiders. You never saw Rob address the Chamber of Commerce. They were very lonely in Peterborough. They couldn't wait to have people visit them. They'd drive us from Port Hope to Peterborough. They'd put up with our kids!

Chapter 16

BEARDING THE BEARD

As a journalist, RD had a sensible distrust of other journalists. But as an author, columnist, playwright and personality, he could not dodge his own share of media scrutiny.

ROSAMOND BAILEY

In 1952, *Maclean's* magazine sent someone to do an article on my father. The writer, June Callwood, came to Park Street to interview my dad. Contrary to my father's feelings about this, he seemed a real power in the world – people came to interview him!

From "The Beard," *Maclean's* magazine, March 15, 1952, a profile of RD by June Callwood:

> The people of Peterborough, like those of most communities, have a well-developed knack of keeping track of one another's goings and comings. The appearance of Davies and his actress wife, who dresses like a ladylike gypsy, led them to expect something exceptional, like opium parties and orgies on the lawn. Disappointingly, the Davieses are the most circumspect couple in Peterborough and the orgies on the lawn have been directed at weeding the tulip beds. Peterborough has reluctantly come to realize that, as a Bohemian, Davies is a fraud.

JUNE CALLWOOD

"As a Bohemian, Davies is a fraud . . ." Did I write that? Good for me!

I was still early in my working life at *Maclean's* – I was 27 but looked younger.

Maclean's editor Ralph Allen did most of the assigning. He or Pierre Berton phoned and said, "We think we'd like a piece on Robertson

Davies and can you do it by such and such a day?" *Maclean's* was then a biweekly. We worked a few weeks in advance.

So I phoned Robertson Davies and said *Maclean's* was interested in doing a piece on him. On the phone he was civil and courteous. Nothing suggested he'd be as difficult a man as he later was.

Before I went, I read everything he wrote. I saw the rumbling humour, the intelligence, the wit . . . his disdain for most of Canada, everything he saw here being far too crude. That struck me as kind of adorable. So I was looking forward to meeting him.

I must have driven to Peterborough. I don't know if I went to the *Examiner* office. I think the interviewing was always at the house on Park Street.

He was magisterial and I was awed. Who did we know in those days who had a beard? And a strange accent? Now I would call it mid-Atlantic, the accent of a Shakespearean scholar. He *projected*, as well.

When I did an interview I always thought chronology was helpful. So at Park Street we started with his childhood. I'd read his books, and I had done whatever research you could in those days, getting clippings in brown envelopes.

So I said to him that he had played in *Oedipus, King of Thebes*, by Sophocles, at Queen's. I guess I mispronounced "Oedipus." I suppose I pronounced it phonetically. I hadn't finished high school. He corrected me in such a patronizing, unkind way! It was *scathing*. I just gasped. I was scared. I continued with the interview as best I could.

He was very hostile throughout that whole interview. I felt there was something about me that had put him off, that I was not senior enough, that everything told him that I wasn't the right writer. . . . After the Oedipus correction, I was the meek scribe and he was the performing lion. I was cowed.

JENNIFER SURRIDGE
He was not impressed with June Callwood. He didn't think she knew anything. At the time of the first *Maclean's* interview, she was very young.

JUNE CALLWOOD
To write the story I also went around Peterborough, around the neighbourhood. I went into stores. I wanted to know how people felt about him, and I got nothing that was useful. People said, No, they hardly ever saw him. His name had drawn a blank, except for the clothes. As for

people being invited into his house, I couldn't find any. It looked like he lived in a cocoon. I found someone from the *Examiner* and couldn't get anything from him, either. So I concluded that as a newspaperman, Robertson Davies was not being a pal, hanging around with this staff. People didn't *dislike* him – they were puzzled. They'd never known anyone to act like that.

JENNIFER SURRIDGE
I remember RD and I were once talking about "the truth." I was about 15. I said, "What is the truth?" RD said, "The truth is what is good for someone else to know." . . . We had had this thing in our family: *You don't tell.*

GWEN· BROWN
He did not like the fact that June Callwood was interviewing other people about him. I think he used the words "getting the dirt on Robertson Davies."

JUNE CALLWOOD
I had written about the Happy Gang, a comedy troupe who thought I was there to be their publicist, and they all told me how they hated one another – so I wrote about the "Unhappy Gang." So yes, Davies was right to be worried about me. Come to think of it, I was a pain in the ass. I guess I had a reputation.

Maclean's, continued:

> Mrs. Davies is horrified when admirers suggest she must be a great help to her husband. "That's ridiculous, of course," she observes. But she does permit him to work uninterrupted evening after evening. . . . "Permit me!" snorts Davies. "I'll have you know that I am master of this house and it is run to suit me."

JUNE CALLWOOD
When he was talking about what was "permitted," and his being "master of the house," Brenda was not in the room. Most of our interviews were in his study. But when he said, "I am the master of the house," you have

to remember that it was the 1950s. That was the normal male preroga-
tive. That whole thing about "This house is run to suit me" – if Brenda
had been in the room when he said it, I might have picked up that he
was kidding or teasing. I knew her to be a very much more complicated
woman than she let on to me. Was he saying this as a parody of his role?
If so, I would not have been so unkind as not to give him [credit for]
that. When he said it, I wasn't offended. I was probably delighted that
he was in character. The more he dug himself in, the better for my
piece. . . . A few times we had tea in the living room. I remember the
kids were so quiet and civil. They only spoke when spoken to.

JENNIFER SURRIDGE

RD was very private, and he wanted to protect his privacy very badly. . . .
He wanted people to know only what he wanted them to know. I don't
recall his ever saying anything. It was just the sense that what was in the
family stayed in the family.

JUNE CALLWOOD

Then I went to the Peterborough Little Theatre and I watched RD
direct. He was patient and kind, and he gave bloody good direction.

When I think about it now, I am reminded of Tyrone Guthrie. At
Stratford, a few years later on, I heard Tyrone Guthrie say to an actor,
"You've got to fuck off a lot faster than that." I'd never heard a director
talk like that!

RD was totally engaging as a director, loving his business, loving
what he was in, and very endearing.

But the other thing about our interview was, he told me about his
experience with what he had thought was Hodgkins' disease, and he
told me, "This is off the record." But everywhere I went afterwards,
everyone told me about it. His wife referred to it casually, and friends
did, too.

So I wrote about his cancer scare. When the article came out,
Davies went to my editor, Ralph Allen, and said that my ethics were
hugely in question. He said that he had put me under a solemn promise
not to mention it.

I realize now I had made a huge mistake in not warning him. But
again, the tone he used and the words he used with Ralph were very
derogatory and not only of my ethics. I think he used words like "this

snip of a girl" – that wasn't the phrase, but it was in that category. Ralph called me on the carpet. I gave Ralph all my sources for saying that RD had feared that he had had cancer. I said everyone in town knew it.

But for years after the *Maclean's* article appeared, we were famous for not liking one another. If we were in the same room or at the same party, we would manage to stay at opposite ends.

Then, about the time he got to be master of Massey College at the University of Toronto, someone said to me, "You know, Robertson Davies is beginning to like you." So the next time we were in the same room, I made a point of going up to him and saying in a genial way, "Hello, Robertson."

And he said "Hello, June!"

It was a colourless little exchange, but I went away and I thought, "We've fixed that!" The sting had gone out of it.

Years later, I was at some media gathering – PEN or something. Arnold Edinborough gave some speech and it was full of that man's self-conceit. In the audience there was lots of eye-rolling. Then Robertson Davies got up – and I liked him for this – and he said, "Usually it is a huge pleasure to thank Arnold Edinborough for a speech," and added, and I remember the words, "but not on this occasion!"

That's when I really began to like the old rascal. And I always liked the writing. I remember as Marchbanks, Davies wrote a description of a cough "like coal going down a coal chute." I'd thought, "What a writer!"

Chapter 17

LEAVEN OF MALICE

To everyone but RD, Rupert's pride in Arthur and RD was obvious. But with his first-born son Fred, who had less luck, or talent, for business, Rupert's relations were more difficult.

MICHAEL DAVIES
(My uncle) Fred had a very tempestuous relationship with Rupert. But I always got along with him. One time, in the 1960s, I was in St. John's, Newfoundland, for a newspaper convention and I had my name tag on: "Davies/Kingston." This chap said, "Would you be a relation of Fred Davies?"

Now, ninety-nine times out of a hundred, when people asked me a question like that, they'd say, "Are you related to Robertson Davies?" But this time, it was Fred. This man said, "Fred Davies, what a guy! What a guy." He had known him during the war. He said, "He could rustle up more booze and girls when the convoys came in!" So Fred was who you needed for a party.

I remember Fred one time driving me back to Trinity College School from Kingston. He was a very fast driver. He had a Ford convertible. He came roaring into the courtyard of the school. After I got out he gave me $50 and he said, "Don't spend it all in one place."

A newspaper that Rupert had given Fred to run, the *Kincardine Review-Reporter*, fared poorly, so Fred tried other jobs. On New Year's Eve 1947, he sent his youngest brother a breezy, friendly "Dear Bob" letter (on letterhead which read "George Fredrick, Photography") asking if *The Peterborough Examiner* would help to underwrite a trip to Nassau in exchange for a series of travel articles and photos. RD's reply was cool and formal, and contained some specific suggestions.

Dear Fred,

When the articles on Nassau are ready, let us have them and let me know also when you want the payment for them by sending me a bill. . . . May I make a suggestion about the Nassau articles. A point which we have been trying to stress in our local tourist articles is that holiday makers must be offered something more than an opportunity to catch fish if they are going to come to a resort district in large numbers. If you could, in one of your articles, give us some idea of the entertainments provided for visitors in Nassau.

With every good wish, I am
Yours sincerely
Robertson Davies
Editor

One of the running jokes in RD's second Salterton novel, *Leaven of Malice*, dealt with the sad lot of editors importuned by pushy freelance writers. Fred never read it – because on March 6, 1954, before the novel came out, Fred, who was by now living in Nassau, was killed in a car crash.

BRENDA DAVIES
There was a phone call in the night. I presume it was Rupert. Rob had never got on with Fred – Fred had oppressed him and been nasty – but it was a shock. He may have been drunk. Fred was a magnificent driver, so if he hadn't wanted it to happen . . .

MICHAEL DAVIES
Could Fred's death have been a suicide? I doubt it. I don't remember any talk at the time. He'd been at a party and was driving a very fast sports car, an Austin Healey, and he hit a palm tree head-on. He was crushed by the steering wheel. Did he deliberately turn off the road? We'll never know.

BRENDA DAVIES
Rupert took it very hard, very hard indeed. I think Rupert hadn't gotten on terribly well with Fred and I think he felt guilty. Fred's children were only teenagers when it happened.

MIRANDA DAVIES

I vividly remember when RD told us that Fred had been killed. RD probably told us in quite a straightforward way. After he said that he had written to Fred's daughters Kathryn and Jane, who would be very distressed, I said something appalling like, "Why would they care when he had been such a horrible father?"

My father was *shocked* at my hard reaction. He gave me a little reprimand for being so unfeeling. He himself was not sad – he detested Fred – but he was distressed about the girls and about how it would affect their mother. . . .

If he felt that Fred's suicide might be related to a genetic predisposition in his family to depression, he might have said this to Brenda, but he did not say it to us. My parents had strong boundaries around some things that were adult and what was for children. They had a sense of responsibility not to talk about Fred like that in front of us, even though they were subversive about adults in other ways.

Later that year came the publication of *Leaven of Malice*. It opens with the editor of the Salterton newspaper learning to his horror that an engagement announcement linking the son and daughter of two rival university professors is bogus. It was placed in the paper as an act of malice.

JEAN RICHARDSON

The *Whig-Standard*, I remember, had a women's page, and a social column. When I was a little kid, I'd phone the paper and pretend to be Mrs. H or Mrs. D, and say things, and they would be reported! And whoever I had been impersonating would be indignant!

BEA CORBETT

I've always thought this was where *Leaven of Malice* comes from.

Among the novel's many satiric targets are small-town newspaper readers and university faculties, both of whom, to RD's eye, are too sure of their prejudices.

ROBERT FULFORD

Davies, I believe, absolutely nailed those people . . . people who believe that the purpose of a university is to confirm the views you already have.

Whatever RD's failures as a commentator and a human being, he would *never* say that. He would *never* say, "Let's read a lot of books and find out we were right all along." He was, as he says in *Tempest-Tost*, "an advocate of ornamental knowledge."

That same year, Rupert Davies suggested that his youngest son move from Peterborough to take over as editor of the *Whig-Standard*. Arthur, the *Whig*'s publisher, had a good relationship with his brother, but – more sensitive to family dynamics than Rupert – opposed this plan. So RD suggested his friend Arnold Edinborough.

ARNOLD EDINBOROUGH
Arthur and Rob were two very different people. Rob had a beard and dressed in a way to attract attention; Arthur had a gammy leg and was a very retiring person. Arthur did a lot around Kingston, but you never heard his name. And I never met a more level-headed, fair-minded man. He ran the *Whig* very well and made a lot of money. . . .

When Rupert interviewed me for the job, I told Rupert I knew nothing about newspapers. He said, "That's what endears you to me."

This may have been Rupert's position, but RD kept a close eye on his protégé. In a 1955 letter to Edinborough, he wrote:

> I have felt for some time that the editorial page of the *Whig* has a very dirty and uninteresting appearance and you and Arthur might be interested in considering some improvement. . . . Since I am getting franker and franker in this letter, I might as well say that I think that for years the editorial page of the *Whig* has had a dull and neglected look entirely unappropriate to a newspaper published in an important university and industrial city. Anything that can be done to make it look authoritative and tasteful will be a step towards improvement and (*) *though I hesitate to say so* I do not think that you will find a better model than the editorial page of the *Examiner*. You will certainly wish to discuss this with Arthur, and I am convinced that after a very short discussion you will be struck with the force and logic of what I have just said. It *will be a long and uphill*

struggle, of course, but *you must not be discouraged* and *in a few years* you will be within sight of your goal.

With patronizing good wishes, I am,
Yours sincerely,
RD

Ralph Hancox was another RD protegé. A high-school dropout from England, who later became editor, president and CEO of Reader's Digest Canada, Hancox joined the *Examiner* in the mid-1950s. He was soon promoted to writing editorials, cultural and foreign features.

RALPH HANCOX
He was an extraordinary editor in that sense. At *The Peterborough Examiner* he sent me down to Stratford to review. He sent me to Germany to write about postwar German reconstruction. I was sent to Washington. And he encouraged me to apply for a Nieman Fellowship to Harvard.

RD also advanced the career of Fern Rahmel, the high-school teacher whom he had coaxed into theatre.

FERN RAHMEL
I wrote book reviews for *Saturday Night* – under Rob's direction, of course. He went through the *Examiner* and *Saturday Night* with a red pen and a stern eye. He never assigned me, other than to deliver a pile of books and say, "See what you can do." As a review editor he didn't talk to me much, and I think he kind of let things stand. He was not a micromanager.

Rob thought that *Saturday Night* magazine needed someone with a critical eye to catch some of the mistakes that were offending him. So he got me a job in Toronto. I was chief cook and bottle washer, copy editor and so on. I've always been grateful to Rob for making it possible.

In order to have more free time to write and to travel with Brenda, RD proposed that Arnold Edinborough take over his work as literary editor of *Saturday Night* magazine. There were other advantages, too ...

September 20, 1954

Dear Arnold,

Speaking of novels, my own novel has probably reached you
this time, and if you see fit to do anything about it in *Saturday
Night*, that is your affair. It is always rather embarrassing to be
reviewed in a publication in which you have some connection,
but on the other hand it is nice to have a review in a paper
like *Saturday Night*, so if you choose to say anything about it
my blushes will not absolutely burn me up.

**With a book jacket designed by Clair Stewart, *Leaven of Malice* enjoyed
better sales than *Tempest-Tost*. It won Canada's Leacock Medal for
Humour in 1954, and appeared on the recommended list of the *New York
Times Book Review*. But there were some critical reviews, too, and they
haunted RD.**

RD (letter to Horace Davenport, 1955)
I am very happy about the fine reception *Leaven of Malice* has received
in the USA. Apparently it is what publishers call "a sleeper" and is
gaining ground all the time. Has been reprinted within a month of
publication. Dramatic rights have been sold to a Broadway producer.
Very nice. But it is my old friends, the Canadian critics, who assure me
that I am no better than I should be, and have much to learn, presum-
ably from them.

One critical review was written by none other than Arnold Edinborough.

ARNOLD EDINBOROUGH
Though I enjoyed that novel, I felt that after all the satirical peeling
away of layers of sentiment, there was nothing left. In the peeling, something was missing, something human, warm and wise. . . . I said it was
a little stagey. Those earlier novels were informed by a cranky point of
view. There's a lot of Marchbanks in the Salterton trilogy. The early
novels are condescending, and Canada was changing – he was no longer
preaching to the unconverted. . . . He took umbrage at that. He certainly had one skin too few. In the 1960s we had not so much a chill or
a coldness, we just didn't see much of each other. . . . I think it may well

be that I became more critical of his work. I don't think he liked that very much.

JENNIFER SURRIDGE
RD never forgot a bad review. He could get twenty-five wonderful ones and never forget a bad one. He would wish terrible things on those who gave him bad reviews because of what he called a "vengeful strain in my nature."

Chapter 18

THEATRE DREAMS

Although turning with more interest towards fiction, RD continued to see himself in the early 1950s primarily as a mentor to Canadian theatre. As he said in public speeches at the time, "Good Canadian theatre is not a thing to be looked forward to in fifty or a hundred years. We have it now, and the time to support it is now." His ideas informed the paper he was invited to submit to the Royal Commission on National Development in the Arts, Letters, and Sciences in Canada (known as the "Massey Commission" because it was co-chaired by Vincent Massey, father of RD's Oxford friend Lionel). The report was published in 1951.

JAMES EAYRS (professor, journalist and friend of Vincent Massey) When Vincent co-chaired the Massey Commission, he wanted it to work by bringing the Right People together. He had a genius for getting the Right People. If you're trying to bring a culture up by its bootstraps, how can the project be anything but elitist?

RD's submission touched on everything from the importance of better training for actors to the establishment of a national travelling theatre company.

BRENDA DAVIES
Rob gave a draft of his submission to the Massey Commission to me to read. I thought it was a bit dull and would be much more lively as dialogue. So he revised it in the form of an eighteenth-century play. . . . It was great.

DAVID GARDNER
A lot of theatre people did not like his contribution to the Massey Commission. It was a dialogue involving characters called Trueman and

Lovewit. . . . But what he wrote looked like a diatribe of reasons why *not* to have a Canada Council. He essentially said, "Don't finance theatre companies, just love them and go and see what they do."

ARNOLD EDINBOROUGH
The submission to the Massey Commission was typical of Rob. He did not want to write like everyone else. It's a pretty savage piece. He couched it in fictional terms because he thought he could be more out-rageous. He had books – his plays – to be bought and didn't want to queer the pitch.

MAVOR MOORE (actor, playwright, arts administrator)
Rob used to talk to me about his work on the Massey Commission and all that jazz. We'd run into each other in the lobbies of the Royal Alex and in movie theatres. I read Rob's chapter on theatre for the Massey Royal Commission, of course, and I quoted it frequently. He clearly, wittily, described the situation I knew so well. The Massey Report theatre section must be one of the most quoted Royal Commission chapters ever.

Writing for the Commission brought RD close to Vincent Massey. Both were Oxford and Balliol men, and men of the theatre; Vincent's brother Raymond Massey was a bona fide Hollywood film actor. As the Davies-Massey friendship deepened, RD was heard to remark that he had three fathers: Rupert; Tyrone Guthrie, his "father in art"; and Massey, his father in Canadian public life.

JAMES EAYRS
I am astonished to hear that RD thought of Vincent as a father figure. I can't think of RD as a younger man. They both seemed like grand old men to me. I was very much more in awe of RD than of Massey. RD was a pretty impenetrable person. His disguise was pretty heavy.

In 1952, after the Massey Report's publication, English Canada acquired something close to a national theatre when the small town of Stratford, Ontario, announced the establishment of an annual Shakespearean festival. Massey supplied key funding and Tyrone Guthrie was hired as artistic director. Guthrie invited RD to join the board of governors. RD also wrote program notes and gave lectures and seminars.

ROBERT FULFORD
The impact of the Massey Commission was not immediately understood. We did not know that when government said they would do
something, that they would do it. And in fact it was six years later that
the Canada Council started, and two or three years after that they actually started to give out the money. In retrospect, the Massey Commission
was important, but at the time no one thought it was important.

　　But Stratford! Everything I said about the Massey Commission is
in reverse for Stratford. It was immediately apparent in 1953: it was
unbelievable! These were by far the most gorgeous productions that I
had ever seen. That was amazing. And so was the participation of a star
like Alec Guinness, or James Mason a year or two later. It seemed like
a bit of a miracle. These were people you knew about. They were giants.

**Those involved in that first year recognized RD as one of the miracle
workers.**

ALEC GUINNESS (letter to RD, July 29, 1953)
　　. . . This whole enterprise has been tremendously exciting –
　　quite the most stimulating experience I've had in the theatre
　　– and I *do hope* SOMEONE has thanked you adequately for
　　your moral and practical support which I know was so heart-
　　ening to many when things looked grim and doubtful. Hope
　　we meet again.

　　Sincerely,
　　Alec Guinness
　　P.S. Am re-reading *Shakespeare's Boy Actors* with great pleasure.

**Together, RD and Guthrie wrote books about the new festival – *Renown
at Stratford* (1953) and *Twice Have the Trumpets Sounded* (1954). RD produced a third volume, *Thrice the Brinded Cat Hath Mewed* (1955), alone.
Meanwhile, RD gave Stratford supportive coverage in his newspaper and
in theatre reviews in *Saturday Night* magazine. Privately, he was critical
of many Stratford productions, as his theatre notebooks attest, but he
restrained his public critiques because he wanted to see the young festival prosper.**

LISTER SINCLAIR (writer and CBC producer)
He was decent in the same sense as was Bernard Shaw, who was very, very good at not going after people who were doing their best.

ROBERT FULFORD
Davies was on the board of the Stratford Festival, and reviewing the plays. At the same time, Herbert Whittaker was a drama critic – and was a close friend of Robertson Davies and was directing Davies's plays. . . . So, no question, there was a clubbishness about cultural journalism.

Canadian culture at this period was being reconstituted by British people, not Americans – or else by Canadian-born, British-trained people such as Alan Jarvis at the National Gallery, Vincent Massey, who was more English than the English, and Lister Sinclair at CBC. All these arts were dominated by people with a British sensibility. And Robertson Davies took this tradition, which was built into our culture, and extended it after those others had mostly died or gone home. He was constantly enlarging it: *enlarge, enlarge, enlarge.*

RD also went out of his way (with Brenda's help) to encourage the next generation of actors and theatregoers.

MARTIN HUNTER
When I got to the University of Toronto in 1952, we did a festival of one-act plays. Robertson Davies came to town to adjudicate. It was a miserable, snowy, winter night. We had originally planned to do a play that was totally outrageous, Jean-Paul Sartre's *The Respectable Prostitute*. But the play also called for a black actor, and there weren't any black students at Trinity. So we had to change to some one-act play by Arnold Schnitzler.

After the performance, Davies told us, "I have driven all this way to see a play of the French avant-garde and you have given me a piece of old Viennese cheese!"

We won no kudos, but we invited him back to Trinity for a warming drink. He drank with us in the Trinity Buttery and was very charming. Eventually, he said, "I don't know what's happened to my ride." So we went out and stood with him and waited in the snow. After fifteen minutes a car went by with a very angry woman driving it. She said, "Where have you been? I've been waiting outside Hart House!"

This was, of course, Brenda Davies. I only noticed then that she was rather cross. I now know why: Brenda could be exasperated by him, but not without reason. I never saw him embarrassed by her or by this. He was a baby looking to be cared for.

In 1952, at the request of his old school, Upper Canada College, RD wrote *A Masque of Aesop*, a costume comedy replete with both classical references and school in-jokes. Clarke Irwin published two editions of this pageant for young people, one illustrated by Grant Macdonald, and RD gave the royalties to the school. Of all the plays he wrote in the 1950s, this was probably the most performed.

JOHN FRASER (then a schoolboy at UCC)
I have a very vivid memory of my first meeting with Robertson Davies. . . . I played Cricket in *A Masque of Aesop* in the UCC Prep. The play called for Cricket to be bonked on the head with a large mallet made of sponge. I remember RD coming backstage to check the mallet. He said, "You can't trust boys."

RD preferred writing to directing, and was delighted to oblige when Tyrone Guthrie asked him to write a play for Stratford. The result was a Canadianized, updated version of Ben Jonson's *Bartholomew Fair*. But after Guthrie left Stratford in 1955, the play was dropped. Discouraged and angry, RD started to work with a company that promised a better relationship, Toronto's Crest Theatre, where producers Murray and Donald Davis, strikingly handsome brothers of English gypsy descent, were mounting and starring in original Canadian plays with their sister Barbara Chilcott. In 1955, the Crest put on RD's *A Jig for the Gypsy*.

ROBERT FULFORD
I saw Davies's plays. What came through with them was disdain for the "thin gruel" society, the repressed society of Toronto. In the middle of the play *A Jig for the Gypsy*, there's a gypsy – that's Barbara Chilcott – asserting the powers of the unconscious. She had an incredibly good gypsy costume. The play was an attempt to assert the life force, dark and beautiful.

BARBARA CHILCOTT

I first met him, it must have been 1952 or '53 at Stratford. I'd done *Shrew* for Tony Guthrie. Davies had written those books, *Renown at Stratford* and *Twice Have the Trumpets Sounded*. And I had done Davies's play *At My Heart's Core* for the Straw Hats. I was Mrs. Stewart. . . . I found that play interesting, but I wasn't wildly excited about it. A bit bookish, wordy?

But I really just remember meeting him while rehearsing *A Jig for the Gypsy* at the Crest. RD came to visit at the Crest and I found him a bit intimidating. The beard, for one thing. There's a photo of me standing with him – he's carrying a clipboard, I am in costume. This was a posed photograph. I don't think he was trying to direct me, but I think Herbie Whittaker, who was the director, would have given way to Rob. I think Herbie respected Rob as a playwright, and also Rob's whole manner could be a bit intimidating. I'm sure this photo was taken during dress rehearsal; I think I was hoping he was pleased. It was very important to me to have him pleased.

DAVID GARDNER

I was Jesse Fewtrell in *A Jig for the Gypsy* at the Crest Theatre, the production that Barbara Chilcott was in. My memory of this was that I was really padded out, I was huge. Then RD came in and looked at me in costume and said in his nineteenth-century way, "I miss something."

I said, "What?"

He said, "Your pants should be shrunk down so I could see your scrotum. Shrink them so that you have half a watermelon down your leg."

We didn't do this. But it was perfect Rob.

After the *Jig* was up, the Davis brothers proposed more collaborations. RD wrote *Hunting Stewart*, which the Crest mounted in 1955, to good reviews (except *The Toronto Star*'s Nathan Cohen, who called it "laborious"). For the 1956–57 season, the Crest asked RD for a third original play. RD started work on a pageant involving Casanova. Then he and Brenda held a fateful dinner in Toronto for the English playwright J.B. Priestley, and invited their friends from the Crest. Barbara Chilcott arrived at the dining room at the same moment as her brothers.

BARBARA CHILCOTT

I hadn't seen either of the boys. We all arrived at the same time at the University Club, which had an entrance with wide double doors. The boys were in dark suits and I was in a black dress. We all came through the double door at the same moment. It was our arrival that caught Priestley's eye – because that's the entrance we made in the play he later wrote for us.

After dinner, we were sitting around in the University Club, talking, and J.B. said, "Have you three ever played your own relationships?"

We said, "No."

J.B. said, "Why not?"

One of the boys said, "There isn't a play that is written that way."

J.B. said, "Oh, nonsense. There must be."

A few days later, Murray was having a cocktail party. J.B. Priestley came in and handed a note to him. The note said, "You are absolutely right. There is no such play. I'll write one for you."

Through the summer of 1956, RD laboured over the Casanova piece, titled *General Confession*. In September, he learned that the Davis brothers had postponed his play and had instead booked Priestley's latest, *The Glass Cage*, which the celebrated British playwright had written just for them.

BARBARA CHILCOTT

Rob definitely had the feeling that the boys (my brothers) had betrayed him. I knew nothing about it.

When I finally read *General Confession*, I thought the parts were great. As for not doing it at the Crest, I don't know that it would have filled eight hundred seats. But then, practically nothing did! We'd all have been quite good in the parts written for us. But the play did not really have a strong story line.

Bad reviews, betrayals – and still RD dreamed of making his mark in theatre. In 1956, New York producer Joe Hyman bought the rights to RD's novel *Leaven of Malice*. When RD's Old Vic mentor, Tyrone Guthrie, expressed interest in the project, RD hoped that at last he was on the verge of a breakthrough.

Chapter 19

IN SEARCH OF A
SECOND WIND

To the outside eye, RD's life in the 1950s was by most standards enviable: he had a supportive wife, three clever, attractive and healthy daughters, a successful journalism career, plays that toured, award-winning books, and a position of influence in his community.

EB ZEIDLER (architect)
I met him in 1951. I was 25. He was very respected and kind of feared in town. I had emigrated to Peterborough because, when I was a student in Germany, I had heard a lecturer who said Canada needs architects. I lived on Water Street, and Robertson Davies would walk past every morning to his office down Water Street. He was a very imposing man, a terrific guy.

Sometimes I would drive to work in my Volkswagen and I would stop and say, "Would you like a ride?" He'd say, "No, I have a principle of walking." But he liked to talk to me. So he would get in. We talked about everything.

In 1953 or '54 I was asked to do a church, Grace United Church. My design of brick and wood and cast stone was modern. There was a big argument in the congregation, who thought that my design was *too* modern.

UELI SCHALLENBERG (Ueli of Switzerland, barber and hair stylist)
Eb Zeidler is a client of mine. And Eb told me that people hated this church. And it was by a young *German* architect. Then RD wrote an editorial in the newspaper saying what a great church it was. So Eb says the lesson is, Always pick up a hitchhiker. Everyone respected RD so much up there. If he said something was good, it was good. This may have changed Eb's life.

EB ZEIDLER
In the midst of all the negative comments, this editorial was a pleasing thing, a positive thing. Not to the hard-core minds, of course. But the main arguments against my church disappeared. His editorial was like the word of God.

So was RD's insistence that the *Examiner* maintain high grammatical and stylistic standards.

RD (Memo from the editor, May 1956)
Will you please take care that no headings or reports appear in the *Examiner* in future in which a party is "thrown," or a deed, a crime, an imposture or a joke is "pulled." We are becoming much too careless about these colloquialisms, which tend to appear particularly in headings, and unless we check them now they are likely to become *Examiner* style – which would be most regrettable.

He may not have liked to read about jokes being "pulled," but RD pulled some of his own.

RALPH HANCOX
He loved practical jokes. At one point, he was at home sick, but he wanted to look over what we were putting in the paper. We sent editorials over by taxi. Shortly after, I got a package; it was a homemade catalogue and a letter appealing for funds to Help the Homebound Handicapped. The catalogue was for things like "egg cosies" and "egg yolk wipes." All whimsical stuff. Of course, I could tell it was RD's handwriting.

With his managing editor, Ralph Hancox, he launched an "Advice to the Lovelorn" column in the newspaper. The two men gleefully invented the pathetic queries. And RD tried to scandalize the city's chief librarian, Robert Porter, by forging a document that implicated one of the founding matriarchs of Peterborough in a sex scandal. RD artificially aged it with tea stains, and the document was taken so seriously that it had to be suppressed.

VAL PORTER (wife of Robert Porter)
We still have that paper! It's very well done. . . . But he was always very encouraging. I'd said to him that we were trying to get an orchestra

started in Peterborough. He said, "When you get started, invite me and I will come."

We had our first concert upstairs in the old library around 1959, a terribly warm night in May. . . . Here's his review of the first performance of the orchestra: "The ensemble shows great promise. . . . Their playing was always musicianly but there has not been enough rehearsal time yet to achieve a unified tone, and the humidity on Wednesday night was unfriendly to string instruments. . . . The intention was always clear even when the execution did not equal it . . ." It's absolutely wonderful, encouraging – but those of us in the orchestra were very aware of what he was saying, *and not saying*.

RD felt his newspaper had a mission to encourage people, but he did not duck controversy.

ANN DUDAS
When my father, Judge John N. Kennedy, became a judge in the county court, city of Peterborough, in 1953, he looked at how police evidence constructs a court case. Robertson Davies questioned whether he was trying to control the police. I think he thought that my father was a very activist judge. It was a way of getting a story. My father didn't like the way the editor of a local paper would go at him in public. He thought they should do this in private. I think Robertson Davies was very good at stirring things up.

BRENDA DAVIES
The *Examiner* was somewhat resented, as it reported on the town's news. Such things as arrests for drunken driving, reported from the police, were much disliked.

RALPH HANCOX
At one point there was a commission into the police force in Peterborough. . . . The story was that a furniture store had been broken into and the police went to investigate. It was rumoured that after the thieves made off, the police had helped themselves and taken some of the furniture. And there was a house of ill repute in town, which, it was said, was being protected by the police. Davies was called as a witness because the *Examiner* had published editorials on the police. At one point, he was asked to check a date. When he gave it, the commissioners asked how

he could corroborate it. He said it was in his private journal. So his private journal was subpoenaed. He went through the roof! He protested very loudly. I suspect he felt invaded.

ROSEMARY HOEY
I remember very well the controversies between the Catholics and Protestants in Peterborough. I was a student at St. Peter's and I remember Grade 11 "religion classes" very vividly. Davies's editorials were often the topic of the day. I remember one priest advising us to have our parents cancel their subscriptions to the *Examiner*, especially over the abortion and euthanasia issues. Given my part-time job as a cub reporter for the *Examiner*'s youth page and for any special events that came along, I was sometimes asked what Mr. Davies was really like, and did he ever comment or edit my copy. He never did. And he was always very friendly to me.

In fact, for a man sometimes labelled an Edwardian sexist, RD encouraged women reporters.

PENNY SANGER
I was at the *Examiner* in the late 1950s. . . . RD told me I was the first woman news reporter he'd hired – and I had to fill in for the women's page editor when she went on holiday. He rarely came into the newsroom, though I remember looking up from my work in the newsroom to see his checked trousers and purple waistcoat hovering over my desk. You can imagine the reaction of the rest of the newsroom to the clothes. . . . When I rose to writing editorials at the *Examiner*, I remember thinking, "This is the best job ever."

RALPH HANCOX
I'd start each morning at five reading all the papers. Then we'd spend the morning discussing the editorials. Then I'd be packed off to do the research. We'd meet at 5 p.m. and he'd look over what I'd written, and sometimes he'd say, "Well, if you're going to say this, you've got to take into account that. . . ." He didn't write much by this time. He'd do maybe one editorial a day and I'd do three or four.

He chewed gum at his typewriter. Once, he offered me a piece of gum and I said, "No, thank you." He said, "I quite understand. You need powerful North American jaws for this stuff." He also smoked a pipe and blended his own pipe tobacco. There was a Dutch element to it. I could smell it, because I, too, liked Dutch tobacco. He was not a constant smoker, but moderation was not a personality trait of RD's.

Another young Englishman won RD's attention precisely because of his lack of moderation.

ROBERT SUNTER

The newspaper was a place of great camaraderie; it had a good atmosphere. I worked there for quite a few months. Never saw Robertson Davies. Then one day, my editor sent me out to review a movie – *Hercules*, with Steve Reeves. I wrote a brutal review, made fun of it. My review was vicious. The next day, I was at the office when the newspaper came out – midmorning, as I remember – and I looked up my review. They had left the byline off. I was growling, very annoyed.

At that very moment, in came Robertson Davies to the newsroom, his hair and beard blowing in the wind. Robertson Davies *never* came into the newsroom.

A hush fell. Everyone looked up.

He waved the paper and said, in a booming voice, "Who wrote this?" He was brandishing my review.

I said, "I did," thinking, "Oh dear, I'm going to be fired."

He said, "Come with me!"

We went into his office, and he said, "How would you like to try writing editorials?" So I tried my hand at it.

The next day, I handed them to his secretary, Moira Whalon, who was his gatekeeper. And then he called me in and said, "You're hired."

This was a whole new direction for me. Robertson Davies was an extraordinary mentor. He would never criticize you; he would say, "Hmmmmm, why did you come to that conclusion?" You'd take the piece away and think about it and think, "Yep, this is what I should do." He could praise. Or he could say, "You've taken this in a direction I didn't want to go in."

I never knew what side of an issue he would take. He could, and did, switch directions. Sometimes we'd discuss an editorial and Ralph Hancox would say, "But didn't we argue the other way a month ago?" And he would say, "Ah, yes . . . consistency is the hobgoblin of little minds . . ."

He wasn't a Liberal or a Conservative. He was independent in his thinking. He had enormous common sense, and if things didn't make sense to him, he was against them. The main thing was, he expected a certain style. Ralph Hancox and I both write in a sort of Robertson Davies style. We were all on the same wavelength. We'd come from England.

It was clear to Sunter that no matter how successful RD was as a newspaperman, there was more behind the mask – and it was also clear that his real interests lay elsewhere.

ROBERT SUNTER
At that time, my domestic life was difficult, because my wife was suffering from mental illness. I had to put her into hospital. Robertson Davies was very empathetic. I was warmed by the fact that he would take the time, late in the afternoon, after we had sat around mulling over the next day's editorials, to talk with me about it. This was also the time when we would talk about theatre. I was doing some theatre reviews. And he always wanted to talk more about my reviews than he did about the next day's editorials.

Although a powerful presence in public, RD nursed the private conviction that by middle age he had not yet created for himself or his family the life he had dreamed of.

SASSY WADDELL
This is absolute speculation, but maybe they were also at that stage in their lives when RD realized he would not be the next Shakespeare and Brenda realized she was not going to be the next – Vivien Leigh? So they were at that stage of giving up their dreams. But this is absolute speculation.

RD (letter to Horace Davenport)
Recently I met a friend of mine, an actor, at a party; we were both getting ready to celebrate our forty-second birthdays; we sat in a corner and had a perfect orgy of self-doubt, shattered hopes, unfulfilled ambitions and general misery, and emerged much brighter. In one's early forties, one knows oneself; one knows that one is not really Leonardo, and one is faced with the job of doing the best one can with the few morsels of talent that one can muster. The man in his forties is old

enough to have lost some of his appetite for praise, but he is as sensitive as ever to blame. His glories seem mean, and his youthful dreams, as in the words of the Old Testament, but menstruous rags. He knows himself half-lunatic, three-parts fool, knave, charlatan and gull. He is conscious of his aging body. He is a pitiable mess. Yet in this abyss he is upborne by the knowledge that he really can earn his living, and that he has persuaded a woman to live with him and that seems to endure him pretty well, that he has children who are far better equipped for life than he. He is also conscious – if he is you, H.W.D., or me – that there are people who envy him and wish that they could do what he does, and who would love to topple him off his perch and seize his job and its emoluments. This knowledge sustains him, somewhat, as does a feeling that if he can wade through the Slough of Despond he will get his second wind, and do some very neat work before he dies. So cheer up. You have always had a fine talent for gloom, but you know damn well that you are an enviable man.

Chapter 20

A MIXTURE OF FRAILTIES

Music had made RD's childhood and his parents' unhappy marriage more bearable. Brenda had trouble counting beats, so RD took it upon himself to encourage his children's musical education.

MIRANDA DAVIES
It was great when I was little. Daddy would play *Pop Goes the Weasel* on the piano and I would stand at the top of the keyboard and play the POP! He bought me a recorder, and he could play the recorder. I learned to play from the chart of scales. But I was so disappointed when I said, "Daddy, let's play duets," and he said, "I don't play any more." I really wanted to make music with him! But he knew his limitations. He knew he was a fumbler on the keyboard.

RD (letter to John Espey, March 7, 1947)
My eldest daughter Miranda shows signs of unusual musical ability, and we are fussing about getting the right teaching for her; I teach her now but I am a born genius ruiner, being explosive and impatient when I should be tactful and torpid.

MIRANDA DAVIES
I studied piano. . . . He'd hear my pieces and he'd tap my shoulders. It was heavier than a tap, and it was in rhythm. It was very daunting.

At school, Miranda and Jennifer joined the BSS choir. To encourage them, RD sought the advice of Dora Herbert-Jones, the family friend from Wales who collected Welsh folk songs.

RD (letter to Dora Herbert-Jones, March 1957)
It is shameful of me not to have written to you for such a long time. . . .
I am writing to you now to ask if you can give me some information
about the Royal National Eisteddfod and also the International
Eisteddfod which has been held at Llangollen for some years past. I am
asking this on behalf of the choir of the school to which our older girls,
Miranda and Jennifer, are now going. It is the Bishop Strachan School
of Toronto and it has achieved a good reputation for the work of its
Chapel Choir. . . . Brenda and I are very happy that our two girls have
been able to get places in this choir, as the musical training is first rate
and I feel that good choral training is second only to orchestral training
as an introduction to real musicianship.

When RD wrote this letter, he was deep into the writing of his third novel,
the story of Monica Gall, a talented girl trapped in a dull job at the
Salterton Glue Works. Then Monica wins a scholarship to study singing in
London and discovers a wider world. Was it a coincidence that by 1957
Miranda, who was then about Monica's age, was about to graduate from
BSS and showed vocal talent?

BRENDA DAVIES
I think that *A Mixture of Frailties* was a fantasy about making it in
England. It had more to do with *his* wishing for success than about the
education of a young girl. *He* is Monica Gall, not Miranda. He would
have very much liked to be a big success in England.

JENNIFER SURRIDGE
Both Rosamond and I feel strongly that the books were not about us.
RD was concerned about Miranda, of course. He was more concerned
about Miranda than me or Rosamond because she had a career he
understood. But Rosamond and I feel that the books were about *him*.
He did not approve of Scott Young, Neil Young's father, who was
writing about his family as fodder for his newspaper columns. RD didn't
do that.

However, RD did ask Miranda to read his new novel, *A Mixture of Frailties*,
in galley proofs before publication.

MIRANDA DAVIES

We all knew he was writing about a singer by the time the book was in galley proofs. But he kept his writing very close to his chest. He felt the magic would leak out. I suppose it is similar to psychoanalysis. It is kept within the container so it doesn't disperse, so it can be used. . . . I remember vividly being at Hawthorn Gardens, Rupert's house in Toronto. I was 17 and out of boarding school for the weekend. Daddy asked if I would like to read the galleys and I said, "Oh gosh yes, I would love to!"

Father left me entirely by myself to read at my own pace. I wouldn't have dreamed of putting a mark on the proofs. I just said how much I'd loved it. Every word. I'd read the earlier books and I found *A Mixture of Frailties* more convincing in its characterization of a woman. I liked *Mixture of Frailties* enormously. But I think it spoke less about the training of the singer than the management of oneself. . . .

It strikes me with a dull thud that when we went to Wales with the BSS choir in 1958, I decided what I wanted to do. And that I resolved to be a singer only *after* I had read *A Mixture of Frailties*.

With his third Salterton novel, RD decided to be more hard-nosed about marketing his writing. Besides, he had been annoyed with Clarke Irwin since the early 1950s, when the editors rejected a proposed Marchbanks book on the grounds that the humour was too vulgar. In the mid-1970s, Ashley Thomson, a graduate student at the University of Toronto School of Library Science, interviewed RD for a thesis on RD's evolving relationship with his publishers and his sense of himself as a professional author.

ASHLEY THOMSON

Davies's relationship with Clarke Irwin came to an abrupt and bitter close around 1956 or '57. The split between them, however, had been widening since the early '50s, when Davies acquired a New York agent [Willis Kingsley Wing] who was to act as the "go-between" between him and the company. That Davies himself abandoned the casual relationship of the '40s attests not so much, one suspects, to the increasing demands made upon his time by *The Peterborough Examiner* . . . but to his growing feeling that his writing was no longer just a pleasant pastime, or a source of modest fame, but a product to be marketed for all it was worth.

As long as W.H. Clarke was around, nothing happened, for he

enjoyed Davies's great respect. The same cannot be said for Clarke's wife, who took over the company after the old man's death. And when one of her first moves was to ask Davies to drop his agent and let Clarke Irwin act in his place, the author rebelled. He simply refused to entrust his fortunes to a company which in his opinion . . . gave every appearance of "Wanting to take all the gravy for themselves." Looking back, he has no regrets about his decision. Even though his agent gets 10 percent of his profits, he feels that over the years he has done enough for him to be "worth every cent."

Wing submitted *A Mixture of Frailties* to a new Canadian publisher, Macmillan of Canada, and in England to Chatto and Windus, which had published the earlier Salterton novels. Chatto rejected *Frailties* on the grounds that it was not as funny as the earlier Salterton novels. So Wing sent it to Weidenfeld and Nicolson.

TO RD FROM WILLIS KINGSLEY WING
17 July 1958
GEORGE WIDENFELD [sic] ENTHUSIASTIC DAVIES FRAILTIES. KNOWING YOU OFFERING ELSEWHERE HE OFFERS TWO HUNDRED FIFTY POUNDS ADVANCE AGAINST ROYALTIES WE TO SUGGEST. WHAT IS YOUR OPINION AND RECOMMENDATION. PLEASE CABLE. WINGS.

A Mixture of Frailties was published by Weidenfeld and Nicolson in England and Scribner's in the United States. German and Dutch editions followed. Reviews were good (including Arnold Edinborough's in *Saturday Night*) – though a few readers were appalled to see a man with three daughters writing so frankly about a young girl's sexual explorations.

ROBERT FULFORD

When he was starting to write his column for the *Star*, we talked about *A Mixture of Frailties*, and he told me that a number of people in Peterborough were scandalized by the young girl, Monica, having sex outside of wedlock. They thought that wasn't a good thing. RD said that people were displeased by this – as if sex outside of marriage was always wrong. He said these people could not be more stupid or narrow-minded. He said that sex can be virtuous inside or outside of wedlock, provided your body is in the keeping of your soul. He was trying to say this about his heroine Monica's sexuality.

Chapter 21

LOVE AND LIBEL

By the end of the 1950s, RD was in the front ranks of Canadian letters. He'd had mostly good reviews for three novels. His Marchbanks books were Canadian favourites. His *Saturday Night* columns on new Canadian writing had led to a collection of criticism, *A Voice from the Attic*, published by Alfred Knopf. In 1959 he began to write a syndicated column on books for *The Toronto Star*, the largest newspaper in Canada.

ROBERT FULFORD
At the *Star*, I edited his column. He never fussed. I didn't do things to it. Then the books pages floated off and became part of Nathan Cohen's domain, when Nathan became entertainment editor. . . . I know Davies didn't like Cohen. He, Davies, had this horrible habit of referring to people without naming them; he fearlessly attacked the anonymous. He'd make references like "loud-mouthed theatre critics who freely denounce their betters" – well, what other loud-mouthed theatre critic was there? . . . And Nathan Cohen couldn't possibly have liked Davies.

When RD wrote extra lines for *The Merry Wives of Windsor* when *Merry Wives* was at Stratford, RD was so pleased that no one had caught him. I quoted him boasting that no critic could tell the difference. Then Cohen wrote me a note saying, "It's true, I didn't notice the difference, but every time I see *Merry Wives* it seems to get longer . . . ," the implication being that RD had lengthened an already long play.

By now, RD had reached the age of 47. And it finally looked as if his devotion to theatre would be repaid. In 1960, he wrote to Horace Davenport:

Brenda and I hope to be in your part of the country in November. A play of mine, adapted from *Leaven of Malice* and now called *Love and*

Libel, begins rehearsal in Toronto in two weeks, and will open there in November, and go on to Detroit. . . .

It is being done by the Theatre Guild and is quite an elaborate affair, with an army of actors – about sixteen, and understudies who also appear as a crowd – and more scenery than the Oberammergau Passion Play. . . .

Theatre people are assuring me that the experience of having a play done in New York is a destructive and shredding one. Everyone sings this doleful lament, even Jacques Barzun, who is thought to have more philosophy. Perhaps it is so, but I must say that at 47 I am damned grateful to have the chance; if I am ever going to make a mark other than a rather local and tiny one, I had better get busy and do it. However, I am now too old, and have had too many plays done by quite good companies, to be simple-minded about it; neither am I capable of being destroyed by failure or driven mad by success. The play is quite a decent piece of work and the production will be first-rate. If it fails, well, it fails, and not the first good piece of work to do so. However, Guthrie's plays do not fail ignominiously, so un *flop d'estime* is probably the worst I have to face.

In October 1960, after months of writing and rewriting to accommodate Guthrie and the stars' various demands, the play opened at Toronto's Royal Alexandra Theatre.

LISA BALFOUR BOWEN (Arts journalist)
When the curtain went up, the set was dominated by a huge double bed. I was very young and impressionable in those days, of course, and I found this a daring, racy image which for me conjured up SEX with a capital *S*. I thought, "Jeepers, this guy is not the stuffy person I had imagined at all." I don't remember much about the play. However, it has stuck with me as one of the first original pieces of Canadian theatre I had ever seen.

RAMSAY DERRY
Our group of Miranda's friends were like a claque. We went to the Royal Alex for *Love and Libel* as RD's guests – a gang of us sitting together in the top balcony. My sense is that it was a big, lavish production, with a lot of people, a lot of stuff going on. I remember a sense of being at a

show that was very well done, filled with interesting stuff, but not getting off the ground. I remember there was a sense that there's a joke there, but you were not quite made to laugh, whatever that mysterious process is. It was a production that had not quite jelled. . . . I am sure he came on stage and took a bow. He was such a magnificent and imposing figure, and I was 22 or so. You couldn't possibly imagine that he was nervous or insecure. It took me a long time to grasp that.

VAL PORTER

The first and only play of RD's that I saw was *Love and Libel*, at the Royal Alex. I may even have gone to Toronto by myself. I thought it was wonderful that something he'd done was going to New York and I wanted to wish them well. Everyone desperately wanted it to succeed for him. There were wonderful scenes in it, but my feeling was neither he nor Brenda were very happy about it. Rob did not usually seem uneasy – he carried himself with confidence and assurance. But there was a sense of unrest about him on that occasion.

FERN RAHMEL

There had been an attempt by Guthrie to get peculiar effects. I remember there were peculiar lighting effects. I'm not a lighting person, but I know when lighting is *wrong*.

RD had a good idea of what had gone wrong with his play well before the American leg of its tour, and it started with his "father in art," Tyrone Guthrie.

ROSAMOND BAILEY

He'd worked with Guthrie, whom he'd admired all his life. Mum always said Guthrie wanted to be a writer himself, and he was jealous of Dad. She always said Guthrie was bad luck for Dad.

In 1972, in response to questions from Elspeth Cameron Buitenhuis, a graduate student who was working on a biography of him, RD described the difficulties.

RD

I had known Guthrie since 1937 and there was no difficulty about working with him, as it appeared. He asked me to prepare a detailed plan for the play, which I did, and on July 8th of 1959 I went to visit him at his home in Eire – Annagh-ma-Kerrig, Doohat, Newbliss, County Monaghan. My plan was for a dramatization that would have been fairly close to the storyline of the book with the editor, Gloster Ridley, acting as the character who linked the various elements in the story together. Guthrie's first comment was that nobody was interested in editors, and he proposed that the part of the editor should be cut out entirely.

It was necessary that a new version be prepared, and I worked on it with him from July 10th to July 30th and we emerged with a script that he liked but which I felt was loose to the point of incoherence. On March 23rd, 1960, Guthrie and I met in Toronto to work on casting the play, as he wanted to do it with a group of Canadian actors. The management that was putting on the play, which proved to be the Theatre Guild, wanted further revision. . . .

Two significant facts happened around this time. On March 13th I had dinner with Jacques Barzun, who, when he found out that I was working on a play for Broadway, said, over and over again, "It will kill you; it will kill you." Later in May, I spent some time with Miss Julie Harris and her husband, who, when they heard what I was doing, said, "Your hair won't get any whiter but you can still lose it." . . .

There was endless rewriting, and after rehearsals began on October 9th, I rewrote new portions of it every day. What I very quickly discovered was that the author in these circumstances is the last person whose opinion is considered, and he is expected to listen to the opinions of everyone else connected with the production, even in quite a modest capacity. Guthrie was determined that the play should be tailored to suit a plan of production which he wished to try, in which the scenery was changed in front of the audience and all the necessary furniture was hauled up to the flies, or descended from the flies, on wires. There were times when it was clear that the writing was vastly less important than the wires. . . .

The star of the play, the late Dennis King, was no stranger to egotism, and more than once after rehearsal he would come up to me menacingly and say, "Either I have six new sure laughs in that scene by tomorrow morning or I walk out." The result of this was that by the time we went on the tour, preliminary to going to New York, the play was a mud pie in which everyone's ideas had been incorporated but from which coherence and relevance had almost entirely been excluded.

The tour was dismal except that we had a very jolly two weeks in Boston, where the play was given a warm reception by the newspapers and played to packed houses. We opened on Tuesday, December 6th, in New York and closed the following Saturday.

AMY STEWART
He was a tremendous admirer of Tyrone Guthrie. Unfortunately, Guthrie did a terrible job on Rob's play in New York. We flew to New York to see Rob's play open. That was such a humiliation and disappointment.

I remember a big, round table at that restaurant where everyone went – Sardi's? I remember Rob was very reserved. He would never admit to anything wrong. It was sad. Everyone knew it was a failure.

CLAIR STEWART
I think we had a bit of Champagne to lessen the sting. Brenda was very stoic. She kept a stiff upper lip.

AMY STEWART
I've never seen her defeated. . . . Guthrie himself was a bit subdued that evening.

RD (letter to Elspeth Cameron Buitenhuis)
The humiliation of having to work under everyone's direction on *Love and Libel* did much to convince me that the theatre was no place for me.

MARTIN HUNTER
RD had put some of his own money into it. And Tyrone Guthrie just walked away. RD had been counting on him as a father figure. He said, "I called him my father in art, but he abandoned me." . . .

In the 1960s I remember being at the Royal Alex and seeing Brenda and Rob and saying, "Rob, aren't you writing another play?" He said, "Oh, no, I don't have the talent or the temperament." . . . If you're repeatedly told that your work stinks, you stop doing it.

ROSAMOND BAILEY
When I was 13, after the debacle of *Love and Libel* in New York, he decided that he'd never write a play again. He was devastated by that.

ARNOLD EDINBOROUGH
He was a very despairing person. Rob desperately wanted to be a drama-
tist, but he never had an ear for the working man's vocabulary. His plays
were curiously stagey. We know, my wife and I – we've acted them.

In a curious way, Rob realized the theatre wasn't the place to say
what he wanted to say; I remember when he was writing his novels,
he . . . exploded! It was a question of literary capacity: rather than let
someone else, an actor, shape your character, the novelist could tell
people what the character is. Rob was never a theatre man in my view
– but he was a commentator on human nature, and his view of Canada
is better shown in his novels.

Chapter 22

RETURN TO THE
IVORY TOWER

It used to be said of Canada's largest English-speaking city, "Toronto has no social classes,/ Only the Masseys and the masses." By 1960, this was no longer true, thanks to the emerging wealth of Jewish, Italian and Hungarian immigrants, but the anglophilic, philanthropic Massey family was still prominent.

ROBERT FULFORD

In the mid-1950s, when Louis St. Laurent was prime minister of Canada and Vincent Massey was the governor general, Prince Philip was in Ontario and said to Vincent, "Her Majesty would like to appoint you to be a Knight of the Garter. . . ." This was way, way better than being appointed to the House of Lords, and Vincent was ecstatic. This was *so* important to him. But Vincent had to check it with the Canadian government. St. Laurent didn't like it and [his successor, John] Diefenbaker didn't like it. Neither said no, but there hadn't been a knight appointed from Canada since the 1920s.

One of the few places where this impasse was raised as a moral and political and national issue was in the editorials of *The Peterborough Examiner*. RD said, "Give Vincent the Garter." This didn't do any good. But it must have been very heartening for Vincent.

Vincent Massey had many other reasons to value RD, of course: a shared background at UCC and Oxford, his wit, his love of theatre, his wide-ranging intellect. These attributes must have been on Massey's mind when, in 1959, he convinced the Massey family's foundation to establish an all-male residential graduate college at the University of Toronto on the model of Oxford colleges. On December 31, 1960, just weeks after the humiliation of *Love and Libel*, RD was taken by limousine to Batterwood, Massey's country residence.

RD (diary, December 31, 1960)

I had an intuition it was about the College, & probably the Mastership. Had not Hugh MacCraig, the astrologer, said that I should spend the latter part of my life among young people, & be something of a sage and prophet? . . . How often is one given the opportunity to shape something which is of significance to large numbers of people?

BRENDA DAVIES

The new enterprise was a godsend to us. We had been twenty years in Peterborough, and Rob felt that he had done all he could with *The Peterborough Examiner*, and we had just endured the failure of *Love and Libel*. A new direction was just the thing we wanted most.

ROSAMOND BAILEY

My father asked Rupert whether he should take the position and Rupert said, "Yes, it will put you above trade." This, from a man who had been born above a tailor shop in Wales! Rupert's comment on the position at Massey gave my father the sense that he had done something of value. I find that very touching: where Rupert had come from and what he gave his son.

RD (letter to Arnold Edinborough, August 21, 1961)

Brenda told me your news at lunch today [Edinborough was buying *Saturday Night* magazine] & I take Underwood in hand to congratulate you most heartily. This is the reward of boldness. . . . Long may you dare and may your daring bring you everything you want. It is the daring ones who make the wheels go round.

I feel this strongly because I am doing a spot of daring myself, in a direction that seems superficially to be the contrary of your own. I am leaving the comparative ease of being publisher of a paper for the certain unease of running a particular sort of college; I am leaving a world were few people cheek me for one where aged profs sneer at me because I am not, and never will be, their notion of a scholar; I am also making certain sacrifices of money in the hope that new world will keep me alive, as I am sure that another twenty years of provincial journalism would wrap me in the sleep of intellectual death. I am also canning my *Star* column, at Christmas,

I expect. It pays handsomely but it is whoredom. . . . To write about Corvo and Logan Pearsall Smith for housewives in Sioux Lookout is all right for a while, but in the end it makes one a Tinpot Pontiff. . . . The *Star* can take their money and ingest it anally, if I make myself clear. . . .

I embrace you in the spirit,
Rob

JENNIFER SURRIDGE

RD saw this opportunity as a way to get out of Peterborough, a wonderful opportunity. But the Masseys were not easy people. There was basic resentment in the family that Vincent wanted to do the college. The rest of the family thought that the family money should be spent on other things.

BRENDA DAVIES

I think some of the Masseys felt that Vincent was building a monument to himself . . . which of course he was. Rob had to negotiate among these Masseys. He could make Vincent Massey laugh, which lightened the atmosphere. But he used to say to me after these negotiations, "Why did I get into this?"

Another problem: RD hadn't graduated from high school, and his only degree was his Oxford B. Litt. He knew that his new university colleagues would greet his appointment with skepticism.

TOM SYMONS

And the assumption had been the head of the new graduate college would be a great pooh-bah scholar. I was on the President's Advisory Committee and was present on the occasion when Claude Bissell told the committee that Robertson Davies would be Massey College's first Master. The reaction was stunned. Not hostile. Stunned. Then some good people gave the lead.

Northrop Frye said, "That's a really good appointment."
Marshall McLuhan did, too.
After they had spoken, no one said anything negative (and they would have)! There were some academics at the University of Toronto

who felt that the headship of a graduate college should go to a person with a lifetime in academe.

I didn't feel that way at all. I rejoiced when I discovered that it was RD who would head the new college. . . . He would open windows to a wider world for the students. I liked him enormously. He combined solemnity and fun in a way I've never encountered in another human being.

It helped that in 1960, RD's friend from Peterborough Gordon Roper, then a professor at Trinity College at the University of Toronto, had arranged for RD to teach drama courses two days a week at Trinity College at the university, a job to which Brenda drove him from Peterborough. Michael Peterman, a U of T student at the time, was later a colleague of Roper, and a biographer of RD.

MICHAEL PETERMAN
At first, RD was not well received. And Gordon was very angry with his colleagues for that. But being at Trinity put Davies in a fabulous position to be snapped up by Vincent Massey. One of the things about RD was that once he had adopted a role, he really sashayed about. He must have seemed overdressed for the part at Trinity.

RUPERT SCHIEDER (English professor, retired, from Trinity)
Gordon had this supreme devotion to the Master. Was he shy? I guess that was the excuse for the way he was: the Master, in the Henry James tradition. The Great God. . . . When I heard that he was coming to Trinity to teach, I probably groaned inwardly that we were going to have to warm to him. I liked his books very much. But I didn't like dealing with him.

I shared Gordon's office, which was a bit of a nuisance. Gordon and I were on intimate terms, but Davies and I were on formal terms. I think he invited that. We kept our distance.

I'll tell you an odd thing. Gordon was quite devoted to RD, and he was bound that the old man would teach at Trinity. At first, there was no one in RD's classes. The students wouldn't go. So Gordon said, "This man is a genius. You *must* attend this man's lectures."

LISA BALFOUR BOWEN
Rupert Schieder was one of my professors at Trinity. A lot of professors like Rupert, professors with tenure, wouldn't have appreciated a person without a university background being brought in. I was taking honours English and Davies was teaching, not a course but a casual group of honours English students. It was about Irish theatre – "John Synge: The Real and the Ideal."

At the time, I thought Davies's delivery was dull, meandering and unfocused. I hardly took a note. We were used to professors who made us focus. At the time, I found Davies an old, fusty fuddy-duddy. He just went round and round.

RUPERT SCHIEDER
The students would complain to Gordon, and Gordon would tell me – but Gordon would have liked us all to have appreciated Davies. When he was appointed to Massey, I suspect probably a good many of us in the university faculty felt that Massey was a good place for Davies . . . a sort of special, *outside* place.

Ernest Sirluck, who had been lured back to Canada from the University of Chicago to become the University of Toronto's dean designate of graduate studies, was given theoretical jurisdiction over Massey. He joined the Massey College Corporation.

ERNEST SIRLUCK
Like all professors at the University of Toronto, at the outset, we had some trepidation about Massey College. It was not merely that Robertson Davies was not an academic. It was that here was what was called a college, with no faculty, no teaching role, no academic standing. It was obviously aimed to reproduce the conditions of Vincent Massey's Oxford experience and his yen to be an English aristocrat. It didn't allow women to be a part of it, and yet it was a college in the University of Toronto, headed by a person with no academic standing, aiming at a social presence that most professors regarded with hostility and antagonism.

Once he had agreed to enter this skeptical academic world, Davies looked for talented allies. He brought from Peterborough his secretary,

Moira Whalon, and Colin Friesen, a young assistant manager of the Peterborough branch of the Bank of Commerce.

COLIN FRIESEN

One day, I got a call from Rob Davies. He said he'd like to meet me in Toronto at the University Club. I thought, "What in heaven's name have I done that this man would want to meet with *me*?"

I went to the club and I was sitting on a chair in the hall. RD arrived in that aristocratic way and he said, "Mr. Friesen." I jumped up and said, "Yessir," as if I were still in the air force.

We had lunch, he gave me a glass of wine, which was lovely, and after lunch he said, "Would you join me in the club library?" That's when he said, "I have recently been elected Master designate of Massey College. I have twenty-seven letters on my desk applying for the bursar's position. I shall not open a single letter until I have talked to *you*."

I was a banker, and a banker has tunnel vision. I said, "Sir, I had no idea you were going to approach me on this."

He said, "What do you think?"

I said, "I'd prefer if you gave me the opportunity to discuss this with my wife."

He replied, "If you hadn't said that, I would not have proceeded with my intentions to hire you."

I gave it a lot of thought. RD waited. He gave me so much scope and time. I couldn't make up my mind. Finally, I wrote to the bank and resigned. Then I got a terrible cold, which turned out to be pneumonia. I had no pension. It was Christmas. I went to the hospital and the doctor took X-rays and said, "You have cancer of the lung." And I had three lovely little daughters crawling around on the floor at home. I was so terribly sick. A week later, the doctor came back to me and said, "I'm awfully sorry. We read the wrong X-ray."

So I came to Massey with a new lease on life. In a monetary sense, I would have done better staying at the bank. . . but at Massey I was so completely *nourished* – I don't think I could have had a better life than having met RD and serving at the college.

Work began – with much input from the Massey family, which included architects such as Hart Massey, people with strong views and no particular affection for RD.

JENNIFER SURRIDGE

RD had to be a diplomat among Ron Thom, the architect, and Vincent Massey, and the others, which cost him a lot. The reason I know it cost him a lot was from his diaries. He would come out of meetings incredibly frustrated and think through how he would have to solve these problems.

But it was a wonderful time for RD. I think all his creative juices went into Massey College. He found the motto. He found the crest. He found the George Santayana quote that went onto the wall of the dining hall. He was in all the meetings about the furniture. They went into endless detail, which drove him mad, but he got a lot of creative bang out of it. He was creating this thing he thought would make an enormous difference. . . . A great deal of what the college is today is RD. He enjoyed being with young people. He always said it was ghastly to be limited to friends of your own age group.

Then it was time to move from Peterborough. This proved to be more of a wrench than RD or Brenda anticipated, particularly after Scott Symons, an expert on Canadian furniture then at the Royal Ontario Museum, came to scout out the place.

SCOTT SYMONS

My brother Tom Symons and Robertson Davies are both very proper, very decent, very considered in their deportment. FOOFs: Fine Old Ontario Families. It also stands for snotty and inbred!

My brother was to be the first president of the new Trent University in Peterborough. Tom asked me to go to Peterborough and speak to Robertson Davies at his house, Marchbanks Towers on Park Street. I went down to Peterborough with my wife Judith and stayed with Davies and Brenda at Marchbanks. His view was that Judith and I and he were all FOOFs. My grandfather, William Perkins Bull, turned down a viscountcy because his wife told him that Canadians do not have titles. And Judith's father owned National Trust. Davies and Judith got along famously.

My wife and I thought RD was a case. He was the sort of guy who drank his morning coffee out of a bowl – and watched you watching him as he did so. I liked the guy, but he was a mountebank. Very much the chatelaine of Marchbanks Towers.

He showed us the whole place, and we examined the house in

terms of possible acquisition. Lovely gardens! It was well kept, a small chateau – and you *felt* it. I remember the big front room, and the study. He kept a photograph of himself and myself in the toilet. God knows why I graced the toilet. It didn't take us long to realize that this house would be *the* place for the future president of Trent to live. But after we tried to buy it, Davies tried to keep it! You never knew if he was coming or going.

TOM SYMONS

There is no question that RD treasured the house at 361 Park. He had some moments when he wasn't entirely happy with Peterborough, but both he and Brenda loved the house and found it very, very difficult to part with it.

When I was chairing the committee for Trent, Rob and Brenda were kind enough to have me several times to the house. Of course, I fell in love with the house, and just about then the announcement was made about Rob and Massey. So I asked if I could buy the house. They would not sell the house, except to someone who cared about it. They decided I would do – and we shook hands without benefit of clergy or realtor. And for a very fair price. Rob did not believe that realtors or lawyers were indispensable.

After a few days, Rob phoned me and said, Would I understand if they changed their mind about selling the house? The thought of selling it had given them a very restless time, and they'd been fretting.

I said, Of course, I understood. They said they wanted to try to keep it for a summer home or a retreat away from Toronto. And they did do that, for a summer. But it didn't work out very well. Rob didn't drive. And this house is a substantial property to maintain.

Then they explored the possibility of moving the house, the whole house, closer to Toronto, because they liked it so well. But they found that this would be so costly . . .

And then they kindly remembered how much I had loved the house, and they allowed me to buy it for the same price as we had discussed. This story reflects on the depths of their feelings about Park Street.

In the garden, we still look at flowers that pop up in the spring that Brenda put there forty-five years ago. The house has just been designated a historic monument, the oldest brick house in Peterborough. The plaque outside says the house is known as "Marchbanks." Its antiquity, and the Robertson Davies connection, make it special.

BRENDA DAVIES

The Park Street story was a little like that. First, Scott Symons came
with his wife to look at it, and he patronized the daylights out of us. He
was working at the time for the Canadiana Gallery at the Royal Ontario
Museum, and so he came in and ran down all our furniture! We knew
Tom Symons wanted Park Street. We thought he was buying the house
for the new university. So we charged him just $25,000. We had bought
it for $23,000 and we had altered it and put in a good deal of work. It's
true we did take our time in making up our minds, and we did toy with
the idea of moving the house to the land we had bought in Caledon. It
was not a practical idea at all, just a fantasy. In the end, we sold it to
Tom because it was impossible to keep. Tom called it Marchbanks
Towers. He didn't ask us if we had called it that!

**At last, in October 1963, Massey College was completed and ready to
open its gates and ready to become the new home of the Davies family.
For the several inauguration ceremonies, RD took on a role of scriptwriter
and stage director.**

COLIN FRIESEN

Vincent Massey said that donors usually handed over the keys to a
building, but he found this impractical; instead, he handed over the
Founder's Cup, a symbol of community life, and a visitor's book to rep-
resent hospitality. "Community and hospitality," he said, "will belong
to the life of this place."

Dr. Davies followed with a speech of acknowledgment and grati-
tude punctuated with the usual Davies wit. . . . Near the end of the
speech, a junior fellow advanced and shouted, "Cease and suspend this
endless flow of tripe. May I come forth?"

At this point, all the speakers began to use verse! The junior fellow
introduced himself as a *Terrae Filius*, a son of the Earth, and a critic of
the Establishment. He repeated all the harshest criticisms of the college.
From then on, each of the participants spoke his own verse. At the end,
Mr. Massey invited the junior fellow to join the master and himself. As
the three drank from the Founder's Cup, the bell in the tower chimed.

Chapter 23

MASTER OF MASSEY

RD laboured valiantly to make Massey into a community where creativity, curiosity and a sense of tradition could flourish. He also tried to find a place for himself within the university community, particularly the Senate, which he was required to join.

ERNEST SIRLUCK
We met every third Friday of the month. Robertson Davies was always there, but he never spoke. You can interpret that in several ways. You could say, as a novelist, he was gathering material. Or you could say he was uninterested in the subjects we were debating. But I interpreted that as his continued unease about his academic qualifications. And it is true, the bulk of the university professoriate did not consider him to be one of them. He knew that people were saying that he had no qualifications.

At first, some professors were reluctant to have anything to do with the new college.

JOHN POLANYI (Scientist, Nobel Prize winner)
I was made a senior fellow from the day the door opened at Massey College. I was the first senior fellow with an exotic name. I didn't think I wanted this. I'd been to Princeton, and I'd seen a warmed-over Oxford, so playing games here in Toronto didn't appeal to me. I turned it down.

When my refusal came to the ear of the other youngish senior fellow, James Eayrs, he phoned me up and said, "You've just signed your death warrant at the U of T." I made skeptical sounds . . .

When I met Davies, he was such an imposing figure. He came into a room like a galleon under full sail, a beautiful sight. Davies marshalled all his forces, and wrote to me charmingly. . . . His forces far exceeded mine. A few weeks later, I was led by the ear into the Round

Room at Massey College by Robertson Davies, and there was Jim Eayrs laughing into his sleeve. It turned out to be a lovely association. It's a wonderful place.

Eayrs, a young and gifted professor of political science, had ghostwritten much of Vincent Massey's Romances lecture "Canadians and Their Commonwealth," which was delivered at Oxford, and he had worked on Vincent Massey's autobiography, *What's Past Is Prologue*.

JAMES EAYRS
He thought well enough of my efforts to help get me invited to join the first group of Massey College senior fellows. The kind of people there then were the head of the university [Claude Bissell], the dean of graduate studies [Ernest Sirluck], and the ineffable John Polanyi, who was distinguished even then, years before he won the Nobel Prize.

In due course, a letter from the recently appointed Master arrived. I wrote back and demurred. I said I had a lot of journalism going. Only after I sent the letter did it occur to me that Robertson Davies had more journalism going in a day than I had in a year, plus all his novel writing and literary enterprises. He didn't point that out in his reply, but said something like, "So far as your projects being impedimenta, rather, they are precisely the kind of accomplishments that we want!" So I caved in.

In RD's vision, the new college would be renowned both for scholarship and traditions of hospitality. He asked a noted Sinologist, W.A.C. Dobson, to help organize "high tables" – formal dinners to which eminent guests would be invited and, after dinner, given port and snuff in the Upper Library.

PETER BRIGG (former junior fellow)
Bill Dobson ran these high tables with his old buddies like Northrop Frye and the port and snuff and cigars and walnuts, just as at Oxford. Bill had done his studies at Oxford and fully understood its culture, whereas Davies had an Oxford B. Litt. but must have felt somewhat of a colonial there. I think that at the beginning Dobson was a shadow of the Oxford Davies had admired.

MICHAEL PETERMAN
At Massey we learned such things as, "The port must be passed to the left," so that if someone to your *right* said, "May I have the port?" it had to go to the *left* and all around the table.

JAMES EAYRS
The part of the high table dinner set in the Senior Common Room was notable for its refreshments. There prevailed a certain gluttony among us – no, that's wrong – an appreciation of the finer things of life. . . . I always felt that Rob, true to his attention to detail, paid close attention to the supply and presentation of the cashews, the walnuts, the circulation of the port and the cognac.

MARTIN O'MALLEY (former Massey journalism fellow)
Someone used to say of Massey under Davies, "O to be in England. Now that England's here."

KILDARE DOBBS
I first became conscious of Massey College when a Southam fellow from western Canada complained to me, "They don't have salt in proper shakers, they have the salt in these little buckets." He was indignant! He also told me that at Massey they played croquet and wore gowns. Jim Eayrs said it was "a place where tradition goes all the way back to 1963."

PHYLLIS GROSSKURTH (writer)
Mavor Moore and I married in 1966, and then I was invited to dinners at Massey College. It was because of Mavor – I didn't have any illusions about *that*. Davies would assemble us all in a line – man, woman, man, woman, man, woman – and we'd go through the Common Room in dinner dress. The students were looking very amused. I was embarrassed. But it didn't bother RD at all. . . . After dinner, he'd adjourn with the men to the library and we went with Brenda to the drawing room in the Master's lodging. I never knew what to call Brenda. She was "Mrs. Davies."

JAMES EAYRS
The occasion I most vividly recall was when Harold Town [a celebrated abstract artist] was our guest at high table. After dinner in the dining

room we repaired as usual to the Senior Common Room, where a table was well set with silver, crystal, nuts, port and cognac. On this occasion, Harold was in what his friends might call good form. For a guest, he behaved rudely. Everyone was looking from the Master to Town to the Master and then back to Town.

ELIZABETH EAYRS
It was Town and gown!

JAMES EAYRS
When the Master turned to him and asked, "Mr. Town, perhaps you'll tell us from your artistic point of view what you think of Massey College?" Town was leaning back in his chair and meditatively fingering the light switch and said something like: "Look at this light switch! It's so damned ordinary! Like everything else in this place, I suppose." He was clearly out to inflict maximum pain with minimum effort. Like everything else in Massey, I think the light switch was specially designed by the architect, and Town was set to destroy the place. The only thing he did not destroy was Rob's imperturbability.

Another version of RD's encounter with Town is recounted by John Fraser and Robert Fulford. It goes like this:

One day RD agreed to give Town a tour of Massey. After he had sneered at the quadrangle, the bell tower, the upper library and the fountain, RD took him to the subterranean chapel designed by Tanya Moiseiwitsch, designer of the Stratford Festival stage. She had created for Massey a crypt-like place of worship with a Greek Orthodox ambience. Town pronounced it an excrescence and said it was the worst thing about the college. RD said, "At that point I heard rolling thunder and a booming voice from on high which said, 'Go forth, Mr. Town, and never darken Massey again.' To my surprise I discovered that voice was my own."

While keen that Massey College host the talented and influential, RD and Brenda also worked to make junior fellows feel at home.

FATHER HAROLD NAHABEDIAN (former junior fellow)
In November 1965, there was a massive power blackout. The lights suddenly failed all over Ontario and the Northeast states, and 25 million

people were without electricity. It must have been just at suppertime. We were in the Great Hall and suddenly we could not see our dinners. I remember he came upstairs carrying a great silver candelabra for us. "Gentlemen, I bring you light."

ROSAMOND BAILEY
Mum was extremely shy, but she would invite young girls from St. Hilda's College to dinner. A lot of the guys were far from home, so it must have been nice for them. And Mum thought it would be great to move to Massey College and her daughters would meet eligible bachelors . . . but they weren't interested in us, they were only interested in my father!

BRONWYN DRAINIE (broadcaster, magazine editor)
I did my M.A. in 1969–70, when the college was still all-male. As female students in Davies's classes, we were called upon to come to dinners and cocktail parties at Massey College and to be a sort of decorative element. The ratio in these gatherings was four or five (males) to one. Before these dinners, Brenda and Rob would move the few females around the room. You'd be chatting with a group of three or four gentlemen and you would suddenly feel a hand at your elbow. . . . "Now, why don't you come over to this group and sparkle . . ." You sat at one table for the soup course, and they'd move you to another table for the main course, and another for the dessert. It felt very odd.

Other junior fellows empathized with RD's attempts to civilize the mob.

MICHIEL HORN (former junior fellow)
I never saw Davies angry, but I did see an angry letter he wrote to a grad student, someone from the States, who had been rude to the cleaning staff who came into his room too early. As I recall, RD wrote that it is not the part of a gentleman to be rude to the serving class. He had a sense of Victorian noblesse oblige.

MARGARET ATWOOD
There was also a story, which is certainly untrue, that Robertson Davies had not permitted a laundromat to be installed in Massey on the ground that "gentlemen do not do their own washing." But he never said that.

JIM DUGAN (former junior fellow)
He resisted requests to install a washer/dryer in the college because, as he was quoted in *The Toronto Star*, "a gentleman doesn't wash his own socks." One of the residents of Massey College – protesting this position – took a pile of dirty socks out into the courtyard and washed them in the goldfish pond, in full view of Davies's office. The Master relented and installed a washer/dryer.

By the late 1960s, Massey, which had been built with wealth from the Massey-Ferguson farm machinery empire, inspired an anti-Massey, known as Ferguson College, which had its own mock Master. Ferguson College played a role in the curious incident of the fish in the night.

DAVID KLAUSNER (former junior fellow)
Let me tell you the fish story. It is such a good example of the way Rob didn't take things personally. This was around 1969, when there were goldfish in the pond in the quadrangle at Massey. I think they were eventually taken out because the engineers used to sneak in and pour detergent into the pond, which made nice bubbles but killed the fish. However, in 1969 there were fish.

Somehow, word got around that the Massey College quadrangle pond was to be cleaned and stripped of algae. The graduate students worried about how the fish would be cared for while this was going on. One night, a group of people – I am ashamed to admit I was one – stole the fish with nets from a pet shop. The fish were loaded into three double-bagged green garbage bags and removed from the college via the northwest men's room, which had the only window in the entire building that opened wide enough to get the bags through. The fish were taken to Ferguson College three blocks away, and there they were put in the bathtub.

Colin Friesen, the bursar of Massey, was certain the fish had been murdered, flushed down the toilet. He called the police. About six of Toronto's finest began going house to house, floor by floor, checking all the toilets in the building for a trace of golden scales.

JOHN BROWNE (former junior fellow)
Well! the next morning, the police are there. And the caretaker is opening all the drains. He's saying that drunken junior fellows have flushed the fish down the drains. I could see this was getting totally out

of hand. So I had a friend send a telegram to Colin Friesen from Florida. It said:

ALL IS WELL. HAVING A WONDERFUL VACATION. SEE YOU SOON. THE FISH.

The next day, things were even tenser. RD was saying nothing, but there was a witch hunt under way. Friesen kept saying, "Who did this?" It was really getting out of hand.

DAVID KLAUSNER
Towards the end of the week, after the pond was cleared out, three heavy-duty garbage bags of fish came back through the bathroom window and were replaced in the pond. The thing was, Rob never said a word. I suspect he was delighted and was creasing up in his beard. But Colin insisted that fewer fish had returned, and therefore several had been killed. We think we brought back more fish than we removed. We think some had been pregnant.

A couple of years later, the chaplain of the college instituted a prize for the best non-destructive prank of the year. The prize was a large mug with a fish on it. Rob approved the cup.

As Massey developed its legends, it was also developing a reputation as a place of music.

ASHLEY THOMSON
I recall a blond law student who had the habit of riding around the quadrangle on his bike, whistling classical music as he went. I don't think Davies particularly approved of the bike riding. But one day he was overheard to say to the person standing next to him, "His Bach is worse than his bike." Not bad.

From the start, there was a Massey choir. Bruce Ubukata, organist at Grace Church on the Hill, was one of its early directors.

BRUCE UBUKATA
On Sunday evenings, the great majority of choristers had put in at least one church service, some as many as three, but we would get ourselves there and carry on from 7 till 9 or 10 at night. We'd go to the basement of the Master's lodging, his library. Always, at 10 o'clock, you could

count on Brenda to bring platters of sandwiches and cake and beer and Canada Dry Ginger Ale in wicker baskets. . . . One year, on the first of March, in came Welsh rarebit, specially done for St. David's Day.

RD would be present all through the rehearsal. He would use this period to become reacquainted with his library. As Churchill says, if you haven't time to read all the books in your libraries, you should at least make time to finger them. So RD could spend nearly all evening in the stacks, listening to the singing, and he was very much ready to be brought into the discussion.

We'd ask him, in a Shakespearean song, should it be "*Jug, jug poo-wee?*" And, "How should we do the *too-wit, too-woos?*" And he would give us a deliciously improvised answer, or he would go off and look it up. I often wondered if he would have liked to join us.

Once, around Palm Sunday or Holy Week one year, he expressed amusement when I told him that I had seen printed instructions on how your Sunday school class could make its own palm cross. He really took off on *that*. He said, "Oh yes, in my childhood there were all sorts of books that could give you pious exercises, *Fun for Little Catholics* . . ." and then he improvised several improbable crafts, ending with ". . . or making a Cistercian alb out of blotting paper."

Yet he did preserve the common touch. One of our members did not converse at the lively intellectual level of the others, but RD would always praise her lemon tarts. Her son had to write a high-school essay on RD's novels, and RD had the boy come in and helped him on his essay.

On other occasions, the common touch eluded RD.

FATHER HAROLD NAHABEDIAN

I applied to go to Massey College in 1965–66. I think by that time he had withdrawn a little from the college, because he was so roundly criticized for several initiatives, such as posting the conversation topics before high table. We saw little of him. Once, he came and sat next to me and I said, "How do you like being Master of Massey College?" He said, "What a question!" and he got up and left.

In fact, it was a good question. Sometimes, RD did not like being Master of Massey. Throughout the 1960s, the college required him to spend more and more time on administration, and on wrestling with its financial requirements, which had not been fully funded in the initial Massey bequest.

COLIN FRIESEN
There were many stresses in the early years over how the college would be funded. . . . He'd say, "Let's have you do your best in not increasing the fees, because I believe that the poor should have the same opportunity as the rich – in fact, it's even more important." Money was always on our minds.

ERNEST SIRLUCK
Around 1965–1966, when he was depressed about his work, he said to me that he was pretty downcast. I tried to cheer him up by launching into a discourse about the importance of what he was doing. He stopped me and he said, "Ernest, you know what I'm doing: I'm running a boarding house."

More annoying than the student tenants was the eminent Sinologist W.A.C. Dobson.

IAIN DOBSON
My dad was a founder of Massey College. He was a very self-effacing human being. He won the $50,000 Molson Award, he got the Order of Canada and was a member of the Harvard Board of Overseers for twenty-two years.

For the first few years of Massey College, until 1967, Brenda and Rob and my father, Bill, and mother, Pearl, were great friends. My memory of them is hazy, but there are lots of letters from Robertson Davies around, inscriptions in books – "With fond memories to Bill" – that sort of thing. Then my parents separated in the fall of 1967, and Dad moved into Massey College. RD arranged for a room for me as well. I lived at Massey from 1967 to 1971.

PETER BRIGG
Dobson was the under-the-blanket son of a Scottish nobleman. He knew Vincent Massey from quite a way back. Vincent had consulted with Bill about Massey before he had consulted with Rob, or so Bill told me. I think Bill had always thought he'd be made first Master of Massey. Bill Dobson was a wonderful man, but very egotistical. A scholar of his stature had some right to an ego.

JOHN BROWNE
Was Dobson agitating to be Master of Massey? I think he would have taken it if it had been offered. He opened his rooms to junior fellows informally, which Davies didn't do. We had long conversations about Chinese and the Romance languages – but also about how the college could be better than it was.

IAIN DOBSON
The problems were not because of my dad, but because of his strong feeling that a university should be a place where senior and junior fellows could socialize and be part of a community. . . . Dad became a lightning rod, and a lightning rod has a great deal of ground around it. At the time he felt that students got a bum deal, that's his phrase, when they became teaching assistants, when they were excluded from university decision-making.

DAVID KLAUSNER
There was no love lost between W.A.C. and Rob. W.A.C. was on easier terms with the grad students, but he was a major-league shit-disturber. I was part of the Dobson crowd, but we had fun far too often at others' expense. I can see now why Rob didn't like him. In the bar, they would be at opposite end of the room.

On rare occasions, the two men clashed in front of other Massey fellows.

IAIN DOBSON
I was there for the Night of the Green Ghost. Seven or eight junior fellows had started drinking sherry in my father's rooms – his fortnightly sherry party – along with Clarke Davey, then managing editor of *The Globe and Mail*, and Dalton Camp, the Tory strategist, who were among the robust guests.

I'm the one who, at 10:30 at night, said "Let's order in a pizza." I remember there were two limos parked outside the college, waiting for the important people. I suppose Clarke Davey would have been one.

I got six pizzas and gave one to the limo drivers. The guys in Dad's rooms said, "Give them another, we'll be a while." So I did, and then we all trooped into the Great Hall to eat our pizzas. There was a woman, and at one point she was certainly on Dalton's lap, but I wouldn't want you to think we'd called in a hooker. She was one of the guests. And there were antics with the pizzas.

DAVID KLAUSNER
The ceiling is two storeys high in the dining hall, but at the high table, which is raised on a dais, it is much lower, and somehow a piece of pizza got stuck on the ceiling, where it hung, tomato and cheese curling down.

Memories of the details differ somewhat.

IAIN DOBSON
I don't remember a piece hanging from the ceiling by a string of cheese, but I remember tremendous humour and outstanding conversation, and that it was getting quite loud. People were giving speeches and generally carrying on. Then . . . The Gown appeared at the top of the stairs.

The Gown was floor-length, crushed velvet, very expensive, with embroidery on the collar. Then a booming, imperial voice announced, "My ROOM is on the other side of this WALL! I shall see you ALL in my office at nine in the morning." Then, as the image pirouetted, the voice of Dalton Camp protested, "But I won't be here."

DAVID KLAUSNER
Suddenly, at the far end of the hall, there was an absolutely brilliant, beautifully executed *Harrumph!* It was worthy of the stage! My recollection is that RD said nothing. He merely glared and then turned on his heel. Dalton Camp finally broke the silence and said, "Who was *that*, Banquo's ghost?"

We, the guilty ones, went through the next few days on tenterhooks. Rob knew perfectly well who we were. But nothing was ever said about it. One of the nicest things about Rob was that he did not pursue these things. There were no repercussions.

IAIN DOBSON
The big issue between Dad and Rob had more to do with Rob's insecurity about running the college. The rules, which the porter tended to enforce, were Victorian. It was as if the College were a dormitory for 16-year-olds! But these were mature people! The problem wasn't Dad, it was that RD was attempting to run a boy's school. . . . If there was a

trigger, it was Dad's separation from Mum, which RD couldn't explain to Brenda. Was Vincent's death another trigger for the falling-out between RD and Dad? Dad was never deferential to Vincent, and RD was, no question. Therein lay another source of acrimony.

RD was also upset by Dobson's dealings with other Massey staff.

COLIN FRIESEN

Because I hadn't finished my degree, Dobson felt I was not adequate to be the bursar at this college. Now, the Master was full of tricks. At one corporation meeting, he spoke to the group unexpectedly. He said, "There are some of you who feel that Mr. Friesen is not up to being the bursar of the college, and I want to discuss why you feel this way." Well, my face was burning! RD went on: "Let's decide right now if we want Colin Friesen to remain." Every hand went up but one . . . and then with the slightest bit of reluctance, Dobson's hand went up. So it was unanimous!

ERNEST SIRLUCK

I want to tell you a story you won't hear from anyone else about Rob. It is about the time I disappointed Rob. He came to see me and said something like, "Dobson is wreaking havoc in my college . . . he gathers the fellows around, gives them drink and talks about how things could be better at Massey and more like Oxford. He's clearly trying to replace me. And I would like you to try to get rid of him for me." This was the one time Rob ever interpreted Massey College as coming under the jurisdiction of Graduate Studies. He usually took the position that it was autonomous.

I said, "On what grounds can I get rid of him?"

He said, "Disruptive influence."

Now, Dobson had collaborated with Claude Bissell on a project that Claude Bissell really liked. Dobson would translate Chinese poems into English prose, and Bissell would reorganize this into poetry. So Rob was asking me to interject myself into Massey College and to throw out a senior scholar placed there by the president of the university, a collaborator of the president on an artistic endeavour. I said, "This is not in my jurisdiction. The only person who can do this is the president."

Rob rose and said "Thank you" and left quickly. He was very disappointed in me. I know that Rob did not ask Bissell to remove Dobson, because I asked Bissell and he said that he knew of the problem, but that he hadn't been asked.

IAIN DOBSON
All that happened was that RD kicked Dad out of his rooms. . . . He sent Dad a notice that the corporation was going to use his rooms for other purposes. We knew this was coming. RD waited until he had a proxy board. There was no scene, no confrontation.

PETER BRIGG
Davies basically threw Dobson out of his apartment and then, when the elections came up, Dobson was not re-elected as a senior fellow. This was not a nice business. I saw what it looked like when two powerful old men had a fight. Dobson told me that both Northrop Frye and Claude Bissell had offered to resign their senior fellowships at Massey over his failure to be re-elected, but that he had dissuaded them. A man who had less insecurity than RD, wise as he was – and I think of him as a very wise man – would have handled this situation differently.

IAIN DOBSON
Claude Bissell knew about all this, but RD had administrative control of Massey College and that was that. Claude arranged for Dad to move to the most luxurious digs, a mansion on the east side of Queen's Park – I think it's now the School of Theology. And on a clear day, you could see Massey College.

Chapter 24

TWO DEATHS

Burdened by Massey responsibilities, RD had little time to himself.

BRENDA DAVIES
After the theatre fiasco in New York – it was such a disaster and so agonizing – this period in the 1960s was not a creative hiatus. He concentrated on the college and he did not have time to do much writing.

Until 1966, that is, when the impresario Nicholas Goldschmidt invited five major men of letters, including RD and novelist W.O. Mitchell, to create a pageant for Canada's centennial in 1967. Still bruised from his Broadway failure, RD must have felt some trepidation. With good reason, according to Mitchell's son Orm and daughter-in-law Barb.

ORM MITCHELL
It was to be a two-hour pageant, and they had been given five or six months to do it. RD was the overseer and was to write the frame and the Ontario section. . . . It was a patchwork thing. W.O.'s section was a three-part skit about Prairie con men. From what we can gather, it was a silly, silly piece. But W.O. sent it along to RD and RD quite liked it – at least, W.O. said that RD said he was pleased.

The contributors met for a preview performance on October 6, 1966, at the Academy Theatre in Lindsay, near Peterborough.

ORM MITCHELL
What happened was that some parts of this play were supposed to be funny, so Davies was laughing at the stuff he thought was funny, but he was *not* laughing at the framing material (which was *not* supposed to be funny). But particularly for the framing parts, the actors hammed it

up. Years later, W.O. used to do a falsetto voice to re-enact this melo-dramatic scene where Freya, the Viking settler amazon, who is pregnant, tears open her bodice and whets her sword across her breasts to scare off marauders. In Lindsay, that brought the house down.

W.O. felt that the production was a hodgepodge and the only sal-vation was to play it as farce. But RD was so upset he walked out at the intermission and said it was a mockery. He was just fuming. And the reviews were bad. The Lindsay newspaper said something like, "Is this the product of Canada's best writers?"

W.O. did not want the centennial play to go on to Ottawa. But Davies felt Lindsay had mocked it and he wanted it played straight. And, much to W.O.'s dismay, Nicky Goldschmidt was also very keen to have it go to Ottawa. W.O. later said, "I'm looking at this church-basement shit, and Davies likes it!!"

BARB MITCHELL

Robertson Davies and W.O. were the only two contributors who went to the Ottawa Little Theatre when it opened on January 11, 1967. Davies wrote to W.O. afterwards and said that he was sorry that the players had mucked up W.O.'s writing. Something like, "I expressed keen dissatisfaction with the production and was shocked by the wanton disregard for the text." But the production was panned in Ottawa, too.

MIRANDA DAVIES

I get the impression that this struck very deep. It revivified memories of disappointments with the play *Love and Libel* and what was dearest to his heart, which was theatre.

Just two months after this blow came another: RD's father died on March 11, 1967.

MICHAEL DAVIES

Rupert had been out to lunch that day with an Anglican bishop, had felt bad at lunch and was dead by midnight. It was very quick. Rupert's funeral was quite elaborate. He was laid out in the drawing room at Hawthorn Gardens. An awful lot of people came to pay their respects. I think we were all in a – I was going to say state of shock, but not really. He was an important person in our lives, but he was 87.

As for RD's comment that he was unable to write *Fifth Business* until someone died, well . . . pleasing Rupert was important to Robertson, I've been told.

MIRANDA DAVIES
I was still in Toronto when Rupert died and was absolutely grief-stricken. Still am. I would go to bed in tears and have no idea if anyone else in the family was grieving. It was perhaps a relief for Father, who felt he never had praise or recognition for what he was doing, for what he had done. I remember staying home one night just after this when they went out, and I remember thinking *they* were having a good time while I was at home thinking about Christ's betrayal – my God, my God, why has Thou forsaken me? I sometimes wonder if I was grieving for the whole family.

Rupert's will left almost nothing to his surviving sons; everything went to his grandchildren.

MARTIN HUNTER
His father thought he had no head for business, was Rob's sense of it. I remember he told me, "Although I am an executor of my father's will, I am not a beneficiary."

JENNIFER SURRIDGE
With Rupert's will, RD was hurt. It wasn't the money issue – that Rupert's money had skipped a generation and was being left to the grandchildren – it was Rupert's thoughtlessness. RD was very hurt. But he told us that although it was hurtful, it was a relief to him: he wouldn't have to provide for us. He saw it as just Rupert being high-handed, as usual.

And then, on December 30, came news that Massey College's founder, Vincent Massey, had died. In one year, RD lost two of the three most important men in his life.

PETER BRIGG
They had become quite close, RD and Vincent, and RD asked us all to go to Vincent's funeral. Thirty or forty of the junior fellows went, wearing our gowns as requested. Massey had had a state funeral in

Ottawa but was laid to rest in the Anglican churchyard in Port Hope. It was freezing, and they had to get a pneumatic drill to dig the grave.

Afterwards, we went to Batterwood, and Davies was doing his thing, helping people feel at ease. I remember him saying, "Mr. Brigg, I would like you to meet Walter Gordon." Yikes! This was the former finance minister of Canada, and at the time he was president of the Privy Council. In addition to all the celebrated people there, Batterwood had a stunning array of Group of Seven paintings. There was a lot of liquor flowing, too, as the family, including Hart and Raymond Massey, and close friends such as RD, were at the end of a difficult public week. RD was very formal at that funeral . . . he believed in the formal public world and he was probably hiding his personal grief at losing a friend. That RD's father had died several months earlier . . . this double shock had such an impact on him.

Chapter 25

INSIDE THE
MASTER'S LODGING

Keen to make Massey the Canadian manifestation of all he had loved about Oxford, and anxious to realize his patron Vincent Massey's vision, RD felt himself as Master of Massey to be under considerable pressure. It was important to keep up appearances and a sense of authority. For a proud, shy man with three lively daughters to do this under any circumstances would have been tricky. To do so in the exuberant, iconoclastic sixties was impossible. And RD was still smarting from recent debacles.

JENNIFER SURRIDGE
The sixties were a terrible time for RD.

MIRANDA DAVIES
What was the most painful aspect of the sixties for him? The Dobson stuff was ghastly, and the pageant thing in 1967 – the appalling disillusionment. It was the collapse of his aspiration for the Canadian spirit.

ROSAMOND BAILEY
There had been after *Love and Libel* a great disappointment, a huge letdown. So it was extremely important to him that Massey College do well, because it represented the things that had *saved* him. Oxford had saved him when he couldn't get his Grade 13 and after Queen's. Oxford gave him success and it gave him theatre, which got him a job at the Old Vic. . . . Then he came back to Canada and became – a journalist. So of course he would want to create something that had been of such enormous value. Of course, he was trying to bring his best to its creation.

JENNIFER SURRIDGE
You must know he was prone to depression and suffered from what he called "the Black Dog." Brenda rode out his depressions. She encouraged

him to walk, and was at one time trying to get him involved with yoga. But he was not incapacitated by his depression. He could do everything he was supposed to do. I never knew he had depression until I had grown up.

He would go up and down in his feelings about the college. Sometimes he felt that he was just an innkeeper. Junior fellows either wanted to change the world, or they would come to him and say things like "I am going to Oxford for four months, can you rent out my room while I'm away?"

RD was not of the personality to take these things lightly. He spent a great deal of time thinking about his position at Massey. He felt there wasn't an appreciation among students of what he was doing. *And* he was having trouble with Dobson. *And* they didn't have enough money at the college, and he was never good at raising money. He had a lot of trouble sleeping – in fact, he had trouble with that throughout his life when he got upset. So in this period he would get incredibly tired, and they, the parents, had no way of getting away from the college.

ROSAMOND BAILEY

I had been in boarding school at Bishop Strachan School, and I was just ecstatic in 1963 when I could live at Massey and go to school by day. I thought Massey was my salvation. I was 16, and we had not lived together as a family since I was six and Miranda was 12 and went off to boarding school. This idea I had that we would all be back together and wasn't that great was a little naive. . . . In fact, living at Massey was very difficult for me.

In Peterborough, our house had a lot of grounds. At Massey, when I woke up in the morning, someone would be cleaning the windows of my bedroom.

It was difficult for my mother. The college was a creative effort as much as a novel or a play. That meant my father would want to come home and sit and stay in, and my mother would have been home all day and she would want to go out. There was a disjunction. . . . Dad was so caught up in the college, and in its problems such as money. This meant there were strains and stresses on my father that I only knew about later. You had the coming together of the college and the breakup of the family at the same time. It must have been very stressful for us. It was not obvious on a daily basis, but there were just these bitter encounters.

I'd bump into my mother coming in the kitchen door and I wouldn't apologize. I was a teenager!

MIRANDA DAVIES

I do remember Rosamond, when we were living at Massey College, slamming through the kitchen door and slamming it on Mum, which bruised Mum's finger. She felt that our Peterborough life had been uprooted and we had been dropped into this public world. There were these tensions. And Daddy couldn't bear the reproach, that we didn't think Massey was 100-percent perfect. . . . I used to have bad dreams about the residence at Massey being invaded and our privacy being overrun. I certainly remember the theft of our name plate.

BRENDA DAVIES

There was a break-in at Massey. They stole our antique barometer, which had been hanging in the front hall. So I started locking the door. You know, students feel they have a right to things. Students are larcenous, you know.

ROSAMOND BAILEY

One night, the three of us were in the kitchen at Massey; the parents had gone out. The engineers had a residence across the street, across Hoskin Avenue. They saw the three girls in the kitchen, because we had left the shutters open, and so they decided to do something goofy. They rolled a giant snowball across the road, and left it at the kitchen door.

Such antics upset RD and Brenda, who were dismayed that their girls were attracting mischief and attention. RD was like Mr. Webster in *Tempest-Tost*, who "came of a generation to which any girl, until she is married, is a kind of unexploded bomb."

JENNIFER SURRIDGE

He started off *years* before we began dating, talking about "Goatly," as in "When Goatly comes to call . . ." He'd make a big joke of it. Was RD intimidating to our dates? Omigod! He didn't think anyone was good enough for his daughters, and he was overcome by a sense of What Would People Think, by what was going on in the Master's lodging.

BRENDA DAVIES
Rob was very old-fashioned in some ways. All fathers are in this situation. But it was worse at the college. There were no secrets. We had to avoid scandal. If Miranda came in late, people would know.

MIRANDA·DAVIES
From 1964 to '65 I was having an affair with George, a young man I had met as an undergraduate. George was in advertising, a man of a terribly, terribly black disposition. He had been a magician's assistant, and I thought that part of his attitude to advertising was a manipulative one [tricking the public through illusion]. Of course, he didn't see it like that. It was a difficult relationship for me. I was going to his flat and then coming home late at night. I was coming into the Master's lodging at all hours. Which was a problem.

Daddy and Mum didn't say much to me. But they called George in to meet with them, and they asked him his intentions. The upshot was that I went on living at Massey and I broke up with him. This reflects Daddy's anxiety about his daughters and the idea of the "time bomb" of unmarried daughters – the terrifically public exposure of what this meant for him.

JENNIFER SURRIDGE
I don't remember a lot of occasions when dates came to pick us up!

In 1960, I was 18. I was lonely and they were away a lot. It's astounding how much they were away. . . . After I graduated from BSS, I got a job at the *Examiner* and I had a local boyfriend. He was a printer in the press room at the *Examiner*. They didn't like that. He was German, too, and they didn't like that, either.

RD and Brenda anticipated that at Massey their daughters would meet interesting college men.

MIRANDA DAVIES
The first few years at Massey, we all took part in the Gaudy Night. Daddy's lyrics for Mendelssohn's *Lift Thine Eyes* were so clever! There was one verse which contained the words "Sapere Aude, hark to the Bull," and I distributed the words so that on the bottom line I sang, "Sap- sap-, sap-," which was hilarious. That year was great. But . . .

The second year, Daddy wrote a skit. The great political brouhaha that year was about Quebec possibly seceding from Canada. The device for the skit was that Massey had seceded from the University of Toronto and become self-sufficient. The three of us, his daughters, were dressed for the Gaudy as three cleaning ladies of Massey. I was Italian, Jenny was Canadian and Rosamond was Polish, and there we were with our mops and pails. As Massey was cut off from the rest of the university, the only means of propagating the species within Massey was with the cleaning ladies. So the cleaning ladies were to discuss the junior fellows as possible mates, one being a chap who had introduced croquet to Massey.

Daddy had written a line for one of us to say – something about someone who knocked his balls into the pool. Well, we three girls went along with this without a peep, though my boyfriend George hated it. It was a very odd position to put one's daughters in. We were the tools of his wit. He was Pandarus. The underlying message was he wanted to marry his daughters off to junior fellows.

Soon enough, the Davies girls did make friends with Massey men.

MICHIEL HORN

I remember at his house [the Master's lodging] admiring his wonderful-looking books, many first editions, including a set of Nonesuch Dickens. I said, "Clearly, these cost a lot of money. Does your father get it from teaching at the University of Toronto?" Jennifer replied airily, "Oh, no, Daddy has an independent income." Some of the junior fellows resented the family's wealth, and thought, "Who does he think he is?" But of course, he knew who he was. I liked him a lot.

There was one junior fellow, Robin, who was a real man about town (he later died of AIDS), and the night of the Founder's Gaudy – a big event with Vincent Massey, Raymond Massey, Hart Massey – in Robin's rooms the mighty gathered: the stunning Barbara Amiel, later Lady Black; *The Globe and Mail*'s theatre critic, Herbert Whittaker; and on this night, Jennifer and Miranda were there. There was a great deal of drinking before dinner, and then Jennifer urged, she *dared*, me to ask Raymond Massey about life in the operating room. I had never watched television and was scarcely aware that he was Dr. Gillespie in *Doctor Kildare*. In any case, after dinner we all went to the Common Room and I went up and asked my question. He was very frosty and said, "That's just my television personality." But from this, Jennifer realized that I was agreeable to things, and we developed a neo-platonic friendship.

Massey at the time was an all-male college and got a reputation early on for attracting gay men, but each of the daughters at one time or another was dating one of the Massey fellows. I was invited to things where Jennifer wanted an escort, and I went to the Davieses' for dinner on three or four occasions. The Davieses were always extremely correct and affable about this. And I had the good sense when I was there to let Robertson Davies do the talking. I enjoyed him – and understood he was Master in more ways than one.

In 1968, when Robertson Davies sold *The Peterborough Examiner*, several fellows speculated about how much money he would have made from that sale. Their idea was two to six million dollars [in fact, Arthur, RD and Fred's widow Kathryn, sold it for $3.1 million]. Clearly there was a lot of mazooma about. This explained how the Davieses lived in such quiet, understated elegance. His wife drove a Jag. Everything was in quiet, good taste – almost excessively so!

In 1963, Jennifer began to date Tom Surridge, a graduate student in psychology from Jamaica who was in residence at Massey. Their relationship caused a stir around the college, and in the Master's lodging.

ROSAMOND BAILEY
For Tom and Jenny it was extremely difficult. We sensed that we were watched all the time.

JENNIFER SURRIDGE
At the time Miranda was going out with George, Tom and I were working on our marriage plans. Tom had moved out of Massey because it was not easy for him, he was marrying the Master's daughter. . . .

When Tom and I bought a car before we were married, the parents nearly had a fit – imagine: to make a commitment to buy a car when we weren't married! It seemed like the end of the bloody world. Everything that happened in the family was just a trauma. If we had been in a normal family house, it wouldn't have been such a big deal. . . .

RD used to say, "When Goatly comes to ask for your hand . . ." So when Tom asked me if he should go and see my father, I said yes. Tom made an appointment with RD's secretary, Moira Whalon. She made it in the afternoon and Tom said, "Is it possible to make this in the evening?"

ROSAMOND BAILEY

I remember when my sister and Tom decided they were going to tell my parents that they were getting married . . . they were so tense, the atmosphere was vibrating. But the evening they were to tell them, my parents decided at the last minute to go out to the movies. This was horrific for Jenny and Tom, who had to get ready to do it all over again.

RD played a role in planning his middle daughter's wedding.

JENNIFER SURRIDGE

We had wonderful music at the wedding. RD chose it all. I remember standing outside the chapel as I was to go in and be married, and Miranda and RD were having an argument about which beat to go in on! I said, "Oh come *on!* It doesn't matter! Let's just get married!"

ROSAMOND BAILEY

I remember the wonderful party we had for them, with good food and music and dancing in the Common Room. That was an absolutely wonderful occasion – Jenny's wedding, where Dad was Master, King of the Castle.

When Jenny and Tom split up for a time, and Jenny was in England with Sassy, Tom asked me out to lunch. He was lonely and I was Jenny's sister, and I guess he wanted to talk. So we went out for lunch. We did not even bring up the subject of Jenny.

Later, I went to Dad's office to borrow a book on George Bernard Shaw. Dad said, "I'll lend it to you if you tell me what Tom said about Jenny."

I said, "He told me nothing. I have nothing to tell you."

He said, "Then I'm not lending you the book."

My mum was furious. This was very unusual. She said in a low voice, "Now I know why young people leave home."

This was what made living with him so difficult. You were either with him or against him. It made the bar pretty high. He once called one of my former boyfriends "the Pig." He could take up a bias against someone as an expression of loyalty, but underneath his reactions to people were far more nuanced. My mother thought it was wonderful that he could denigrate people who'd hurt his children! She hadn't had a father to protect her, so she thought this was protective . . . but there was a problem: if you made up with someone, and you were again happy with them, RD had meanwhile backed himself into a corner. . . . Dad was so fascinating, we wanted him to think well of us. He had such a high standard, such high ideals of relationships. Love. Honour. Chivalry. You wanted to live up to that, to be that thing which he could imagine . . . You pretended to be something you weren't.

JENNIFER SURRIDGE
Some of RD's codes were very, very old-fashioned. When I was a child I walked into the dining room one morning and he told me, "First of all, you haven't washed your face. Second, your blouse and skirt don't match. Go upstairs and change!" Later, when I wore miniskirts, he had a bloody fit! By then I was in my twenties and married!

ROSAMOND BAILEY
There were rules, and you were expected to know them. Dad said there was "a language of socks." A gentleman's socks were long; my father wore garters. My first husband, John Cunnington, when he was a medical student, came to visit, and he made two impressions, one bad and one good. He came over in white socks . . . which was horrific. White socks connote athletes! And he took off his shoes at the door. I suppose gentlemen have servants who will clean up after them, so they aren't supposed to take off their shoes. . . .

But the other thing John did was right. At Massey we had a cook, and John would always greet the cook and say, "Thank you." My mother liked that. My mother said, "It's so important to thank the staff."

There were all these rules which we knew, and not everyone else did. It was very anxiety-creating, because sooner or later someone would blow it. It was my job in the family to poke fun at this and cast doubt on it and undermine it. Or was this a case of my trying to provoke feeling out of him? Whatever it was, I paid a high price for this. He was identi-fied with the college, and if I cast doubt on it, that was to reject him. He began to see it as a personal attack. He was always in control – and when he wasn't, he had a very cold anger.

MIRANDA DAVIES
We did not lack for sexual education. I was given a sex manual – by both my parents – when I was the age of 12. But I also remember my father saying he was ashamed of being so Old Ontario and puritanical to mind so much about Rosamond's pregnancy. But you see, he was then in the public eye. We were all in the public eye. Earlier on in our lives, the message was, "Please come to us if you are ever in trouble, do not go to an abortionist." But when it happened, the treatment was very different: the shut door.

ROSAMOND BAILEY
I was at Bishop's University, and by Christmas in 1968, I was pregnant and it became more and more clear to me. John and I decided to get married.

I said, "Let's just do it and tell them after."

John said, "You have to tell your parents."

I said, "Are you *kidding?* You don't know them."

He said, "No, we have to do the honourable thing."

So we went back in February to Toronto to see them, at home, at Massey. We sat down after dinner. None of the others were there. They probably thought we were going to announce that we would be travelling in Europe together in the summer. . . . We sat down and John said, "We have come with good news. Rosamond is pregnant and we are getting married."

My mother burst into tears. To see my mother cry, RD was even more furious. Then he said, "You're not the first little Welsh girl to whom this has happened."

BRENDA DAVIES
"You're not the first little Welsh girl" – that was Rob responding to a nasty shock. That voice sounds like Florence. Florence didn't like the Welsh.

JENNIFER SURRIDGE
When Rosamond got pregnant, the household nearly collapsed. The parents had hissy fits. It was 90 percent because of the college: that People Would Know. It was such a big deal. It caused them to have a total bird. It shocked all of us to the core.

MIRANDA DAVIES

I remember talking to him in the laundry room of the Master's lodging at Masscy. And he said, "I wish I could be different. I wish I were not so Presbyterian. I cannot help it."

ROSAMOND BAILEY

Then – this was February – Dad said, "You've got to get married right away. The baby won't be born until August."

John, who was 21, said, "No. I am graduating in May and it will be a celebration." For him, it wasn't to be a hush-hush affair, but a celebration.

To my dad's credit, he said, "I have a vision of you walking down the aisle, great with child, in running shoes, and this does not make me proud of myself." In other words, a vision of the ridiculous, that I and therefore *he* had been made to look ridiculous – but he was *not* proud of this reaction. He was trying not to respond that way.

All this stuff was going on at home and RD was writing *Fifth Business*. When I went to an analyst and told her that the man was different in fact than in his novels, the analyst didn't believe this could be his way of seeing the world.

JENNIFER SURRIDGE

In 1969, we'd had this big family drama. And in 1970, there was this book!

Chapter 26

FIFTH BUSINESS

On May 10, 1969, Rosamond Davies married John Cunnington in the Massey College chapel. A month later, RD and Brenda moved to Clair and Amy Stewart's country house in Caledon, where RD finished the manuscript of *Fifth Business*.

BRENDA DAVIES
He read it to me as he went along. He was ready to change it at my suggestion, but I only made a few, at a practical level, such as a character needing a little more explanation or background. I was not surprised at the content of *Fifth Business*. But I was thrown all in a heap by how good it was.

While RD wrote, Brenda oversaw the construction of a Davies country house on land that the Stewarts had sold them, overlooking the Humber River Valley.

CLAIR STEWART
Fortunately, the architect was a great friend, Bill Fleury. You can't tell most architects what you want. Bill Fleury was the exact opposite, anxious to give you what you wanted.

Rosamond and John's first child, Christopher Cunnington, was born on August 31.

JENNIFER SURRIDGE
Rosamond had refused to be married right away, which was another Big Deal. And RD didn't want baby Christopher brought to the college because people would see how big he was. And yet RD was writing

about everything! Here was this tight-laced person who would go into his room and write about everything! *Everything!*

The book that would so astonish the Davies children, and the world, was written in the form of a letter to an authority figure – ostensibly the head-master of a boy's school, Colborne College, modelled on Upper Canada College. The narrator hero, Dunstan Ramsay, a teacher at Colborne, is responding to a profile in the school newspaper, because he feels that the article's author has underestimated his true character and accomplish-ments. In fact, RD once remarked that he was amazed that so few people realized that Ramsay was writing to God.

STEPHEN BONNYCASTLE (English professor, now at Royal Military College, Kingston)
I taught at Trent from 1971 to '72 and my next-door neighbour was Gordon Roper. When *Fifth Business* came out, he said, "Stephen, you've got to read this book." I did, and I was bowled over. I loved it.

Then Wilfred Cude wrote an article in the *Journal of Canadian Studies* about Dunstan Ramsay being a saint. I thought this was so wrongheaded I had to reply. To me it seems an artificial part of the book that Dunstan is so offended by an article on his life in the *Colborne College Times* on his career. It's only a school paper! Why should Dunstan sit down and write a long, outraged reply – the text of the novel – because some young person underestimated him?

As Master of Massey College, RD had spent the previous decade living among people who underestimated him. But there were other factors that spurred him to write.

ASHLEY THOMSON (M.A. thesis)
This plot had been simmering in Davies's mind throughout the 1960s, but for most of the decade he was unable to do anything concrete on it, for other commitments took up his time. . . . It was only in the early summer of 1969 that Davies felt himself able to get down to *Business*. He began by collecting extensive notes on the subjects that would inter-est him in the novel – rural Ontario at the turn of the century, the war, magic, hagiography. . . . Even so, as he confessed to the Montreal *Gazette*, when he began writing, "events and characters develop(ed)

unexpectedly (so that) the ends of my novels are often a surprise to me." For example, "*Fifth Business* was to be much more a novel of revenge than in fact it was finally."

A few weeks after the birth of his first grandchild, RD delivered the *Fifth Business* manuscript to his secretary, Moira Whalon, for fact-checking and copy editing. In December it was ready for Macmillan of Canada, where it was read by Ramsay Derry, a friend of Miranda Davies who had joined the firm as an editor.

RAMSAY DERRY

I recall a conversation with Rob, who said, "I'll be sending in my manuscript, and I've done something different. I don't know if you're going to like it."

I thought, "Oh dear." I thought of him then as a grand magnificent has-been. I thought, "'Something different'? Gosh, what if he falls flat on his face?" So when the manuscript arrived, I was rather anxious.

I took the manuscript with me on the train to Montreal. I was about thirty-five pages in and I had that sense of "Ahhh, this is the real thing." The hair really did stand up on the back of my neck.

I came back from Montreal and I came into the office Monday and I said, "Robertson Davies has done a magnificent novel. Can I phone him and tell him?" [Macmillan's publisher] John Gray was very cautious. He said, "We'd better get more readings." So poor RD didn't hear from us for weeks.

ASHLEY THOMSON

The reaction of the other members of Macmillan's manuscript committee who make the decision to publish was far less enthusiastic. According to Derry, "They did not like it very much," for it seemed too enigmatic, too "different." No doubt their attitude was affected by the news which came in shortly after Derry handed in his report that Scribner's, the American publisher of *A Mixture of Frailties*, had turned down the manuscript, according to Derry, on the grounds that it was not one of Davies's "funny novels" and that it "wasn't of interest to anyone."

Despite their misgivings, the members of the manuscript committee did not feel that they could go that far. *Fifth Business* was, after all, "a new Davies book" and people would want to read it. On March 15, 1970, the decision to publish was conveyed to the author at a meeting between him and the committee convened at Toronto's exclusive York Club.

RAMSAY DERRY
By then, Viking New York had also said yes. So we had our meeting in the York Club with the Canadian and English Macmillan publishers. It was the end of the day and we were having drinks in those round tables in the club. The conversation was going round and round.

ASHLEY THOMSON
Evidently, everyone hummed and hawed. . . . What in fact [Macmillan executives] would have him do was explain his title. When this finally came out, Davies appeared to have been expecting it.

RAMSAY DERRY
Alan Maclean, managing director of Macmillan London, wanted an explanation of the term "fifth business." I remember the expression on Rob's face. As he fished into his pocket and pulled out a scrap of paper, he looked like a conjurer about to startle us. He passed the scrap around and it was written in his beautiful italic handwriting.

On the scrap was a definition of "fifth business," its source cited as Thomas Overskou's *Den Danske Skueplads*, an obscure account of nineteenth-century theatre in Denmark.

RAMSAY DERRY
I didn't know at the time that the quote was bogus. But I knew he was capable of that. I'd read the novels and I knew he was capable of mimicry. It didn't surprise me years later when I found out it was false.

Then the editing process began.

ASHLEY THOMSON
Robertson Davies did not like editors. He seemed to feel that John Gray at Macmillan was trying to tamper with his text. He pointed out that Viking in the United States had not made suggestions.

RAMSAY DERRY

And RD could not always control his disposition to make a joke. He had created characters such as Libby Doe and Gloria Mundy . . . Ah yes, those were the unfortunate jokes that got in. There were more like that – false rings. I do not recall anyone in the office making more marks on the manuscript than I, and I was uneasy as I did so. I was his daughter's friend. I thought, "Can he take this?" But he was totally professional, he responded with amazing speed and either made the changes or said, "No, no, this is why this is there . . ." He didn't accept all my suggestions, he just considered them. There were no big issues, but lots of to-ing and fro-ing . . .

Within a year of the book being published, a young man doing library science, Ashley Thomson, said, "I'd like to do my M.A. on the making of a bestseller. Can I come and talk to you?" I said yes and RD said yes. I told him, "The one thing you must be able to do as an editor is you must not be afraid to ask stupid questions. That is the editor's job. Just ask." Then he went to interview RD. RD told him, "Editors are damn stupid people who ask damn stupid questions."

For example, on the American [Viking] author proof of *Fifth Business*, galley page 43, Davies's text had been edited so that Dunstan Ramsay remarked: "As a historian by training . . ." RD's handwriting has corrected the correction, in red pen, to "As *an* historian by training," with a note: "Ramsay would certainly have written 'an historian' so please forget your house style & change it." On page 71, the proofreader wrote beside a passage about the aged Mrs. Dempster, "OK? She's 71 and lived about 10 years after she was isolated." RD's written response: "Dear editor, 71 is not really old – especially to people over 50. How old are you? Under 30, I'll bet. May God preserve you for another 60 years. RD"

ASHLEY THOMSON

It was decided to allow Viking to produce the book for all three companies in order to effect economies of scale. Directly and then indirectly, this decision was to prove to be the most controversial one taken in connection with the book. The item that may have suffered directly from the arrangement with Viking was the dust jacket.

The jacket featured a stylized portrait of a magician in coffin grey, based on the image of a Chicago card shark rather than the Magnus Eisengrim character in the book. Perhaps trying to shock the graduate student in his office, RD jokingly remarked that the book jacket had been designed by "a trendy young Negro in pink pants and a purple shirt with his hair in rollers – a sort of flower child."

ASHLEY THOMSON

When he commented on the book jacket design, I said, "Well, what would you have put on it?" He said, "Breasts! Breasts! *Breasts!*"

That put me on the floor. I tend to encourage people when I talk to them. I'm a good audience. I egged him on. People can be more forthcoming when I just go with the flow. When he got going, I glommed onto the outrageous jokes.

Despite their misgivings about the book jacket, RD and his Canadian publisher got on with the job of promoting the new book with the Viking jacket design. Acceptance by the Book-of-the-Month Club and the Literary Guild made that easier. And on October 29, 1970, Macmillan hosted a publication party, inviting about 150 friends and media people to a party at a floating restaurant on the lakefront – roughly the place where the *Fifth Business* character Boy Staunton commits suicide by driving into the water. A stone is later found in the corpse's mouth.

RAMSAY DERRY

I was determined that *Fifth Business* would have a big launch party. As party favours we handed out lake pebbles stamped with RD's signature. Everybody came, including [the prominent novelist] Morley Callaghan, who had been in seclusion. He came in a well-timed arrival, flanked by his two sons, made a sub-regal passage through the party and then departed. I recognized that Callaghan sensed he was being challenged!

Canadian reviewers were at first chary with their praise.

WILLIAM FRENCH

I was appointed literary editor of *The Globe* in 1960. The general opinion was that Davies was old-fashioned and stuffy. . . . It was really *Fifth Business* that attracted my attention. . . . I wrote: "Davies is so heroically old-fashioned, so impressively erudite, so puckishly disdainful of current fashion, that he will not only dazzle his faithful admirers, but may successfully woo the uncommitted." I didn't realize at the time that he didn't like that review.

RD remained chilly towards French for years.

JIM DUGAN (former student)
Davies was my thesis adviser between 1976 and '78. . . . In one gathering we got onto the subject of capital punishment. He was clearly in favour. Someone said it was just a form of legalized revenge. Davies moved in quickly with, "So what's wrong with revenge? It's the most deeply satisfying of all human emotions." *Fifth Business* is a great revenge saga.

The best revenge was provided by the British and American reviews of *Fifth Business*, as journalist Peter C. Newman wrote in 1973.

PETER C. NEWMAN
The New Yorker said it was elegant, *Esquire* saw it as being "as masterfully executed as anything in the history of the novel," Saul Bellow claimed it had taught him much, John Fowles looked on with admiration. . . . The international response boggled Davies's acquaintances. "My God," said a fellow professor, "it's fulfilling Rob's sanest dreams."

MARTIN HUNTER
Although he had come to Trinity College as a published writer in the 1960s, the grandees of the English Department were very mean to him. Then suddenly Rob wrote a novel which got a favourable review in *The New York Times* and the grandees had to eat crow. He was quite happy for them to eat crow. He was acknowledged by McLuhan and Frye. Because of the Vietnam War we were getting a lot of American students at the university by the early 1970s. They were coming for McLuhan, and Frye – and Davies. He became a star. And people running the university noticed. They like stars, because that helps them attract money.

As a star, RD was suddenly in demand by the media. CBC's Peter Gzowski, host of *This Country in the Morning*, a popular national radio program, interviewed him together with an eminent psychiatrist and poet, Dr. Vivian Rakoff.

VIVIAN RAKOFF
The Deptford trilogy books were different from his other books. . . .
They, the earlier books, were colonial pastiches of Edwardian literary
genres. They were jokey, insidey. Everybody was in costume. They were
jocular and too sparky by half. I interviewed RD on a CBC radio show
hosted by Peter Gzowski and asked him why the Deptford books were
different from the previous novels. And he replied, "People had to die."

MARTIN HUNTER
When *Fifth Business* came out, I wrote to him and he replied, "You
know there were a lot of things I couldn't write about while my parents
were alive." RD's father was a very vigorous, energetic, successful man.
He married a Canadian of United Empire Loyalist and Pennsylvania
Dutch extraction. She was probably the one who was encouraging to
her sons and interested in the arts, but as Rupert became more successful she was left at home . . . like Leola Cruickshank in *Fifth Business*.

Those closest to RD agree that he felt freer to write after Rupert's death,
but they reject the notion that *Fifth Business* is autobiographical.

BRENDA DAVIES
Was Florence Leola? Martin Hunter would say that, wouldn't he? People
love to pin down characters in novels to real people. Write this down:
"Writers take from their accumulated experience to create characters.
They get a great deal from their unconscious."

MICHAEL PETERMAN
In his writing, RD is always talking about the big spiritual adventure. . . .
Mrs. Ramsay in *Fifth Business* is probably closely modelled on Florence
Davies. The story is always Davies as hero-adventurer, constrained by
people who fail to see his imaginative qualities.

Still, when the novel came out, other family members recognized archetypes.

KATE BRAY
There's a huge amount in Robertson's writing that just shrieks of
family lore.

MARTIN HUNTER

When I visited Arthur at his home in Kingston, I do remember Arthur said, "You know everything in Rob's books comes from his life." I do remember that.

Family members did agree that it was time to reassess RD.

MICHAEL DAVIES

Only with *Fifth Business*, when we all got a copy, was there a collective realization that Robertson had hit the big time. I remember that was the watershed. Before that, I remember, Rob wrote books . . . but I don't think I read the novels.

The family members who were most astonished were his own daughters.

JENNIFER SURRIDGE

When *Fifth Business* came out, I went to Sassy Waddell's cottage for the weekend. It was cold and rainy . . . not a nice weekend, so I read a lot. I read *Fifth Business* and I could not believe he had thought of all these things. All these people doing and feeling these things.

I thought my father was trying to be the most straight-laced person in the world – and it was very irritating. He had been a more open person in Peterborough. By the time we were living at Massey he revealed himself only to Mum. So I had no idea that he had thought of these things! These feelings! Mrs. Dempster in the pit having sex with the tramp! I was so amazed, I called him and I said, "I cannot believe you wrote this book! I am so impressed." It just blew me away.

For a while, writers of RD's daughters' and his students' generation remained skeptical.

GEORGE JONAS (writer)

In some ways he was an outsider in the 1960s and 1970s. . . . Imagine, being one of the significant authors in English Canada, and yet your name is not mentioned in Peggy Atwood's book *Survival* [her critical analysis of Canadian literature]. . . . If Peggy was in tune with her times, then RD would have seemed out of tune with his times.

MARGARET ATWOOD
When I wrote *Survival*, *Fifth Business* was a new book and I didn't catch up with it until after I had written *Survival*. I wish I had.

Because of this generational gap, *Fifth Business* failed to win Canada's biggest book prize. The 1970 Governor General's Award for Fiction went instead to *The New Ancestors*, a first novel by a young man named Dave Godfrey, published by a small press, House of Anansi.

RAMSAY DERRY
The House of Anansi was bringing out Margaret Atwood, Dennis Lee. There was no doubt that RD carried the old Canadian imperial sensibility. . . . When Dave Godfrey's *The New Ancestors* won the G-G, it was a zeitgeist decision.

ASHLEY THOMSON
Davies's reaction reflected a mixture of amusement, disdain and indifference. As far as he is concerned, literary politics more than literary quality determine the winner. At present, "the *Tamarack Review* crowd" is responsible for selection, and he has it from an informed source that "this bunch would rather commit mass suicide than give me any kind of prize!"

True enough, Kildare Dobbs, a co-founder of the *Tamarack Review*, had reviewed the novel in the Spring 1971 issue in terms both admiring and mocking.

> A brilliant staging of the WASP Imperial myth . . . what prompts the outpouring is Ramsay's anger at the illiterate tone of an attempt at his biography in the school's *College Chronicle*. . . . The whole novel can be read as a kind of Upper Canadian dream.

RD had his revenge on Dobbs not long after.

KILDARE DOBBS
I liked Massey College and I wrote to Davies, "Why don't you give me rooms at Massey?" After the review came out, I went to a book launch

at Massey. And the Master burst out of the door between his office and
the Common Room and charged me like a bull and said, "I'm very surprised to see *you* here."

I said, "I like it here!"

He said, "I've a mind to write the papers and tell them you've asked
me for a room."

I said, "I wish you would."

He said, "You're not welcome here!" and he rushed off.

But the Toronto literary scene was too small for the feud to continue.

KILDARE DOBBS
About a year or two after Robertson Davies had driven me forth and
said I was not welcome at Massey, I was sitting a place away from him
at dinner at the Albany Club. The woman between us said, "Do you
know one another?" And Davies said, "Oh yes, there's been a little difficulty about a book review" . . . and I realized he was hurt. And I didn't
want to hurt him. So we got along that evening – we were well house-
trained. It was a kind of reconciliation.

A couple of years ago, I was staying with friends in Oslo, and Liv,
my hostess, who was 90 at the time, was reading Robertson Davies. She
reads in four or five languages. She said to me, "Do you know this man?"

I said "Yes, and I don't like him."

She said, "You ought to, he's a good writer."

MARGARET ATWOOD
Years later, when I was in Norway, a publisher told me that *Fifth Business*
was "an egg of a book." He meant a whole, perfect, book.

Chapter 27

DEPTFORD PRODUCES
A TRILOGY

RD always insisted that he didn't set out to write a second trilogy but that the insistent demands of his publisher, his readers and the characters he had brought to life pushed him to surprise himself. By this time, he was surprising a lot of people.

DAVID CRONENBERG (former University of Toronto student and then a fledgling film director)
It was around 1969 and I was shooting *Crimes of the Future*. The architecture of the buildings I was shooting in was very important. I wanted the space of Massey. My remembering is that *Fifth Business* hadn't been published because I seem to recall thinking that he, Robertson Davies, was a playwright *manqué*, a bit faded – that he'd had his day. But still, I thought of him as a lovely character. I liked the university and the idea that I would wind up at a place like Massey College. I liked the idea of a "Master" – somebody of great education and depth and culture.

One day as I was shooting in the quad there – me operating the Arriflex camera on a tripod, and with one or two actors, and no sync sound – *he* wandered by. He asked if he could have a peek through the lens. He was twinkly, very twinkly. I felt he was completely benign, supportive and curious. Little did I know that I would later read a book with a cinematographer as a character (*World of Wonders*) – but I believe that character was based on Ingmar Bergman, not me.

I thought it was a very nice irony that he should explode with *Fifth Business* and become *hot*. A whole new career at his age. That was a nice lesson – that he suddenly emerged as a new creature, a new butterfly. You'd have thought he was the Master of Massey College and that was it . . . and you'd be *wrong*.

RD was already at work on a sequel to *Fifth Business*. His publishers dubbed it *Sixth Business* and urged him to complete it for publication in 1972.

RAMSAY DERRY

There was pressure to produce a second book fast. He always was working hard and was used to working to deadline for newspapers. I don't remember us setting a schedule, but that may have been the case. When the manuscript came in [April 1972], it was originally called *Son and Stranger*, which I rather liked, but others didn't.

In the bottom of my heart I was very uneasy with that novel. It was filled with interesting stuff, but I felt it didn't have the narrative strength of *Fifth Business*. I desperately wanted it to be a success. But I knew it would do nobody any good – me or Davies or the company – if I expressed uncertainty.

There was the big quarrel about finding the right title. I was roiling around with *The Manticore* much more. And with this book there were more areas where we said, "Will you reconsider this? Will you do this differently? Is this the way an industrialist's funeral would have happened?"

That novel had a lot of social history. It was important to get David Staunton's story right – get too much wrong, and the magic of fiction is undermined.

Almost certainly by then the publisher of Macmillan, John Gray, had retired. I felt it was all on me. I haven't looked at the book since then. I don't know if I let him down. I was unhappy with it at the time.

Like *Tempest-Tost*, whose writing was preceded by the death of Florence Davies, and *Fifth Business*, which was written after the deaths of Vincent Massey and Rupert Davies, *The Manticore* was created as RD learned of the death of his third "father," Tyrone Guthrie, on May 15, 1971. *The Manticore* was published in October 1972.

RAMSAY DERRY

The launch of *The Manticore* was a lugubrious affair. The party favours were gingerbread men flown in from St. Gall in Switzerland. It was held at Halloween, at the Mackenzie House right next to our office. It was a narrow little house, and the party did not get off the ground. People were all tumbling around. I recall an excruciating exchange between Marian Engel and Davies. She was a young writer coming to pay obeisance. Davies did not handle it well. He was condescending . . . tactless. I was pained for him. I was pained for her. I remember thinking, "Oooooh." I was fond and admiring of Davies, but I knew he could be capable of social misfires.

HOWARD ENGEL
I don't remember any unpleasantness. I do remember Marian thought he was rather frosty and unapproachable, but most people thought that. As far as I can recall, it didn't rankle Marian.

The Manticore follows the attempts by David Staunton, son of the deceased Boy Staunton (he who threw the snowball that launched *Fifth Business*) to deal with his own alcoholism and his conflicted feelings about his father. He sorts this out through a Jungian therapist, Dr. Johanna von Haller.

VIVIAN RAKOFF
The novel is always a rearranged piece of autobiography. . . . The writing of a novel has been called "permission to confess in public." . . . What writers write about tells you what they are preoccupied with; what RD wrote about was unmasking. Now, the mind rarely produces nonsense. It produces puzzles, but not nonsense. So here is a gent who seems to be in costume, the cape and the swagger. This is a declaration of a disguise and inside is something more authentic, more vulnerable. . . . Davies could tell truths about his parents, about the family, because he was given the Fool's permission of the aesthetic form. He could tell truths that he could not tell in real life.

RD might have liked this notion; he and Brenda had been studying Jungian theory since the late 1950s. But this had not altered his capacity for intellectual contradictions. At the very time that he was producing a book in which two powerful, intelligent women help a man to understand his own soul, the Master of Massey was devoting considerable energy to resisting the admission of women fellows to the college.

BRUCE BOWDEN (Massey junior fellow)
I think the critical acclaim from his novels made him more confident in dealing with people like me. . . . My first year, 1971–72, was the year the college decided to go co-ed. Davies was vociferously against this

idea. "If you accept the principle of separate bedrooms," he would say, "you must accept the principle of separate floors. And if you accept the principle of separate floors then you must accept the principle of separate residences." Of course, most of the junior fellows did not accept the first premise.

MARGARET ATWOOD

Women weren't allowed into Massey, but you could be snuck in after hours illegally. Rumours went round, some untrue, that Robertson Davies glued hairs on the doors to see if they had been opened in the night.

JOHN BROWNE (Massey junior fellow)

In my first year I was invited into the Master's study and was served sherry and was told that the admission of women was against the founder's wishes. . . . When I pressed him – Would it lead to the withdrawal of the founder's money? – he would get into vague things about the Massey *family's* wishes. Then, I suggested, we should talk to the family. . . . It was clear in my conversations that RD was not prepared to go to the corporation to ask about the admission of women.

Bruce Bowden, later registrar of Trinity College, and James Carley, later professor of English at the University of Toronto, were junior fellows at Massey in 1970 and attended a question-and-answer session in the Upper Library. About thirty students confronted RD, who responded with the fable of the camel who put its nose into the camel-driver's tent. Meeting no resistance, the camel eased in a foot, then another . . . Soon the camel dominated the tent. There was no room for the camel-driver.

JAMES CARLEY

Of course there were objections to this comment from the junior fellows. I do remember that meeting as somewhat confrontational. But RD's stance was not so outrageous; there were still single-sex colleges at other universities, and at Oxford well into the 1990s.

BRUCE BOWDEN

Finally Ian Scott, the incoming Don of Hall (the leader of the junior fellows), and Bill Fong – *not* one of Davies's admirers – decided to contact the Massey family directly. They wrote letters to the younger generation of Masseys, arguing that women should be admitted. By now the relations between the Master and Colin Friesen on one side and students on the other side had really deteriorated. There was a lot of tension. We were at loggerheads. There may have been talk of our going to Claude Bissell and asking for a new Master. By this time W.A.C. Dobson was gone, but he had created cliques at the college. So some of the senior fellows also held it against Davies that he was implicated in the hatcheting of Dobson.

In spring 1973, I was elected 1973–74 Don of Hall . . . I knew that the consensus was there had to be democratic change. I had no contact with RD that summer. But Douglas LePan and Robert Finch came to speak to me and went out of their way to say there did not need to be tensions. LePan was particularly pressing. It could be that LePan was protecting his old friend RD, but what he said to me was there were many senior fellows who agreed that things had to change.

In May 1973, an hour before the annual meeting of the Massey Corporation, RD invited me and the outgoing don, Ian Scott, to his office. He sat us down and told us that he had received a letter from the Massey family that stated that they would not object to having women enter the college. Then he turned on us very fiercely, sitting forward in his chair, and, raising his voice, said that we had "ruined the college." He asked, did we know what we had done, and said it was a great tragedy.

When I spoke of this years later, Moira Whalon's reaction was that it was not true: Davies had welcomed women. Ian Scott and I started to wonder if he had been play-acting with us. . . .

The report that came to us from the May 1973 meeting of the corporation was that RD walked in, read out the letter from the Massey family – the one which undercut his position – and then declared his support *for* the admission of women.

And even as RD was defending the Massey policy against the admission of women, he was championing the careers of certain women scholars.

ANN SADDLEMYER (scholar and later Master of Massey College) I came to the U of T in 1971 when the Drama Centre was still young. I was cross-appointed to the English Department at Victoria College and the Drama Centre, and was put on the search committee for the centre's next director.

Rob recognized that I was new, and trying to prove myself in a new world as a full professor. I liked Rob very much, and from the beginning, though I was also in awe of him. We had both lived in Kingston, both gone to Queen's and both been students in England. We had had to adapt to a new (old) world. I had not been a student at U of T either. . . We were both outsiders. We both felt uneasy about being at the university, and Rob recognized this in me. The only parallel I can draw is with the Irish going to England. You know you'll never belong.

As I say, I was on this Drama Centre search committee, and at our first meeting Rob and Clifford Leech of the English Department met me at the door of his office and said, "We want to put *you* on our list of candidates." Then they sent me away – and I was made the director. I am pretty sure it was Rob who decided I would be the new director. He was absolutely not a sexist – he was *not* an old-fashioned man. I could always count on him.

As editorial writers from *The Peterborough Examiner* could have explained, RD was quite capable of reversing a position and arguing eloquently for the other side. Students found this confusing.

BRUCE BOWDEN

I still do not know how to square the RD I knew at the college with the RD of the fiction that was starting to come out. Or the private man. When we went to his residence for dinner, he could defer to his wife as hostess – or engineer conversation so that it would flow towards her background in theatre, where she had expertise. And clearly he thought very highly of his daughters. Although we at Massey thought of RD as a misogynist, he did not smother his family.

That fall, when I took up my position as Don of Hall, RD contacted me and we acted from the start as if we were a team. . . . RD and I worked all that year to ensure that the transition to the admission of women went well. I really came to like and respect this man.

VINCENT del BUONO (former Massey junior fellow)

You'd have to be careful with him. He was very provocative and you'd have to be sensitive enough to decide if he was just trying to get you going or if he was sincere. He was always crafting. I'm not sure that his opposition to women in the college was just a case of his being true to Vincent Massey. By the time I was in residence, women in the college was a complete non-issue for him. People would tease him – Bruce Bowden and others would tell war stories about the fight to get women in – but RD had moved on.

While RD could reverse an ideological stand with relative speed, it took much longer for him to forget an emotional confrontation, as John Fraser, then a *Globe and Mail* journalist, noted.

JOHN FRASER
My first visit to the York Club with RD, he saw John Browne and crossed the street to avoid him.

And it took him years to understand how profoundly the institution of the university was changing.

ANN SADDLEMYER
At the time, it wouldn't have occurred to him that I would one day be Master of Massey College. Yet when I did, he was enormously support-ive and generous, while appropriately keeping his distance.

When the second Deptford novel came out, Canadian reviews were mixed. RD didn't care – or so reported Patrick Scott of *The Toronto Star* in a February 13, 1973, article titled "Public is behind Robertson Davies even if the literary mafia is not."

PATRICK SCOTT
"I know they must regard me as something of a dilettante," he says without visible rancor. "I don't frequent the 'in' cocktail parties for one thing. . . . And I don't write in a garret or on a grant; in fact I don't even write full-time, which may be my worse sin of all." But if Davies is not discernibly bitter over the tepid reception accorded his newest novels by the Canadian critical establishment – *The Star*'s Kildare Dobbs initially found *The Manticore* "curiously dry and cerebral" but later said it was one of the year's best novels; *The Globe and Mail*'s William French yawned simply that it was "tedious" – he certainly is bemused, as he can well afford to be.

Scott's article went on to cite popular and foreign reaction, which as with *Fifth Business* was far more adulatory.

> Exceeds the Mark
> *The Manticore*, which was published by Macmillan only last fall, has exceeded the 6,500 mark in Canadian bookstore sales (3,000 books in Canada is considered an authentic hit), has been bought by 15,000 more Canadians through the Book of the Month Club and has been on *The Star*'s own bestseller list for 13 consecutive weeks. In addition, and perhaps even more significant, sales of *The Manticore* in the United States have passed 13,000 – a remarkable American reception for a distinctively Canadian novel. . . ." Anthony Burgess reflected in the *Chicago Tribune* that "*The Manticore* is one of the most elegant novels to come out of North America in a very long time – a masterpiece."

The Manticore was named to the shortlist for the 1972 Governor General's Award for Fiction. Critic Robert Fulford was on the jury.

ROBERT FULFORD
There were two other people on the jury, and I can't recall their faces or even their sexes, but I remember what they said. They said, "*The Manticore* just isn't as good a book as *Fifth Business*." I told them, "But he didn't get the prize for *Fifth Business!*" And besides, *The Manticore* was better than the other books we had on the shortlist that year. Here, he'd been deprived of the one award that he *had* to win. My arguments swayed them. He got the Governor General's Award. Of course, he was probably still disgruntled, and well he should have been.

By the mid-1970s, RD produced World of Wonders, the third novel in what has become known as the Deptford trilogy. By the time he delivered the World of Wonders manuscript, his editor, Ramsay Derry, had left Macmillan and Douglas Gibson had taken over the Davies file. With the exception of The Lyre of Orpheus, Gibson would remain RD's fiction editor for the rest of his life.

DOUG GIBSON

I forget what sales figures *World of Wonders* reached, but the sales were really quite extraordinary. *Fifth Business* had not sold in huge quantities, surprisingly, but book by book he was getting to three or four times as many copies sold – a very marked progression. What I recall most vividly about those earliest encounters was my hearing either from RD or from Moira Whalon, his secretary, that the manuscript was now complete. I'd race up by cab, pick it up and then it was a point of pride with me that I would get back to him first thing in the morning with my comments. I had the sense that, like so many of our best writers, he was immensely unsure of what he had just completed, and genuinely uncertain as to whether he had wasted the last three years of his life. It was important to me to set his mind at rest. . . .

With *World of Wonders*, what pleased me most was the richness of it all, on the train with the circus folks, the magicians and the monkey.

Clearly, the 61-year-old novelist still took boyish delight in magic, an interest shared by Vincent del Buono, Massey's Don of Hall in 1974.

VINCENT del BUONO

RD's interest in black arts was connected to my interest in astrology, and I did his horoscope. He's a Virgo, August 28, 1913. He was amused by our reading of his chart. He has a Mars-Saturn conjunction in Gemini, which is thought to be a very maleficent force. He would have understood that. He was very much a person with a controlled sense of power. He was in touch with that side of himself. We were both big men and he once said to me, "Large people like you and me need to keep our defences up." It was almost that there was a softness or a goodness in us that he sensed needed to be protected. He was a very good student of Jung. He understood the role of the Trickster who, when you think you're going in one direction, takes you in another. He understood that Jung's Trickster exists within you. He was always conjuring.

World of Wonders is the story of master magician Magnus Eisengrim, who, it emerges, began life as Paul Dempster of Deptford, Ontario, Canada. As a child, Eisengrim/Dempster was kidnapped by Willard, a magician in a travelling circus who trained him to be his assistant. When the child was not being forced to manipulate magical contraptions, Willard, a pederast, would rape him.

DOUG GIBSON

The book's pederasty theme concerned me, in a minor way. I may have said something like, "There goes the public library market." In those days it was a daringly frank treatment of child abuse. And child abuse is never easy reading or easy publishing. RD knew there would be resistance, but he said it was an essential part of the plot.

As usual, *World of Wonders* attracted better reviews outside Canada than within it.

DOUG GIBSON

Time magazine reviewed the book, saying that "Davies is not only Canada's finest novelist but also one of the most gifted and accomplished literary entertainers now writing in English." As I recall, Britain was late in catching up to Robertson Davies, but he was already a huge success in Canada and in the United States. And only when 90 percent of the reviews were in did Davies start to relax. That would be later in the publishing process than for most people.

Even the good reviews failed to completely satisfy RD's self-doubts, or so some of his drama students suspected.

BRONWYN DRAINIE

What did seem to get his back up was his place among the other greats of CanLit. He was at great pains to distance himself from the Margarets Atwood and Laurence, from Marian Engel, even from Mordecai Richler. He saw himself as of a different generation, a bearer of a kind of anglophilic tradition which he saw as a kind of bedrock Canada . . . which these others were somehow in the process of betraying. . . undermining some of the things he felt were the ties to Empire, which he saw as important.

ARLENE PERLY RAE (former Davies drama student)

Someone had said in a review of one of his books that he would be remembered as one of the minor authors of the twentieth century. He told our drama class: "Do you have any *idea* how great it is to be a minor writer of the century? Everyone has heard of the greats. But how hard it is to be even considered among the minor writers?" Was he trying to convince himself? He really went into it, the argument. He convinced *us*.

When the Deptford trilogy came out in paperback, the books reached a young Los Angeles filmmaker.

NICK MEYER
I discovered *Fifth Business* on the paperback rack at Hughes Supermarket at the corner of National and Sepulveda Boulevard in West Los Angeles, next to the frozen-food section, in 1971. I saw the edition of *Fifth Business* with a blurb on the back from *The New York Times*: "*A marvellously enigmatic novel . . . elegantly written and driven by irresistible narrative. One thinks of* The Magic Mountain *and* The French Lieutenant's Woman, *although Mr. Davies hardly needs Thomas Mann and John Fowles to prop him up . . .*" So I read it. Then I wrote a letter to Davies saying how much I had liked it – I was just a fan at this stage. . . . I wrote a very careful letter: I wanted it to show that I was clever and to show him that I had understood the book and understood the references. I got a very perfunctory reply. It was polite enough, but it showed that I had failed to impress him or to establish any kind of connection. Then I started giving *Fifth Business* as gifts to people – the paperback copy, given my income in those days. I gave the book to a friend of mine, a film producer, who said, "This would make a swell movie."

The problems around bringing *Fifth Business* and the other Deptford novels to the screen would be a persistent annoyance for RD for the rest of his life.

Chapter 28

THE FALSE GOD
OF THE THEATRE

An academic life fraught with student and administration politics, a creative life at its most intense and productive – and yet RD made time for his old love, the theatre. Sometimes he was a part of the performance.

CHRISTOPHER NEWTON (later director of the Shaw Festival)
I remember him in a box at the National Arts Centre. It was 1969, the opening of the centre, and the National Ballet was performing. In the middle of the performance, the elevator beneath the orchestra went crazy and the orchestra came rising above the stage and then sank from sight, playing all the while. The leader of the orchestra tied a white kerchief to his bow and we could see it wave as they slowly sank into the pit. I remember that Rob put on a pair of pince-nez. The whole effect of the beard, white tie and tails – he was performing, even as part of the audience. He was scrumptious. Just lovely.

ANNE WALMSLEY (former University of Toronto student)
Here's what I recall. Sometime between 1974 and 1978, when I was at U of T, my friend Brigid Higgins was in a play staged at St. Mike's where Robertson Davies was in attendance. The final scene is a dance of death in which the seven sins, including Brigid costumed as a peacock (Vanity or Pride) cavorted around the performance space. Robertson Davies was in the front row (his massive beard was so unmistakable). As I recall, one of the actors grabbed Davies's hand as he danced past – and Davies joined the dance.

However, from the 1960s on, RD's taste in drama – his passion for melodrama, pageantry and long disquisitions about ideas – were seen as wildly out of step with the kitchen-sink realism then favoured across the

English-speaking world. Davies knew this, yet defiantly chose not to change his style.

RD (letter to Horace Davenport, May 1968)
. . . such talent as I had for writing for the stage is now hopelessly old-fashioned, and not only am I unable to take to the new techniques – I don't want to, because they are totally unsuited to saying the kind of thing I want to say.

Sometimes, RD's blend of Edwardian form and Upper-Canadian material still found sympathetic directors and appreciative audiences – as in 1973, at the Lennoxville Theatre Festival in Quebec's Eastern Townships.

WILLIAM DAVIS
I became director of the Lennoxville Festival in 1971. It's hard to believe, but at that time Canadian plays were so scarce – they'd get one production and never be seen again. So in 1973 we did *A Jig for the Gypsy*, and my cousin Barbara Chilcott was available to reprise the role she had done at the Crest Theatre. I think Donald Davis, her brother, directed it.

William Davis wasn't aware that, more than a decade earlier, RD had written a play for Donald Davis and his brother Murray at the Crest Theatre, only to be sidelined when they chose instead to produce a play by J.B. Priestley.

BARBARA CHILCOTT
This was in the 1970s. By then, the fashion in theatre was that dialogue was at a minimum, so for people who considered themselves "with it," RD's dialogue would seem old-fashioned, very literary. But I enjoyed it more the second time. It was a more lively production. In this second production, Harry Somers's music helped a lot. And my costumes were better.

ROSAMOND BAILEY
I remember going to see *A Jig for the Gypsy* in Lennoxville. It was a great production. My friend Mary Pirie was in the cast. One dress rehearsal, I remembered Dad sitting with the director, and he and William Davis were discussing how Mary should say her lines. This was before we had

the term "up talk." Dad considered it to be typically feminine to raise your voice at the end of an idea, in inquiry. Gendered speaking – I hadn't thought of it this way.

The success of *Jig* at the Lennoxville Festival was a balm for RD the play-wright. That autumn, there was more good news from the University of Toronto's Hart House Theatre.

MARTIN HUNTER
I was supposedly artistic director of Hart House Theatre, but I was under the thumb of a committee of directors led by Ann Saddlemyer who told me what I could do and could not do. At one meeting, Ann said, "Martin wants to direct a play by Rob." That was fine – but it was news to *me*. Typical Ann, bulldozing her way through things!

RD was delighted. So I read several plays, including *General Confession*, which he had written for the Davises at the Crest. I looked at *General Confession*, but as I said to Rob, "This is a play for mature actors, and I can only get young actors." Which was true. But I also thought *General Confession* was Rob at his worst, absolutely loaded with Jungian theory, and pretentious and didactic. It could have been done well, but not by my students.

In his office, I had seen a copy of *Love and Libel*, the stage version of *Leaven of Malice*. I said, "You know, what I'd really like to do is *Love and Libel*." He said, "Oh no, that was such a painful experience." I said, "Just think about it." A few days later, he said, "If you really want to . . ."

I said, "I'd also like to go back to the book, and insert two sequences." I'd remembered a dream sequence as one of the strong ele-ments that I'd liked when I saw it at the Royal Alex. . . . We did some work on it. I also realized that there were some too-long scenes that were overwritten. The Humphrey Cobbler role had been padded to accom-modate the American actor Dennis King, who was to play Cobbler in New York.

This was not the Cobbler RD envisioned, and with Hunter's production he tried to get it right at last.

MARTIN HUNTER
Rob told me, "I wouldn't say this publicly, but the character of Humphrey Cobbler and his wife, Molly, was based on the home life

of Tony (Tyrone) and Judy Guthrie." . . . Rob wanted Brenda to play Molly. But when I assembled the cast for a reading, he arrived and said, "Sadly, Brenda won't be able to do this, as her mother is ill and she has left for Australia." I recast the role with a very attractive Irish woman. Rob took an instant dislike to her. He said, "She's turning this into an Irish joke." I thought she was fine.

Other participants have sunnier memories of the production.

FRANCESS HALPENNY
I became dean of the Faculty of Library Science in 1972. And it was not long after that we put on this production of *Leaven of Malice*. . . . We had a splendid cast . . . it was a very amusing play. I played a very domineering character, a very possessive mother. There was a famous scene where she is getting into bed and trying to keep her son from heading off for an evening's entertainment. I had a voluminous nightgown to get into. And we had a set of corsets under it. As I was getting ready for bed, I kept handing my son things – out I would thrust layers of clothes and then a pair of corsets. It absolutely brought down the house and caused quite a stir at the university: a dean of a faculty doing a little striptease!

REED NEEDLES (actor)
When we did *Leaven of Malice/Love and Libel* in October 1973, I was the son, Solly Bridgetower, and I remember RD watching the rehearsals and speaking to all of us very crossly. He said to me, "Reed, you have no idea who Solly Bridgetower is, no idea." So I said, "Tell me what you want." He said to me, "Solly is ingenuous, but by no means feckless." So I thought, "Right, I'll go home and find out what the distinction is." RD gave notes to Rex Southgate, who was playing the professor, a character who in the play says something like, "You are like many in your generation, a brassy, undereducated pup. . . ." RD felt that way as a teacher.

MARTIN HUNTER
As we were rehearsing, Rob came in and sat at the back of the theatre. I thought, "Here's trouble!" But Rob came up afterwards and said, "You've edited this much more cleverly than Tyrone Guthrie." I should have cut it more! Another thing I did was to add songs, which frankly kind of pepped the thing up.

REED NEEDLES

He came and spoke to us on the night of the dress rehearsal. He said,
"You're not very good. This is not the play I had written." But it was
hard to translate *Leaven of Malice* – a 1950s play set in the 1930s – to
the 1970s. It made no sense to us. A tempest in a teapot, in a small
town, made no sense to kids in the 1970s who were concerned about
dying in Vietnam. So the play was out of its time. In the end, though,
it worked for the academic audience at Hart House.

MARTIN HUNTER

The play was a success for two reasons. John Fraser at *The Globe and
Mail* and Urjo Kareda at the *Star* wrote very positive notices. And,
because it was a story about the university community, the university
community *got* it. It was on the strength of this production that Tony
Van Bridge, then the head of the Shaw Festival, said he wanted to do it
at the Shaw. I wrote him and said, "Tony, I do have a revised script and
musical notes." I never heard back. The play was not as much of a
success at the Shaw. It was always an ensemble piece, not a vehicle for
star actors. But I think Rob was grateful that the play was kind of
redeemed by these productions. And Rob was very welcoming to me
and most supportive through my time at Hart House Theatre. He was
more encouraging and positive about my work than all the rest of my
colleagues put together.

   About this time, Leon Major, who had been a director at the Hart
House Theatre, was talking with me and I said, "Leon, you know Rob
has not been writing plays lately, but he is now a successful author and
he has matured. You should get him to write for you."

So, in 1974, RD again put aside some of his other work to write a play. It
was to be called *Question Time*, and involved an Inuit shaman who comes
to the medical and spiritual rescue of a Canadian prime minister who has
crash-landed in the high Arctic. It featured long dialogues about the
nature of heroism.

RD (letter to Horace Davenport, 1974)

. . . The new piece is to be a fantasy; the director suggested casually that
I write a Canadian *Peer Gynt*; I hope that the noun rather than the
adjective is the conclusive factor in what emerges.

The play opened at the St. Lawrence Centre on February 25, 1975.

MARTIN HUNTER
When Leon put it on, it was not a success, and it was not well received. I think there was an element of the mean-spirited Toronto critic thing: "So, just because you're a successful author you think you can write plays. Well, you can't." Nothing annoys critics more than something they can't destroy.

IAN ALEXANDER (former junior fellow)
A number of us from Massey made up a party and we went to see *Question Time* at the St. Lawrence Centre in 1975, a little late in the run. RD knew that we were going, so he sent me a note afterwards, when we were back at Massey. It said, "Thank you for yr note & good wishes for the play: it came at a time when encouragement was most welcome, for a playwright is a defenceless creature. . . . I hope *Question Time* was to your liking."

I replied with some positive generalities. Because frankly, a number of us weren't entirely sure what to make of it, or even whether we had enjoyed it all that much.

Given that the critics, audiences and even sometimes the casts weren't enthusiastic, why did RD keep on? In part because theatre was one of the few pleasures he shared with his parents. More rewardingly, it was a passion he shared with his wife. In 1974, at Grace Church on the Hill, Brenda directed *Noye's Fludde* (*Noah's Flood*), a fourteenth-century miracle play set to music by Benjamin Britten.

DEREK HOLMAN (composer and conductor)
Arnold Edinborough was to be the Voice of God. But one night he was not able to be at the church, so Rob came in his place. Rob, who was standing in the back, in the gallery, made some error in the rhythm of his text and got out of step with the music. I corrected him brusquely. In his big, booming voice he said from up in the gallery, "Alas – I am but a False God."

JOHN FRASER
I remember reviewing his wife's production of *Noye's Fludde* at Grace Church on the Hill. RD was very proud of his wife pulling it off. He

was very proud on her behalf. He said, "That review is going into the archives . . . and I have control over them, you know."

Contemptuous of most critics, RD developed a fondness for *The Globe and Mail*'s John Fraser. Like RD, Fraser had tempestuous times as a student at Upper Canada College. Like RD, he was widely read and loved a good gossip. In 1977, when the University of Toronto's Drama Centre commissioned RD to write a play for the university's sesquicentennial, Fraser interviewed him about the new project.

JOHN FRASER (*The Globe and Mail*, March 5, 1977)
> Robertson Davies, the *playwright* Robertson Davies in case anyone had forgotten, is back in business again, with a new drama called *Pontiac and the Green Man*. And if anyone thinks that Davies has become benign as he surveys life at the pinnacle of his career . . . they may be in for a sharp shock. . . .
> "I am told there is cruelty in my writing," [says Davies]. "Often the cruelty of life is that it is such a great avenger. It's in the Bible, you know: you reap what you sow. People who lead mean lives reap meanness. I describe it and then get accused of being cruel." . . .
> Getting even is an important part of understanding him; he is a believer in the therapy of revenge.

Back at the Old Vic, Tyrone Guthrie's secretary used to tell her boss, when press coverage was good, that it was "fair to lamb." RD used the phrase in his diary entry on March 5, 1977.

RD (diary, March 5, 1977)
Fraser's article in the *G & M* today & v fair to lamb. He is a perceptive young man and discerns what is plain enough – that I am shy and sensitive – but what also eludes the blockheads who feel that anyone who has attained to any success must inwardly celebrate Mass to himself all day long. He has also sensed both the vengeful strain in my nature and my observation of the Biblical pattern of a man reaping what he has sown.

The play RD was writing for the university's sesquicentennial was to be based on the first play ever written in Canada, Robert Rogers' *Ponteach*

(1766). RD's play-around-a-play proceeded from the fact that Rogers had been brought to trial in Montreal in the late 1760s for treason and stirring up the Indians against the British. RD set the play at the end of the trial. The British generals who are prosecuting Rogers re-enact *Ponteach* as further evidence against him. Martin Hunter directed the production, and Derek Holman composed the music.

MARTIN HUNTER
Pontiac was one of the worst experiences of my life. . . . Rob had written a parody of *The British Grenadiers*, but Derek wrote music that was too modern, cacophonous and discordant. Rob didn't think the music worked. Derek didn't seem to think the play was good. The music school didn't want us there. The orchestra, which we decided to take out of the pit and put backstage, didn't want to be backstage and said, "Then why don't you just use recorded music?" We were all at each other's throats. Rob's idea was this would be a wonderful spectacle, but it was like a school pageant.

LAURIER LaPIERRE (broadcaster and writer)
All I remember was that it was a negative experience. Excruciating! I remember Robertson Davies came sometimes and that he was meticulous. Fussy, in other words.

DAVID GARDNER
I was Captain Rogers. And it just didn't work. It was not a happy production. I don't remember tempers flaring, but I like the word "vulnerable," which is not a word usually used with Rob. There was always the flamboyant Rob. And I sensed that he was vulnerable doing *Pontiac*.

MARTIN HUNTER
Nobody involved felt good about *Pontiac* – Rob, me, Derek, the actors. I don't imagine Brenda had much fun. People kept stamping out. They were at sixes and sevens. When the *Star*'s Gina Mallet wrote her review, she demanded, "How the hell was this thing cast? It looks like it was done over brandy at Massey College!" Which was more or less true . . .

After so many setbacks in RD's playwriting career, *Pontiac* turned out to be one more. Still, he could not suppress his own theatrical nature. When he was not writing for the stage or directing, he brought stagecraft into the simple act of walking down the street.

ELSPETH CAMERON BUITENHUIS
One day I was walking down St. George Street and I saw him walking past the Sidney Smith Building. He was a sight to behold. You could not help but notice him. People were turning their heads. He was tall, and he was wearing an all-brown outfit, a wide-brimmed hat tilted to one side, rather eighteenth-century. And a longish coat, brown, with a cape around the shoulders. And he was carrying a walking stick, which he flourished with each step – he flipped it up in rhythm as he walked. It was a remarkable sight. This was either the late 1960s or 1970s, and this kind of outfit would have been very eccentric.

REED NEEDLES
We would pass each other on the street on Devonshire Place. I wore a hat in those days – an Australian hat, black – and I carried a walking stick because I had a bad knee. He'd be wearing a black fedora, his Marchbanks hat, and he would be carrying his cane. We would see each other approaching, and as we approached he would raise his cane and waggle it in a friendly way. I would do the same.

   He did not think I waggled properly. And he thought that as an actor, I should know these things. So one day he took me to the long covered walkway outside the Trinity College Buttery, and we went up and down and he showed me how to swing the stick properly. One puts it down every fourth step, not every second.

The cane was not the only object RD used to dramatic effect.

MARTIN O'MALLEY (Southam Fellow at Massey)
At the Christmas Gaudy, he'd recite his ghost stories, and I just loved hearing him speak. He'd time his glass of sherry so, as he came to the end of his story, he came to the end of his sherry, and you'd hear the chink on the lectern. His timing was exquisite.

REED NEEDLES
After I became fights master at Hart House Theatre, we were doing a production of *Macbeth* with fights that went everywhere – and at one of these sherry parties, Professor Davies said to me, "Ah Reed! I have

something for you!" He pulled out a medal of St. Gerard and told me, "He is the patron saint of wounds. Though this medal is a little worn, I think you will find it most efficacious."

Actors and drama students could count on RD for support and arcane knowledge when it came to theatre classics. But he was uncomfortable with contemporary Canadian drama, which had grown vigorous since the Massey Report, thanks to government funding for the arts. After seeing David Freeman's *Creeps*, the first play ever put on by Toronto's Tarragon Theatre (it later won a New York Drama Desk award), he told Ann Saddlemyer that he disliked the subject.

ANN SADDLEMYER
Rob said he didn't think "those kind of people should be onstage." Dragons onstage were okay, ogres were okay, and there was a "looner" in the attic in *What's Bred in the Bone* . . . but he was really upset by seeing a play about the mentally retarded. There's that Edwardian ambivalence.

His discomfort with contemporary theatre resurfaced when young people came to him for advice about careers in modern theatre.

REED NEEDLES
In the late 1970s I was in Hart House, engaged by Michael Sidnell to be production manager. I'd signed a three-year contract. But I only lasted two years. In those years we were doing thirty to forty shows a year. The theatre was used several nights every week. I was feeling bad about leaving, about breaking my contract, but what to do?

I went to Massey to see Professor Davies. He sat behind his desk in the Master's office, with his fingers steepled. He had a breathy voice, which I now understand to be an asthmatic style of speaking, the voice of someone with respiratory problems. It was a memorable voice. . . .

RD said, "Hart House is a man-killer. It has killed better men than you. My advice is not to be next."

I said, "Really?"

He said, "You, Reed, are an artificer. By that I do not mean artificial. I mean that you are someone who can make something out of nothing. And that talent means you can do something other than Hart House."

I said, "But I need money to live . . ."

He said, "If you need money, come and ask me for it."

I was astonished. Then he reached behind his desk and pulled out a morning star, one of those medieval weapons, a ball with points on it attached to a chain. He said, "Some benighted undergraduate thought I might like this. I can think of no better recipient than you." He gave it to me and then patted me on the shoulder, and saw me off from the door of his office.

I never saw him alive again. And that was very sad.

Chapter 29

TEACHER

When RD first began to offer courses at Trinity College in the early 1960s, he had not yet hit his pedagogical stride.

RAMSAY DERRY
He would give a beautiful exposition and then he would say, "What do you all think?" We'd be silent. We were dumbfounded, we were dazzled. But we were silent. And he'd say, "God, you're a dull lot." He was better at talking to us than at getting us to respond.

But in due course RD's teaching style was animating classrooms.

JOHN WHYTE (former student)
He said of *King Lear*, "Without the experience of three daughters, you won't understand this play . . . *Lear* is about people who need more love than you can rightfully claim from people." I thought he was very eloquent about that.

As well, we were doing Synge and he would just wax poetic about the mysticism of the people of the Western Isles. He was in awe of the powers of their creation, of conjuring the life beyond the life of reason. We all live by the Fates. In a way, this course with him was life-changing, even though taking it made me feel on edge.

JIM DUGAN
Up to the time that I met Davies, all my professors of literature had been of the generation educated into anti-Victorian backlash. They were students of Evelyn Waugh, Aldous Huxley, D.H. Lawrence, the critic F.R. Leavis, et al., who hated the Victorians, and Dickens in particular. I was taught to scorn Dickens. Davies took me aback once in his class by stating that Charles Dickens was the greatest of all English prose

stylists. He was very "retro" in this view. Then I read more Dickens, and it was a great discovery for me.

RD's idiosyncratic tastes got a cool reception from some colleagues, but others appreciated his willingness to teach unfashionable subjects, such as nineteenth-century drama.

JIM DUGAN
Davies's knowledge of the eighteenth and nineteenth centuries was astonishing. His only academic credential was a B. Litt. from Oxford, but he had read *everything*. He'd read obscure memoirs, unknown novels and essays. Many people know about the Victorian "penny-dreadful" novels; Davies is the only person I ever met who had actually read many of them. He once said that the way to get a real feel for a past age was to study the secondary and tertiary writings – the "discards." Davies had the comprehensive knowledge of a specialist scholar plus the deeper feel and intuitive grasp of the sensibilities of the ages that scholars often lack.

PETER BRIGG
To this nineteenth-century theatre course, Davies invited Michael Booth, then chair of drama at Guelph University, as a guest. Already Michael was beginning to be regarded as a pre-eminent historian of nineteenth-century British theatre and melodrama – he is the editor of the *Oxford Nineteenth-Century Plays*. . . . It was a three-hour class, and Michael came as the expert. But as the class wore on, it became clear that RD knew as much, if not more, than the expert. RD had spoken to some of the very people Michael was talking about. This wasn't a pissing contest, it's just that RD knew more, and Michael was quite respectful, and perhaps a little surprised.

CAROLINE Di GIOVANNI
Once, he was describing kid gloves, and how you had to wear kid gloves in that time because the streets of London were so filthy. Toffs wore gloves to the theatre. And then he told us about the way they made kid gloves. To soften the leather, he said, they had to rub it over and over in animal feces. That talk stuck out in my mind . . . the minutiae of making kid gloves.

To favoured students, RD seemed loyal and fair; to others, he was tough and capricious.

CAROLINE Di GIOVANNI

He was not a harsh marker. I think he treated me with those smelly kid gloves! When I was there in 1973–74 in the University of Toronto Drama Centre in the first year of my work towards a doctorate, my classmates included Arlene Perly and David Gardner. It was quite a congenial group. A friend said, "You will enjoy RD's class, it is very *bracing*." That word was exactly right. RD was engaging and challenging. You were on your toes. He was kind and gentle but it was clear: you had to be up to snuff. You were privileged to be there.

ARLENE PERLY RAE

When he was my thesis adviser around 1973 or '74, I had to defend a thesis about whether a certain poem by Milton was originally intended for the stage, or just oral performance. I argued that this poem had been intended for the stage. My proof was that Henry Irving had actually performed it. The professor who was head of English said no. And after I had finished my defence, Davies stood up for me. This meant the world to me. He was so loyal and so articulate, and he waited for the right dramatic moment and then stepped in with the right thesis and proof. Afterwards, I saw the two of them walking across the quad, still talking and arguing.

DAMIANO PIETROPAOLO (former drama student)

In 1975–76 I was in the U of T Drama Centre doing a Ph.D. on Catharsis and Performance in Renaissance Tragicomedy. We in the Drama Centre were not only doing course work, we were engaged in productions. We were all involved in an ambitious production of Ibsen's *Peer Gynt*, directed by a man who did not believe in rehearsing without the whole ensemble present. And this had a negative impact on our ability to finish our term papers for Davies.

Davies had this habit of having a glass of sherry with his students and chatting with them after class. So we felt things were informal enough that we could approach him to give us all a postponement until after the Christmas break. All of us approached him after class and asked for an extension over the Christmas holidays because of our rehearsals for *Peer Gynt*.

He drew himself up – and said no. He said that anyone whose paper was late would be penalized severely. There would be no extension. We should finish our essays. And he added, "Ladies and gentlemen, may I remind you that I, too, am in *Peer Gynt*?"

Well, yes – he was the voice of the Great Boig. Which meant he was involved for maybe forty-five seconds. The voice was pre-recorded. So Davies had taken a cab to the recording studio and recorded his bit and then gone home, which took him an hour and a half, tops.

This said to me that he had a mean streak. And that he lorded it over his students, and took centre stage. In this, he was like another of my professors, Marshall McLuhan, who once told us, "All the theatrics in this class will be provided by *me!*"

When RD provided the theatrics, Massey College was his stage.

ELSPETH CAMERON BUITENHUIS
When I think about Robertson Davies, what comes to me is visual. He was a very *picturesque* person. I first saw him when I was visiting friends at Massey College. The study where he worked faced into the quadrangle. It was night, and the quadrangle was all dark, except the window, where his study was illuminated, and he was sitting, wearing an elaborate dressing gown – crimson or burgundy. It was a framed picture of the artist at work. I remember thinking this was so odd, so unusual. You were meant to take notice of a performance.

PETER BRIGG
Have they told you how he arranged his study at Massey? He had his eighteenth-century desk against the east wall, with the chair facing it. You would sit to talk to him with your back to the light of the windows. His chair was high and hard, yours was soft, and when you sat in it you would sink. So, you were looking at him as you were sinking down, and the light coming behind you made his glasses opaque. You could not see his eyes. You could not read him. This was calculated, I think, but how will we ever know? But he was very aware of how to shape things.

JIM DUGAN
I spent several weeks one year in the British Library, and researchers have to present a "bona fides" letter to be allowed to request books and

examine materials. I arrived at Davies's office to request a letter from him, which he typed and then signed. I have a very clear memory of how he held his pen: curl loosely the fingers of your right hand, place the pen between the index and the middle fingers and hold the pen perfectly vertical, with the fingers lightly gripping the pen in two places: at the crook of the fingers and between the tips – with the thumb lightly touching the pen below the fingers.

In signing, his whole hand moved, the pen never changing position within the grip, never tilting off the vertical. I also think now it took more like twenty seconds to sign his name. His signature looked as if it was engraved. At one of his sherry parties, he railed once against people who were careless about their signatures, telling us about one that "resembled a patch of barbed wire."

RD's theatrical bent manifested itself in teaching methods that were informed by a keen sense of pacing and performance.

REED NEEDLES
Professor Davies was one of the last people I remember who, when he came into a classroom, everyone would stand up. They would all rise and remain standing until he had reached his desk. He established a kind of order at the outset of the class. . . . The first time I was in his class, RD said to us all, "You can sit there in silence and be thought a fool, or you may open your mouth and prove it." So of course, as we students did not want to be proved to be fools, we all stayed quiet. And listened to him lecture, which was wonderful.

Two things I remember very clearly: he never used fillers – he never said "um" or "er" or "ah." He spoke specifically without pause. And he never spoke in the passive voice, which gave his lectures a richness.

ARLENE PERLY RAE
I remember RD talking to us about the stage whisper. He thought it was underrated. A wonderful tool. Instead of shouting, you could get everyone's attention with a whisper.

CAROLINE Di GIOVANNI
RD did not move around himself during these discussions. His *voice* was the presence. We were all seated around the long table. His strong

eyes . . . he could command and with his concentration . . . this was his acting trick.

Some women students found him old-fashioned and sexist. But on this, as with so many observations about RD, there's no consensus.

BRONWYN DRAINIE

I remember the feeling, as I was sitting in his class, of having been rather gracefully but definitely cut off if Professor Davies didn't think I was expressing an interesting thought. In anyone else, it would have been rude. I remember thinking, "Ooooh, I wouldn't want to be this guy's daughter."

ARLENE PERLY RAE

He did treat women differently. He thought we were the Muse and we were the truly creative ones.

MARTIN HUNTER

Davies could be quite mean. He played favourites, he had scapegoats. I remember him talking about a New Zealand girl and he talked about "her flat antipodean mind." Looking back, I ask, What's this antipodean thing? His wife was Australian!

The New Zealander was very likely Fiona Farrell, who later became an award-winning novelist. In her 2004 novel, *Book Book*, she creates a character, Kate Dobbs, whose experiences in RD's class at the University of Toronto are modelled on Farrell's own.

> *A democracy of supermen*, he muses. His voice is rich, his brows most definitely beetle. He regards the students seated around the table over half-frame glasses. "Do we agree?" he says. "And if not, what would we propose as the ideal form of government?"
>
> The students doodle knotted lines on their notepads. They crosshatch all the capital letters in SUPERMAN. Assessment for the course, is, however, based on the quality of their reply so finally they are all flushed out onto open ground.
>
> "Some form of socialism, I suppose," says Kate when it is her turn.

"Indeed?" says Robertson Davies. "And what might we mean by the term socialism?" He gives the word a hollow beat. Kate feels herself step out onto an icy street with her back to the enemy.

"Some form of government that guarantees equality of opportunity for all," she says. She can hear her voice rise at the end in the New Zealand fashion, signifying some lack of conviction, but it had worked for her, this socialism, so why should it not work for the world?

"For the purpose of engendering universal happiness, I presume?" says Robertson Davies. He has put a stone in the snowball. Kate can feel it coming. No matter how carefully she treads, the ball will hit her between the shoulders.

"Well, that's a lot to ask of any sys—" she begins, but Davies is speaking.

"*A lifetime of happiness!*" he declaims as if centre stage at the Old Vic. "*No man could bear it! It would be hell on earth!*" Kate looks around the table. None of the other students will meet her eye. She is on her own, out here on slippery ground. She makes one final desperate appeal.

"I just think there might, you know, be a chance that people might be happier, you know, that there'd be a more kind of general happiness under a socialist government than any, you know, other kind of universal government I can think of, if you see what I mean . . ." She has lost them. Lost the other students, not to mention the chance of an A— in this course anyway. She is rapidly sliding toward a B, maybe a C. Robertson Davies takes out a pocket watch and turns the little knob on its top rapidly back and forth. "What socialism will look like when it takes it final form," he says, "we do not know and cannot say. Do you know who said that, Mrs. Dobbs?" Kate shakes her head. He holds the watch to his ear to check its steady reliable click. "Vladimir Ilych Ulyanov," he says. "Whom history knows as Lenin."

The ball lands. Kate feels the ice slide down her collar.

Davies responded to his students according to their backgrounds.

JIM DUGAN

Davies was initially offended by my American accent and some of my colloquialisms. After my comprehensive oral, he told me I had to improve my diction if I was going to discuss the eighteenth century, and that I should learn to talk like Oliver Goldsmith in Goldsmith's "Citizen of the World" essays!

In one of my early dissertation chapters, I described a character as being "savvy." Davies wrote back to say that he had grown to find my style charming – he had grown fond of my "Yankee barbarisms" – but "savvy" just would not do in a thesis.

Even speech patterns of Canadian students came under RD's scrutiny.

JOE MEDJUCK (former student)

He took a liking to me and he heard my M.A. thesis defence. It was to be in an office with RD, Clifford Leech and McLuhan, for whom there had been a substitute at the last minute. . . . I was sitting outside the examination room and I could hear them all talking about *me*. I heard RD saying, "He's a nice enough young man, but we must teach him to speak English." He thought I spoke funny. Well, I do. I mumble.

SKY GILBERT (former student)

The first class with him, Robertson Davies went round the room and asked people what their background was, meaning place of birth and ethnic/racial background. It was very politically incorrect, and of course would not be permitted today. A friend of mine said he was Jewish, and RD said, "Well, you would like Israel Zangwill" – I can't remember the Edwardian playwright's name, but it was something like that. My Jewish friend quit the class because of RD's stereotyping him. The implication was clear, and RD had no qualms about it: we should be interested in studying things that had to do with our ethnic origin . . .

RD kept students on their toes with his theatrical style of responding to their work.

IAN ALEXANDER

We quickly came to recognize the telltale sign of boredom or disapproval from the Master. For instance, if he removed his spectacles and began clicking the earpieces together, you knew you'd lost him. One memorable morning, while the designated presenter was in full flight, Davies stood up and moved to the door. "Please continue," he intoned. "I shall return shortly." As I recall, the poor discomfited individual broke down completely and did not return for the rest of the semester.

ANN SADDLEMYER

[In Ph.D. examinations] I used to see him get bored if the questions went on and on. He would pull out his pocket diary and make notes. I never saw him doodle – but I would see him deliberately reach into his inner pocket and make an entry. And then I knew he was bored.

REED NEEDLES

I was auditing a graduate class in theatre. Because I was not enrolled, I did not have to write assignments. The one time I handed something in, I got it back with a single line through it, and the word "drivel." I was hurt.

How RD felt about a topic depended in part on who introduced it.

DAVID GARDNER

Doing my thesis with Davies was wonderful. It was the history of theatre in Canada. I began with the Vikings and we worked closely together, but all the research was my own. *The Theatre of Neptune* was one of the first performances in Canada, done on a boat on the water off Halifax in 1606, in Shakespeare's own lifetime, and it is still celebrated in Nova Scotia. It has heroic figures and canoes . . . Rob was very intrigued by this.

RAY CONLOGUE

In 1974, when I was doing an M.A. at the Centre for the Study of Drama, Davies did a course in the history of Canadian theatre. In the first class, he began with a mention of the *Théâtre de la Neptune en Nouvelle-France*, the Marc Lescarbot play performed in 1606. He acknowledged in his gracious fashion that since the French had been here first, they ought to be mentioned. That accomplished, he leaped two and a half centuries to Toronto of the 1860s and was very enthused about touring British theatre companies . . .

Remember, this was 1974. Canadian nationalism and authentic Canadian roots were very big then. I had taken a course in anthropology and studied the Kwakiutl Winter Ceremonials on Vancouver Island. It seemed to me that Davies would be fascinated to learn that for centuries the Kwakiutl built wooden stages with trap doors, had on-stage dialogue among several actors, and used hinged masks to effect transformations one character to another. Davies heard me out in silence. Then he hunkered down into a bearded squint – you know, squinting with one eye while stroking his beard – and said something like "How very, very interesting. But of course we won't be discussing *that* sort of thing in this course."

And how RD felt about students depended on how they handled the challenges he threw their way.

REED NEEDLES
It took me months in class before I had the courage to ask him something. I said, "Professor Davies, you previously said such and such, is this not inconsistent with what you are saying now?"

He looked at me. "Reed. For a moment, I was afraid you were right. But you are not. And I will show you why . . ." And he did. It wasn't a putdown – it was as if I had handed him a cue.

One bitterly cold day, I remember finally challenging him. I said, "Professor Davies, last week you said such and such. And this week you said . . ."

He looked at me and said, and I remember this very clearly: "Reed. Were I Herod, in the midst of the Massacre of the Innocents, I should pause, merely to consider the confusion of your thinking." The translation: "What a stupid question."

I went home that night and called Father and said, "I've been savaged by Professor Davies." Then I repeated what he had said.

Father said, "Oh, he's just quoting from Christopher Fry's *The Lady's Not for Burning*. Go read it."

I did and went back to class. This time I was ready. I said, "Professor Davies, when you were quoting Christopher Fry last week . . ."

This time he raised not one but both eyebrows, and he said, "Someone has been doing his reading."

Because his students regarded RD as a formidable character, when he revealed his empathetic side, it surprised and moved them.

PETER BRIGG
My first wife, Stella, was killed in an accident – it was 1977 and she died in the ambulance on the way to hospital. Likely, RD was a reader of obituaries. I had left Massey in September 1970, yet RD had Moira Whalon get in touch with me. He said, "If Peter ever wants to see me . . ." and she relayed the message. I went to Massey a month and a half later. We talked for about an hour.

He said, "Well, how's it going?"

I said, "I don't think I'm grieving properly. I haven't cried over this."

He said, "Peter, grief is very personal and very individual. You must do it the way you do it."

That statement freed me. Stella was 35 and she had had a tough life. RD said, "You have to think, 'She has fulfilled her destiny.' You have to ask, 'What did her life mean to those who love her and those who knew her?'" That was a strange idea about destiny, but it made a kind of sense. It was comforting in a distant way. He certainly wasn't a shoulder to cry on. But this was very important for me.

SKY GILBERT
When our class had our final luncheon, served by his wife in our classroom, Davies took the time to question us about our out-of-class activities, asking what we did in our spare time. . . . One girl said she had a job as a waitress. Davies looked very concerned. He tactfully said something like, "Ah, that must be very difficult for you." His wife, who was serving soup, helped out. "Oh dear," she said, "it's not as horrible to be a waitress these days as it used to be. Lots of nice respectable girls have jobs as waitresses these days." I always took this as an example of Davies's complete disassociation from the realities of modern-day living.

But overall I would say he was a wonderful teacher and both charming and intimidating. Old and opinionated and judgmental . . .

but very witty, very smart and not the least bit academic. As I am a professor now, I rather covet that aspect of his style. I try to copy it.

REED NEEDLES

To me, RD was Dumbledore . . . benevolent, wise, perspicacious. He had a vicious wit, and he showed me enough of the dark side of his wit that I would be careful not to waste his time. He despised "smatterers" – people who did a little bit of something. He wanted you to *love* something. He gave me advice because he knew I was thinking of becoming a teacher. He said, "Be eccentric, but never be boring."

Chapter 30

AMONG WRITERS

In their dreams of an ideal gentlemen's college, Vincent Massey and RD envisioned a place where writers, journalists, poets and scholars could mingle and enjoy one another's company. But, as a writer himself, RD was only too aware of writers' tendency to stand back, judge and compete. So he told his former student, Bronwyn Drainie, when she interviewed him for CBC Radio.

BRONWYN DRAINIE
He said to me in our *Sunday Morning* interview that there was a distant, cold side to him, that writers by their nature were outsiders who observed, and that they were "rather cold fish."

The college hosted a writer-in-residence program – for older and more established writers, as RD insisted – and inevitably, Massey turned up in these writers' subsequent books. W.O. Mitchell's 1984 novel *Since Daisy Creek* was written a decade after his Massey residency, and has several Massey-like scenes. (However, Mitchell's son Orm and daughter-in-law Barb insist that Mitchell also drew on a college at the University of Calgary and a former U of C president.) Mitchell's protagonist describes this composite college as a place of

> ritual plagiarism. By the new of the old. The worst kind.
> Colonial . . . I never want to see that silver snuff mull again,
> even if the Master took a pinch from it himself. That would
> be refreshing. He should be forced to snort some so he'd
> sneeze his ass off. God knows how long it's been since he had
> a reflex that hasn't been calculated.

BARB MITCHELL

W.O. must have gone to be writer-in-residence at Massey in the fall of 1973 because in June 1974, he thanked RD for the experience: "It has been a beautiful and quiet eye in the middle of the urban storm."

ORM MITCHELL

W.O. felt that Massey's attempts at high sherry parties and high tables were an extension of RD's facade. He was amused by that and took delight in it – and by the big event when the U of T engineers put soap suds in the Massey pool. W.O. was quite sympathetic to the engineers taking a dig at this pretension.

In *Since Daisy Creek*, Mitchell writes a passage about someone dropping detergent in the college pool. It creates an exciting foamy mess, but kills the fish and infuriates the Master.

> "[I saw] the guy in the flannels and the blue blazer."
> "The Master!"
> "Up to his knees in the first pool, yelling at people to forget the ones floating on top and rescue the ones under water. He kept shouting 'Bloody engineers!'" . . .
> "You think it might have been somebody from Engineering? Why should the Master–"
> "He's got a Matthew Arnold complex. Considers Engineers and Education faculties the worst of the barbarians, unfit for either junior or senior fellowship."

ORM MITCHELL

W.O. used to tell us the soap suds story with delight. But it is the same kind of scene that Robertson Davies would have loved, as in *Leaven of Malice*, when Humphrey Cobbler plays music that shouldn't be played in church.

BARB MITCHELL

But I don't think W.O. and RD had real camaraderie. I would say your dad was friendly with Margaret Laurence and Tiff Findley and Alice Munro, whom he called "Sweet Alice." But I would say W.O.'s feelings for RD and Margaret Atwood were . . . respect.

Edgy respect was probably a better way to characterize RD's relationship with Margaret Atwood, at least at the early stages.

MARGARET ATWOOD

Even at Massey, he was vulnerable. He wasn't an academic and there was university resentment because he was an artist. My sense of his vulnerability was reinforced several years later when he said to me, I don't remember where, "People tell me you don't like me."

I said "*Whaaat?!?*" I liked him fine!

But people don't ask that question unless it's on their mind. Young people do cause older ones anxiety . . . it reminds them of looming mortality, the generational issues. I found that early on when I was interviewed by older people who were fearful – they thought I was judging them.

Another prominent Canadian novelist, Timothy Findley, known to friends as "Tiff," met RD as a young stage actor in Kingston in the 1950s. His partner, Bill Whitehead, recalls Tiff's experience – in 1977, after he had written three novels – on finally being invited to Massey High Table.

BILL WHITEHEAD

That night, Tiff found he was seated on the left of the Master himself. On the Master's right was a world expert on – cement. Throughout the dinner, Rob was totally occupied by the world expert on cement.

He finally turned to Tiff and said, "So, Findley, how are things?"

Tiff said, "Master, I am thinking of writing a play about Elizabeth I, and I understand you wrote a book about Elizabethan boy actors."

RD looked at him and said, "Oh, I can't remember. That was so long ago," and he turned back to the expert on cement.

After a long time, he turned back to Tiff. Tiff had another conversation topic ready – this time he said, "Master, I hear you knew Thornton Wilder, my mentor. I'd love to know what you thought of him, as a man or as a writer."

Davies said, "Humph. Repressed homosexual," and turned back to Mr. Cement.

From its inception, Massey offered a year's residency program for visiting journalists, known in RD's day, and for years after, as the Southam Fellows.

Martin O'Malley, then a *Globe and Mail* reporter, was a Southam Fellow in 1972–73.

MARTIN O'MALLEY

I remember he had a walking stick. He wrote, "Of what use is an establishment figure if he does not look like an establishment figure?" I'd read *Fifth Business* and his Samuel Marchbanks stuff. I just loved it. He liked cats, and I remember once he said, "Happiness is a cat-like emotion. You can't chase after it. . . . Just leave it alone and it will rub up against your leg and leap into your lap." I loved that!

He'd often say the journalism part of his career gave him the muscularity of his prose. After a full day of committee work, he was trained to sit down and write. Davies also used to say, if he had writer's block, he'd just walk around it. Journalism taught him to do that – to just sit down at the blank page and do it. He and E.B. White were inspirations and models. They had the same idea about humour. E.B. White once said the laurels go to the serious writers, the Brussels sprouts to the humorists.

The idea was that the Southam Fellows would mix with the junior fellows and broaden their outlook. Sometimes, the process was reversed. The night the junior fellows invited the lady known as "Miss Gates Ajar Honey-Pot" to high table is a Massey legend.

COLIN FRIESEN

No sooner had we sat down at the table after grace than, from the far entrance, this young lady, who had disrobed and was clad in only a G-string, came forward carrying a silver tray with a bottle of Champagne, which she presented to the Master. The Master accepted her gift graciously and thanked her, and she left amidst laughter and applause from the offenders.

BRENDA DAVIES

When the stripper came, Rob kissed her warmly on the cheek. He later said in his diary that, having three daughters, this sort of thing couldn't throw him. Rob was amused by highjinks. Vincent wasn't there when the stripper came. I expect he found out. But Colin Friesen was very nervous. Vincent was a lot broader-based than Colin thought. He'd been around.

MARTIN O'MALLEY

At one point, Betty Lee, one of my fellow Southam Fellows, wanted to invite Xaviera Hollander, the Happy Hooker, to address us. Perhaps she got the idea because we'd had a high table and this stripper ran in. But then I got a call from the professor in charge of the Southam Fellows. RD had asked him to call *me* and head off this embarrassment. The next day, I schmoozed with the others and I said, "The Master seems to think this is kind of tawdry."

We all agreed that RD must have been really upset if he had made this entreaty. I convinced my fellow journalists not to invite Hollander by saying, "Do we want our whole year to be known as 'The Year of the Stripper'?"

I thought it quaint that RD didn't phone me up directly and ask me to head off the Hollander invitation. He didn't want to be seen as prohibiting her. . . . For all I know, he would have loved to have a brandy and a heart-to-heart talk with Xaviera. But he didn't want it to be a Massey thing with her as official guest.

As RD's reputation as a writer grew, so did demands that he become involved in writers' causes. Margaret Atwood and her partner, the novelist Graeme Gibson, went to recruit RD for one.

MARGARET ATWOOD

In the early 1970s, I'm with Graeme and I'm in my early thirties. Davies is in his early sixties. We were forming the Writers' Union of Canada, and Graeme and I went to his office at Massey. He was sitting in his Masterly chair, and he was backlit. The light was shining through his beard. And you could see the face underneath. It was a very different face from the bearded presence. The face under the beard was sensitive, vulnerable, anxious, not the magisterial presence, the magician who says "I command you" – none of that.

Graeme and I said our *blah-blah-blah* Writers' Union speech, and when we'd finished, without missing a beat, Davies replied, "I'll join." Right away! He knew the situation of writers in Canada. He knew how we were treated.

The Writers' Union was formed to share information so that writers who were offered fifty cents for their world rights would know they were being taken. It was to be a mutual help organization and a group lobby, and it was to plug the loophole in our copyright law so that American publishers' overruns of our books could not be shipped to Canada and sold or remaindered – a situation that denied the Canadian writers any royalties. We were lobbying against that. I remember the then consumer and corporate affairs minister asking us, "Don't you want the consumer to have cheap books?" This was our situation and Davies knew the disrespect, the snotting-upon, that writers got, because he had been a professional writer for some time.

Some writers sought out RD not for moral support, but just because they liked his stuff.

JOHN IRVING (American novelist)
I came up to Canada to do background [research] for *A Prayer for Owen Meany*. The only people I knew in Toronto were Graeme Gibson and Peggy Atwood. They told me to look up RD.

He had written a very funny, and to me enjoyable, review of *Hotel New Hampshire* in the *Washington Post Book World*, and he had heard a story that at Harbourfront a woman had thrown her underwear onstage during one of my readings. I don't remember this happening, but once he wrote about it, it happened. His *Washington Post* review made reference to this event, and to my "rock star" persona. . . .

He said Henry James and I could meet each other in Heaven and teach each other things. Then he wrote me a letter, and I wrote back. Writers like letters.

So I came up here to do some work on this book and to meet Davies. At this time I was living in New York City and sharing an apartment with my oldest son, who was in acting school. I was still wrestling in those days. A couple of days before I came, I broke one or more of my toes wrestling, and my shoes didn't fit. I had to borrow a pair of my son's shoes – as opposed to borrowing just one of his shoes and really looking like a clown. And I couldn't find any shoes but his wrestling shoes. I imagined Davies as a formal fellow, so I dressed conservatively for the meeting in Toronto – but with wrestling shoes two sizes too big. And I was walking with a limp.

A former girlfriend of mine had learned that I was going to Toronto to have lunch with Davies, whom she admired, and she came along. The girlfriend would have made an unfavourable impression on most people of RD's generation. She was very forward.

We all met at his club. The York Club. Edwardian! All the waiters were even older than he was. Everyone was about to fall down. In his collected letters, his impression [of that lunch] was every bit as awful as mine.

Actually, RD's impression of the lunch was a very happy one, or so he told his editor at Viking New York, Elisabeth Sifton, in a letter in 1982:

I have an odd adventure to relate. For some months – about a year – I have been receiving very kind and praising and humble letters from John Irving, author of *The World According to Garp* and *Hotel New Hampshire* – fan letters, no less. He says I am his ideal among living writers. Well, I am totally unaccustomed to this sort of approach from anyone, let alone immensely successful and popular novelists. Recently he came to Toronto to give a reading and wrote to ask if he could take me to lunch. I replied, as a boy educated at Upper Canada College (the Eton of the North) ought to do, that I couldn't think of it, and he must allow me to take him to lunch. I nominated the York Club, the second stuffiest club in Toronto, and told Brenda to get herself a Big Mac somewhere as We Authors were going to have a heavy session. So prompt on the hour, Irving arrived, splendidly dressed, but to my astonishment wearing running shoes which I gather are all the thing now among the younger fashionables, though in my young days we were assured that they "drew your eyes" and caused the feet to give forth a powerful fragrance, like a hot motor tyre. But what really surprised me was that he had a lady in tow, who was introduced simply as "Rusty" but who after a while emerged as Mrs Guinzberg-as-was, the ex-wife of the former head of Viking. . . . She proved to be a nice and funny lady and Irving was delightful and we had a high old time. Brenda – who might just as well have eaten with us and not been banished – turned up later and we all got on like a house on fire.

JOHN IRVING

At the lunch, we talked about the writers we liked and the writers we didn't. It was kind of a contest. We were wrestling the conversation away from the young woman. . . . Whatever his disapproval of the young woman I was with, he paid her a great deal of attention. At one point she got up to go to the ladies' room, and we were alone. He then leaned forward, and with a gesture to everything around us, he said, "Isn't this *awful!*"

I couldn't tell if he was reading my mind or if he loved the stuffiness because it suited the impression he wanted others to have of him . . . certainly a young "rock star" like me.

The friendship between RD and John Irving lasted for the rest of RD's life. But it had an unlikely beginning: a year before this lunch, RD wrote a letter to the American literary biographer Leon Edel which shows him at his most critical.

There are people who cry up John Irving as a writer of significance, and when the *Wash. Post* asked me to review his book I read all of his novels in order to prepare myself and I could find little in him. . . .

Of psychological insight or subtlety, of sensitivity to the nuance of language, of any perception of the insubstantiality of passion, there was not one crumb.

JOHN IRVING

That letter to Leon Edel? Oh, yes. Brenda was horrified and afraid of my reaction when the letters were published. . . . In retrospect, I find it funny. I think if he were sitting here with us he would not dispute that he was a snob. Some of my closest friends in the book world are great snobs.

RD could be offended by the younger generation of writers in principle until he got to know them in person.

BRONWYN DRAINIE

He was outraged that a wave of political correctness was more influential than excellence and that he was being hounded to write references for grant applications by young writers he didn't think were all that good. . . .

It's fascinating that when RD's book of letters [*For Your Eye Alone*] came out, that he laid out Irving's shortcomings as a writer for all to see. And yet they developed a warm friendship. What could Irving have thought when he eventually saw that letter of Davies's?

JOHN IRVING

The more he became familiar with my work, the more he saw that it was every bit as nineteenth-century as he was. He loved Dickens and I loved Dickens. And I felt, on subsequent meetings with him, more at ease being myself. I'm a pretty good cook. I may have cooked for him and Brenda on several occasions. He did like to eat. I cooked better than anything he'd get at the York Club!

JANET TURNBULL IRVING (literary agent, and wife of John Irving)

My first encounter was my convocation from BSS [Bishop Strachan School], in 1973. He was the speaker. I had had an extraordinary teacher, Liz Stimpson, and she was all over us about *Fifth Business* being the most mind-boggling novel. Somehow the school had asked Robertson Davies to do the commencement, as he'd had daughters at the school. I'd actually won the English prize that year, the Elizabeth Stimpson English Prize. He called my name and then he shook my hand. It was mind-boggling. . . .

I told him when he and Brenda came to dinner at our apartment at St. Clair and Spadina that he'd given me the prize at the commencement. He proceeded to relay the entire speech he had given at BSS thirteen years before! It was about being at UCC and peering at BSS girls. It almost made me cry. . . .

That night he and Brenda came to dinner, I remember he then kind of wandered off to examine the bookshelves. I was mortified. He stood there with his hands behind his back and went through my stuff, all the Penguin paperbacks, the bestsellers . . . all kinds of embarrassing things.

On June 6, 1987, John Irving married Janet Turnbull, who had been his literary agent and was also RD's literary agent, in the Bishop Strachan School chapel. RD read from the scripture at the ceremony.

JOHN IRVING

He did not trust the Bishop Strachan School chapel to have a King James Version of the Bible. Just to be sure, he brought his own.

My two sons were my best men at the wedding. One of them, Brendan, could not be at the rehearsal. He arrived just before the wedding, barely on time, tying his tie as he came through the door.

He had not met Rob. I hastily introduced the wedding party, but Brendan had his back turned to the altar. Then Rob emerged from behind it with his Bible in one hand. Brendan turned and saw Rob, with the white beard, framed by stained glass, with the Bible, and Brendan turned white as if he had seen a ghost. Brendan said to me afterwards, "I thought he was God."

For some of RD's growing legions of fans, that description was not so far-fetched.

ERIC WRIGHT (novelist)
Around 1988 I went to a crime writers' convention in Moscow. Roger Simon [creator of Moses Wine detective books such as *The Big Fix*] came up to me and said, "You're Canadian. Do you know Robertson Davies?" As if he was saying Alice Munro! So I became aware of how good RD was when I went to Moscow. You never really honour your own. I knew him here and had accepted that he was a man you made fun of. When I read the Deptford trilogy, I shut up.

As for rube Canadians who persisted in misunderstanding RD, he never lost the habit of mocking them.

JOHN IRVING
We were at a dinner party in Toronto at someone's house, and we were bored. I felt sorry for the host and hostess making a great to-do about having John Irving and Robertson Davies, but he was seated between two women who were obviously not bowling him over. You could always tell when he was entranced: there was a lot of give-and-take. When he was bored, he'd talk all the time, because he needed to entertain himself (I recognize that syndrome in myself: if I am having a good time, Janet doesn't hear from me).

Anyway, that night he told the story of another dinner party – when you start remembering stories about an awful dinner party, it is by association – and he was telling of a mixed-media artist who used to render women's reproductive organs onto dinner plates. You can imagine Rob's delight in telling this to the two ladies on either side of him: of eating your dinner from a plate where you find "your lamb chop is on a vulva."

He was up to great mischief that night. I thought our hostess was going to pass out.

I looked at Brenda to see if she would secretly admonish him. But she is the consummate actress.

Chapter 31

RETIREMENT,
THE LIFE OF A DOG

In 1980, RD turned 67. His hair had gone white. He was reluctant to admit just how white.

UELI SCHALLENBERG
I started trimming Davies's beard and eyebrows around 1980. His beard was an organized mess. It looked ragged, but he liked it that way. I trimmed the beard . . . very carefully. He never said how he would like it. He expected me to know. Sometimes I had to cut the hair out of his forehead – so fast! – because as soon as I did he'd pull his head back. There was a power struggle between him and me, but I couldn't let him walk around with hairs coming out of his forehead.

In the beginning when he came here, I used to dye his eyebrows. His eyebrows! He was very hairy and he was fussy about his eyebrows. I had to be very careful.

Age intensified RD's perennial struggle between his desire to uphold and defend traditions, and to keep his mind open to new ideas and technologies.

BRENDA DAVIES
Rob never had a computer. He decided against using one. It would have driven him crazy . . . and he thought they caused people to write too much and not revise.

JULIET GUICHON (former junior fellow)
One afternoon in about 1989, I was working in my Massey College room when I stepped out for a minute. As was the custom, I left my door open. Returning quickly to get back to work, I stopped at the threshold of the door. Standing deep in the room, at my desk, was Robertson

Davies. A formidable figure with his long beard and round abdomen, the Master Emeritus had an office on my floor.

Even though I had seen him coming and going, he had not greeted me despite my shy smiles. Now he was where I thought *I* was supposed to be. Urgently searching my memory, I rapidly realized that there had been no Junior Fellow briefing for this situation.

"Hello?" I suggested. He replied, "Yes, I was just looking at your computer."

Even in 1989, the equipment before him was ancient. In fact, it wasn't a computer but a word processor – and a monstrosity at that, accompanied as it was with a huge sound cover to reduce the noise of the printer. I tried to explain that this antiquity had been a bargain, sold at a discount by the law firm for which I'd articled because the firm was upgrading to real computers. Given his obvious interest, I wanted him to understand that this thing was seriously outdated. I thought I was getting through.

"Yes," he replied. Then, pointing to a side table, he asked about the object on top. "Is that part of your computer?"

"No," I replied. "That's my radio." With that, Robertson Davies backed out of my room.

Being among Massey College's young people intensified RD's self-consciousness about his age.

ARLENE PERLY RAE
He knew I'd paid my way through university by working as a stewardess on Air Canada, and he complained to me that on airplanes people thought of him as old. "Why do people give me priority seating and treat me as if I am old?" he'd say. I suppose in the 1970s he was in his sixties, not much older than we are now. But he always *seemed* old . . .

RD (letter to Arnold and Tish Edinborough, 1980)
I had an unseemly wrangle with some undergraduates who were hog-wild for Canada to open her doors to all U.S. draft dodgers, and who were convinced that all criminals – especially sex-criminals – are SICK and need love. . . . I got myself into trouble when I said merrily that I had had almost all the childhood diseases, but false compassion had not been one of them; this was in answer to a boy with a mouth like a hen's

ovipositor who asked me if I had not been more liberal in my opinions before I GOT SO OLD . . .

Although past retirement age, RD let himself be convinced to stay on as Master of Massey College for another term, until 1981.

MIRANDA DAVIES

RD was very concerned about his departure from Massey. Men are so concerned about retirement. They feel their jobs define them. Though he had another role in his life, as an author, he still felt anxious about Life After Massey.

He had created it, and it was his community, with his old colleagues from Peterborough, Colin Friesen and his secretary Moira Whalon.

COLIN FRIESEN

Even though the Master always had the answers, he'd never allow himself to make a decision until he'd come to me with a discussion. He always included me. He'd say, "You know, Colin, I am going to be entertaining a number of journalists from all over the world. Who do you think should be included from Canada?" Why would he ask *me?*

Moira Whalon made him look tall. He wasn't terribly accurate in many of the things he wrote. Moira was so observant, and she did the proofreading in such a way that she caught many things. She was doing his fact-checking. The whole staff at Massey was a family. We just loved each other.

Finally it was time to exchange the role of Master for that of Master Emeritus.

ANN SADDLEMYER

There was a bit of a fuss . . . because Moira Whalon, Rob's secretary, went to act as secretary of the committee to select a new Master, and Douglas LePan, a consummate civil servant, moved that it was not appropriate to have Rob's secretary at the meeting. Moira returned to Rob's office very distressed. When I tried to calm her, Moira lashed out at me and called me "Pollyanna."

Rob was in the office. He said nothing directly about the meeting, but remarked to me about how upset Moira was. . . . And yet Douglas was right. The committee could not have talked about how they wanted to choose a new Master, and what changes they wanted in Massey, if Rob's secretary had been there.

To the end, RD professed ambivalence about academic life.

IAN ALEXANDER

I spent two wonderful years living at Massey, while acquiring an M.A. and completing the course requirements and comprehensive exams for my Ph.D. Then I spent a year *not* writing my dissertation. A tempting professional opportunity had been offered to me in broadcasting. Confused and ambivalent about my future, I visited the Master. I was somewhat surprised when he encouraged me to take the job. He reminded me that he himself had been a working journalist for many years before coming back to the university. I felt that he had given me permission to leave. . . .

A few years later, when he was retiring as Master, I wrote to thank him. He replied: "I always had slightly cold feet when I advised a Ph.D. student to get out of that grind . . . but increasingly the university world reminds me of the medieval church – a scattering of saints, a few hundred worthy men and thousands of scaredy-cats who couldn't face the world and sought protection in Mother Church or the Alma Mater. . . . It is astonishing to look at the history of the Renaissance and see just how little of the new learning and the new world emerged from the universities. It was the men of quality outside who did the serious work."

There was in this a putdown of academic life. Now I see that he, too, was an outsider in the academic environment and felt shy about it, but he made a virtue of that.

After RD's successor was named – it was to be Patterson Hume – the Massey fellows gave the founding Master a special send-off.

BRONWYN DRAINIE

Ann Saddlemyer was a specialist in Davies's drama. She contacted me about when he was retiring from Massey. She decided to have a huge evening for him in the Great Hall at Hart House. The evening would consist of a play which she would write, made up of a pastiche out of Davies's own plays.

This was the darndest play! Frankly, none of us really knew Davies's drama except for Ann. We didn't know what the hell we were talking about. We found the script such a puzzlement. It didn't have any real plot. Just bits and pieces from all his plays. We managed to get together for about two rehearsals. We just shook our heads through all the rehearsals. How could you find any motivation from all this? What was *this* about?

ANN SADDLEMYER

The Drama Centre presented it as a beautiful production and we even had a fire-breathing dragon, which was quite marvellous. My sense was, the audience loved it, and all the more because it was all spectacle and melodrama. But it is true that the actors had very little time to rehearse. They wouldn't have had time to develop or really get into their characters.

BRONWYN DRAINIE

On the night, in the Great Hall at Hart House, there was Rob in the front row with Brenda and close friends and relatives and the thronged masses behind him. Once the play started, we'd come up with lines and suddenly there would be a great guffaw from Rob. He was the only person *getting* it. It would be line, line, line . . . huge guffaw from Rob. Line, line, line, huge guffaw. That was the craziest audience I've ever played to. His reaction was all you heard. You were playing to an audience of one in a house of five hundred.

RD (letter to Ian Alexander, August 19, 1981)

The farewell party was great fun, wasn't it? My wife and I, being incorrigibly theatrical and incorrigible Dickensians, referred to it between ourselves as *The Great Bespeak for Mr. and Mrs. Crummles* [a reference to the eccentric but kindly theatrical couple in *Nicholas Nickleby*]. What an honour to be treated to a Masque, and laughter and music and excitement, instead of the usual ghastly banquet, with a tedium of speeches and the presentation of an engraved muffineer at the end. Best of all was to see so many friends, young and not-chronologically-young.

That fall, the University of Toronto gave RD an honorary degree. And Massey College named its library in his honour, commissioning a bronze bust by the sculptor Almuth Lutkenhaus, of RD at his most stern and Jovian.

JENNIFER SURRIDGE
Did you see how shiny the nose is? RD knew you could have a great deal of talent, but you still needed luck. He was somewhat superstitious, so it's lovely that at Massey College now, the students rub his bronze bust nose for luck.

Massey College gave the Master Emeritus a permanent office in the northeast corner, overlooking the quadrangle. From this office RD wrote, advised, counselled and gave interviews.

PHYLLIS GROSSKURTH
My goodness, he was vain. One time I was doing a piece on [the Jungian analyst] Marion Woodman for *Saturday Night*, and I went to see him. He was being interviewed at the same time by a guy from *The Globe and Mail.* He kept joking, to get a rise out of the *Globe* guy. And there was an electrician around. He wanted them to laugh and pay attention to him. He was telling me awful things about Marianne Woodman so they would all hear. His face was wreathed in pleasure when he heard them all laughing. He would say, "Don't print this," and then tell a terrible story. I had to tone it all down for my article.

The spectre of retirement raised in RD anxieties over money. The Davies family had made $3.1 million with the sale of the *Examiner* (although the majority of that went to the majority shareholder, Arthur Davies). And Rupert had left his grandchildren, including RD's three daughters, well provided for. Yet RD joked about his dread of ending up in poverty.

RD (letter to Horace Davenport, February 11, 1995)
You must abandon all thoughts of the Country Poor Farm. I know that is not easy because such images are bred in the bone. In my family, the dread was of an institution called the Workus – which being interpreted as the Workhouse, familiar from the works of Dickens and the hobgoblin of every right-minded Welshman of the nineteenth century. . . . I have been known to hold this terrible possibility over the heads of my daughters, who receive it with unfilial mirth. With those of your nation, it is the Poor Farm.

JENNIFER SURRIDGE
He had unrealistic feelings that he was poor, and you could explain to him that he wasn't, but that didn't help.

RD's feelings about money came as a surprise to a former student, Damiano Pietropaolo. As a CBC radio producer, he went to interview his former professor for a documentary on Oscar Wilde.

DAMIANO PIETROPAOLO
Davies had been a member of the Old Vic, when in that company there was an older person [Ben Webster] who had worked with Oscar Wilde. Davies told us lovely stories . . . we thanked him profusely. We assumed he, as the great scholar attached to the university, often did this sort of thing, but as we were packing up our interview equipment and leaving, Davies took me aside and said, "Mr. Pietropaolo, if you should offer me $100 for this I would not be offended." I had assumed that he was beyond money, but I was reminded sharply that he was a canny Ontarian with a sense of what's what. I recovered and said, "It's in the mail!"

MARTIN HUNTER
His books are all about money. In the first trilogy, it's the conflict of the inheritance. In the second trilogy, it's the problem of Boy Staunton and his wealth. And the rich are a big theme in *What's Bred in the Bone*. . . . Davies loved to talk about people with money. He'd say, "So-and-so has used his money well."

MIRANDA DAVIES
He certainly experienced his retirement from Massey as a massive loss. He feared that he'd become a nonentity. This was a huge spur to his investing everything in his literary career.

RD (letter to Ian Alexander, December 10, 1981)
I am retired. What does this mean? It means, my dear friend, the LIFE OF A DOG, for I have more work to do than ever, and no efficient Moira to carry most of the detail. (Poor Moira is having sad trouble with her eyes – glaucoma – and is greatly worried though she is very brave. Indeed, the College is hard hit, for Roger has just had a heart attack. Change and decay in all around, I see, Oh God, I wonder, will the next be me – old hymn.)

Since retirement I have been rushing to complete a program of writing articles and the libretto for an opera, all promised by December 15. Ever at my back I hear, the horrid deadline hurrying near. But I am beginning to see the light at the end of the tunnel. Just one more article – on ceremony for a magazine called *Parabola* – which must be whipped off this weekend. After Christmas I must take care not to take on so much.

When he and Brenda vacated the Master's lodging, they moved to a condominium, Oaklands, located north of Massey on Avenue Road. A nearby park was named in RD's honour in 2007.

JENNIFER SURRIDGE

When he and mum moved to Oaklands, he went over the condominium contract with the lawyers. He was very canny.

By 1982, work was becoming more difficult because of a cataract that clouded the vision in his right eye. In December 1983, the problem came to a crisis as he was returning from Massey to Oaklands.

RD (diary, December 20, 1983)

At an intersection crossed the road in front of a car that was waiting for me. . . . Was thrown to the road, but the car was able to stop, and the driver hastened to pick me up; a young man who recognized me, and was put into a canaries because he admires my books. Picked me up, and my briefcase and parcels, and drove me home, v. kindly. Felt shaken but not ill, and had no serious injuries.

But RD was severely bruised. His doctor told him it would be five weeks before he was over the effects.

MIRANDA DAVIES

I remember after his first fall, on Dupont Street in Toronto. I spoke sharply to him about going to the lights to cross the street. . . . I think he was touched by my concern and he told me he had taken it to heart.

RD finally had surgery on his right eye in 1986 and on his left in 1992. Poor vision was just one of his physical tribulations.

JENNIFER SURRIDGE

He had asthma. And he had allergies and thought he had a tricky heart. . . . When he was older, it was hard to know [what he had]. . . . He was not a fan of pills. He had a hard time taking pills. He had real health issues, but he also had melancholia, up-and-down moods. Along with the Black Dog would be physical manifestations of depression. He'd be lethargic, unable to do anything but read (which was his work anyway). A lot of the time he'd say in his diary, "Not feeling well today." But then he'd do a massive day's work. The output was prodigious! Unbelievable! He was incredibly, intensely busy.

RD interspersed hours of concentrated writing with long walks. At Oaklands, he would process down Avenue Road to Massey or his favourite restaurant, Le Rendez-Vous. At Windhover, his house in Caledon, he rambled around his domain while Brenda gardened with the help of a groundskeeper, Theodor Henkenhaf.

THEO HENKENHAF

Always he would roam around the property by himself, for what looked to me like stressful, strenuous and energetic walking. He usually carried a big stick. In the early years it was for protection, because we had rabid foxes on the property.

I told him once that I was reading *Tempest-Tost*. He said, "I am not very proud of that one. I'll get you a better one." He gave me *Fifth Business* and said it was better. It certainly was funnier. I am told I am in one of his books, something about gardening and how it is done. But I don't remember which book. He certainly didn't ask me if he could or couldn't put me in!

At the Davieses' property there were oodles of rocks, and Mr. Davies enjoyed the rocks. Therefore we made use of them. He built little creatures of rocks. There is a special name for these in the Inuit language – *inukshuk*, that's the name. He built these creatures himself. A lot of them got knocked over by wild animals.

Mrs. Davies, Brenda, was always the one to do things maintenance-wise, and Mr. Davies was the creative ideas. He had many different ideas about his stone pile. I know he brought some stones home from England to Caledon. He did not advertise this. Maybe some of the stones weren't supposed to be exported.

UELI SCHALLENBERG
You know the big piles of stones at his country place? He told me that he had a good friend who went to King Arthur's grave and picked up many little stones and sent these stones and RD put them under his big stones. So under RD's big stonepile are little stones from King Arthur's grave. I told Brenda about this. She didn't know what I was talking about. But there was a bit of mysticism about *him*.

THEO HENKENHAF
He called them "Hen Stones" [after megalithic standing stones at Caer Hen Eglwys in Wales]. He mentioned several times to me how old these stones were, how many millions and millions of years. . . . Quite often he would be talking about things and I would just stand there and listen. He did not need or expect me to comment.

NORMAN JEWISON (Caledon neighbour)
He loved rocks. He knew all the names of rocks. And he knew the gossip in the Caledon area, too. He knew the murder stories. A man who lived on Third Line in his late eighties had a son who was killed under strange circumstances. It was claimed that people had murdered him. Robertson would go on about the strange circumstances. He knew a lot of local history – for a guy who never hung around the feed mill. Which *I* did.

Among the neighbours in Caledon, the only people I know he had contact with were the Stewarts. I was making maple syrup and he'd say, "How can you be a farmer out here, there's nothing here but rocks!" and then he'd talk about these poor Irish farmers who emigrated to the Caledon-Mono area "to farm these terrible hills."

UELI SCHALLENBERG
I told him about an enormous hickory tree at my farm. I said I'd wanted to see how big it was, so I hugged it. And . . . it felt good. When I told him this his eyebrow went way up. He said, "This is very interesting. I know of an Indian tribe who hug trees for energy."

THEO HENKENHAF
There are springs on the property and we made three ponds. . . . At this particular pond, he would watch the wildlife, the wild turkeys, the deer.

Mrs. Davies was more the photographer, but Mr. Davies would just want to get close to the wild animals. And he could move very quietly, sometimes to within thirty feet. He had quite a few mysterious ideas about these creatures, and about ghosts and spirits. To me, these were just ideas. They were not in the understandable world. But he got deeper.

Chapter 32

THE CORNISH TRILOGY

RD was thinking about a new trilogy even before he had completed his three Deptford novels. He told Martin Knelman this for an article that appeared in *Saturday Night* magazine in June 1975.

MARTIN KNELMAN (journalist)
Davies writes his novels during the summers working on a strict schedule at his country home in the Caledon Hills. It takes about two years to write one, so with luck the one after *World of Wonders* might be out in 1977. There's one good satiric subject he's thinking about, and that's university life. "The world of business where people compete for money is very innocent compared to what I've seen here," he confides. "Here there isn't much money, so people compete for power and prestige and titles, and that is really cutthroat." But don't expect that book quite yet: "I wouldn't dare write about that until I am retired and safely out."

RD began his novel about university life in 1979 and completed it in 1980. Published in 1980, the year before he retired from Massey, *The Rebel Angels* has as its protagonist a beautiful young half-gypsy girl, Maria. Was he inspired by the young Barbara Chilcott, who had starred in *A Jig for the Gypsy* two decades before?

Many readers detected in this novel some sly portraits from RD's life. Massey College seemed to be recast as Ploughwright College (a reference to the Massey family fortune coming from manufacturing tractors).

RD (letter to Horace Davenport, August 19, 1981)
A new novel comes out in October. Called *The Rebel Angels*, and it is obviously set in the Univ. of Toronto . . . and is truly intended as a celebration of what a university is – in our sad times a guardian of culture and humane feeling against a rising barbarism. Nevertheless a place full

of human creatures of a special sort, with all the passions and whimwhams inseparable from their human condition. There is a murder in it, which may annoy some people, who think academics never kill (except with malice, ill-will and treachery, which are not thought to count). But this is a real murder, and, I flatter myself, in a good university tradition of homicide. . . . [The novel] contains no portraits, pays off no old scores.

Surely RD doth protest too much. Many readers were sure that the novel was indeed portraying real people and paying off old scores. One of *The Rebel Angels'* creepier characters is Urquhart McVarish, an academic with claims of a pretentious Scots ancestry, an impressive war record and a swollen ego. McVarish was suspiciously like RD's real-life Massey nemesis.

ERNEST SIRLUCK
Now, Rob had a long-standing rule that he would not create a character in his fiction based on a real person. And then he did base a character on W.A.C. Dobson, as he saw him. That character came to a horrifying end. When *The Rebel Angels* came out, I asked Rob, "Is this character based on Bill Dobson?" And he looked at me and tilted his head and put one finger to the side of his nose and said, "It is safer not to say." Pretty well everyone recognized Dobson and thought it was rather a mean revenge. I thought it was beneath Rob. But he was so *angry*.

The terrible and undignified end RD created for McVarish shocked David James, professor of engineering and senior fellow of Massey College, and Eluned MacMillan, a family friend and granddaughter of the Welsh prime minister of England, Lloyd George.

DAVID JAMES
After *The Rebel Angels* came out, I was talking to RD. I told him I enjoyed his stories and their strong sense of Ontario identity – I'm from Belleville – and he understood that world precisely. Then I mentioned that particularly gruesome murder . . . and the knitting needle up the nostril. Hmmm. I said I didn't think it was possible that such a thing would occur among academics. RD replied, and I remember this exactly, "My boy, you don't know your colleagues!"

ELUNED MacMILLAN
In one of his books, *The Rebel Angels*, there are two professors, and one puts a pink ribbon up the other's . . . and then kills him. I was shocked. I said to Rob, "That's disgusting." I said I was shocked and he turned on me snappishly and said, "That's exactly why I wrote it. I wanted to shock *you*."

Happily for RD, there were plenty of other people for whom *The Rebel Angels'* scatological references and weird characters (such Ozias Froats, a scientist investigating medieval alchemists' experiments with human excrement) were simply part of normal life.

JAMES CARLEY
I organized Rob to get an honorary degree from Rochester, and at Rochester they stayed with the great Dickens scholar George Ford and his wife, Pat (ex-Canadians, and great friends of the Bissells). One weekend, the Fords came up from Rochester to my wife's family farm, where we were having a visit from my cousin, Sir Francis Avery Jones, England's great ulcer specialist, who had almost singlehandedly built up the first clinical and research base on the peptic ulcer, and his wife, Joan. Sir Francis founded the medical journal *The Gut*. . . . The Stewarts came – not Clair and Amy, but their son Tim and his wife, Nalini. What I remember is George Ford was talking about shit and Victorian hygiene and bad sanitation and Dickens. Avery Jones was talking about how the digestive system produces shit . . . Rob was talking about shit: it figured in his newest novel. I will never forget our dinner at the farm that night.

Another of *The Rebel Angels'* strange characters was a defrocked monk named Parlabane. He was inspired by someone at UCC who used to tell RD about the joys of sodomy, according to a letter RD sent to Horace Davenport in 1985.

Your passages on the rectum, anus, sphincters, etc. turned my mind to a subject much in the news these days, and of curious interest – i.e. sodomy. This was an aberration I do not understand, though years ago I had a friend – the model for John Parlabane in *Rebel Angels* – who was much given to it and carried on ecstatically about its pleasures. To my astonishment I see it now recommended as a diversion for married couples, provided (as these articles invariable say) "that both partners are squeaky clean."

However, some Toronto journalists, including a Southam Fellow at Massey, were convinced that RD had based Parlabane on a Toronto writer he knew, who had left his wife in a scandal.

MICHAEL ENRIGHT (journalist and broadcaster)

Bob Fulford told me that the character of Parlabane in *The Rebel Angels* was based on Scott Symons. Fulford said, "I've never asked Davies about that." I was then a Southam journalism fellow at Massey and I said, "Hell, I'll ask him."

One night in the Master's lodging, I guess I had had a lot of port or madeira, so I asked, "was Scott Symons the model for Parlabane in *The Rebel Angels?*" RD said, "I don't talk about my work in detail." Then he paused and lowered his voice and said, "Scott Symons sucks cocks, you know."

My visible shock was the desired response. I didn't know where to look. I didn't know if the women sitting nearby overheard. I said, "Oh dear me, yes. But isn't that, er, usual with homosexuals? That's what they do?" RD was twinkling. His eyes were alight. He said, "But he *talks* about it!" I got the feeling that he wanted to tell me the naughtiest thing he knew. He was so pleased to convey this information.

The Rebel Angels was published in the United States and the United Kingdom in 1982, to mostly wonderful reviews. In *The Observer*, Anthony Burgess wrote that Davies "stands out as internationally important and undoubted Nobel material." Burgess began to lobby the Swedish Academy to deliver the Nobel Prize in Literature to his favourite Canadian writer. But when RD began to promote the book in person in the United States, he met with some odd responses.

DOUG GIBSON

The review that made a huge difference for this book, and for RD's work in general, was John Kenneth Galbraith's front-page treatment in the *New York Times Book Review*. But on his promotion tour for *The Rebel Angels*, some publicity person for his U.S. publisher had sent him to a Black Christian radio station in Washington – this person must have thought his novel was a religious book. And when the Christian radio interviewer realized what sort of writer RD was, he decided to make the most of it. He told his listeners, "We got a guy here, who says Matthew, Mark, Luke and John *didn't know Jesus!*"

So RD informed his scandalized audience that scholars had questioned whether any of the writers of the Gospels had actually lived at the time of, or had actually known, Jesus. Well! The phone lines lit up. The listeners phoned in and Davies later did an imitation of them protesting, "Matthew, Mark, Luke and John, they *walked* with Him! They *talked* with Him!!"

When he told this story to my class at the Banff Publishing Workshop, I was laughing too hard to notice that some of the younger members of the class were offended by RD telling this with an Afro-American accent. I didn't recognize that some of the more politically correct people did not like his imitation of the outraged Christian callers.

In 1983, while researching the second book of the Cornish trilogy, *What's Bred in the Bone*, RD and Brenda joined an Art Gallery of Ontario trip to Vienna, Budapest and Prague to look at private art collections. One of the trip's organizers was Jane Zeidler, wife of Eb Zeidler, the young immigrant whose modernist church RD had championed in Peterborough, and who was by now a leading Canadian architect.

EB ZEIDLER

On that trip we sometimes travelled by night, and late in the night, driving through the mountains, Rob would tell marvellous stories.

JANE ZEIDLER

This was a terrific trip. We went to the Albertina [art museum in Vienna]. There was a beautiful reading room with great windows, and we had to wear white gloves to look at works like Albrecht Dürer's *The Hare*. Our guide in Vienna, George, took us everywhere. Someone on the bus said something about Freud. George said, "We don't like him much here in Vienna." Rob said, *sotto voce*, "George, your anti-Semitism is showing." I don't know if George heard. *I* heard.

Back in Canada, RD compiled more research for the book, and was interviewed by Eluned MacMillan's daughter Ann, a television producer.

ANN MacMILLAN

I interviewed him in his office at Massey while he was writing *What's Bred in the Bone*. He showed me his filing system and he pulled out a clipping: GUILLOTINE FINALLY ABOLISHED BY FRENCH NATIONAL ASSEMBLY.

I asked him: Why are you interested in the guillotine? He said: "Well! *Every*body is interested in the guillotine. Aren't *you* interested in the guillotine? Aren't you interested in a man lying down with his hands tied behind his back, putting his head on a block and a big knife coming down and cutting it off? Isn't that interesting?"

Rob once claimed that he could smell evil. He talked about having worked with a man who had a revolting smell. According to Rob he was later arrested for being a spy.

What's Bred in the Bone, published in 1985, is about attempts to write the biography of Francis Cornish, art collector, painter and forger. Cornish, who first appears in *The Rebel Angels,* comes from Blairlogie, a remote, rough Ontario town much like Renfrew. *What's Bred in the Bone* struck many readers as the work closest to RD's own bones.

BRONWYN DRAINIE (*Books in Canada* article, 1985)

This is the darkest of all Davies's novels, but not in the sense of the exotic darkness of the bear cave in *The Manticore*. *What's Bred in the Bone* is probably as close as Davies will ever come to the Age of Anxiety. The wit, the eccentricity, the arcana are all present, but much subdued, and behind them you sense a man totting up his personal accounts.

When the character Francis Cornish defended his penchant for painting in the manner of three centuries before, RD seemed to be asserting his insistence on writing an old-fashioned page-turner of a novel. In Cornish's own words:

> How else was I to get attention for my picture? If I had made
> it known that I had painted a great painting in an old style,
> how many of you would have crossed your doorstep to see it?
> Not one! Not one!

BRONWYN DRAINIE (*Books in Canada* article)
And Francis has other concerns. He is consumed by the fear of being second-rate because his aesthetic impulse takes him entirely toward the past rather than the present.

Cornish's childhood in Blairlogie mirrors RD's in Renfrew. Francis, too, is pelted with snowballs on his way to school, and taunted by kids sewn into their long underwear for the duration of winter. Blairlogie's leading citizen is a Catholic multimillionaire senator, inspired by Renfrew's real-life Senator M.J. O'Brien.

MARGARET MacKAY GIBSON
I do not know *what* Renfrew people thought when they read *What's Bred in the Bone!* There was something very special about Renfrew. There were a lot of very nice people there. There was an active University Women's Club in Renfrew. It was *not* way out in the sticks!

But certainly, there was a division in the town between the Catholics and the Protestants. Senator O'Brien was an RC, but he was fond of my great-grandfather. I wasn't keen on *What's Bred in the Bone* because Robertson Davies took on the Senator, and made the O'Brien family do terrible things. . . . My daughter Sarah says Robertson Davies is impish.

RD gave another of the novel's characters, Aylwin Ross, a career trajectory very much like that of Alan Jarvis, the director of the National Gallery of Canada from 1955–1959.

ROBERT FULFORD
That's the closest *roman à clef* portrait in Canadian literature I know, and I know quite a few. As I read *What's Bred in the Bone*, I could hear Alan Jarvis talking. It was the most perfect depiction – in fact, it was better than perfect: it was Alan without the ahs and ums and hesitations.

Writing in the October 1985 edition of *Saturday Night*, Fulford commented:

Like Jarvis, Ross commits the National Gallery to buying certain paintings in Europe without being sure of financial backing from the government. As Jarvis was, Ross is refused support for his purchases

and publicly disgraced. . . . At this point we find one notable difference between novel and history. Ross kills himself immediately; Jarvis
took a dozen years or so to kill himself with alcohol. . . . Davies shows
no noticeable sympathy for Ross, and perhaps Jarvis's many friends
across the country will resent that.

ROBERT FULFORD

Why did I complain in the article that Davies gave Jarvis short shrift?
Davies was using the material as he wanted to, not as I wanted him to!
I sound a little silly to me. Maybe I found the sadness of Jarvis's decline
sadder than most people. He inspired a lot of people. He made the
National Gallery an important place. But Alan was a misogynist. He
once said to me, "I find women reduce the level of conversation to
pointlessness in two minutes" – and Alan was gay and married, which
was a terribly cruel thing to do to his wife. She had no idea he was gay.
When I think of it now, RD could have made him out to be a monster,
which he didn't.

**As RD's readers had come to expect, the novel was studded with arcane
details.**

RD (letter to Mrs. Linda Benn, January 20, 1987)
Many thanks for your letter of January 9th. All the ear-wax references
in *What's Bred in the Bone* are absolutely authentic. My copy of Krafft-
Ebing's book is pre–First World War and I think it is rather different
from more recent editions and certainly it contains the case of the man
who would like to eat his mistress's ear-wax. It is also true that Nicholas
Hillyard used ear-wax as part of the enamel-like paint that he used in
painting miniatures.

I am delighted to have the information you give me about Japanese
use of this fascinating substance in painting. I take enormous pleasure in
such odds and ends of knowledge and like to include them in my books.

**In 1981, the year *The Rebel Angels* was published in Canada, Davies turned
his curious and well-stocked mind to working with composer Derek
Holman on a fifty-minute children's opera, *Dr. Canon's Cure*. The process
of creating an opera turned into the subject of RD's third Cornish novel,
The Lyre of Orpheus, which Macmillan published in 1988.**

ARNOLD GOSEWICH (former music and publishing executive)
I had become president of Macmillan in 1980–81. My basic job was to make sure the company made some money. The way to do that is the amount of profit you make from your books, so pricing is important. All of Robertson Davies's previous books had been priced below $20 at that time. So I did due diligence.

The first Canadian book I had to deal with was *The Lyre of Orpheus*. I realized that in this author we had the equivalent of a rock star – revered, loved, known. I felt we had been undervaluing his work, and I wanted to raise the price of the new novel. I got a lot of resistance in the company. I think we priced it at about $22.95. The book sold well. Robertson Davies told me he was very pleased. We made money and he made more money. I was pleased that everyone turned out to win, most importantly the author.

Chapter 33

AN AMBASSADOR ABROAD

As RD's books won more readers abroad, the Canadian government turned him into an unofficial cultural ambassador, giving him more reason than ever to cross the Atlantic. Besides, in the early 1980s RD and Brenda acquired a flat in London.

BRENDA DAVIES
Richard Wernham, a junior fellow at Massey, found London frightfully expensive, so he decided to have a club and sell weeks at the apartment he planned to buy for a twenty-five-year period. He asked Rob if he'd like to join. RD loved the area where the apartment was, at Pont Street just behind Harrods.

Buying a share of the Pont Street apartment entitled RD and Brenda and their family to two weeks in London every year.

BRENDA DAVIES
Mornings at Pont Street, we'd have cereal and tea. He didn't like tea bags. He'd have a great big cup. He always read *The Times*. We'd go to Harrods Food Hall and we'd walk about London. We'd always go to the theatre. . . . Mostly when we were over there he'd be interviewed for radio shows and do articles for *The Times*. He worked at the dining room table. He wrote by hand, and would deliver handwritten articles to *The Times*. And we always went to the Old Vic.

Another London destination was the Heywood Hill Bookshop at 10 Curzon Street, Mayfair. Not only was it well-stocked with a knowledgeable staff willing to ship books anywhere in the world, but the proprietor was a Davies admirer.

JOHN SAUMAREZ SMITH

In 1978, somebody who worked here went to Yale and said, "By golly, there is a trilogy that is not available in England, John, and it's a knockout."

So I got the Penguin paperbacks shipped over and she was absolutely right. . . .

I must say, there was skepticism at first. I'd say to people who come here for their books, "You must read this Canadian novelist."

They'd say, "Canadian?" or "David Robertson?"

And I'd say, "No, Robertson Davies, and I would like to meet him."

We have many American customers at the store, including Arthur and Nina Houghton, as in the Houghton Library at Harvard. Nina is the sort of person who would read all the works of an author. When she was done Trollope, she said, "I've had such a good time in the nineteenth century! But now I feel I must try and find someone who is more my century."

I said, "Nina, let's think. Have you read anything by Robertson Davies?"

She said, "Never heard of him." She rang me back six weeks later and said, "You weren't half right! Is there anything I can do in return?"

I said, "Don't you feel you would love to meet him? I'd give my eye teeth to meet him." Arthur and Nina said, "We could fly him down."

And so they arranged for me to have a blind date with Robertson Davies at Wye Plantation in Queen Anne's County, Maryland. This would have been around 1980. By the time I got to Wye Plantation, there they all were having a whale of a time, and Rob and Brenda were enjoying the lavish hospitality – really, because this was not about a grand weekend but about a love of reading.

Once conversation at Wye Plantation was about books of magic. I asked him about the magic in his books, particularly in *World of Wonders*, and how he had known so much. He said, "I did that by reading up."

Various things came out of that weekend, not least that Robertson Davies said to me, "The Swedes like me, I get on quite well in France, but not in the Old Country. Is this something to do with England and Canada?"

I said, "You have a fan club in Curzon Street."

Saumarez Smith was eager to introduce RD's books to English readers, and to introduce RD himself.

JOHN JULIUS NORWICH (historian and television documentarian)
I suppose it was John Saumarez Smith who first recommended the books. After I read the Deptford Trilogy I was absolutely thrilled. I wrote him a fan letter and I got a fan letter – no, a delightful letter – back. So I said, "Do let us know next time you're in London." And so they came to dinner. I did not recognize my old school in *Fifth Business*; I had gone to Upper Canada College in September 1940. I don't remember him mentioning at dinner that this was his old school, too. Instead, the talk was about history and the theatre. With his huge white beard he looked like the prophet Isaiah. I remember him as full of life, and gusto and fun.

Alas, other encounters reinforced Davies's sense that the English still looked down on Canadians.

JOHN SAUMAREZ SMITH
When he came to visit the shop on Curzon Street, he saw Trumper the Barber next door.

> ***Geoff Trumper, Court Hairdresser and Perfumer, 9 Curzon Street, Est. 1875, Unique Preparations for the Hair and Scalp, Shaving Creams and soaps of the purest qualities. All Manner of Toilet Requisites.***

Trumper has been there since Noah's Flood. Robertson Davies said to me, "Can they be relied upon?" I said, "Yes."
But when he came out of there he said, "They were snooty. They thought I was a 'colonial.' I am not sure I'll have my beard trimmed there again."

Far more gratifying were encounters with readers. And near-encounters.

JOHN SAUMAREZ SMITH
After RD had just come here on a visit, into the shop came an Australian painter, Jeffrey Smart, who said to one of us, "John [Saumarez Smith]

persuaded me to read Robertson Davies and I am mad about him. I do wish I could meet him."

John Francis said, "You've just missed him by two minutes. Or perhaps he is still out on the street. You may see him there."

Jeffrey rushed out, and there on Curzon Street was a man with a long white beard. He went up to him and said, "I have to tell you, I enjoy your books immensely." The man was not Robertson Davies. But in fact he was himself an author, and had written a book of war memoirs. This comment made his day, it made his week, it made his year!

The next day, I told RD this story when we were having lunch at his club, the Athenaeum, and he started laughing right down in his shoes, and the laughter rolled and rolled. He had a wonderful laugh. Orotund.

There were also trips to New York and Washington, where again RD was called upon to play cultural ambassador.

WILLIAM FRENCH (in *The Globe and Mail*, October 23, 1984)
NEW YORK – An impressive guest he makes, with his Father Time beard, impeccable attire and urbane speech. . . . Many of his novels are well known in the United States and, if attendance at the reading was indicative, by students at NYU. Despite the allure of Manhattan's other attractions, the auditorium in which he read was full, with listeners sitting in the aisles. . . . Davies gave them a treat by reading from his just-finished novel, *What's Bred in the Bone*, to be published next year. The passage was typical of his style, erudite with a quirky edge. It concerned an embalming in a small Ottawa Valley town in the late nineteenth century, and the audience found it highly comic. Davies was suffering from a pesky cold, but tried his best, in the tradition of the acting profession of which he was once a member, not to let that interfere with his performance.

Before reading from his new novel, Davies asked rhetorically how Canadian writing differs from American, and if it has any distinctive flavor. . . . [he] then proceeded to give some satirical examples, using a variety of dialects. One concerned a hissing Quebec heater, delivered in the patois favored by William Henry Drummond. The audience loved it. "That kind of writing," he added, "has lost its relevance for most Canadians." The great fact about Canada is the land itself, Davies said. Everyone's temperament is conditioned by the land. This does not make us a merry, ebullient people, but we are not professionally melancholy either, like the Scandinavians. But the climate and feel of the land provide the ground bass of Canadian writing, and it does have a certain melancholy tone.

WILLIAM FRENCH
The Globe thought the event was important enough to send me down to New York to cover it. The cultural attaché at the Canadian consulate picked me up in a cab at my hotel, and then we picked up RD and his wife at their hotel.

The atmosphere in the cab was decidedly chilly; we did not have a conversation. Perhaps he was concentrating on what he was going to say at the university.

In January 1986, the American chapter of the human rights group PEN invited RD to take part in its annual conference. RD and Brenda flew to New York to speak alongside Alice Munro, June Callwood, Margaret Atwood and former prime minister Pierre Trudeau.

MARGARET ATWOOD
I remember him at the PEN Congress in New York City. We were staying at a grotty hotel and the elevator was broken. Some of the rowdier ones among us were going up and down in the service elevator. He used the back stairs. We saw him in the lobby and he announced, "I have just fallen down the stair!" I said, "Oh! Oh! Are you hurt?" He said, "No. But I'm cross."

Meanwhile, because RD's novels in translation were doing well in Germany and Scandinavia, in the fall of 1986 the Canadian government sponsored a tour that took RD and Brenda from Oslo to Helsinki, to Stockholm and then Copenhagen.

MARGARET ATWOOD
We both stayed at different times in Scandinavia with the same Canadian cultural attaché. He had a dog who could open doors with

his nose. A big dog. So you would be brushing your teeth and suddenly there would be a dog nose poking up your bum. We both had this happen. I know because he asked me, "Did you stay at that place in Scandinavia where that dog would goose you with its nose?"

RD and Brenda were in Scandinavia in September 1986 when they heard that his name was on the shortlist for the Nobel Prize in Literature. And not for the first time; they were also informed that Anthony Burgess, among others, had been lobbying for a Davies Nobel for at least two years. This was followed by more good news.

FELICITY BRYAN (London literary agent)
I was an agent at Curtis Brown, this would be about twenty years ago. Rob was repped by Curtis Brown. . . . I took the Deptford trilogy with me on a holiday to France. I read it, and I was bowled over. When I came back from France I was spouting over about this tremendous writer. Then I read *What's Bred in the Bone*. I sat down and I wrote a long fan letter to Rob. And then *What's Bred in the Bone* was coming out in England . . . I've never worked so hard on getting reviews. We had wonderful reviews for it. And then it was shortlisted for the Booker Prize!

I phoned him while he was on tour in Sweden, to tell him about his being shortlisted. We had not yet met at that point. But over the phone he was very funny and very pleased!

JOHN SAUMAREZ SMITH
At the time, I had two sons at Winchester School, and they told me that the head of the English faculty, a Mr. Wyke, was a great admirer of Robertson Davies. I said to Mr. Wyke, "I gather that you're a fan of Robertson Davies. Would you like me to arrange for Mr. Davies to come down and talk to the boys?" He said, "That would be sensational."

The Tuesday before we were to go down, Felicity Bryan rang me up and said, "John, you and I should be very proud: Robertson Davies is on the Booker Prize shortlist." So I rang up Rob and said, "Congratulations! But will it still be all right for Tuesday?" Rob said, "John, I won't let you down. And as you drive us down to Winchester School you can tell me about the Booker."

I said [with] the Booker list . . . there was always an agenda that was not always going to produce the best sort of decisions. . . .

That day was one of those magical days. Even as Rob and Brenda walked from the college to the cathedral, the cathedral choir was practising. And it was so beautiful it brought tears to their eyes . . .

Just before the talk, Rob stood before some of the boys. He took out an envelope and said to one of them, "It will appear quite soon that I have given one or two lectures, but I want you to have some pleasure in this. So I will speak for twenty minutes and then I want you to ask questions. I know from experience that this often means there is a horrible pause. But this time there won't be – because here are six questions, and I am very good at answering these questions." A brilliant trick!

Then he spoke. He was very informal and he made them laugh. Afterwards, the boys asked questions for an hour and a half. And they never asked his six questions.

JENNIFER SURRIDGE
Being shortlisted for the Booker Prize – on top of hearing that he was being considered for a Nobel! . . . But RD was a great worrier and he realized that winning these prizes would have meant a whole lot more time away from his work. . . . He never believed he deserved to win. Too much of a Presbyterian background.

His diary shows that he was tortured by hope.

RD (diary, September 26, 1986)
The Nobel and Booker have stuffed my pillow with thorns . . . no Stoic, I.

RD (diary, October 20, 1986)
I have a fit of the Black Dog and am downcast all day, wholly irrationally. I feel I have been weighed on the balance and emerged 15 ounces to the pound.

The winner of the 1986 Booker was to be announced on October 22, at a gala dinner in London.

FELICITY BRYAN
That evening, the Booker evening, I picked them up in a taxi at Pont Street. There is a photo at the flat . . . Rob is in black tie and smoking a cigar. He is wearing his big black ring, and is looking right at the camera.

Here's another photo from that evening, of Rob wearing a black bow tie and a burgundy velvet waistcoat, looking very smart. Brenda is in a sequined dress, navy or a dark teal blue, with a red scarf at the neck. . . . Gosh, she's an elegant woman.

RD (diary, October 22, 1986)
The evening of the Booker. Fatigue has gone beyond the point when a night's rest can do much to dispel it. . . . A man from the *Toronto Star* affects a familiarity I do not understand for I know nothing of him. . . . Win or lose it means little, but it consumes a great deal of energy and spirit. A great throng and two policemen keeping a wide swath to a great car. We dress and Brenda looks very elegant. Felicity calls for us and we drive to Guild Hall, to the crypt for champagne and meet celebrities. . . . Denis Healey. . . . Talk with Margaret Atwood and Graeme Gibson. . . .

Atwood was shortlisted for *The Handmaid's Tale* and RD was shortlisted for *What's Bred in the Bone*.

MARGARET ATWOOD
He gave good interviews. This was the first time two Canadians had been on the shortlist, and he talked about how the English were all saying, "How curious! How odd! Two *Canadians!*" And he said, "The English are just a little late in discovering what the rest of the world has known for some time."

FELICITY BRYAN
That year, alas, the judges gave the Booker to Kingsley Amis for services rendered.

RD (diary)
As predicted, Amis. . . . He speaks ungraciously, thanks no one. . . . Clearly pretty well boozed up. . . . Dora Herbert-Jones used to rave about Amis and what a handsome young man he was. Now a swollen wine-skin.

FELICITY BRYAN
I was furious, of course. But I believe that year was the first time in history that the judges announced the runner-up.

RD
I was runner-up. Mrs. Healy told me afterwards one of the judges weakened. A lot of cheering and I had many supporters. Another interview with Margaret Atwood, and we had a jolly indiscreet time.

MARGARET ATWOOD
On Booker night, when we both lost, we did not commiserate. Self-pity is not appropriate at these things. How very Canadian of us! "We were both pleased to be there and it was very nice to be on the shortlist." If it mattered deeply to him, it didn't show. In 2000, when I won the Booker, I thanked him, which was a very Canadian thing to do: to thank All Those Who Had Gone Before.

There was to be no Nobel Prize, either, something that rankled in a small but persistent way for the rest of RD's life. And increasing demands that he travel and give public performances were hard on an older man with breathing problems, a tricky digestive system and a nervous disposition. On a 1988 trip to Sweden, RD fell ill. So did Brenda.

JENNIFER SURRIDGE
There was an asthma attack. . . . In his diary there is a line through Denmark, France, Switzerland, over which he has written "cancelled due to illness." He writes, "I have travel fatigue beyond the usual . . . Hot bath . . . I feel ill. Cannot sleep til 3:30. My throat is raging . . ." They cancel a reading, rearrange interviews. Then they stay an extra day. By now he's throwing up . . . "I am taken to hospital. For two and a half hours am tested, X-rayed, interrogated . . . Bronchial asthma and a wee spot of pneumonia behind the heart."

BRENDA DAVIES
Oh God! He had asthma, and it eventually put him in hospital. First we got colds, and I remember asking the cultural attaché for a steam kettle so we could have some steam. When he was hospitalized I was terribly worried about him. The Swedish woman in charge of the readings came to the hospital to translate for us. Then we went to recuperate at the house of the Canadian ambassador to Sweden. We stayed four nights, until Rob was well enough to travel. There is nothing worse than being sick in a foreign country and you can't talk to people.

RD (diary, September 1988)
Brenda worries and makes emergency plans. Think about next novel . . .
Have awful reflections. Is this the end? Not death but the end of reflective life?

JENNIFER SURRIDGE
That's the kind of thing he said all the time: "Is this IT?"

RD (diary, cont'd)
Doctor prescribes suppositories which I thought went out with Galen . . .
We arrive at Stockholm . . . Given excellent whiskey and then to bed.
Begin Molieresque work with suppository. I am feeble. Is this age or
illness?

JENNIFER SURRIDGE
He sees the doctor on September 14. Then he has a reversal – he
coughed so terribly he gave himself a hernia. He writes: "I hate being a
worry to B[renda] and a burden to [his embassy hosts] the Brownes.
The doctor [Olsson] asks if I am of a nervous temperament. B replies
with such stagey affirmation, Olsson laughs: 'Ho! Ho!!'"

September 17, he writes: "Vague and trembly. I hate the sense of
physical inadequacy. I am quite stupid enough without taking drugs to
emphasize it."

They go to the airport and Miranda and Les [Woollerton, her part-
ner] meet them at Heathrow. They stay with Miranda at Marlborough
Crescent in London. "We watch Miranda's tape of early Ingmar Bergman.
Powerful but I think I did it better in *World of Wonders* . . ."

Then he goes to the Heywood Hill Book Shop.

An interest in books was a good sign that RD was on the mend.

Chapter 34

THE GAY QUESTION

While at Oxford, RD had confessed in a letter to Eleanor Sweezey that he had, for one one-week period at Upper Canada College, had a crush on another boy, who was acting a female role in a UCC play. At Oxford and in English theatre circles he encountered gay men and women, some of who became lifelong friends. When he returned to Canada, homosexual men such as Herbert Whittaker and Grant Macdonald had the wit and playfulness and love of theatre that RD valued in his companions. But being a small-town newspaper editor, he observed decorum about his social life. So firmly did his Establishment mask settle into place that by the 1970s people were surprised when he proved to be open-minded about sexual orientation. No wonder: RD sent contradictory signals.

ERNEST SIRLUCK
Sometime in the 1980s, when positions on this subject were not as evolved as they are now, I was reading a novel by Patrick White, and I mentioned to Davies how good it was. His reaction shocked me. He said, "Oh, that poof!" I knew that Patrick White was homosexual – but this seemed very strange coming from Rob. I was taken aback.

It was as if he perceived that his duty as Master of Massey was to defend conservative Establishment values despite his basically open mind.

SCOTT SYMONS
When I ran away to Mexico with John McConnell, around 1967, John was then a day under 17. He was flamingly beautiful, gorgeous red hair, and he was no fool. But legally, he was underage. Which made things awkward – well, illegal. His parents had tried to put him in a gilded cage, but I sent him a telegram: "Take up your cock and walk!" Which he did.

His father was the head of Eastman Kodak, and chair of the premier of Ontario's ad campaign, and [the Premier] John Robarts said he did not want to be the one to put Scott Symons and John McConnell in jail. This was high-level stuff!

After a year, when John and I came back from Mexico, we turned up at Massey College. They say I turned up handcuffed to John? Well, bravo for us! That is exactly what we would have done. I do remember stating, "They are not going to separate us!"

Robertson Davies would not have been rude to us. To be rude to John McConnell would be like being rude to John Robarts. So they showed us in. I remember that evening challenging Robertson Davies. I said things like, "You're a joke!" I challenged him in his own house. I would have come in with four funnels steaming. And Davies always had four and a half funnels steaming. I must say, we liked each other's bravado and panache! I still remember him sitting in his den at Massey, pulling on his beard.

Robertson Davies was a pompous asshole. And if anyone was a certifiable snob, it was Davies. He tried to impress us with the port, the cigars, the rituals. He couldn't outsnob us! But he made me laugh. He *was* witty. It's coming back to me – that night at Massey *he egged us on*, bless him! After he told me I'd end up in a Mexican jail, he said to us, "What you should do now is go out and break a few windows!" Robertson Davies was conventional – but he was on our side.

In fact, RD even saluted Symons in one of his Christmas Gaudy ghost stories, "Conversations with the Little Table."

I am sure that many of you are acquainted with the book on Canadian furniture written by the great expert on that subject, Scott Symons; in it he asserts that Canadian furniture, at its finest, has a sensuous quality that can be, under certain circumstances, positively erotic. He says – and I have no reason to doubt his word – that on one occasion during a meal a dining table caressed his leg. Ghosts I can cope with, but erotic furniture destroys my self-possession.

People who had known RD since their childhood were also unsure of his attitudes.

JAMIE CUNNINGHAM

After *Fifth Business* I wrote him a letter of congratulations and I realized when he replied that he must have been inquiring about as to what was going on with that Cunningham boy. Maybe my brother-in-law, Martin Hunter, told him that I was an actor and that I was gay, because RD wrote me back a letter thanking me for my note, and he wrote something like "I applaud you for the intelligence and courage to be yourself" – which I took to mean "being an artist and being out." I took it as a thumbs-up.

ANN SADDLEMYER

Douglas LePan had been very distressed by Rob's *The Rebel Angels* and its gruesome homosexual murder. He told me that at High Table. I don't think he took it personally, but he didn't like the book or what it did to Massey. And Douglas didn't think Rob knew anything about [LePan's love for a young man named] Patrick until *Far Voyages* came out in 1990. Douglas came to me and said that he was going to publish this book of erotic poetry – that he would be coming out with a book about Patrick. He told me that he was very nervous about giving the book to Rob because their relationship went back to before Oxford. But when he did give Rob the book, Rob was very formal – but very encouraging.

MARTIN HUNTER

The whole sexual thing in RD's books is intended to shock and be outrageous. But that's just RD showing off. He was not interested in sexual experimentation himself, but he was interested in other people and their idiosyncrasies. I can tell you one story: Douglas LePan had an office at Massey after he returned from a stay in Bermuda, and he had left his wife and had published a book of homoerotic poetry. RD went to him and said, "Douglas, this is very brave of you – not that I have ever given much attention to that side of my character." RD wasn't saying that he was homosexual, but that he seemed to regret that he hadn't explored that side of his relations with other men.

Chapter 35

THE RELUCTANT

BIOGRAPHEE

For a man with a strong sense of privacy, all too aware of his own contradictory values and sympathies, the last thing RD wanted was an intrusive,
investigative biographer. For years he hoped that his friend Gordon Roper
would produce the definitive Robertson Davies biography and pre-empt
other would-be explorers of his psyche.

JUDITH SKELTON GRANT
Roper's desire was to make people understand RD's books better. The
article he wrote in 1972 about *Fifth Business* and Jung grew out of years
of friendship with RD. He told me how he remembered the big black
Bollingen books of Jung arriving at RD's. It was Roper who opened
Canadian eyes to the Jungian influence on RD's writing.

MICHAEL PETERMAN (Trent University professor of English and colleague of Gordon Roper)
Gordon saw RD's talent and watched his development closely. Gordon
could see the passion and the talent, the seeds of something that was
percolating.

But by the early 1970s it was clear that Roper was not going to complete
his RD biography project any time soon, and by this point RD's growing
literary reputation was making it impossible for him to evade the attention of other biographers.

ELSPETH CAMERON BUITENHUIS
I interviewed him for my M.A. thesis, which was published as a book
in 1971. I was then at the University of New Brunswick and I had come
to Toronto for this. I went to see him during the day, and the Massey
quadrangle fountain was going. I interviewed him in that same study.

It was my first of hundreds of interviews, and at the time I was just 21 or 22. He was not friendly. He delighted in a cat-and-mouse game, intimidation. I had a tape recorder, and the noise of the fountain almost masked the interview. I'd gone in with a list of questions, something I never do now, and my questions were probably naive. I was so nervous – and he did not try to put me at my ease. Instead, he sort of pontificated. I felt I was in the presence of a very important person who had no time for me, or for anyone else for that matter – it wasn't personal and I didn't take it personally.

When Buitenhuis attempted to follow up her interview with letters, RD's response was crushing.

RD (letter to Elspeth Cameron Buitenhuis, July 14, 1971)
Your letter of July 7th just reached me. . . . I am not surprised that McClelland and Stewart refused to give you information about sales; publishers generally take this attitude and I am in agreement with them because I think that such information, if made public, encourages a false standard of judgment and is also information which I think an author is unwise to let out. I would not consider making public what my income is, or how I get any part of it. . . .

I am sending you a sheet which contains some information about my life. It is substantially the same as what appears in *Who's Who*. As is always the case with such summaries it conveys no sense of the reality whatever, but I have not time to write an autobiography . . .

What do you want to know about the Greek names in *Eros at Breakfast?* If you are looking for some sort of symbolic meaning there is none.

I suppose you know that Professor Gordon Roper, of Trent University English Department, is working on a book about my writing which will be considerably more extended than yours. Possibly if you want answers to detailed questions you might apply to him as he has given some years of study to many things about my work which are not clear in my mind at present.

Elspeth Buitenhuis's thesis was published by Forum House in 1972 as a paperback, *Robertson Davies*, edited by William French. Lacking access to her subject, the author had only produced an eighty-page biography.

RD disliked it, and urged his friend in a letter written on August 23, 1972, to step up his own work.

I am anxious that you should become the Received Authority about me, for there are getting to be a few theses, and that awful, coarsely contrived mess by Frau Buitenhuis, which students must turn to if they turn to anything, and they are dreadful. This is delicate to say, but you know very well that I do not regard you as my trumpeter or apologist, but as a scholar who by native wit, training and personal knowledge and sympathy with me knows what I am struggling to do, and I want your voice to be heard. It will be impossible then for anybody to ignore it; but at least the kind of nonsensical rubbish that depicts me as a sort of queeny, snuff-taking intellectual clown will have to go. Canada is such a bloody *belittling* place, and the brass-bowelled lack of intellectual curiosity displayed by Frau Buitenhuis is very common.

ELSPETH CAMERON BUITENHUIS
At a conference I heard Frank Davey say that Canadian literature had almost no bibliographic or biographical material on its writers. I decided to write on Davies, and sent him a letter. He must have said no. . . . He had reason to be worried because he was not at all a truthful man. . . . He was a pompous lecturer, more of a performer – because he was a failed actor. As a writer, I don't think he was interested in sex. He was much more interested in food.

JENNIFER SURRIDGE
Gordon Roper did work on a book about RD but he never got on with it. He was writing it in the early 1970s. Then someone named Michael Peterman took it on.

MICHAEL PETERMAN
Gordon's nominal reason for not doing the book on Robertson Davies was ill health. He was going blind, he had angina and he had to live with the reminders of rectal cancer. I was on my first sabbatical, so about 1978–79 he called me and said, "Would you be willing to complete this book with me?" He had been working on the Davies study for G.K. Hall since the 1960s. What I also remember is that RD wanted to

be written up, big time. Hence his impatience in anyone's failure to deliver with promptness.

I had first met Davies when I was a grad student at Massey in 1970. I'd come back from Princeton to do my Ph.D. I also knew W.A.C. Dobson, who retired up here in Peterborough in a little Regency cottage and who had an extraordinarily deep-seated dislike of Davies. At Massey, Davies would invite people to a dinner party, and then Dobson would somehow get hold of the list and invite everyone to a sherry party first so they'd be too drunk to go to the Davies dinner party.

RD could create enemies very quickly, and to my mind he didn't necessarily read people well. Gordon always maintained that he was a very shy man. But RD's disguises were not only modes of self-protection but of self-assertion and aggression.

When I got involved in the biography, Gordon had done about a hundred pages of text, most of it uncritical. Gordon's problem was that he liked Davies so much and saw so much promise in him he found it hard to be critical. Gordon's first hope was that we would do it as a joint book. But after I read everything he'd done, I was thinking, "This book won't go far academically." I told Gordon, "I am going to start over. I have to seek a different tone and approach."

I did an overview chapter and two chapters on the plays. I took them to Gordon's house. At some point, he looked at me, paused, and then he said, "I don't have any objection to what you've done, but I will have to take my name off it."

I was trying to create a critical point of view. Roper's manuscript would have been hagiography. Gordon said to me many times that it was hard for him to get a critical distance from Davies . . . so we, Gordon and I, reached this interesting parting. It was a mark of Gordon's generosity that he said to me, "I will have to take my name off it – but keep up the work and keep reading it to me."

Being young, I was being overly aggressive. I had to tone it down over the process of the five or six years I was working on the book. There's a wonderful postcard that RD sent to Gordon in 1983: "When's Peterman going to be done with Ma Moodie [Susannah Moodie – I was doing research on her] and do me?" When I saw it, it took my breath away. He was *very* annoyed with me – *whew!* very annoyed. When *he* did a book, he got it done. He could never understand people who took a long time over a project.

I did interview RD for my book. I found it a bit of an awe-inspiring experience. He was very guarded but helpful, but when I honed in on something, he really bristled and bridled. I remember almost backing into the wall in the early 1980s at Massey College, on this question of who was the "common man." I questioned how much he knew about the phenomenon that he so readily labelled. He talked as if he really knew the common man. My sense was that he really didn't. I always said, "To know your gardener well is not to know the common man."

Michael Peterman's *Robertson Davies (Twayne's World Authors Series)* was published by Twayne in 1986.

MICHAEL PETERMAN

RD's comment on my book was that it was written in "Quaker Oats prose" – wasn't that a nasty slice-and-dice! I guess it means the book was a consumer product. He was also saying, "This writer is a small-city man" because Quaker Oats had a factory in Peterborough.

There were no personal encounters with him after my book came out, but I did get the sense that he disliked the book and he disliked me. Maybe he wanted a sycophant-ish, positive book and I did say I didn't think the plays were up to scratch. But I still tell people that I think *General Confession* should be performed and that others are very good.

In 1995 I had a Fulbright scholarship and I was at Princeton. I heard that one of the readers coming was Robertson Davies, but I was never formally told. And this was odd because I was the senior Canadian Studies scholar on campus at that time. Nor was I invited to the small dinner that was held in Davies's honour. I heard later from someone in the dean's office that Davies had explicitly said, "I will come and do the reading, but don't invite Peterman to the dinner."

In the late 1970s, when Peterman was just starting his work on RD, another academic, Judith Skelton Grant, produced a small critical biography (*Robertson Davies*, McClelland & Stewart, 1978). Then she proposed to produce an anthology of his journalism and a collection of his criticism.

JUDITH SKELTON GRANT

What was troubling him when I was working on this project was that people might think that he was over the hill, something that had never crossed my mind, given how productive he was. After all he had just completed the Deptford trilogy, had written a couple of new plays and a book about Leacock, and had published a collection of speeches, all in less than ten years.

At the end of the meeting he said "Okay, go ahead" . . . so I went off and began to re-read his columns and articles, and to make decisions about what might be included in the two collections I had proposed.

In 1977–78, after I had gathered piles of photocopies from which my eventual selection would be made, and many of them were faint and hard to read, I took the stack to Davies. I wanted him to make excisions before I got each collection balanced. He was a very hard worker. He removed only a few individual pieces, among them several articles on Tyrone Guthrie because he was planning to do some writing on that himself. It was not a case of self-censorship but of utility, of not wanting to scoop himself. . . . But in the main he said, "It's your book, you make the decisions."

I had four sections for *The Enthusiasms of Robertson Davies*: Books, Characters, RD himself, and Marchbanks. I took in masses of material. Davies went through the manuscript in a week and a half. Then he didn't want to see it again until it came out in book form. He was surprised that *The Enthusiasms* had a good sale in the United States. He wrote me a couple of notes. He said he had doubted that the collection would be of interest and was surprised and pleased with the response.

The other book [I did, *The Well-Tempered Critic: One Man's View of Theatre and Letters in Canada*, 1981] revealed that he was an astute critic of our national literature. He'd recognized the key works in the Canadian literature canon as they were published, in his reviews in *The Peterborough Examiner* and *Saturday Night*. He'd been calling it right.

We only had two or three meetings over those first books – a first, stiff meeting and then three or four others. He had me to dinner with my husband, John Grant, at Massey. I think he truly thought I was a graduate student. I remember John and I arriving at the Master's lodging at Massey, and Davies saying, "You didn't tell me you were married to the chief economist at Wood Gundy." That was a whole new angle on me, one which he hadn't grasped. He wasn't at ease with economists. If he had treated John as a normal person who loved to read books it would have been easier for both of them.

In the spring of 1981, Skelton Grant began to consider a full-length biography of RD.

JUDITH SKELTON GRANT

It was April or May 1981 when I approached him about writing his biography. I was so sure he'd say no that I had committed myself to writing a short critical book about the Canadian short-story writer Mavis Gallant. I'd finished both of the collections and he'd read them both. And all the questions in my mind were biographical. I wondered what sort of life had produced the books he wrote. Where had these interests come from?

I was certain that he'd say no. I'd heard him say, "The thought of some graduate student grubbing through my papers makes my skin crawl." But I couldn't turn away from the work I'd done in the collections without at least asking about a biography. So I went to ask if he might be willing to have a biography written. I said, "I'd very much like to work on a biography of you." To my total surprise, he said, "That would be great." You could have knocked me down with a feather. I started one year later.

About a month before the interviews for the biography started, we had the Davieses to dinner at our house. With them we had Sister Benedetta, an Anglican nun, Ann Hutchison and James Carley (James had been a junior fellow at Massey). I wanted people he'd feel comfortable with. And the chap from National Trust who was Massey College's financial adviser, Austin Seton Thompson, and his wife. Thompson was a broadly read person with a twinkly personality who was a good addition to a dinner party. My intention was to make it clear that I was on equal ground with Davies: I was *not* a graduate student but a professional, and able to entertain him at an interesting dinner party.

I remember Austin quoting the actor Garrick saying of Oliver Goldsmith that he "wrote like an angel but spoke like Poor Poll," and saying that he'd always wondered who Poor Poll was. Three people at the table spoke up: "Polly Parrot, of course!" It was that sort of dinner party. People had a command of quotation and a broad range of literary reference. RD sparkled and so did everyone else. It was a wonderful dinner party.

Afterwards I said to my husband John, "I think we're starting things off right." And John replied, "But RD was nervous," showing me the paper serviette from the place setting where RD had been sitting. It had been shredded. And yet, that evening, RD had shone.

As the interview process began, RD laid down some ground rules.

JUDITH SKELTON GRANT
While I was researching the biography, Davies did some funny things. We talked about the resources I would be able to use. I asked about diaries, and I pointed out that they would be very helpful, as they would give me access to what he was like at a particular point in time without the overlay of memory and the distortion of looking back. He made it clear that he'd give me access to a great deal of material, but not all. I had a list of people and he had a list, and as we talked and I worked, the list expanded. What I hadn't grasped – and what I realized later – was that the questions that I thought would be hard, the psychological ones, were easy because he had thought so much about them. The questions he found hard were about facts, though he had an astonishingly good memory.

Skelton Grant did one interview a week for twenty-six weeks, for an academic year. She recorded these conversations, which typically lasted from 10:30 until noon. Anything on the tapes was fair game, but RD had control over which documents he allowed his biographer to use.

JENNIFER SURRIDGE
In the beginning, RD was quite enthusiastic about Judith Grant. He thought she would do it well and not make it into a big exposé. He got in touch with all of us and said she was doing this book and would we talk to her? She came to visit me in Ottawa and we talked for quite a while.

But as her questions became more penetrating, RD began to complain in private letters to his close friends that she had "no bowels of compassion."

JUDITH SKELTON GRANT
What did he mean when he said I had no bowels of compassion? I have no idea, but I did discover that he was very mercurial and very dramatic in the way he expressed himself in private utterance.

Meanwhile, RD was sorting out his feelings about biographers as he always did – through writing. He was at work on *What's Bred in the Bone*, in which the character Simon Darcourt wrestles with the difficulty of discovering the truth about the elusive Francis Cornish. Darcourt is not the only biographer: the story is narrated by all-seeing angels, who have more insight than the poor humans below.

JUDITH SKELTON GRANT

He certainly thought a lot about the role of the biographer. He'd written a hundred pages or so of *What's Bred in The Bone* on yellow newspaper pads, the paper with a dull finish. He had written the whole first section, in which he has Simon Darcourt meet with Arthur and Maria and say, "It can't be done, I can't write this biography, there must have been formative childhood influences and I cannot get my hands on them."

Davies had finished writing that section when he phoned and asked me to come down to his office. He then read all that opening section to me. Then he stopped, looked up at me and asked, "Well?"

I said, "I can hardly wait to read the rest." He said, "Well, are you concerned about that passage as a biographer?" I said that I had just written a speech based on RD's *Saturday Night* magazine reviews of biographies of writers and artists, [in which he had written that] a biography of an artist is almost impossible to write. Most of an artist's adventures are internal, and therefore discussing or making a life emerge is not easy to do. I had prepared myself for writing RD's biography by reading all these reviews. I said, "I can't take what you've just said personally, as directed solely at me, because you've said it so often before."

He said, "Fine! As long as you are okay with it."

Afterwards, it did occur to me that he was including a biographer in *What's Bred in the Bone* because he was himself the subject of a biography at the time, and that experience was stimulating all sorts of reflection. I did find after I had read *The Lyre of Orpheus* that Simon Darcourt scores about 85 percent in terms of his subject, and comes up with some highly original methods of research. He was indefatigable, and while he didn't lick everything, he got the essence and much of the detail of the life of his subject right. I looked on that as a report card. Davies wrote about biographers because every writer has to use the fodder that is most engaging his energies.

Then came the crises – starting with RD's first version of his years at Oxford. When Skelton Grant began to question the timing of RD's studies, RD admitted frankly that he had glossed over his breakdown. He revealed that he had failed his first year, and consulted with Dr. Gillespie. Then he spoke of unrequited feelings for someone in Kingston in the early 1930s.

JUDITH SKELTON GRANT

At the end of our first chat about his time at Oxford, I gave him a list of half a dozen people associated with that period in his life, whom I wanted to discuss during our next interview. Dr. Gillespie was on the list. I thought Gillespie was someone Davies had worked for, given the way he'd spoken of him in a CBC interview. (I transcribed every interview Davies had done for the CBC and thus was well aware of many details, which Davies had thought were irretrievable. That's where I got Dr. Gillespie's name.) I did not know that he had been Davies's psychiatrist.

And after the first interview on his Oxford period, I spent the weekend with a British friend who'd been to Oxford. I said, "There's something wrong here with the chronology of the Oxford period." And my friend said, "It should have taken him two years to do this, and yet it took him three." So I went back the following week intending to ask him about the Oxford chronology and about Dr. Gillespie. But before we began he said, "I think we'd better start over." He revealed that he had not told me about Eleanor Sweezey, the woman he'd fallen in love with in his final year at Queen's University. Nor about his breakdown at the end of his first year at Oxford. He had not told me about his counselling sessions with Dr. Gillespie. He had not told me that he had flunked his exams at the end of his first Oxford year.

At that time in RD's life, in his early twenties, he had continued to press his affection for Eleanor Sweezey, both by letter and on visits home to Canada.

JUDITH SKELTON GRANT

I could tell that talking about the relationship was truly difficult. We went back several times to the love affair, as he got more comfortable talking about it. It took him a whole year after telling me about her existence to tell me her name. And several months after that I went to Montreal to talk to her and hear her side of the story. Before I went

to see her, RD went to see her and had lunch with her. I suspect that
the reason he went to see her again was to make sure that she would say
little to me.

Skelton Grant found Sweezey in Montreal. She was a single woman who
had had a successful career as a medical artist. She agreed to speak with
Skelton Grant, and offered to let her stay in her sister's apartment.

JUDITH SKELTON GRANT

I arrived on a weekend when Eleanor was under great emotional stress.
Her sister (a powerful person in her life, who had interfered in her relationships with men) was on life support in a hospital, which was visible
out the window of her apartment where we were talking.

She, Eleanor, loaned me her sister's apartment, which was in the
same building. Her first statement as I arrived at her door was, "I have
letters I didn't return to Rob. Do you want to see them?" I said, "Yes!"
But I also assured her: "RD owns the words. I cannot quote from the
letters without his permission." And I told her that she owned the physical letters, and her permission too was necessary if I were to quote from
the letters.

That was the weekend that Eleanor thought that she had to decide
whether to pull the plug on her sister; it turned out after the weekend
that she didn't have to make that decision after all. I found her very
blunt, unguarded.

For the previous six months, RD had been preparing a typescript
of the letters he had written to Eleanor Sweezey from Oxford, for my
use, to give me access to his young self. However, the fact that I had only
his typescript rather than the letters themselves meant I could never be
certain what he had edited. He certainly removed all evidence of what
he called the "sugar syrup," the lovesick young man.

I saw that side of his young in-love self only in the letters to
Eleanor that remained in her possession. She also had a letter that one
of Davies's Oxford friends had written to her, a twelve-page, thoughtful
exploration of RD's state of mind in the time of his breakdown.

When I went to see RD after my interview with Eleanor, he said
"I've completed the typescript of my Oxford letters for you – forty
single-spaced pages!"

I said, "I'm delighted. Thank you." But my rule for myself was that
whenever I learned something that would make Davies uncomfortable,

I told him. So I continued: "You should know that she kept twelve letters." He replied: "That crook! What's she going to do with them? Publish them in the *Star Weekly?!*"

I said: "No, they are mementos that prove that she, who never married, was once loved by someone exceptional. I think that if you wrote her a letter and asked her to have them returned to you after her death, she would do it." So far as I know, he never wrote that letter.

I quoted a couple of snippets from those letters, but nothing from the sections expressing his despairing love. They were not vivid. They were abject. I thought I could do a better job at evoking his state of mind than those letters.

RD wrote his own version of this conversation in the margin of his copy of the précised letters from the 1930s. The note is dated 1983.

1. Judith Grant tells me that EAS has kept some of these letters and shared with her, which throws a new light on her apparent renunciation in returning them to me as being all she had saved.
2. JG has a different story: EAS gave her a tale of romance uncompleted for a variety of reasons, but JG thinks she was a coquette – to use an old-fashioned term – who liked to receive love but would not or could not give it.

Skelton Grant also tracked down a Swedish woman, Birgitta Rydbeck, on whom RD had developed a crush in his early days at the Old Vic.

JUDITH SKELTON GRANT
I contacted Birgitta because RD had made a note in the margin of one of the travel diaries that I was allowed to see, when he and Brenda were in Sweden and he wanted to look her up. He had written her contact information in the diary. So I wrote to her and asked if she had letters or recollections that she would be willing to share. I said I was pleased to be able to reach her because it was important to see what RD was like earlier in his life, from someone who had no overlay of memory from what he was like later. She wrote back the most marvellous letter in Swedish English, based on her diaries and on her letters home from England to her mother. In this letter she said she still had correspondence from RD but she would not release it unless RD approved.

When I told him this, his reply to me was, "Nobody would want to know what was in those letters . . ." pause . . . "*Everyone* would want to know what was in those letters, but they are *not* to know." Afterwards, Brenda let me read them.

DOUG GIBSON

It is true that he was nervous about being the subject of a biography. He would groan theatrically when asked how things were going with Judith Skelton Grant. But he greatly admired her thoroughness.

Yet another issue of control emerged over Grant's request to see how RD worked on his novels.

DOUG GIBSON

A significant exchange he had with Judith had to do with whether she would see notes for the first two volumes of the Cornish trilogy, *The Rebel Angels* and *What's Bred in the Bone*, while he was working on the third one, *The Lyre of Orpheus*. He wrote no to her request and gave three reasons, and the greatest of these was that he was not comfortable with putting his life under a microscope.

Davies used to say, "People ask me where I get my ideas from. I say, 'You might as well ask a spider where it gets its thread.'" By definition he is talking about something that wells up inside him, and it is not surprising that a spider would be reluctant to share the source of its thread.

JUDITH SKELTON GRANT

He certainly wrote his agent in New York and forbade him to let me see anything recent, though I could see the archive at Columbia University, which was very useful. But I think he regarded the biography as a psychological adventure. Psychological adventures interested him.

Ultimately, RD grew annoyed because Grant's biography, like Roper's project, was taking so long.

JENNIFER SURRIDGE

He began to feel put upon about the biography as time went on. As the project took about ten years, he felt it was a long time to "be got at" by someone else.

RD (letter to Gordon and Helen Roper, August 27, 1992)
Judith Grant seems no nearer to producing her book. But I can read her mind; she wants me to die so she can end it properly. I hope to disappoint her.

JENNIFER SURRIDGE
He was given every chapter to read as she wrote it, and Mum read them, too. By then he didn't want to be so involved. He had more than enough to do, and as he got older he got crankier about work imposed on him by others. So there was a lot of groaning.

Robertson Davies: Man of Myth was published in 1994 by Viking Penguin Canada. Friends such as John Philip Stead told RD that Skelton Grant had done a very fair job. But RD was unhappy.

RD (letter to John Stead, April 1995)
I accept your judgment of Judith Grant's book; I am the worst possible critic. Of course I am aware of how much she has missed of the self-doubting, maggoty-headed jackass that lies beneath the showy exterior.

JOHN SAUMAREZ SMITH
The woman who did his biography – RD called her "Boswellina." (Brenda may not like my saying that!) RD said of that biography, "The book has lots of research and that's what a biography is all about. But the book is not about ME."

Because so much of the book's account of Davies family life had been filtered through the prism of RD's memory, *Man of Myth* annoyed other family members, particularly Fred's daughters Kate and Jane.

KATE DAVIES BRAY
A lot of what people know about my father is coloured by Robertson's biography. I still to this day do not understand why Judith should not have spoken to us or my mother. One thing my father never, ever did was manage my mother's money. Her money was her money. There were a tremendous number of misconceptions on the part of Robertson with regard to my parents. Robertson would have said these things to Ms. Skelton Grant! That he would think my father married money and then spent the rest of his life managing it! It makes me laugh. Robertson

had a much more dramatic view of things than the rest of us did. He had some clay feet, very clay feet.

And RD kept complaining about his own portrayal in *Man of Myth*.

RD (letter to Horace Davenport, November 20, 1994)
You have said so much about Judith Grant's book that I feel strongly but cannot quite bring myself to say to her. On the whole I think that it is a creditable production but I am vain enough to think that as a portrait of me it lacks verve and the failure to distinguish between the significant and the insignificant makes it a sad muddle; several friends have told me that they have essayed it and have broken down in early pages.

JUDITH SKELTON GRANT
I found it difficult to cope with the way he reacted to its publication. He said he hadn't read it, and had given it to his secretary to read. This was slighting in the extreme. He truly did not want to answer questions about it, and one way to do that was to say that he hadn't read it. But things grew awkward enough that I went to see him at the Oaklands [his condominium] with my husband John and gave him a presentation copy. I wanted to remind him that I was a real person, who had done a lot of work, and that the least he could do was be civilized. The following year he wrote me a postcard, and a couple of months later a letter. We were embarking on a new project – a collection of his letters – in the months before his death. We would probably have had a congenial relationship had he lived longer.

RD (letter to Judith Skelton Grant, May 1995)
By chance last night I picked up the TV program *Imprint* which proved to be about literary biography, and as I watched it, with gaping mouth, I realized how gently and considerately you treated me in *Man of Myth*. . . . Prominent among the panelists – indeed Top of the Pops – was your old pal Elspeth Cameron, looking, I must say, splendid. . . . I am sure you have heard the latest news of Elspeth. She has COME OUT OF THE CLOSET. . . . The men of the literary world may now breathe more easily, but you Women of Letters had better watch your step.

Chapter 36

FILM FLAM

From his boyhood, when he had thrilled to *The Phantom of the Opera* in Renfrew's O'Brien Opera House, RD was enchanted by the movies. Until late in life, however, he maintained film was, as an art form, inferior to theatre. Still, he was acutely aware that movies were making some of his fellow writers rich and bringing their works to wider and wider audiences. For years the screen was the object of RD's contempt – and his yearning.

NORMAN JEWISON
I think I first met Rob at Clair and Amy Stewart's, his neighbours and mine in Caledon. I was on the next concession road over and I knew them and they invited me to dinner and I was introduced as "that filmmaker." He then immediately expounded on how awful movies were. But I realized that he was *au courant*. I'd always thought that he'd be a secluded guy. But he was hip, very hip. He was cool, very cool. When RD talked to me about my movies, it was *The Thomas Crown Affair* that he liked. . . . the erotic chess game! He told me that he and Brenda liked to go to "the senior citizens' showing" because you could not only get senior rates and get good seats, you could come out in time to have a decent dinner and a glass of wine. He had it all worked out.

Because he loved movies, RD was obsessed by the fact that his own novels were not being made into feature films. But not for want of trying – Nick Meyer, the young Los Angeles filmmaker who went after the rights to *Fifth Business*, spent a good part of two decades trying to get the project into production.

NICK MEYER

Herb Jaffe and I became close when he produced *Time After Time*, which I had written. Herb read *Fifth Business* and said, "It's terrific, but I don't see how you could make a good movie out of it."

I agreed with him that it was too complex a story to figure out a structure that would work. I said, "I know it might well be beyond my capabilities – but you never know till you try."

Herb said, "Your candour is refreshing," and because he had just seen my movie *The Seven-Per-Cent Solution*, he said, "Nick, I'll take a flyer and option this novel for you."

In 1976, Herb Jaffe bought the rights.

JENNIFER SURRIDGE

RD sold the film rights to the book outright on the advice of his agent. This wouldn't happen now. At that time he thought that $50,000 sounded pretty good, and his agent thought this would be a good deal. The deal sounds so different from what I'm now acquainted with as a film deal. No reversion clause! But RD sold it outright because he was so astounded that they wanted it.

Meyer began working on the script, and soon acquired the rights from Jaffe.

JENNIFER SURRIDGE

RD had been quite chuffed when Nicholas Meyer bought the rights. RD had liked [Meyer's film] *The Seven-Per-Cent Solution* and thought that a good film might come out of Meyer and *Fifth Business*.

NICK MEYER

When I was actually writing the script, I flew up to Toronto and met him. Robertson Davies struck me as he struck everyone: the Mephistophelean persona, the bushy eyebrows, the big beard, the love of ceremony. He had me to a high table at Massey College. He may have told a ghost story.

We had dinners in the late 1970s and early 1980s, when I'd come to Toronto to see him. He talked about theatre and opera. He figured me for someone who was literate – not an inaccurate perception. But my dad was a New York analyst with a certain degree of skepticism about Jung, so we did not get into Jung. One of the things about *Fifth Business* which I liked is that there isn't a lot of dogma. *The Manticore* is steeped in Jungian dogma.

I was heavily influenced in my adaptation by Orson Welles's *Citizen Kane* and I always described this movie as "*Citizen Kane* with magic." I used to say, "This is a film about four people whose lives are inextricably entwined . . . the little boy who throws the snowball grows up to be the Canadian Charles Foster Kane."

NORMAN JEWISON

It was only when Rob and I started having dinner together that he asked me to read a screenplay of *Fifth Business* by Nick Meyer. I knew Nick Meyer. He had a lot of talent as a writer-director, and had enormous respect for the Deptford trilogy. But after he finished his third rewrite of the screenplay to *Fifth Business* he felt that Rob didn't like it and wasn't treating him with respect, so I think he threw up his hands and moved on. RD told me that he met with Nick and kind of put him down. From what he was telling me, it was pretty clear: "This is rubbish!" and "How disappointed I am!" This is not a healthy approach when the screenwriter owns the rights and is the guy who's going to direct.

NICK MEYER

I showed Davies the script and I remember he was quite pleased and quite surprised. And I was surprised, too. I can't recall any problems. He did not drive me away, and if there are letters mentioning issues with a film script, I can't remember any issues.

As time passed and no *Fifth Business* film project was announced, Canadian producers began to inquire after the rights to the novel.

GARTH DRABINSKY

God, it's been a long time! But the story of my involvement with *Fifth Business* is a simple one. In the early 1980s my film-producing partner Joel Michaels and I were very much dominating the Canadian film industry – we'd been nominated for, and won, numerous Genies – but it was becoming more and more difficult to find material with potential to be produced as an independent Canadian movie. I had read *Fifth Business*, and I was attracted to making a movie of it for the same reason

I was attracted to E.L. Doctorow's *Ragtime* a decade later: each has an epic dimension.

One day, while speaking with writer-director Nicholas Meyer, I discovered that he, too, had a connection with *Fifth Business*. He's the key to my story. Nick told me that he'd locked up the rights and had already written a screenplay from the novel. I thought it was odd that an American filmmaker had the rights to this quintessentially Canadian novel – this Canadian masterpiece. I said, "Let's make it." But Nick Meyer insisted that he wanted to direct it.

And Meyer held the rights.

NORMAN JEWISON

When Rob told me how his agent had negotiated away the author's rights in perpetuity, I was stunned. I'd never heard of that in my life. I've dealt with a lot of agents and a lot of copyrights. Signing away for from two to five years is normal. I said many times to Robertson, "Rob, how stupid are you? Don't you have a lawyer? Don't you have common sense?" I was just shocked.

GARTH DRABINSKY

I didn't want to produce a film version of a great Canadian novel with an American director. It needed to have a Canadian sentiment and perspective. I reasoned that *Fifth Business* could be the book to finally compel Norman Jewison to direct a film based on Canadian material. I used to scream at Norman, "This is the film we've got to make!"

In 1985 I had just made a deal with MCA to become a major shareholder in Cineplex Odeon. I thought Norman would have been able to bring a gloss to the intricacies and complexities of *Fifth Business*, its magic and illusion. . . . I loved the fact that we follow the story of five characters (principally Dunstan Ramsay), and that everything in the story flows from the single act of throwing a snowball. But in the end, Nick Meyer would not let go. Even though *Fifth Business* had become a passion of mine, I moved on.

Enter Janet Turnbull, not yet married to John Irving, and employed by the New York literary agency Curtis Brown.

JANET TURNBULL IRVING

My impression was that Curtis Brown opened an office in Canada because Robertson Davies wished to have an agent in Canada. Clearly, they had asked RD if he'd be amenable to my being his agent.

The big surprise about dealing with him was that he seemed almost helpless. He was just in despair about many things. He'd say, "Explain to me how Hollywood works. Why can't I get my film rights back?"

I know he was haunted by the issue of the rights to *Fifth Business*. He did not understand how he had achieved the stature he had and yet was so powerless over the fate of one of his own children.

NICK MEYER

I wrote the screenplay in 1975 and held on to it for sixteen years – sixteen dispiriting years. In Hollywood, people periodically make lists of the best unproduced movies around. I called my script *Conjuring*. And for sixteen years, *Conjuring* regularly made that list of best un-produced movies.

Joe Medjuck, who had studied under RD, had by this time moved to Los Angeles and become a film producer and co-producer with films such as *Ghostbusters* to his credit.

JOE MEDJUCK

I don't like to drop the names of actors or filmmakers I've worked with, but I'm very proud to tell people I studied with Davies and McLuhan if their names come up in conversation. I remember bragging about it to the actor David Duchovny, who told me he'd been writing a thesis about magic in the novels of Thomas Pynchon and Robertson Davies while he was at Yale. . . .

After I had moved to California, I didn't see Davies again until Rick Butler, a Canadian TV and film producer living in Los Angeles, got me invited to a small lunch for RD at the Canadian consulate in Los Angeles. I was surprised that Davies remembered me. Then I had my picture taken with him and he autographed my copy of *Fifth Business* in his beautiful handwriting.

I believe Rick Butler got hold of Nick Meyer and made a deal to help do the film in Canada. Rick rewrote the script and got quite a bit of interest in Canada, but in the long run was unable to get the film made. Eventually, Nick Meyer gave Rick an opportunity to purchase the rights.

JENNIFER SURRIDGE
After a while RD learned that Meyer had sold the rights, but we didn't know much about who he had sold the rights to.

RICK BUTLER
I first became involved as a writer/producer with *Fifth Business* in the spring of 1986, when I optioned the project from Nicholas Meyer. Before departing for Hollywood to try my hand at getting it produced, I requested a meeting with Mr. Davies. He immediately obliged with an invitation to his "rooms" at Massey College.

He wanted to know why the story of *Fifth Business* so interested me. This led to a spirited, one hour conversation about the book – which concluded with the following question: "Rick, may I give you some advice my father once gave to me? It might be helpful on the eve of your departure for Hollywood." The room fell silent.

"When you meet a man in business for the first time – be an observer. Let him conduct the meeting and do the talking. Listen to him closely – not just to his words, but his phraseology. Observe his gestures, his deportment – and his manner of dress. Note his sense of humour or lack of it. Pay particular attention to how he greets you and how he bids you farewell. Then, when you return to your own place – reflect carefully on the man you have just met. Review in your mind's eye every carefully observed detail. Then, imagine the direct opposite of everything you have just seen and heard. That's your man!"

Joe Medjuck put up part of the money for the Butler *Fifth Business* project.

JOE MEDJUCK
The deal was done through Rick's company, and I was a minor and silent partner – sort of a fifth business. There was a script, which I thought was quite good. Rick was very interested in the "saint" aspect of the novel, something that wouldn't have crossed my mind! I paid Rick to write more drafts.

GARTH DRABINSKY
Rick Butler . . . there's a name I haven't heard in years! When Robert Redford and I were partners in North Fork Productions – we were developing *A River Runs Through It* – we considered *Fifth Business*. Bob read the script and he liked it a lot.

Again Drabinsky tried to involve Norman Jewison.

NORMAN JEWISON

Garth Drabinsky came to me and said, "Robert Redford is a big fan of Robertson Davies and I want to put you two together." This was Garth when he was riding high and had made the deal with Universal [MCA]. But every time someone would say, "Let's make a movie of *Fifth Business*," I'd wind up in front of Rick Butler! Here was this wonderful book – and then to sit in these meetings listening to Rick Butler pontificate! I'd end up in another meeting with Rick Butler! Again and again!

RICK BUTLER

Why has *Fifth Business* been so resistant to film? Many books of real quality are. But I was frankly surprised that a story of such narrative power would be so difficult to bring to the screen.

Of course in Hollywood, you need a bankable star or director – or preferably both – to get a movie made. Tom Hulce, who won an Oscar for his work in *Amadeus*, contacted me for a meeting. We met three times, and got on well, but an Oscar in one year does not guarantee studio financing in a subsequent year.

I came a bit closer with Norman Jewison. We met in his office at one of the studios. Like most directors, Jewison wanted to see a rewrite of the script. I agreed, and asked for a few pages of script notes. He said they would be forthcoming. Instead, through a representative, I was told "Norman's not going to audition for Rick Butler." Next, he dispatched Garth Drabinsky – who at the time was not under indictment in the U.S. – to try to negotiate a "deal" with me. Drabinsky offered a convoluted $7,500 option. After a full five seconds' consideration, I declined. Clearly, Jewison was unable to arrange a better offer through his own studio connections, and unwilling to spend his own money on the project. Thus ended the Jewison phase of *Fifth Business*. The leading "Canadian" director would never make a "Canadian" movie – *Fifth Business* or otherwise.

Next up was Martin Scorsese. I had given my screenplay to his director of development in Los Angeles. Three weeks later she excitedly informed me that Scorsese had read the screenplay on a plane on the way to Tokyo for a tribute to the celebrated director Kurosawa, and was ready to move forward. Next I received a phone call from Tom Pollock,

President of Univeral Studios. He said Marty wanted to make the picture. I asked when. He said the timing was a little uncertain – *The Last Temptation of Christ* that Universal had just made with Scorsese was a labour of love and the studio needed to make some money with Marty before doing a project like *Fifth Business*. He offered me $50,000 for an option. At the time I was living with a big dream in a small apartment in Venice. I explained to Pollock that I had come to Hollywood specifically to make this movie, not to live on option money. He said I should take his offer. I suggested he should make the movie Scorsese wanted to make. The studio President responded that if I did not accept his offer, he would never speak to me again.

He was true to his word.

All this time, Butler was deepening his business relations with Medjuck.

JOE MEDJUCK
Whenever Rick would run low on money I'd buy a greater share of the rights. Eventually, after RD's death, I ended up owning it. . . . But I still stayed fairly silent because I was busy doing other things and knew this was a difficult film to get made.

I knew it would be expensive: the First World War scenes, the sets, locations and large cast. I always had this idea that it was the Great Canadian Novel and should be made in Canada, and Rick doing it was sort of a repatriation. But whenever Rick got close to making a deal somewhere – like when he was close to making a deal at MGM with Stephen Gyllenhaal as director (Steve's a fine director who's also now known as the father of Jake and Maggie) – he'd come to me, because by then I actually owned the rights.

JENNIFER SURRIDGE
Every so often, some news might come out that would get RD excited. Like that Sting might play Magnus Eisengrim. In fact, he didn't know who Sting was, so that news got *me* excited. But then, nothing would happen.

JANET TURNBULL IRVING
Rob wanted his books to be films. My husband always said to me – and probably, too, to Rob – "You don't need your books to be films to be

validated." But Davies was going to this subject *a lot*. There was almost this jealousy – Atwood's books were becoming films, Timothy Findley's books were films, why isn't it happening with *my* books?

It was very difficult to explain to him. . . . My sense of his concern was, "I'm not fully appreciated. I haven't won that game."

Of course, he knew that a screenplay is a contract with the Devil. . . . What had happened to *Fifth Business* informed the way John dealt with *The Cider House Rules*. John took the position that he didn't care if it was *never* made into a film if it meant he didn't lose control. But RD wanted *Fifth Business* to be a movie more than he wanted the Nobel Prize.

Years passed. Meanwhile, RD's Cornish trilogy was also intriguing film-makers. In 1987, Toronto producers John McGreevy and Pat Ferns attempted to turn *What's Bred in the Bone* into a TV mini-series.

JOHN McGREEVY

First we worked with the BBC and a recommended writer from England, William Humble. Pat thought he could do a U.K.–Canada co-production, but RD was not terribly pleased with the first effort. . . .

The BBC had urged the writer, William Humble, to eliminate the angel and the daemon narrators from the script, and so he did. We did not realize that RD regarded them as crucial.

Bill came to Canada and we met with RD over lunch. We tried to defend the script. Humble, like any writer meeting another writer, was a bit defensive. He sort of dug in and said, "That's the way I see the material." But there was no eruption. RD tabled his reservations but then he said, "You people know television. It's your decision." He was very anxious that it be brought to the screen and he sensed the frustration we all went through.

Then there was a change of management at the BBC. The new folks were more interested in street drama, nitty-gritty stories, than they were in *Masterpiece Theatre* projects.

The loss of the BBC support was very serious – the Americans felt that the BBC had given the project a cachet. Eventually, I phoned RD and said, "This is not going to happen." He was very disappointed. Nobody likes rejection.

A few years passed, and then Pat Ferns and I decided to have another go. We thought, if we are going to do this it would be done from Canada.

Guy Gavriel Kay and George Jonas are absolutely superb at bringing to the screen the writer's intention. Both writers believed the angel and daemon were key. And RD was much happier with that version.

GUY GAVRIEL KAY (scriptwriter and novelist)

We did not meet with RD, but we had several exchanges of notes.

RD had only a few caveats with our script. "Caveats," that was his word . . .

He was on the whole very generous about our script, but he noted that we had attempted to save the production money by doubling up two different London men's clubs, so there would only be one set. There was an early scene in the book in which Francis Cornish's father, who is in British intelligence, takes his son to a club, and then another scene involving some other people later in the book in a second club. We made them the same club, but RD sent us a note saying Major Francis Cornish would never have set foot in the second club – it would have been inappropriate for such a father to take his son to such a club.

GEORGE JONAS

He was absolutely right, of course.

JOHN McGREEVY

We designed it to be a four-part series with initial support from CTV, and we were working on PBS and BBC as partners. But the television environment had changed . . . Robertson Davies was not perceived by television executives as contemporary. So again I called him and gave the bad – or sad – news.

RD did not live to see a novel made into a TV or feature film. His family supposed that was the end of it. Then, early in the twenty-first century, they were contacted by Charles Pitts, a young writer and producer with tenacity and a personal interest in RD's work. Pitts had met RD in 1977, during his student days at Queen's – in Watson Hall, the humanities building named after Eleanor Sweezey's grandfather, at an English Club meeting convened by Sarah Edinborough, daughter of Arnold Edinborough.

CHARLES PITTS

Sarah was RD's goddaughter and arranged to have RD come and speak.

Previously, the members of the so-called "English Club" had all written down on little scraps of paper the names of topics or titles for what we wanted Mr. Davies to come and speak on. We put the bits of paper into a hat. I wrote down "The Function of Literature," and that was what was pulled out of the hat. So he came to speak on that.

When he arrived, he had this Santa Claus white beard, the full three-piece suit and tie, or maybe he was wearing a vest. He was very erect and portly, with great presence, and with the bearing of a well-trained actor. Brenda was with him, very much in attendance.

RD said, "The function of literature is to enlighten as well as entertain." He talked about books he loved to read. There were questions, too. When they dried up, I was too nervous to ask mine. This was the thing he had chided us about when he first arrived, about Queen's students being too shy to sit at the front and ask questions. After, he and his entourage left the room and began moving towards the elevator – Sarah, professors, Brenda, the entire English Club – all moving towards the elevator. Brenda saw me hanging back, looking perhaps a bit expectant and hopeful.

She signalled me to come closer, leaned over and said, "Do you have a question?"

I said yes.

She said, "Well, why don't you ask?"

I gestured to the obstructive throng all around him.

She said, "What's your name?"

I said, "Charles Pitts."

She said, "Charles, my dear boy, you must learn that the wheel only comes round once in this life. You must strike while the iron is hot!"

By now we were nearing the elevator, and the elevator doors opened. As she and RD stepped in, she gestured for me to follow, so in I jumped. She looked at me and gave me the elbow and a look that said, "Go on! Now's your chance!" The doors had closed and we had only four floors to the ground floor, perhaps a sixty-second elevator ride. She helped me by saying to RD, "Dear, Charles Pitts has a question." So I coughed out my question, which was "Mr. Davies, do you think there will ever come a time when literature won't be necessary? And that it might some day be usurped by, perhaps, film or television as the primary means of telling stories that teach us the lessons we learn in life?"

He mused into the distance, which in this case meant staring at the top of the elevator door. I am six foot one, but he seemed much taller than me, so I must have been cowering. Then he looked down and boomed, "Not in your lifetime or mine!"

The elevator door opened. Brenda gave me a little wave. I always thought that what she did was profoundly considerate and generous. I never saw either of them again. Or made any further contact until I wrote to Brenda in January 2002.

Pitts had already contacted literary agents about Davies's work back in 1994. He had made a TV movie of Alice Munro's *Lives of Girls and Women*. *Fifth Business* was now atop the list of books he wanted to turn into movies.

CHARLES PITTS

I made some calls to agents in New York City in 1994. Tim Knowlton was very helpful and told me that the rights to *Fifth Business* were held by a fellow in California. His parting comment was, "If there's anything you can do to help regain control of them, it would be appreciated."

So I contacted the fellow Tim had directed me to [Rick Butler], and that individual told me that he would want what seemed like a great deal of money, and in American dollars. Remember that the Canadian dollar was trading in the 70-cent range in those years.

Time went by. I made another film, *Edge of Madness*. When I spoke to Butler again, in the fall of 2001, shortly after 9/11, this figure had gone up. It was more money than we had ever raised before. So I decided to do an MBA to figure out the money side and a plan for what had to be done. In the film world, a writer is like a waiter caught between the kitchen and the customer – you have no power. A business degree can be helpful if you want to take control of what projects you do, to be conversant with the sources of money and to understand the laws of capital. So I did a Queen's executive MBA, a program which has a lot of freedom to pursue independent study.

Queen's allowed Pitts to do his course work around setting up a company to raise funding and secure the rights to *Fifth Business*.

CHARLES PITTS

It was eighty hours a week of gruelling, gut-slogging work without pause for two years straight, 24/7. In the course of doing my work, I discovered that the chap in California [Butler] might not be the sole owner of the rights to *Fifth Business*.

I learned that there was more than one owner. And, in fact, that an expat Canadian producer named Joe Medjuck had an interest in the property. Joe wanted to help and he wanted to get his money back – he'd paid for his portion of the rights to *Fifth Business*. And nothing was happening.

JOE MEDJUCK

One day, Charles Pitts called me to ask about Rick, who he thought owned the rights, and I said, "No, I own the rights."

CHARLES PITTS

In the summer of 2003, I also learned that subsequent to RD's death, a change in the American copyright law meant that U.S. rights had lapsed back to the Davies family. American rights are worth about half of world rights, so you would not want to make a project without American rights – which meant the family had now regained partial control.

By spring 2003, Pitts and Medjuck reached an agreement; in 2005, Pitts signed an agreement with the Davies family, to whom American rights had reverted, giving him rights to *Fifth Business* – and solving the problem of a long-term reversion clause for the family.

JENNIFER SURRIDGE

My own feeling is, a film can only convey a certain amount of plot. A TV mini-series is a better way of conveying the ins and outs of intricate plots. If Charles manages to make a mini-series, that may be the best vehicle.

JOE MEDJUCK

I'd only really gotten involved because Davies was really important to me. I'm from Fredericton, New Brunswick. His nineteenth-century-ness and my 1960s-ness were a contrast. But despite what I do for a living now, I liked being an academic. I never met anyone like Robertson Davies. Even in Hollywood.

Chapter 37

HONOURS AND
GRANDCHILDREN

By the time he retired, RD was a grandfather four times over. Christopher, born in 1969, was followed by his brothers Piers (1971) and Erik (1977) and a sister, Cecilia (1978).

JENNIFER SURRIDGE
RD does tell lovely stories in his diary about looking after Piers and Christopher at Windhover.

RD would take them out as soldiers and they'd march around the property. And then mop their brows with a handkerchief.

Just as Rupert and Florence had seemed old-fashioned to Brenda, so RD (known as "Taid," Welsh for "grandfather") seemed from another era to his grandchildren.

CECILIA CUNNINGTON
My family was pretty formal with my grandparents. Mum always wanted it to go smoothly and they were very punctual, my gran and Taid, very punctual. You tried to be on your best behaviour with him and not drop anything or break anything. He liked kids, but at a distance. And there was a strong sense of private space and public space. I don't think I ever went upstairs at their house as a kid. I never ever saw his study as a kid.

We'd visit three or four times a year, that was it. We went to Stratford every year and to their house in Caledon, always for lunch. At Stratford, we would go to a restaurant or for a picnic for my grandfather's birthday, which is in August: my mum, my three brothers, myself, Jenny and Tom. I don't have many physical memories of Taid. He would hug or kiss. But he would not pick us up.

MIRANDA DAVIES
As a grandparent, I am sure he was delightful and charming. I saw little of him. But there was one incident that chilled me. Christopher was about three and Piers was around two and the others were not yet born.

We were at Windhover and Christopher had been watching *Sesame Street* and was showing off because he knew the alphabet. He went through it all and ended with "W, X, Y and Zee." Taid said, "You mean W, X, Y and *Zed*." Christopher said, "No! X, Y, *Zee*, you dummy." There was silence from Taid. The afternoon progressed.

Much later, little Christopher passed a remark that showed he didn't know something. Taid corrected him, in a voice of thunder, ending with "*you dummy*." Christopher was so shocked, he just cried his eyes out. He was shaken to the core.

What was really shattering to me was that all the women were shaken, too, but we just huddled together in an enclave. Nobody stood up to Taid and said, "Don't talk to a child in that way." Looking back, I feel ashamed that I did not speak up. I remembered Father thundering to me as a little girl, "How *dare* you."

In a 1983 radio interview, RD hinted that he did not mind being intimidating.

RD
When my little grandsons were small, Christmas came and one of the boys gave me a gift. It was a picture of a man I had never seen before, a sort of man in a tin head. And I said, "This is fascinating! Who is this?"

He said, "I gave it to you because it is like you. That's Darth Vader."

I had to have it explained to me who Darth Vader was. He was an archetypal figure, a villain, a very, very powerful person. I thought this was a sort of compliment.

CECILIA CUNNINGTON
My mother told us Taid was very strict and quick to get upset. That's not at all pleasant for anybody. But I don't think I ever saw it. He definitely liked to entertain – because he was shy. And if you're speaking more than you're listening, you are controlling the subjects.

Taid was the focus. He definitely liked to speak rather than to listen. We grandchildren didn't act out enough to get disciplined. Mum would lay down the law before we went.

ROSAMOND BAILEY
When I took my kids to visit them, I'd just be a basket case. There were so many things that my kids might do that could break the rules.

CECILIA CUNNINGTON
Everything there at my grandparents' was on a different level than what we were used to. We would eat at a long table, off plates with gold rims. . . . Taid was a generous gift giver, and the gifts would be accompanied by beautifully handwritten notes – calligraphy on nice paper.

At Christmas, he liked to pass out the gifts and he would read the cards aloud. But it was lunch first and then we would all move as a group to where the Christmas tree was. He wanted to decide what order the gifts went in, and he wanted to see the responses.

He never helped with the serving of meals. He was not lazy, but my grandmother, aunt and mother would help in the kitchen. And I'd help clear the plates. That was not his realm.

And Taid would tell stories that would shock us. I definitely remember the shock value. If my brothers used to drink, he would dramatize things and say, "You'll be the family drunk."

JENNIFER SURRIDGE
Poor Piers Cunnington would turn up at New Year's Day with a hangover and RD would say "Look out, you'll turn out like Uncle Albert, who was a terrible alcoholic."

Finally, Piers asked me who Uncle Albert was. I said, "He never existed. RD made him up."

RD was not only a formidable grandfather. As Master Emeritus of Massey, he kept a paternal eye on the institution he had helped to create. Sometimes, what was happening to it alarmed him. RD had lobbied strenuously to get Desmond Neill of the Bodleian Library at Oxford to become Massey's librarian. But things went sour, in part because Neill clashed with RD over the fate of Vincent Massey's papers.

RICHARD LANDON (librarian of the Thomas Fisher Rare Book Library)
It was Desmond who negotiated that the Vincent Massey papers should be moved from Massey to the Robarts Library. RD felt strongly that he

should have been consulted. Besides, the Massey papers were to be controlled by the college.

I didn't want the Massey papers at the Fisher [the Thomas Fisher Rare Book Library]. They were laundered. If you wanted to know why Mackenzie King and his government denied access to Canada to boatloads of refugee Jews fleeing the Nazis, that wasn't there. There was just massive amounts of junk. The U of T archivist was keen on this stuff. But the loss of the Massey papers to the U of T archives was a blow to RD. When Desmond sent the Vincent Massey papers away, things went from bad to worse.

DESMOND NEILL
I believed that the Massey papers were of national importance, but we had no means of keeping them under temperature controls and we hadn't got enough of the special boxes required to preserve them. They went to the University of Toronto archives because it is essential that archival papers be preserved properly.

According to Neill, he and Massey's new Master, Patterson Hume, regarded it as "imperative that the Master Emeritus approve" the move, and eventually RD did give his consent. But he continued to believe that Massey's founder, one of the most important figures in his life, had been betrayed.

ANN SADDLEMYER
Rob never forgave Pat Hume or Desmond Neill for agreeing to the transfer to the Fisher. Although he'd ultimately signed on to it, he was bitter. There was an event some time later in the Massey library, and Rob stood up to speak and let it all out. I had never heard him be so bitter in public.

At that time I was hoping to get the original Cuala hand press from Ireland – the private press that had published all of W.B. Yeats's work. The Yeats children were closing down the press, and I was able to get the offer of it for Massey. And then it was rejected by the library committee, which must have been Pat Hume and Desmond. I was very cross. Rob was cross.

RICHARD LANDON
Meanwhile, RD told me, the Massey library was an embarrassment. He said to Marie [Korey, Landon's wife] that he was embarrassed that they had named it after him. It was a mess.

After Neill left and Marie came to Massey as librarian, we went to dinner at the Carleys. James Carley said to her, "There are two things you have to overcome with RD: A, your sex; B, your nationality." Marie is American. But in fact, Marie got along well with RD. She is a character in the last, uncompleted ghost story. And he wrote her letters. The first began "Dear Librarian." By the end, they were on a first-name basis.

RD (letter to Marie Korey, February 2, Candlemas 1995)
I have recently been astonished to be elected an honorary fellow of the Morgan Library in New York; this is because a year ago at Christmas time I spoke to the Fellows about Dickens' *A Christmas Carol* and was able to tell them a few things they didn't know about the stage versions of the book. . . .

It was, to me, an astonishing occasion, for I expected the Fellows of a distinguished library to be bearded ancients with thick specs and a lot of food dropped on their waistcoats, but these were New York sharpies in evening dress, and their ladies were wearing enough jewellery to settle the National Debt; but they knew a great deal about books and firmly bore out one of my lifelong contentions – that the rich didn't get rich by being stupid, and beneath a diamond tiara may lurk a thoroughly cultivated mind. I know that this is contrary to the Bill of Rights, or something of the kind, but I swear it is true. . . . I want to send a catalogue of our collection to Charles Pierce, at the Morgan, so he will know what good company I keep.

Again, thanks and warm congratulations on what you and Richard have to done to bring the Massey Library to life after its long sleep under evil enchantment.

Despite his affection for Marie Korey and his strong attachment to the University of Toronto, RD bequeathed his papers to the National Archives in Ottawa.

RICHARD LANDON
This is speculation, but I think RD believed himself to be a national treasure and he *should* be in the national capital.

Public honours mattered to RD, though he sometimes said otherwise.

NORMAN JEWISON

I remember Rob came to dinner at my place in 1981 and I had just received a letter saying I was going to be inducted as an officer into the Order of Canada. You weren't supposed to tell anyone until it happened, but we had a dinner party and my wife said, "These are country folk, it won't matter, we can tell them." So she did. Then someone said, "Let's make a toast." I'll never forget, Robertson clinked his glass and said, "Welcome to the club." This was to remind everyone present that he was a Companion of the Order of Canada, the highest level. When I became a Companion, in 1991, I always intended to tell Rob, "Now I'm *really* in the club."

In 1986, the Toronto Arts Awards gave RD a lifetime achievement award, which was accompanied by a video profile, a mini-documentary.

LISA BALFOUR BOWEN

I'd been a founding member of the board of the Toronto Arts Awards, and I was there at the Arts Awards the night Davies won his lifetime achievement award. I remember being very surprised by his media savvy. The video opened, and there was a pregnant pause before he came on the screen in an enveloping close-up. He was looking right at the camera, very close. Then he said, "Ah, *there* you are." I'd heard of Davies as a comic actor. But until that night I'd never seen it.

The year 1988 brought more honours to RD, notably the $50,000 Canada Council Molson Prize in the Arts. The next year, his work was hailed in an evening-long tribute at the Wang International Festival of Authors at Harbourfront. As RD was now a national treasure, he was called upon to perform public good works.

JOHN RALSTON SAUL (writer)

I was president of PEN Canada, and at the PEN Benefit in 1989 I got Rob and Peggy Atwood to sing. That evening, Rob had a flu and almost no voice. He was sick. I had to pick him up in my car to make sure that the Great Man got to the show on time. But he was a trouper and he came out and sang. He was very funny. He and she – Peggy Atwood – were great performers.

MARGARET ATWOOD

That night we both had horrible afflictions. RD had laryngitis and I had some sort of cold. I thought after that night I'd never talk again, because I had so exerted my voice in singing. I'd used my *Annie-Get-Your-Gun* voice, which meant screaming.

We met before we went on stage to hammer out the words of the song, which we had already decided would be "Anything You Can Write I Can Write Better." There was a dirty verse, too – the dirty words were all added by him. And after the end, he presented me with a rose, which was unexpected. Of course, I blushed.

He *was* a trouper. He was willing to make an idiot of himself in public. It's a very Canadian trait, this willingness to make an extreme idiot of yourself in public for a good cause . . . think of Pierre Berton rolling a joint for Rick Mercer, or Adrienne Clarkson, the former governor general, going on [the TV show] *Corner Gas*. These things come back to haunt you. When RD died, that's what they played on the radio: "Anything You Can Write, I Can Write Better."

The Emmy Award–nominated TV producer Harry Rasky realized that, as a national treasure, RD would be a fine subject for a ninety-minute documentary. *The Magic Season of Robertson Davies* was broadcast on CBC television in December 1990.

HARRY RASKY

I love talking about RD . . . He's a delicious character, a really delicious character.

Before I made the film, we had no relationship whatsoever. I'd seen him, of course. I used to watch him at the opening of Stratford. For years it struck me that he would be off in a corner, aloof. I couldn't help thinking as I watched him in the corner that he was very much wanting to be noticed. I always got the impression that he was trying to imitate someone English and famous. That was when he was a newspaperman, and a spectacularly unsuccessful playwright.

After his novels, I decided to get RD to pose for a film portrait. He refused. So I did a film on Northrop Frye and RD watched it closely. He wrote me a letter and said, "Well, I am a much more difficult nut to crack than Frye." I don't know why he'd say that. In fact, Frye was as close to impossible as you can get. He was very shy and talked in epigrams. Frye loved the film I did of him.

Finally, RD said he would make himself available for a couple of days. Three days at Caledon.

I always suspected there was a very special bond between RD and his father. His father was just the opposite of him. No beard. A senator. In his life, he'd voted for acceptance. He looked like a very strict guy to me. I figured his father would be the force that would make him . . . his father, who was very famous before he was.

Film is a medium where someone doesn't necessarily have to answer a question. It's there in the expression on the face, in the pauses. Dirk Bogarde once told me when I was interviewing him that I was "playing the pauses." But when I met with RD, all my previous perceptions were wrong. It shows how stupid you can be.

RD was extremely likable and very chatty, unlike Northrop Frye, who couldn't chat at all. I was expecting a standoffish, WASPy, uptight guy. I should have known. The Welsh are not WASPs. They're very individualistic and quite marvellous.

RD was Welsh and I am Jewish. We're both outsiders. And there's humour in common. I looked at him as a very smart Jew. Both of us attained fame after a period of almost pleading with people to recognize what we were doing. I talked to him about anti-Semitism and he said he never really thought about Jews except as enemies of WASPs – who were people he thought *he* was against.

RD was being disingenuous. He had often given thought to Jews and Jewishness, had had Jewish friends at Upper Canada and Oxford, and tended to idealize them – even as, on occasion, he slipped into the prejudices of his class and time, as in this letter to Brenda dated March 2, 1942, when he was scouting out a new home at Weller Street in Peterborough.

> My dearest Pink:
> Ma Bannister, who wears a deaf machine, let me in and conducted me round the place, moaning and groaning all the time about how awful they felt at leaving. I was excessively and obviously insincerely sympathetic, in a sort of Jewish way, not yielding an inch.

SANDY YUDIN
I was in the Davies's house once or twice in Peterborough to play with Miranda when I was little. But my impression was the Davies family

was quite proper . . . and I felt that they weren't overly thrilled with our friendship because we were Jewish.

JOHN POLANYI

One thing he surprised me with was when we were talking at dinner in Massey and he said, "I don't think you could ever be Master of a college at this university." There was a time in the nineteenth and early twentieth century when you had to be ordained to teach at a university. . . . I did not take RD's comment to be anti-Semitic, though maybe it was, at a lower level. He may have been trying to shock. But he was being forthright, and challenging to political correctness, as so often. The remark that one should be a Christian to head an Oxford college was meant to be daring, in the Evelyn Waugh manner. A defence of a vanishing age. I once had a schoolteacher who shook his fist at passing aeroplanes. That is how it struck me.

MARTIN HUNTER

Rob was fascinated with Jewish intellectuals at a time when Jews weren't accepted by Toronto mainstream WASP society. You can see, though, that Jews in RD's novels are all upper-class intellectuals – Sir Benedict Domdaniel in *A Mixture of Frailties*, the family of Judith Wolff in *The Manticore*. Rob was ahead of most Anglo-Canadians of his time.

Jews weren't the only topic on which RD tried to deflect his TV biographer.

HARRY RASKY

I thought when we got into those questions on Jung, he avoided them. He was a great avoider. I didn't mind – in a sense, he was dodging all his life. He didn't want to tell you things. There was a moment in the film where I said, "Frankly, you seem to be evasive." He kind of liked that. I never called him on it.

There is a point in the film at which he winks at me. We were discussing Canadian critics. I agreed with him that Canadian critics are low down on the totem pole compared to *The New York Times* or the *Washington Post*. That was a wink where he and I understood between us where one stands – when you're suddenly accepted here after you have never been accepted here.

RD and Rasky shared the impression that honours at home tended to follow honours abroad. In 1986, RD's old college, Balliol, gave him an honorary fellowship. In 1990, Trinity College Dublin bestowed an honorary degree. Then, in 1991, Oxford did so, too.

BRENDA DAVIES
Rob had a black eye at Oxford. He had fallen in Vienna. A car was coming round a corner and I said, "Come on," and off we went. Rob tripped and went down and blacked his eye.

FELICITY BRYAN
The Oxford honorary degree was at the Sheldonian. I got a friend to invite me, and I snapped a picture. June 19, 1991. It was a wonderful day, and Rob loved dressing up. He looked spectacular in a long red gown. He looked fantastic, though one eye was black.

The form is that they, the honorees, "process" to the Sheldonian Theatre. Then the Public Orator extols in Latin the virtues of the people getting their honorary degrees. It might be a distinguished scientist and a distinguished novelist. After this, they process again towards All Souls, through the gate, for drinks on the lawn. Then you go into the Old Library at All Souls for a lunch. It's all formal, all beautifully done at a long table. And then on to a tea party. They did the whole day.

Here are photos of Rob standing atop a staircase in his red and grey robes with a mortar board on his head, one hand on the stair banister, the other holding his eyeglasses. He is wearing a white bib and a bow at the throat. And here on the lawn is Brenda in a straw hat and a beige shawl with Rob as they are processing.

BRENDA DAVIES
He was thrilled by the honorary degree from Oxford. He thought that was the greatest thing that ever happened.

ELUNED MacMILLAN
After RD died, my grandson Daniel was accepted at Balliol College and Brenda said we could have Rob's old Balliol ties. Daniel started wearing them. Then people started coming up to him and saying, "I didn't know you were in the such-and-such club!" "I didn't know you were a cricketer." He'd say, "I'm not!" He realized that RD had bought all those ties,

every Balliol tie, for every kind of society – literary, athletic . . . he'd bought them all.

FELICITY BRYAN
And here's a photo from that day at Oxford of Rob alone, catching the eye of the camera, his mouth open in an expression of mock astonishment – or else he is just about to laugh aloud.

Chapter 38

JUST A CANADIAN

From *A Mixture of Frailties* to *What's Bred in the Bone*, RD's novels involved life-changing journeys to Europe, suggesting that a Canadian had to go abroad to become a full person. Canada dissatisfied him, but it intrigued him.

MARGARET ATWOOD
I often quote Davies's "Canada is not a country you love, it's a country you worry about."

DAMIANO PIETROPAOLO
When Mark Abley and I were preparing that documentary series on Oscar Wilde [for CBC Radio in 1983], Davies wanted to refute the notion that Canadians are boring and conservative. He told us the story of a girl who was deeply in love and resorted to drastic measures to prove it. He said that I, as an Italian, would have the "gumption" to understand this story. This girl was so in love – with another girl – that she wanted to prove herself, so she castrated a taxi driver and attached his penis to herself with Krazy Glue.

I sensed that he was out to shock me, the little immigrant. He certainly shocked me with that story. He told the Krazy Glue story because he said, in effect, "You Italians have the gumption to understand crimes of passion." Or perhaps it was the gumption that I, as an immigrant, was in his office? I was both amused and offended. . . . In any case, Davies said that what made this story particularly Canadian was not the love nor even the castration, but the Krazy Glue.

As RD told Peter C. Newman in an interview:

Because I am a Canadian I couldn't really live anywhere else. I have had chances to do so and have never given it serious consideration. I belong here. To divorce yourself from your roots is spiritual suicide. The expatriate, unless he is really a rather special kind of person, is very unhappy. I just am a Canadian. It is not a thing which you can escape from. It is like having blue eyes.

Returning home after the collapse of his health in Sweden in 1988, RD began work on his most explicitly Canadian novel yet, *Murther and Walking Spirits*. As he prepared to write his tenth novel, he wanted to explore Florence's Loyalist forebears as well as Rupert's Welsh ones. Writing *Murther* exposed RD to uncanny memories of his mother. While working on it in the summer of 1990, he wrote in his diary:

I sit her down and demand to know why she plagues me. She has no answers but her fears of the unknown & inbred suspicion. Tell her it won't do. Knock it off, Flo. Are many men so haunted, I wonder? Can I deliver myself by this Jungian technique of Active Imagination? The Great Mother in negative form. The Dragon, Gorgon, emasculator . . .

***Murther and Walking Spirits* deals frankly with mortality – in fact, it is narrated by a journalist, Gil Gilmartin, who is killed on the opening page. RD checked his murder with two doctors: Horace Davenport's son, Robertson Davies Davenport, and Dr. Rick Davis of Guelph, Ontario.**

ROBERTSON DAVIES DAVENPORT
He was very concerned that he get his facts right. He spoke of how jarring it is for the reader and how embarrassing for the writer when something in a novel was wrong. He had this idea of a weapon in a cane and wanted to know if it was medically possible that someone could be killed with one blow from such a thing. I said yes.

RICK DAVIS
He invited me to lunch at the York Club in 1990 to discuss blunt instruments and death by trauma. But my first involvement with *Murther* goes back to 1988, when I sent him two books for Christmas. One was on near-death experiences, called *Recollections of Death*, by Michael Sabom; the other was an old book about unusual medical information,

Anomalies and Curiosities. RD was quite enamoured with them. I have his letters.

RD (letter to Rick Davis)
How kind of you to send me those books for Christmas! . . . I suppose it is rather disgusting, but I have always been fascinated by human odd-ities, and although I am truly sorry for them I am astonished at the things that can go wrong with the human body and the miseries that the victims can endure. A writer, of course, is by nature curious, and to really know what happens when a sword swallower does the apparently impossible is very satisfying. . . . Your choice of *Recollections of Death* must have been intuitive for at the moment I am embarking on a new novel to which that book is strongly relevant.

RICK DAVIS
He was always open to learn. I would send him books and he'd say, "I don't know anything about this. I can't wait to get at it."

Early in 1991, RD sent the *Murther* manuscript to his editor, Doug Gibson, who replied on March 12 in a lengthy and encouraging letter.

DOUG GIBSON
Here are my editorial comments. In marking the manuscript I have failed to exclaim in the margin whenever something especially delighted me. That oversight was deliberate. The manuscript is so rich, so full of good things that I would have marked up every page with my whoops and chatter. . . . In terms of overall shape there are only two areas where the pace seems to slacken a little . . . Samuel and Walter's slow decline . . . [and] the auction scenes. . . .

    By contrast, one area you might wish to consider expanding comes right at the end. It seems to me that while Going's desperate attempts to gain forgiveness for his crime are amusing, the really important theme here – for the reader as well as Gil – is that [his distant ancestors from the eighteenth century] Anna Vermeulen and red-headed Wesley Gilmartin will live on.

In a letter to his American editor, Christine Pevitt, RD's response to Gibson's gently couched criticism veered among outrage, mockery and a form of acknowledgment.

RD

Thursday Holy Week 1991
Dear Christine:

I am sending the fully corrected MS to Gibson today; I have addressed all his numberless quibbles as well as I can, but I *will not* put up with his yearning to flatten everything that is written into something that would get 70% in the Dundee Academy for Serious Boys; he has passion for the well-worn phrase – all his griefs are "deep" – and he has a fear that some old woman in Saskatchewan may not understand every word that is used. . . .

[Same letter, next paragraph] Many of his criticisms were admirable and I am grateful for them. But I won't be turned into a Scotch schoolboy! . . .

[Same letter two paragraphs on] I hope Gibson is back at work soon . . .

With final changes negotiated, *Murther* was published in the autumn of 1991. Although it was a record of intimate family experiences, it struck some readers as oddly cool.

MIRANDA DAVIES
I was chilled in *Murther* when the fathers attend Gil's funeral and they have no sense of feeling, no sense of grief. There was not any understanding of the effect of the death of a child on parents, putative or real. Two men who are supposed to be such close friends – and their complete failure to register any feeling about the death of a child! I was also chilled by the link between Gil and Going via the woman [Esme]. They both sleep with her but she seemed just a figurehead.

Monica Gall in *A Mixture of Frailties* was a believable girl, but this later woman – not. In *A Mixture of Frailties*, when Gilles Revelstoke kills himself and leaves a note, Daddy said he was going to have Monica leave the note, but her character took over. She removed it. The character took over the author; she was *not* manipulated by the author.

Murther **received respectful reviews, but some critics deemed it an interesting failure.**

PHIL MARCHAND

The first time I met him was when I interviewed him for the *Star*. This was after I had reviewed *Murther and Walking Spirits*. And it was a dismissive review, so I was apprehensive. . . . The interview was in his office at Massey College. He had this way of sprawling with his legs out. In the review I had mentioned that he had these stock characters. I was very proud that I had looked up *Fifth Business* and had noted Boy Staunton's second wife Denyse Hornick, and lo and behold, in *Murther and Walking Spirits* she was reincarnated as Esme Baron. I said that you could tell what he thinks of these women by their names . . . I'd be a little less judgmental in that way now.

Davies brought up this issue during the interview, with his characteristic drawl. He said, "Don't you notice that there are characters who recur in your life?" He was out-Jungian-ing me. And I replied, "Oh, of course, Mr. Davies. You're right." And then, at the end of the interview, he said, "The next time I'll try to do better." This comment wasn't blatantly sarcastic, but there was a strong sense of irony.

And of course, *Fifth Business* really had given me pleasure. It's a very good book. I was in awe of him. So "next time I'll try to do better" was the most crushing thing he could have said.

I tried to reply, "Oh, Mr. Davies, I admire you, I worship. . ." I fumbled and bumbled. And he magisterially paid no attention.

JENNIFER SURRIDGE

I was talking to him about his books one time and I said I didn't think *Murther and Walking Spirits* was as successful a book. And he said, "Well, it was something I had to write." I am sure it was good therapy for him. *Murther* was the first time he had ever dedicated a book.

RD dedicated *Murther* **simply "For Brenda." In a newspaper interview [with me, described in this book's Introduction] he remarked, "I don't throw these things around wildly, but I wanted to recognize my wife, the most sustaining influence in my life."**

JAMES CARLEY
Rob and Brenda were wonderful as a team. They so played off each other. I never felt that he dominated her, but that it was like a dance. At one dinner we had, Rob sat at one end of the table and Brenda at the other. Late in the evening, I saw her nod and then he got up and said it was time to leave. They were so attuned to one another.

ANN MacMILLAN
He obviously adored her. He would read her everything. She was an invaluable partner. . . . Brenda was definitely the workhorse of the two. She obviously hero-worshipped him . . . she was almost nervous in his presence.

On February 2, 1990, RD and Brenda celebrated their fiftieth wedding anniversary with a dinner for about sixty people at the York Club. The menu was smoked salmon, Tournedos Rossini, salad with cheese, gateaux and Mumm's Champagne.

JENNIFER SURRIDGE
The parents planned these things far ahead, for months in advance. We, their daughters, had wanted to be involved in the planning. *They* had not wanted that. So we pushed in and just did the flowers. In their marriage it was *them* first.

JANE ZEIDLER
We sat with John and Janet Irving. Douglas Le Pan was on the other side. RD made a speech to Brenda. I thought it would be a "Horatio at the Bridge" kind of speech, but it was small and homespun.

DOUG GIBSON
He understood that marriage, as he once put it, was much more than "four bare legs in a blanket," and on his fiftieth wedding anniversary he said something wonderful about marriage, a summation that a good marriage was "an ongoing conversation." He was a man of whom you could use the word "wise" without irony.

JOHN FRASER

RD said at his fiftieth anniversary that they never had an argument – Brenda never would have allowed it. Successful relationships are genuinely mysterious.

BRENDA DAVIES

He thought marriage was an endless conversation. From the beginning, he sensed that we would be lifelong friends. You have to change together. If you can do that to understand one another, you can have a lifelong marriage.

JENNIFER SURRIDGE

In his diary, he says, "A mighty pow-wow is in progress. Everybody seems happy and in full shout. . . . Claude Bissell makes the toast. I reply in the speech over which I had fretted for a fortnight and it goes very well."

His speech, as I recall, had a lot in it that was facetious and funny. I put my foot in it afterwards and said, "But none of that's true," and he just looked at me.

BRENDA DAVIES

He always exaggerated for a good story. The story was the thing, not the facts. I said extremely little.

JENNIFER SURRIDGE

They certainly didn't rededicate their marriage or anything. They thought that kind of thing was crap. They just gave a war of a party. RD got indigestion later that night – he got indigestion whenever he didn't eat at home! He writes in his diary, "Mary with the seven swords in her heart was very much the model for what I felt."

HARRY RASKY

His wife was a very shy person. When I was doing my documentary, that one clip of her is all they were willing to pose for. She just didn't want to do anything that would distract from him. A lovely lady. But he was the flower, she was the vase.

When we were doing the interview with her he was worried about her – he was hovering, protectively. It was not at all that he was worked up about what she'd say. At least, that's how I read it. They were perfectly matched, as long as she didn't want to be a superstar, which she didn't.

RD enjoyed one aspect of stardom: the platform it afforded him for making outrageous public statements. He made one during the 1992 Walter Gordon Lecture, which was a dialogue between RD and the Mexican author Carlos Fuentes on The Emergence of a North American Culture. In the audience were former prime minister Pierre Trudeau and Ontario's then premier, Bob Rae, who was there with his wife, RD's former student, Arlene Perly Rae.

ARLENE PERLY RAE
I remember he'd written a letter of congratulations when Bob got elected in 1990. When I was his U of T Drama School student, he always said there was very little difference between politics and acting; you are on stage and it's all a big performance. That night at the Massey Gordon lectures, Pierre Trudeau was in the audience. Bob went over to Trudeau and said, "Nice to see you." Trudeau replied, "Nice to see you . . . now that we've lied about that, what shall we talk about?"

In his speech, Davies made a crack about politicians being not very bright. For RD to go on about politicians with those people in the audience . . . a frisson went around the room.

RD (referring in the course of his speech to the ongoing constitutional discussions of the Charlottetown Accord)
We are wearied of the pitter-patter of tiny minds, the hullabaloo, brouhaha and pow-wow of constitutional wrangle. . . . Does the language of our politicians betray any acquaintance with the tongue that Milton spake? . . . This [constitutional debate] is our version of a civil war. But dowdy and dispiriting though it appear, it is the struggle for the nation's soul!

VAL ROSS (*The Globe and Mail*, September 25, 1992)
Fuentes seemed to be enjoying Davies's rhetoric hugely, but during the question period, Davies began to opine dangerously about whether people of oriental races could ever excel at Western music. Trudeau suddenly rose and bolted from the Hart House Theatre. It was unclear whether he was angry, late for another appointment, or overcome with giggles.

As Massey's Master Emeritus, RD felt honour-bound to attend the Gordon lectures whether he was giving them or not. Two years later, the then

Master of Massey College, Ann Saddlemyer, decided that the subject of the
lecture should be The Future of Feminism.

JOHN FRASER
Ann Saddlemyer had asked a more orthodox queen of feminism,
Catherine MacKinnon, to speak. But MacKinnon had bowed out – she
often did this just to get Andrea Dworkin some gigs. Andrea Dworkin's
coming to the Gordon symposium was a source of great dispute.

**Dworkin described herself as a militant and was famous for having
escaped an abusive marriage by working as a prostitute. A contributor to
the feminist erotic magazine *Suck*, she crusaded against male pornogra-
phy and likened heterosexual intercourse to rape.**

BRONWYN DRAINIE
The place was packed. RD was there in the front row with Brenda. I sat
much farther back. When Andrea Dworkin came out on stage, it was a
truly astounding moment. She must have weighed four hundred
pounds. She was in a pair of overalls and a short-sleeved, grubby white
T-shirt and big work boots. And hair that just flew in all directions, and
a voice like a New England Puritan preacher in a pulpit. Just stunning.
You were listening to her, her ideas were completely revolutionary; the
audience didn't know how to deal with it. That notion that "every act
of penetration is abuse" was the really controversial point.

I will never forget her arms, because she was so fat that huge slabs
of flesh hung from her wrists all the way up to her armpits, with tiny
little flipper hands. She seemed like an otherworldly, mythic creature.
Though I didn't accept her argument, she was absolutely mesmerizing
to listen to and watch.

I couldn't help wondering as I was watching her over the top of
RD's head, What is *he* making of all this? After all, in Davies's novels,
he explored Jungian archetypes and was clearly fascinated with strange,
mythic characters, especially female ones, who are part of life but have
this otherworldly quality. So after the talk, I made my way down to ask
him and Brenda what he had thought of Andrea Dworkin.

To my disappointment, his response was extremely pedestrian,
very middle-class. He didn't see her as a fascinating mythic character.
The words he used were something like, "She's a dirty, unkempt

creature. Just imagine coming onstage in overalls! Doesn't she have any respect for her audience?"

That kind of small-town response quite surprised me. I thought he'd put her in the category of these grotesques he'd made such a thing out of in his own writing, like Lisl Vitzliputzli. Clearly, he was fascinated by the bizarre in his own imagination, but he recoiled from it in real life.

JOHN FRASER

That night, Andrea Dworkin gave an astonishing speech. It was like William Jennings Bryant, that extraordinary stump preacher. At the party afterwards, she got into the spirit of Massey – and she loved Massey – though one strident lesbian feminist attacked Dworkin for selling out by speaking to a mixed crowd.

You could see RD revelling in the drama of it, the power of the speaker. I asked him what he'd thought of the evening and he said, "The big woman? She was strangely affecting!" I took from that that he had never closed his mind, that the writer in him was always open to new things. He was totally caught up in the magic.

BRENDA DAVIES

I remember Andrea Dworkin. Quite a good speaker, as I remember. She said she had been a prostitute, and Rob and I had great jokes about that. She was incredibly fat, and we wondered how well she'd do as a prostitute! She did not turn herself out well. I bet she thought we were all frightfully correct.

I am not surprised to hear about Bronwyn Drainie and John Fraser's experiences. Rob could have two different opinions about the same event. I never argued with him because if he was losing he could go round to the other side. You never knew.

Chapter 39

THE NINTH DECADE

RD would turn 80 on August 28, 1993. But as he approached his ninth decade, his desire to write and his love of theatre remained undiminished. In 1991 the Stratford Festival asked Elliott Hayes, a young Canadian who had studied at the Old Vic, to adapt *World of Wonders* for the stage. The production, which premiered in 1992, was directed by Richard Rose.

KEN NUTT (theatre director)
Robertson Davies had had a long love affair with theatre. When my friend Elliott Hayes began working on adapting *World of Wonders* for Stratford, Elliott told me that this love affair largely hadn't worked out, and that in some ways, the love had continued, with Davies's being outside the life of the theatre. . . . My memory is that *World of Wonders* was a very big plot, and at first Elliott felt it might be tricky. But it wasn't – there was no need for a narrator or any tricks – and both Elliott and Davies felt it went well. It took all of Stratford's resources . . . the masque and the music and the magic scene at the end with the Brazen Head. Working with Elliott on *World of Wonders* for Stratford put RD back in the thick of it. Elliott just loved working with RD, and there was a really good spirit about it.

I remember the opening of *World of Wonders*. By the time he got to Stratford this season, Robertson Davies essentially had rock-star status. We had to have him over for dinner at my house because if he went into a restaurant, he'd be mobbed. There were masses of people lined up on opening night, so we had to give him the rock-star treatment. We had to sneak him out the theatre's side door and into a waiting car so we could whisk him back to my place. It was a bit like Beatlemania comes to Stratford.

There was anxiety, too, because there was magic in the production and we all hoped it would go all right. And it did. Most people thought it was great. The reviews were great. I sensed a great generosity on Davies's part. Davies gave Elliott quite a bit of the praise and credit for the success of *World of Wonders*.

Davies was lucky with his novels, and had patches of great good fortune with his plays and librettos – but he was definitely unlucky when it came to film.

KEN NUTT
And then John Schlesinger, the director of *Midnight Cowboy*, contacted Elliott and said he had wanted to direct a film based on something by Davies for a long time. So after *World of Wonders* was over at Stratford, he flew Elliott down to Los Angeles and they talked about doing a film. Everything was just rolling for Elliott, and he was so happy. It was on his way back from Los Angeles that Elliott was killed. It was a drunk driver. All of Elliott's promise, all that talent. He died around 9:35 p.m. on Monday, February 28, 1994. He was 37.

I am the executor of Elliott's literary estate and there have been many inquiries about *World of Wonders*. But it is so big, so costly. . . .

We still have a silver mug, a tankard with a glass bottom, given to Elliott by Robertson Davies. He must have known that giving a pewter tankard was a Hayes family tradition. A wooden box arrived from Birks, with the inscription: *Elliott Hayes, World of Wonders, 1992, from RD and BD*.

RD and Brenda would have personally ordered that mug from Birks. But most administrative jobs were handled by Moira Whalon, RD's secretary, copy editor, fact-checker and gatekeeper ever since he had hired her to work for him back in Peterborough.

ANNE WALMSLEY (from a January 1993 article for *Chatelaine*)
A mutual friend paired the two in 1956 when Davies was editor of *The Peterborough Examiner*. Whalon, then 31, had lived in the city since moving from England at the age of five. A voracious reader, she had graduated from Grade 11 at 15 and proceeded to use her bookkeeping and typing skills in a series of secretarial jobs.

"I had always been intensely interested in literature," says Whalon. "But when I was working in a hardware business, it was dull." On meeting her, Davies was instantly impressed. "Some secretaries are rather impudent or creepy-crawly," recalls Davies, "but I could see that she was a woman of great integrity."

When Davies was appointed Master of Massey College at the University of Toronto in 1963, he begged Whalon to come with him. Her articulate and fastidious personality and her cheerful, friendly nature quickly made her the darling of Davies's crowd. In fact the students were so fond of her they named their hockey team Moira's Marauders. When worsening glaucoma and cataracts forced her to retire from the college in 1984, Davies told her firmly, "You can leave the college but don't you dare retire from me."

But by the 1990s, RD's workload required another assistant to ease the burden on Miss Whalon.

JENNIFER SURRIDGE
Starting in March 1992 I was working for Dad, and I think it caused Moira Whalon some problems. I was younger and faster and I could use a computer. I think it was hard for her, and I was doing all the travel arrangements.

Dad had asked me some years before if I'd consider working for him, and I was quite flippant. I'd said, "You couldn't afford me." In early 1992, however, I decided to leave a job that was getting difficult. I called him and said, "I am leaving this job anyway, but would you be interested in my working for you?"

He said, "Working for both of us."

He was not good at delegation *ever*, but it helped that I was around and working with Mum. I catalogued his collection of John Martin Harvey material that has gone to the National Archives – with my archival cataloguing unchanged! – and his large collection of Victorian plays, which we sold to the University of Victoria for a lot of money. I also did a catalogue of Tyrone Guthrie and Judy Guthrie's letters, also gone to the National Archives, as has the Old Vic material. And I did the travel arrangements: I got Mum and Dad to the White House, which was fun. Hillary Clinton had asked to meet him. He liked Mrs. Clinton. As an employer he was delighted with what I did for him because I would do things he wasn't good at. My being tidy and neat impressed him.

By the time he hired his middle daughter, whom he referred to as "my chief wrangler," RD was writing what was to be his last published novel,

The Cunning Man. Like *Murther, The Cunning Man* opens with a violent death, that of the beloved Father Hobbes, whose high Anglican church was modelled on the architecture, community and practices of Toronto's St. Mary Magdalene.

FATHER HAROLD NAHABEDIAN
I've been here at St. Mary Magdalene for twenty-three years and I used to see Robertson Davies striding down Harbord Street to go to some clinic on Palmerston. In December 1991 he came one Sunday morning to church. I greeted him at the door and he said, "Oh, good morning, how are you?" I was not sure he recognized me. But he must have. I am mentioned in his book of letters about that morning.

RD (letter to Ann Saddlemyer, December 26, 1991)
On Sunday last I went to church at St. Mary Magdalene. Do you know it? It is the highest of the High Church Anglican establishments in Toronto and I have been going there at intervals since I was a schoolboy, for the splendour and magnificence of its services are a great lift to the spirits in our sometimes quotidian manner of life. This time I was delighted to find that the present Rector is an old Massey Fellow: Harold Nahabedian, and as you might divine from his name, an Armenian who has become an Anglican priest; he gave me a most friendly welcome. (How these Massey men do get around!)

FATHER HAROLD NAHABEDIAN
That morning, I saw that he sat in a pew on the south side. The gallery choir could see something else: throughout the service he had his notebook out, and he was writing everything down. He did not stay to the end. I am at the door by the last hymn and he had left by then.

But he made a mistake in *The Cunning Man*, an error only the clergy would know. . . . There is no celebration of the Eucharist on Good Friday. I remember, too, that he spoke – I think in *The Globe and Mail* – of attending a "Black Mass" at St. Mary Magdalene in the 1940s.

VAL ROSS (article in *The Globe and Mail*, October 8, 1994)
Davies is by no means alone in his ironic reverence; it seems to have been a dominant undertone at St. Mary Magdalene's during the period about which he is writing. "They used to have 'black masses' where all the servers would be black porters from the CNR," Davies recalls. "This

is the sort of joke Anglo Catholics go in for. They also went in for dirty little boy stuff. The priests would leave condoms filled with shaving soap for the vicar to find. They were an awful lot of rascals."

FATHER HAROLD NAHABEDIAN

By Black Mass, he did not mean the satanic. He meant some of the servers were black. I did find that offensive. . . .

In the 1940s, some people would come to St. Mary Magdalene for its High Church liturgy and for the music of the organist and choir conductor Healey Willan, but they would be offended by our black servers. But this church had black servers because the rector then, Father Lee Greene, had worked in South Africa, and was a serious opponent of apartheid. He had got rid of his prejudices. For Davies to call this a "black mass" when he was looking back in the 1990s seemed a little . . . odd.

Still, when *The Cunning Man* came out, I bought a copy for myself and for the church. I thought, I must go and get this autographed. And I put it off.

RD had always known that if he wanted to annoy people, he had only to write about religion. In *The Cunning Man*, he also set out to tweak the noses of the medical profession.

RD (letter to Horace Davenport, March 26, 1994)

My next book appears in the early autumn and I shall of course send you a copy pronto, but you may not like it. It is about a doctor, and I assure you I do not pretend to know anything about medicine, but am somewhat critical of certain modern medical approaches, which I think would benefit from a strong injection of intelligent humanism.

RD knew perfectly well that many doctors, among them his close friends, were intelligent humanists. One was Rick Davis, the young GP and bibliophile from Guelph, who had admired RD's writings since the 1980s. At lunch one day, Davis asked RD if he was aware that the University of Toronto had one of the world's best medical museums – off-limits to the public.

RICK DAVIS

He was listening intently. I said, "Would you be interested if I can arrange a tour? It's a closed museum." He said, "Oh yes, I'd be quite interested."

We went early in the spring – April 28, 1993 – to the Medical Sciences Building and knocked. Inside were human specimens in all types of array, all states. We moved at a slow pace. We were always aware that we were looking at parts of *people who had lived*. . . . We stopped in front of a penis, preserved and shrivelled. He just smiled and made a little speech about boys and men. He was being very respectful. At other specimens of disease or malformation, he would say something like, "There but for the grace of God . . ." We'd stop and smile at each other.

Then I mentioned that down below was the receiving area, which is where the cadavers come in. Some are to be wholly integrated into the museum, some are dissected. As we were talking, we turned around, and we saw, there on a table, the torso of a woman. No head, but she had arms, and on her hands she had sparkly nail polish. RD simply said, "That's amazing." That was our visit . . . then he had to go.

RD had now written eleven novels, but he never got over the writer's vexation with the editing process.

RD (letter to Horace Davenport, May 22, 1994)
I do not have to tell you about the irritation of going over what the copy editor has done to one's writing. Mine belongs to a secret group called Friends of the Minimum who make it their task to iron out every idiosyncrasy or personal quirk in one's prose, and to query anything that seems to their minds to be unclear. Their ideal text is *The Bobbsey Twins Go to Atlantic City*; it contains no ambiguities and nothing to trouble the most sensitive soul.

RICK DAVIS
While he was working on *The Cunning Man* was when we really started to get to know each other. My son Emory, then five, was very ill and was at Sick Kids' Hospital. Emory had a very rare and serious disease and we weren't sure if he was going to make it. He was isolated and on transfusions. Davies would ask me how was he doing while I was helping him with his book.

After Emory pulled through, I was able to take him to Massey. RD gave him things to play with and picture books. He was very kindly and went out of his way to make Emory comfortable.

We talked about what a profound experience it is when, as a medical student, you stop and look at what you're doing. I told him that in the dissection classes, the head and hands are done last because they are so personal to an individual. In my medical training, I was the one who had to disarticulate our cadaver's head from the neck. He put that into *The Cunning Man*.

To promote *The Cunning Man*, which was published in the fall of 1996, RD's Canadian publisher (Douglas Gibson Books, an imprint of McClelland & Stewart) sent him on tour with a young man from Sri Lanka whose first novel, *Funny Boy*, had just been published by M&S.

SHYAM SELVADURAI [reprinted from *Writing Life*, a PEN anthology, edited by Constance Rooke]
My publicist enthused about what a marvellous marketing ploy this was. She told me that hundreds of people came out to hear Robertson Davies read and I would sell just a ton of books. I also learned from her that southwestern Ontario – including Toronto, of course – was known as the Golden Horseshoe in publishing. It was the area where the most books were sold in Canada. From this I conceived the idea of southwestern Ontario (our tour would include London, Guelph, Hamilton and Waterloo) as a sort of make-or-break point in a writer's career. . . .

I could not help fantasizing about the readings I would give with Robertson Davies. I imagined the event from the audiences' point of view. Imagined them coming out to hear the old man read, but before he did so, a young Sri Lankan novelist would come up onstage, and he would start to read, and they would be enraptured. A star would be born overnight on the touring circuit of southwestern Ontario.

The part of the reading I was not looking forward to was being in a van for hours with Robertson Davies. I had heard that he could be a curmudgeon and that I would have to be extremely careful about what I said around him as he was liable to fly off the handle if you disagreed with him. It was entirely likely that this might happen. To me, Robertson Davies represented everything I disliked most about Canada and the white male establishment. I had heard that his *Fifth Business* was mandatory reading at various upper-crust university frat houses, those bastions of white male power. Then there was his stint as Master of Massey College, which I had heard was a rather anachronistic institution at the University of Toronto where fellows drifted about in gowns and generally carried on as if they were at Oxford or Cambridge. Having gone to York University, which I considered pluralistic and forward-looking, I looked down on the University of Toronto as stuffy, snobbish and colonial-minded.

A van had been rented for the occasion of our first reading and, once the publicist had picked me up, we made our way to Mr. Davies's home on Avenue Road. Then, there he was, the man, the legend, coming out to us. He had a great white beard and wore a black fedora at a rather rakish angle. Over his black suit he sported a black cloak, and he walked with a cane. He looked the very image of a senior man of letters, and supporting him by the arm was his wife. She herself was rather formidable, sort of like the Queen, with her hair backcombed into a perfectly coiffed helmet and, just like the Queen, she wore a rather severe suit and carried one of those hard handbags.

Robertson Davies was by now in his eighties, and the van was too high for him to climb into. So the publicists had brought along a stool that he could use as an intermediate step. I had been asked to sit at the very back so the Davieses could have the middle row. After much heaving by the publicists, and quite a few tries, Robertson Davies finally made it into the van. He collapsed in his seat panting, then, once he recovered his breath, he wiped his face with large white handkerchief and turned around to me in the back. He greeted me affably and we shook hands. His wife did the same, and then they turned around to the front and we were off.

I had decided that the only way to survive this tour was not to speak unless I was spoken to, and then say only the very minimum that needed to be said, to avoid in any way offending the great man. So we drove mostly in silence all the way to London where we were going to read at the University of Western Ontario.

On arrival, the writers were met by a professor who rushed to welcome RD and help him out of the van. The professor gave Selvadurai what he recalls as a "cursory greeting" and led the party inside.

Finally it was time for us to read and we were led into a hall. It was packed. In fact, there were so many people that they were seated on the steps of the aisle and standing along the sides of the room. . . . I was to go first and I had been allotted fifteen minutes. Then Mr. Davies would read for, well, as long as he wanted. . . . There was a slight smattering of applause as I walked toward the podium. Then I started to read.

Within a few minutes I saw that it was not going well. This was a section I had read many times before and I knew the first point at which the audience should laugh. Here, however, there was hardly a titter when I got to that part and soon I could feel coming toward me the thing that writers at a public reading, just dread – waves of boredom. A woman coughed, someone rustled a program, two men were whispering. A glance at the audience showed me that one elderly man had actually drifted off to sleep. . . .

Now it was Robertson Davies's turn. Or rather, first it was the professor's turn, to give a long-winded and effusive description of Mr. Davies's bio and heap praise upon him. Then the old man, the legend, stood up, straighter than I had ever seen him stand so far. He picked up his cane, gave it a little twirl, a little flourish, and, at this gesture, a thunderous roar of applause swept through the room. He walked grandly up the steps that led to the stage. I could see that he was lapping it up. The professor came forward gallantly to offer him his arm, but Robertson Davies refused it. He made his way up the steps, then stood a moment to catch his breath. The applause was still going on and he raised his hand in acknowledgement of it, then walked over to the podium, put down his cane, slipped on his glasses and began to read. A hush came over the auditorium. The great Robertson Davies read for forty-five minutes, and the audience listened intently. I could feel it, the thing all writers at a reading hope and long for, the waves of rapt attention passing me on their way to the stage.

The applause when he finished was tremendous. Some people leapt to their feet. It went on and on as Robertson Davies slowly (I thought rather *purposefully* slowly) made his way across the stage, down the steps and along the front row to his seat. Before he sat down he raised his hand once more.

Then it was time for the book signing.

SHYAM SELVADURAI

What happened next was not unexpected. The entire audience began to line up to get their books signed by Robertson Davies. The line was so long it actually snaked right past where I was sitting and, occasionally, as people passed by, they stopped to utter some insincere praise with falsely polite smiles on their faces. I think I must have signed two books that evening. I sat at the table for well over an hour, twirling my pen, until my publicist finally took pity on me and said, with a wry smile, "I don't think you're going to be signing any more books tonight." She ushered me back into the lounge. . . .

Finally Robertson Davies returned to the lounge, triumphant. We were loaded back into the van and delayed while the professor made his effusive goodbyes to Mr. Davies, and then we set off back to Toronto.

After we had been travelling a little while, Mr. Davies turned in his seat and regarded me over his spectacles with an odd twinkle in his eyes. "Let me tell you about a reading I once did at a bookstore in Kingston. We arrived in the middle of a snowstorm, having driven all the way from Toronto, to find that nobody had turned up. There was just me, my wife, and the lady who ran the bookstore. The poor woman was mortified, of course, but what was to be done?" He shrugged. "She suggested that perhaps we should forget the reading altogether, but I said to her, 'Madam, I have driven all this distance and I will do my reading.'" He laughed. "So I got up and read to my wife and the woman who owned the bookstore." He gave me a long stare. "I've read to two people and I've read to five hundred, and I'll take anything in between."

I was glad it was dark in the back of the van, for suddenly I was blushing with shame. For I saw that I had misjudged the old man on numerous levels. On the most obvious level, I had let all the hearsay and gossip about him prevent me from being open to knowing him at all. But more important, I saw that the tremendous adulation he had received tonight was something he held slightly apart from him; that his theatricality, the cape, the fedora, the walking stick, the white handkerchief that he brought out periodically to mop his brow, were all part of a theatre performance that in a curious way kept the audience, not to mention the professor, at a distance; a distance I have now come to understand as vital, if one is to return from being an author promoting a book, to that solitary kernel within, from which the work flows.

In 1995, RD and Brenda went on three international promotional tours for *The Cunning Man*.

JENNIFER SURRIDGE

I was making the travel arrangements at that point. It was Seattle in January, England in March/April, the U.S. again in May/June.

RD (letter to Horace Davenport, January 29, 1995)
Since I last wrote to you I have been to Seattle and Portland to speak and rather to my astonishment enjoyed it very much. . . . [A]fter my lecture, questions. These were on the whole first-rate, with the usual boob queries such as . . . Does anybody ever call you Bob? (Never more than once.) Do you use a word processor? (No, but I keep a fourteenth-century Iron Maiden in my study to welcome such visitors as yourself.) But returning by airship I picked up a flu germ and have for the past ten days been under the weather as the flu combines with my old enemies asthma and bronchitis to give me hell.

The trip to England in March was onerous for RD, and his English agent noticed that he was frail.

FELICITY BRYAN
When he came to England for *The Cunning Man* he wasn't terribly well. He told me so. He had to have rests and things.

RD (letter to Horace Davenport, May 29, 1995)
I have been silent from stark necessity: Brenda and I returned a few weeks ago from some business in the U.K. and picked up a germ somewhere along the way; we had almost immediately to go to New York, where the germ got a firm hold, and when we returned we were both very unwell – Brenda the worst I have ever seen her – with some sort of flu-bronchitis which has once again put me in the hands of heart specialists.

That summer he began to research another novel.

JENNIFER SURRIDGE
I did a lot of research for the new book he planned to write after *The Cunning Man*. It was to be about the man travelling in the present day across Canada by train. I got RD prices, schedules and train routes. He wasn't going to take the trip himself, but needed the research. He also wanted Eleanor Sweezey's advice.

When her sister Maggie was alive, Eleanor Sweezey travelled with her to Europe every year. She continued to go on tours after Maggie's death. It was for information on such tours that RD wrote to her on September 25, 1995.

Dear Eleanor (Fr Yr eye alone)

I need your help. You have had a lot of experience with tours and I should think that such tours included quite a few old people; what can you tell me about the sort of romances that develop on such tours (because I know that travel is a great provoker of romance). . . . I am particularly interested in old men, because as you will have already divined, I am writing a book to which this sort of thing is relevant. My suspicion is that old men, who are so often defined as lecherous old nuisances, are driven by a need for romance, understanding and companionship. . . . I hope this letter finds you well, busy, much sought after and happy. And once again I ask for your words of experience.

Love, Rob.

BRENDA DAVIES
Rob wanted to write a last novel about old age because he knew a lot about it. He said he wanted to write "a really good novel." I suppose it's a bit of a burden to have a huge success earlier on.

Chapter 40

DECEMBER 2, 1995

RD played the roles of brisk perambulator and laughing, robust gourmand but privately worried all his life about his health – his asthma, his tricky heart and his tempest-tossed digestive system.

ELUNED MacMILLAN
Brenda told me when they went up to the country, to Caledon, they took all his city clothes. I said, "Rob, why ever do you do that?"

He said, "Eluned, you never know when there's going to be a funeral!"

I said, "Rob, really!!!"

But that was Rob: Welsh! Dramatic! He had that dour judgmental side, too – wily like a Scot. If you're completely Welsh, you're mad! . . .

All the Welsh are hypochondriacs. [My grandfather, British Prime Minister] Lloyd George used to say to his wife, Maggie, "I'm dying of pneumonia." Maggie would say, "No, Lloyd, you died of that last week." I think we used to say that to Rob, too.

MIRANDA DAVIES
He fell ill when I was working with child guidance in London, very ill. It wasn't so much that I could sense a development of his mortality but that I remember I gave him a medication, Night Nurse, which he just threw up. . . . He was hyper-alert even though partly deaf, and very sensitive to sounds and smells. He expressed all this anxiety as a self-preservative. He could throw up anything. This goes very deep to the way the personality is expressed in the body.

This gave me an insight into how much my mother had to nurse and help him; he could not take in that kind of nursing and help. He had a kind of carapace. He could always talk *at* me, always interesting stuff . . . but I could have been almost anybody. I felt this at the time, of the medicine, you couldn't penetrate the carapace. You don't have a real interchange.

RICHARD WERNHAM (former Massey College fellow)
The last time I saw RD was with Ramsay Derry and his wife Trish at RD's place in Caledon. He gave us a tour, he was very proud of the marvellous views, though he said the drawback of a long view was that all sorts of things can pop up in your view that you can't control. Our farm is nearby, and is on land shaped like a bowl. You just see your own property. He said ours was a wonderful piece of land. But I think he really liked being at the top of a hill. It's a good metaphor for observing other people and being slightly detached.

MIRANDA DAVIES
Acknowledging dependency is a very late development. You see a change in his dedication of a book to my mother, at the forefront of *Murther and Walking Spirits*. I did grow closer to him in the last two years of his life. Of course, those falls and illnesses were mortality knocking at the door.

JENNIFER SURRIDGE
By the 1990s he had a heart problem. But I wasn't living at home then and wasn't so aware of it. Also, he pooh-poohed the big health issues. In a way, he didn't want to be bothered by his health in terms of doing anything about it – though he did start using a stationary bicycle in later life. But as for his heart, nobody ever told me.

ELUNED MacMILLAN
I didn't know Rob was having trouble with his heart. I thought he was a bit of a fusspot. He'd make me laugh by saying, "I think I'm on my way out." Bob [her husband, Dr. Robert MacMillan] told me afterwards that Rob had a terribly bad heart and was in heart failure a lot.

DR. VIVIAN RAKOFF
Once at lunch he said – I can almost hear his voice – "I have only one prayer: Dear Lord, let me not die stupid." We all know people who were once strong and capable and who become doddering and drooling and Alzheimerish. That kind of remark, when it comes lightly inserted into the conversation, means the idea has been long thought of. It's *there*.

JENNIFER SURRIDGE
The parents went to Princeton in September 1995. There's a tape of his speech, and he coughed a lot. He wasn't well. Brenda was very concerned. He was *terrible* at helping himself. If he was in a hotel that was too cold or too hot, he'd complain rather than have things fixed. He probably didn't know how to adjust an air conditioner if he wasn't in his own house.

When they got back from Princeton, they went to the airport to pick up a friend of Mum from Australia and they hung around the airport for a long time and he got a chill. This turned into walking pneumonia. Mum and I finally twigged that he had something that was worse than a flu.

DAVID GARDNER
The last time I saw him was about a month before he died. He was not at all well. He kind of nodded at me – it was some university gathering. Brenda was supporting him. This was the dark side of Rob. He knew he was losing his grip and he was angry about it and did not want to converse. "I don't want to talk to you because I don't want to tell you that I'm not feeling well, and I do not accept that I'm not feeling well."

SARAH EDINBOROUGH ILEY
The saddest thing is, I'd asked him to speak at my parents' fiftieth – their golden wedding anniversary. I had written the invitations in gold ink. His reply said: "Gold ink? What's next?" Then he wrote: "Shall I come? Just try to keep me away. Shall I speak? Just try to keep me quiet."

JOHN McGREEVY
My last meeting with RD was at his office at Massey. I remember lots of laughs. I proposed doing a film, *Gaudy Tales*, with RD reading the Christmas Gaudy ghost stories to young people. I had even spoken to [theatre owner] David Mirvish about doing the ghost stories at the Royal Alexandra with an audience.

JENNIFER SURRIDGE
Then he had a stroke. This was mid-November. The stroke robbed him of his ability to speak properly. It was heartbreaking. The local health organization sent some people to teach him how to speak. These ill-educated people to teach *him* how to speak!

He gave me a letter he wanted me to send to Horace, and I typed it up and gave it to him to read. I couldn't understand why it was taking him so long – maybe he had suffered some vision damage. But he knew what was going on. He'd say, "I can't find the words. There have always been words . . ."

THEO HENKENHAF

After he had the stroke, he wasn't speaking well. But he was comfortable enough to talk with me. Mostly we talked about the garden and plans. It was difficult for him to make himself understood. He got very angry when the words would not come out the way he wanted them to. But he would keep trying, and the words came – eventually.

This was hard for him, certainly. To me, he never seemed like a person who would ever get sick! He was a big, strong man. Well, he *looked* strong. Massive. Though I never noticed him lift anything.

He was annoyed at being sick, and at not being capable. But never, as far as I could see, was he worried about death. When he was in the Orangeville hospital, Mrs. Davies quite often drove herself, but I would drive her if she needed me. These people – I'd known them for so long, they were friends.

JENNIFER SURRIDGE

It was unbelievably awful. I was driving up there every day, and that year the weather was terrible. The weather was so bad that one day Mum left Orangeville Hospital and couldn't get back to Windhover. She had to stay in a motel.

When RD was dying and I wanted to call Miranda, Mum said, "No, don't call her." I said, "She has to know and she'll want to come." But this was RD's big thing. He didn't want to be a burden.

JOHN McGREEVY

Late in the year, I called the Caledon house and I said to Brenda, "I'm calling about *Gaudy Tales*." She was terribly frazzled. She said, "Oh, there'll be no more gaudy tales. The ambulance is coming for Rob now."

BRENDA DAVIES

Rob had a second stroke. I remember John McGreevy calling me and I couldn't wait to get off the phone.

THEO HENKENHAF
The last time I saw him? Maybe it was in the hospital, but I don't think I ever went into his room. I was just there to wait for Mrs. Davies. Miranda was there at the last. And Jennifer, of course. Jennifer is the powerful one who can look after everyone else. Mind you, Mrs. Davies can, too.

JENNIFER SURRIDGE
He had a stroke to the brain stem, but in the end, his heart was so strong it was incredible. He had only oxygen from Tuesday to Saturday and he kept going, though the brain stem was completely gone. Miranda sat with him and read him the funeral service.

BRENDA DAVIES
Rob was in a coma. I got the family in to say goodbye to him. Miranda came. I hadn't wanted to tell Miranda to come because I didn't want to admit that it was the end. He finally died in the middle of the night. I remember how badly I felt that I had not wanted to go to the hospital to see the body. It wouldn't have made any difference if I had. But one blames oneself.

RD died on December 2, 1995, at age 82.

BRENDA DAVIES
When Rupert died there had been a big, long thing in the paper listing all that he had done. When Rob died, the newspaper death notice was simple and short.

There was little need to say more. That was being done in handsome and lengthy obituaries across Canada, in *The New York Times* and in London, and in newspapers across the English-speaking world.

BRENDA DAVIES
Then there were three agonizing days while Trinity College prepared for the funeral. I felt utterly ill and at the end of my tether. The funeral was absolutely packed. The grandchildren carried the coffin with Massey men in their gowns and we had a short Anglican service, the English not being up to huge showings of emotion.

DEREK HOLMAN

For his funeral, I was asked if I could write something. I wrote a piece for the choir, an unaccompanied motet on a well-known text, "Justorum Animae" – "The Souls of the Righteous Are in the Hands of God."

BRUCE UBUKATA

I played the music at RD's funeral. I remember peering across the U of T campus and seeing the flag at Massey at half mast. It was bitterly cold and the Harris Revolution [the new Conservative provincial government] was dawning, and I felt as if a particular world I loved was vanishing.

I played for about fifteen minutes before people came in. The music was my choice but influenced by his spirit. I played Vaughan Williams's three choral preludes on Welsh folksongs. He had not specified that, but it seemed appropriate. He had specified Purcell's "Now That the Sun Hath Veiled His Light." The significant thing that I do remember was that last hymn he had chosen was done to a craggy Welsh tune. It was not a particularly well-known one, not one that people could roar out. But his final musical choice was impeccable.

BRENDA DAVIES

The walk out of that chapel was the longest walk of my life.

LISA BALFOUR BOWEN

I was at Robertson Davies's funeral at Trinity College chapel in December 1995. It is a beautiful, narrow, perpendicular Gothic space. To get into it requires going down very steep steps and there is no banister. All the brides who get married there have problems with this perilous staircase. I was standing at the back and my heart went into my mouth when I saw Mrs. Davies nearly stumble on these steps, and I still remember the intensity of that moment.

ELUNED MacMILLAN

When he died, I remember her clinging onto me and saying, "What am I going to do without him?"

BRENDA DAVIES
There was a reception afterwards at Massey. John Fraser [the new Master] put me and the family in the Master's lodging and only brought in certain people to see us. This was a great relief, and very kind of him.

FRANCESS HALPENNY
At Trinity College Chapel at RD's funeral, Rex Southgate and Martha Henry's husband and other members of the cast of *Leaven of Malice* turned up. I remember us talking in the anteroom at the funeral service and we were saying that we all remembered that production of *Leaven of Malice* we had been in as a good experience, as a production that *worked*. And as I remember, the funeral itself was not a sad occasion. It was celebratory.

One of the many Canadian writers who contributed memorials at a service a few days later at Convocation Hall at the University of Toronto was Timothy Findley, who was, like RD, an actor turned playwright and novelist.

TIMOTHY FINDLEY
It was the role he played. The role of Robertson Davies.
    Was he a ham?
    Not by a long shot.
    It was a gigantic presence – yes. But a gigantic presence sums to nothing if there is not a giant inside.
    I suspect only Brenda Davies knows what it really cost him to play the giant as well as to be one. A lot, I would think. He was a shy man, a quiet man. Oh yes, he was.

Family friends had their own memories.

SARAH EDINBOROUGH ILEY
I had to turn off that memorial at Convocation Hall when it was broadcast on the radio. People spoke of him as always acting. I don't believe such people ever really knew him. They said he was an actor. That was crap. They'd met a persona, not the man, and they didn't seem to be able to tell the difference. He just had a natural defence against a lot of interlopers. The person they were talking about on the radio – that was

not who I knew. This idea that he was stuck in the 1920s, or that he was acting a role, or that he was patrician, English, it just wasn't him. Yes, he was moderately eccentric. Big deal. He wore a coat with a cloak part to it. But he could discuss a play, he could discuss a book. He didn't just watch the world at one remove.

Public tributes in Toronto were followed by one in New York City, which the family attended. In the year following RD's death, Brenda and Jennifer formed a company, Pendragon Ink, to act as RD's literary executor, and went to work compiling a collection of RD's book reviews and occasional pieces, with introductions contributed by his editor for many years, Doug Gibson. It was titled *The Merry Heart* (the name he had planned to use for his next novel) and was published in Fall 1996. More posthumous books followed. In 1997 Pendragon Ink produced *Happy Alchemy: On the Pleasures of Music and the Theatre*, edited by Jennifer Surridge and Brenda Davies (Douglas Gibson Books). Though this period was productive, for Brenda it was terrible.

BRENDA DAVIES
I was just in a coma for that first year after his death. Nothing seemed worth doing. The doctor said it was shock. We also had our own service. He was cremated and we tossed the ashes at Windhover and did a little service of our own. I read a poem about transformation. And we did some prayers. There is also a memorial stone at Mount Pleasant Cemetery in the family plot, because people said there should be a stone. It's very simple.

THEO HENKENHAF
At Windhover, I prepared the area by the stone pile for the family's memorial ceremony. We didn't make it too civilized, just cleared it enough so people could walk about. Elderberry is growing out of the stones, dogwood and high-bush cranberry. Most of these things have seeded themselves.

JOHN FRASER
Our last encounter at Massey, I asked him to do a ghost story, to be set in the bibliography room. I said to him, "Now will you come back as a ghost?"

He said, "Well, I'll try. We can't know these things . . ."

He was mock-serious, warm but edgy. No conversation with him was ordinary. Any subject could be made Daviesian . . .

The Theatre of Massey is still his. I do think he play-acted at being a nicer person than he was. And in the end, he did become a nicer person.

MIRANDA DAVIES
You must know my father was a wounded man, wounded from early life. He had thick defences. Part of this was his sense of contempt. There was much contempt at the dinner table. This was the model. This was the way we spoke. . . . Years later I spoke to my father about contempt. I told him that I had been trying to deal with it and that I thought he had a problem with this too. He said, "Contempt? Oh yes! I have more than enough contempt for any one man!" So he recognized the problem. And he grew. Oh, he grew.

EPILOGUE

Since his death, RD's publications have been prolific. Among the books of his writing that have appeared are: *For Your Eye Alone: Letters 1976–1995*, selected and edited by Judith Skelton Grant; her matching compilation *Discoveries: Early Letters 1938–1975*; and *The Quotable Robertson Davies*, edited by James Channing Shaw, all published by Douglas Gibson Books. The Folio Society has produced a collector's edition of the Deptford trilogy in one volume, and Jennifer Surridge's collection of her father's *Selected Plays* has just been published by Penguin [Spring 2008]. She is now at work on two other volumes, *Selected Works on the Art of Writing*, and *Selected Works on the Pleasures of Reading*. RD's first passions, for music and theatre, are also producing persistent echoes. The Stratford Festival put on a well-received production of *Tempest-Tost* in 2001, and RD and Brenda's original version of the Nativity Play has been remounted in Calgary (Christmas 2007). And there is a new opera in the works. All of this musical and theatrical activity was appropriate for a man who gave considerable – if contradictory – thought to the stagecraft and soundtrack of his own life's drama. Although RD's funeral was a simple service, he had given thought to what the soundtrack could have been.

RD (1991 interview, *Globe and Mail*, on the subject of his funeral)
The thing I'd really like would be for my family to organize a party with lots of music, drink and food – good stuff: roasts to be sliced, delicious tartlets, sherry trifle. The drink, good clarets. And the music would be the second movement of Beethoven's Archduke Trio, one of the noblest utterances I've ever encountered.

Of course, the instructions he gave for his funeral weren't like that at all. But this man was hard to pin down.

DEREK HOLMAN

Did he once say that he wanted Beethoven's Archduke Trio played at his funeral? I am pretty certain that he did not say that Beethoven was one of his favourites. I think I agreed with him, and rashly suggested that some late Beethoven was overrated. Some time after that, I spoke warmly of Beethoven on CBC radio, and later Rob called me up and said, "Well, that's not what you said the other day!"

As Master of Massey, RD established musical traditions – concerts, a choir, and music at the annual Christmas Gaudy – for which he would commission original works from Holman and others. One drew on the writings of John Aubrey, the "maggoty magpie" diarist. Another was a homage to Samuel Pepys which included a canon for eight voices.

DEREK HOLMAN

Well, writing a canon, with the same tune overlapping with itself – even a simple one, like Frère Jacques – is a tricky business, and I'm quite sure that Rob knew that an eight-voice canon is quite a challenge. He knew this would keep me busy for a while. And it did. . . . I fancy he recalled with affection the hymn singing around the piano when he was a boy – Rob liked melodious music. I get the impression that he enjoyed Victorian parlour music – Tosti's *Goodbye*!

RD (travel diary, 1989)

My inner music – what plays in my head if I am not thinking of anything in particular, is ballad trash from my youth. . . . Is this my mother's music?

As Brenda had discovered at the Old Vic, RD would help anyone who had use for his musical knowledge.

RALPH NABLOW

Upon arriving at Massey College in the fall of 1968, I was surprised to discover that the college did not have a piano. I expressed this concern to Robertson Davies, who replied "Oh, but Massey College is a temple of labour." In fact, very soon after, the college acquired its first grand piano. One evening when I was alone in the dining hall playing Schubert's Sonata in B-flat, opus posthumous, Robertson Davies came up the stairs, stood beside the piano . . . and turned the pages for me.

In the company of talented musicians, RD could be positively humble.

VICTORIA WOOD

One time, Jade [my husband James Douglas] and I had a dinner party at our house on Boswell, with Lotfi Mansouri [general director of the Canadian Opera Company] and his wife, Midge, and RD and Brenda, and Nicky and Shelagh Goldschmidt. I was with Rob after dinner and I said, "I cannot imagine you being shy."

He said, "I am terribly shy."

I said, "Oh, Rob! I don't believe it. Whoever would you be shy *with?*"

He said, "I am shy with people like *that*" – and he pointed at Lotfi and Nicky and said, "They've accomplished so much compared with what I have done."

DEREK HOLMAN

Rob was certainly musical. And he sang perfectly well, but it is his speaking voice that I remember. Peter Ustinov once said that the English prime minister Harold Macmillan spoke as if he had "a cathedral in his mouth." This made me think of Rob.

Together, Holman and RD collaborated on a children's opera, *Dr. Canon's Cure*. It was well received. But when RD wrote the libretto for a second children's opera in 1983, this time Holman declined.

DEREK HOLMAN

I read it carefully and he made changes in it, but I did not think I could make *Children of the Moon* work.

RD and Holman's friendship was based not only on collaboration but on shared humour.

DEREK HOLMAN

We used to have long talks about improbable hymn texts. . . . An old friend, Canon Cyril Taylor of Salisbury Cathedral, had once sent me an improbable hymn, "Worms, Strike Your Harps." You're aware of expressions such as "the bowels of compassion" and clergymen who signed their letters, "Yours in the bowels of Christ?" Here's something he sent me: "The Bowel Hymn," by Dr. Isaac Watts – or so he said . . . I think he sent it to John Julius Norwich, too. He might well have written it himself. I wouldn't put it past him.

> *Blest is the man whose bowels move*
> *And melt with pity for the poor*
> *His soul in sympathizing love*
> *Feels what his fellow saints endure.*
>
> *His heart contrives for their relief*
> *More good than his own hands can do*
> *He in a time of general grief*
> *Finds that his Lord has bowels too.*

RD's more serious musical work came to the attention of the Canadian Opera Company's Richard Bradshaw, hired in 1989 as its chief conductor.

RICHARD BRADSHAW

I read the Deptford trilogy to introduce myself to Canada. I was a huge RD fan, and knew he'd be a natural to write a libretto, his work is so tremendously operatic. I wrote to ask and he said, not a "No," but a "No, not now . . ."

At Easter, 1994, I went to Paris to St. Eustache to see one of the great organists, Jean Guillou. I went to hear the mass, and we were talking in the church, high up behind, in the loft. It turn out that Jean Guillou *loved* Robertson Davies. We talked the whole way through the mass, interrupted only by calls from the priests – Would he please come down and play for the *Offertoire*? We ignored these calls and kept on talking about Rob.

That June, RD wrote Bradshaw to confess that there was one opera he would like to write. At Oxford he read Apuleius's *The Golden Ass*, the tale, written in the second century AD, of a vain young man whose lover transforms him into a donkey. He can only break the spell through mystical rebirth. RD had used *The Golden Ass* as the fictional opera in *A Mixture of Frailties*. RD wrote to Bradshaw:

I have an idea for a libretto – have indeed had it in my mind for many years – and it is an operatic version of that wonderful old story, *The Golden Ass*, by Apuleius. . . . This story has considerable modern relevance, has a hint of Women's Lib about it, and is sufficiently dirty for modern taste without being gross. . . . You might try it on M. Guillou.

RICHARD BRADSHAW

Jean Guillou wanted to write this opera. So I gave his music to Rob. But it became very clear that his music was too space-age, too jagged – not at all right for Rob's text. . . .

Then we went to the lunch at Le Rendez-Vous. Rob and I had gone backwards and forwards on the composer. The obvious person was Leonard Bernstein, Rob and I agreed. But he had inconveniently died. I said, "Are you sure there's not a Canadian composer who could do this?"

And Rob said, "Well, who?"

I said, "Harry Somers." And Rob said in a booming voice, "Harry Somers? No sense of humour!" Which was not true.

BARBARA CHILCOTT [Mrs. Harry Somers]

A friend of mine from India and I were having lunch at Le Rendez-Vous. We were the only people in the restaurant except for two men. And I recognized one of them by his loud voice. It was Rob, with Richard Bradshaw of the Canadian Opera Company, on the other side of the room. I heard Rob's voice say, "The thing is, Richard, I just don't understand Harry's music!"

Rob didn't see me. If he had heard that, Harry would have told him, "You're not supposed to understand it, just listen to it."

Bradshaw turned to Randolph Peters, a young composer from Winnipeg. After RD's death in December 1995, Peters worked with Bradshaw and Colin Graham of the St. Louis Opera to create the new opera, the company's largest original work in two decades. With a fifty-five-member orchestra, a forty-member chorus and eight dancers, it premiered on April 13, 1999, at the Hummingbird Centre in Toronto. "For rhythmic drive, melodic invention, orchestral colour and sheer joyous entertainment, you won't beat this opera," Bradshaw told the press. "I think it will become an important part of the regular operatic repertoire."

BRENDA DAVIES

The Golden Ass was a huge thrill. It was marvellous. I went to all the rehearsals. Colin Graham did an extraordinary job. It went extremely well and was well received.

More than a decade after RD's death, his other musical ideas are still resonating, even with those whose contact with him in life was fleeting.

DEAN BURRY (composer)

I was born in 1972, and I grew up in Gander, in the province of Newfoundland and Labrador. By the time I came to the University of Toronto in 1994 to do my master's in music composition, I knew of RD.

I remember walking to school on the day of RD's funeral. I was walking by Trinity College as the cortege pulled in, and I watched from the other side of the street.

After Burry completed his M.A., he found work with the COC box office in 1999, when the company mounted RD's *The Golden Ass.*

No one knew I was a composer, but someone handed me a copy of the libretto of *The Golden Ass.* I remember I read it while waiting for a bus. I felt like I had opened King Tut's tomb. I thought, "My God, does anyone on this bus know this is here?!?"

It was while I was in the early stages of writing *The Brothers Grimm* [a children's opera for the Canadian Opera Company] that I saw RD's collection *Happy Alchemy* for sale in a bookstore in a bargain bin. I probably paid something like $4.99. I thought as I read it, "This guy has thought a lot about opera."

Children of the Moon was supposed to have been given a composition by Derek Holman. But for whatever reason, Derek Holman never set this libretto to music. So I went to Jennifer Surridge and she said it had been shelved.

My wife, Julie McFarlane, is a violinist and we were visiting with her family in Kingston. I asked, as opera composers are always asking, Does anyone know of a patron of the arts? A friend who plays with Symphony Kingston said, "Why don't you talk to Michael Davies, the former publisher of *The Kingston Whig-Standard?*" I said, "Is he related to Robertson Davies? Hold the phone! Because I have a Robertson Davies project that I want to do."

They put me in touch with Jennifer, and I met Jennifer and Brenda Davies, in September 2004. In May 2004 the COC premiered my children's opera *The Hobbit* – now, I had not known that RD had studied under J.R.R. Tolkien at Oxford. That really is two degrees of separation! My opera was partly in Tolkien's Elvish, which really is a bastardized form of Welsh. . . .

From reading *Children of the Moon*, I got a sense of RD's encyclopedic mind. I was reading through what is a children's libretto and I had to look up at least twelve words.

Children of the Moon is set in 1901. The style goes back to the old pastoral: the young man and the young woman are in love but they cannot get together, and it takes a gypsy peddler who is a crackpot magician or soothsayer to bring them together. RD was always fascinated with this character of the crackpot magician.

Burry started to research the text.

DEAN BURRY

This gets spooky: the first pastoral was *Le Devin du Village*, by Jean-Jacques Rousseau, written in 1752. Mozart did a parody of it, when he was age 12, in 1768 – *Bastien and Bastienne*. And there was an English translation in 1762 by Charles Burney, who translated *Le Devin du Village* as – *The Cunning Man*!

RD wrote the libretto for *Children of the Moon* between writing *The Rebel Angels* and *What's Bred in the Bone*. *Bred in the Bone* is narrated by the Angel of Biography, the Lesser Zadkiel. And Zadkiel is the name of the gypsy peddler in *Children of the Moon*. . . .

If I wanted to know what RD's thoughts were on opera, I see his novel *The Lyre of Orpheus*, and it's about the completion of an unfinished opera. Holy cow! That's what I'm doing: completing an unfinished opera. I have this sense that RD is my collaborator. And I find a quote in *Lyre*:

> An opera has to have a foundation; something big, like unhappy love, or vengeance, or some point of honour. Because people are like that, you know. There they sit, all those stockbrokers and rich surgeons and insurance men, and they look so solemn and quiet as if nothing would rouse them. But underneath they are raging with unhappy love or vengeance. They go to *La Boheme* or *La Traviata* and they remember some early affair that might have been squalid if you weren't living it yourself. . . . Only they don't think it; very

deep down they feel it, and boil it and suffer it in the primitive underworld of their souls. . . . Opera speaks to the heart as no other art does, because it is essentially simple.

So once again I felt that RD was a kindred spirit . . . and there are things I get to chuckle at that the audience won't ever see. "Enter Fullpail [the cow of the opera's hero, Barney O'Grady]." Now, cows are played on stage by two people, so he makes a joke about that. He says, "She sings a duet with herself in delightful harmony."

This is where RD is looking down at me, the composer, and laughing. He wants a cow yodel. See the stage directions: they call for a yodelling chorus – "at the discretion of the composer." Now, if that's not a gauntlet he has thrown down!

So I am upstairs here at home, learning to yodel, and my family can hear me, from downstairs. They heard my yodelling and they were laughing at me. And I think RD was looking down and laughing, too.

The relationship between a librettist and a composer is close. Encountering RD, even posthumously, has been a pretty intimate relationship . . .

I am working with a Ghost Writer!

PUBLISHER'S NOTE

Val Ross was diagnosed with brain cancer in October 2007. During the next four months she fought a rearguard action against the disease, with every medical weapon at hand and with her own wry gallantry. She did so for many reasons, among them a burning desire to finish this book. Against enormous odds she completed the final chapters, played a full role in the final editing process, checked the proofs and approved of the final cover.

She died on February 17, 2008. Less than a week before that date she wrote the following final part of the book.

ACKNOWLEDGEMENTS

I owe a debt of thanks to many people and institutions for their help in the creation of this book.

First, the institutions. I would like to thank the Upper Canada College Archives; Library and Archives of Canada for my use of the Davies material in their fonds; the Bentley Library at the University of Michigan; and the CBC Archives, where Barbara Brown was notably helpful.

I thank *The Globe and Mail* and *The Toronto Star* for the use of a number of fine excerpts, and especially Shyam Selvadurai and Fiona Farrell for their kindness in allowing me to use their perceptive written contributions.

My thanks to John Fraser at Massey College for so much, including the suggestion that I undertake this book, and to Lynne Suo for her zesty companionship during the research.

Special thanks go to the Davies family for their graceful cooperation, which applies equally to Judith Skelton Grant, Robertson Davies's biographer.

Above all, I thank every single one of those people who appear in the book. Their kindness and generosity in agreeing to be interviewed by me literally made this book possible. All errors that may have crept in during the process are, of, course mine.

Then there are my children, Max, Maddie and Zoe, and my friends, too numerous to list here. Special thanks go, however, to Katherine Ashenburg, Bernice Eisenstein, Angela Ferrante, Mary Janigan, Sandra Martin, Cori Palmer and Emilie Smith-Bowles for helping me through some times when my health made me fear that I might not finish this project.

And thanks, of, course, to my publisher, Douglas Gibson, who made it work logistically.

And to Morton Ritts, forever.

Val Ross
Toronto, February 2008.

INDEX

KING JOHN OF CANADA *by* Scott Gardiner
This savagely funny political satire foresees a Canada that is falling apart –
until the winner of the "Be A Monarch Lottery" takes charge. "A Richlerian
skewering." – *Toronto Star*   *Fiction, 6 × 9, 336 pages, trade paperback*

THE YEARS OF FIRE *by* Yves Beauchemin, *translated by* Wayne Grady
"Charles the Bold" continues his career in east-end Montreal, through the
high-school years when he encounters girls and fights the threat of arson.
"One of those 'great books.' No wonder Beauchemin is considered Quebec's
Balzac." – Montreal *Gazette*   *Fiction, 6 × 9, 272 pages, trade paperback*

STEPHEN HARPER AND THE FUTURE OF CANADA *by* William Johnson
A serious, objective biography taking us right through Stephen Harper's
early days in power. "The most important Canadian political book of the
year." – *Calgary Herald*   *Biography, 6 × 9, 512 pages, trade paperback*

MY MOTHER'S DAUGHTER: A MEMOIR *by* Rona Maynard
Chatelaine's former editor has written the story of her relationship with her
mother in "a wonderfully honest and enthralling book" (Alice Munro) that
will speak to every mother and every daughter.
                              Autobiography, 6 × 9, 252 pages, hardcover

CHARLES THE BOLD *by* Yves Beauchemin, *translated by* Wayne Grady
An unforgettable coming-of-age story set in 1960s and 1970s east-end
Montreal, from French Canada's most popular novelist. "Truly astonishing . . .
one of the great works of Canadian literature." – Madeleine Thien
                              Fiction, 6 × 9, 384 pages, trade paperback

WHAT IS A CANADIAN? Forty-Three Thought-Provoking Responses
edited by Irvin Studin
Forty-two prominent Canadian "sages," including Roch Carrier, John
Crosbie, Joy Kogawa, and Margaret MacMillan, provide essays beginning "A
Canadian is . . ." The result is an important book for all thinking Canadians.
                              Non-fiction, 6 × 9, 283 pages, hardcover

THE WAY IT WORKS: Inside Ottawa *by* Eddie Goldenberg
Chrétien's senior policy adviser from 1993 to 2003, Eddie Goldenberg gives
us this "fascinating and sometimes brutally honest look at the way the
federal government really operates." – Montreal *Gazette*
                    Non-fiction, 6 × 9, 408 pages, illustrations, trade paperback

THE VIEW FROM CASTLE ROCK *by* Alice Munro
The latest collection of short stories by Alice Munro is her most personal yet,
based loosely on her family history. "When reading her work it is difficult to
remember why the novel was ever invented." – *The Times* (U.K.)
                              Fiction, 6 × 9, 368 pages, hardcover

SAILING AWAY FROM WINTER: A Cruise from Nova Scotia to Florida and Beyond *by* Silver Donald Cameron
"Silver Donald Cameron is a wonderful chronicler of small-boat sailors," says Farley Mowat. Armchair travel at its best, this 3,000-mile voyage "offers an exhilarating experience even to the most sedentary of landlubbers."

Non-fiction, 6 × 9, 376 pages, illustrations, trade paperback

RIGHT SIDE UP: The Fall of Paul Martin and the Rise of Stephen Harper's New Conservatism *by* Paul Wells
Canadian politics were turned upside-down between 2002 and 2006. "Wells tells both sides of the story in his trademark style – bright, breezy, accessible, irreverent and insightful." – Montreal *Gazette*

Non-fiction, 6 × 9, 356 pages, trade paperback

MAGNA CUM LAUDE: How Frank Stronach Became Canada's Best-Paid Man *by* Wayne Lilley
An unauthorized biography of Frank Stronach, the controversial man behind the country's most famous rags to riches story. "Lilley, a versatile business writer, has produced a judicious, balanced, lively trip through Frank's balance sheets."– *Globe and Mail*

Biography, 6 × 9, 376 pages, trade paperback

YOUNG TRUDEAU: 1919–1944 *by* Max and Monique Nemni, *translated by* William Johnson
A disturbing intellectual biography of Pierre Trudeau that exposes his pro-fascist views until 1944, completely reshaping our understanding of him. "I was extremely shocked." – Lysiane Gagnon, *Globe and Mail*

Biography, 6 × 9, 384 pages, trade paperback

STILL AT THE COTTAGE *by* Charles Gordon
The follow-up to the classic *At the Cottage*, this is an affectionate and hilarious look at cottage living. "Funny, reflective, and always insightful, this is Charles Gordon at the top of his game." – Will Ferguson

Humour, 6 × 9, 176 pages, illustrations, trade paperback

SORRY, I DON'T SPEAK FRENCH: Confronting the Canadian Crisis That Won't Go Away *by* Graham Fraser
The national bestseller that looks at how well official bilingualism is working in Canada. "It's hard to think of any writer better qualified to write about language than Mr. Fraser. . . . He is informed, balanced, judicious and experienced, and a very clear writer." – Jeffrey Simpson, *Globe and Mail*

Non-fiction, 6 × 9, 352 pages, trade paperback

CRAZY ABOUT LILI: A Novel *by* William Weintraub
The author of *City Unique* takes us back to wicked old Montreal in 1948 in this fine, funny novel, where an innocent young McGill student falls for a stripper. "Funny, farcical and thoroughly engaging." – *Globe and Mail*
Fiction, 5½ × 8½, 272 pages, trade paperback

ALICE MUNRO: Writing Her Lives. A Biography *by* Robert Thacker
The literary biography about one of the world's great authors, which shows how her life and her stories intertwine.
Non-fiction, 6½ × 9⅜, 616 pages plus photographs, hardcover

MITCHELL: The Life of W.O. Mitchell, The Years of Fame 1948–1998 *by* Barbara and Ormond Mitchell
From *Who Has Seen the Wind* on through *Jake and the Kid* and beyond, this is a fine biography of Canada's wildest – and best-loved – literary figure.
Non-fiction, 6½ × 9⅜, 488 pages plus photographs, hardcover

ROLLERCOASTER: My Hectic Years as Jean Chrétien's Diplomatic Adviser 1994–1998 *by* James K. Bartleman
"Frank and uncensored insider tales of the daily grind at the highest reaches of the Canadian government. . . . It gives the reader a front row seat of the performance of Jean Chrétien and his top officials while representing Canada abroad." – Ottawa *Hill Times*
Autobiography, 6 × 9, 376 pages, trade paperback

DAMAGE DONE BY THE STORM *by* Jack Hodgins
The author's passion for narrative glows through this wonderful collection of ten new stories that are both "powerful and challenging." – *Quill & Quire* "A splendid achievement, these stories pulse with humanity."
– Alistair MacLeod   *Fiction, 5⅜ × 8⅜, 224 pages, trade paperback*

DISTANCE *by* Jack Hodgins
"Without equivocation, *Distance* is the best novel of the year, an intimate tale of fathers and sons with epic scope and mythic resonances. . . . A masterwork from one of Canada's too-little-appreciated literary giants."
– *Vancouver Sun*   *Fiction, 5⅜ × 8⅜, 392 pages, trade paperback*

ON SIX CONTINENTS: A Life in Canada's Foreign Service 1966-2002 *by* James K. Bartleman
A hilarious, revealing look at what our diplomats actually do, by a master story-teller who is a legend in the service. "Delightful and valuable." – *Globe and Mail*   *Autobiography, 6 × 9, 272 pages, trade paperback*

RUNAWAY *by* Alice Munro
The 2004 Giller Prize–winning collection of short stories by "the best fiction writer now working in North America. . . . *Runaway* is a marvel." – *New York Times Book Review*   *Fiction, 6 × 9, 352 pages, hardcover*

TO EVERY THING THERE IS A SEASON: A Cape Breton Christmas Story *by* Alistair MacLeod, *with illustrations by* Peter Rankin
Almost every page of this beautiful little book is enriched by a perfect illustration, making this touching story of a farm family waiting for Christmas into a classic for every home. A "winsome tale of Yuletide past." – *Toronto Star*   *Fiction, illustrations, 4⅝ × 7¼, 48 pages, hardcover*

HERE BE DRAGONS: Telling Tales of People, Passion and Power *by* Peter C. Newman
The number one bestseller by the man whose books on politics, business, and history have sold two million copies, *Here Be Dragons* tells the story of his own life, from fleeing the Nazis as a child to editor of *Maclean's*. The *Globe and Mail* calls this autobiography "a work of genius wit and insight."
          Non-fiction, 6 × 9, 744 pages plus photographs, trade paperback

WORTH FIGHTING FOR *by* Sheila Copps
The former Deputy Prime Minister and life-long Liberal tells all in this revealing look at what really goes on behind the scenes in Ottawa. "Copps gives readers a blunt, no-holds-barred glimpse into the seamy backrooms of Canadian politics." – Montreal *Gazette*
          Non-fiction, 6 × 9, 224 pages, hardcover

RAVEN'S END: A Tale of the Canadian Rockies *by* Ben Gadd
This astonishing book, snapped up by publishers around the world, is like a *Watership Down* set among a flock of ravens managing to survive in the Rockies. "A real classic." – Andy Russell
          Fiction, 6 × 9, map, 5 drawings, 360 pages, trade paperback

ACROSS THE BRIDGE: Stories *by* Mavis Gallant
These eleven stories, set mostly in Montreal or in Paris, were described as "Vintage Gallant – urbane, witty, absorbing." – *Winnipeg Free Press* "We come away from it both thoughtful and enriched."– *Globe and Mail*
          Fiction, 5⅞ × 8⅞, 208 pages, trade paperback

A PASSION FOR NARRATIVE: A Guide for Writing Fiction *by* Jack Hodgins
The Canadian classic guide to writing fiction. "One excellent path from original to marketable manuscript. . . . It would take a beginning writer years to work her way through all the goodies Hodgins offers." – *Globe and Mail*
          Non-fiction / Writing guide, 5¼ × 8¼, 320 pages,
          updated with a new Afterword, trade paperback